Gatcha Gacha™

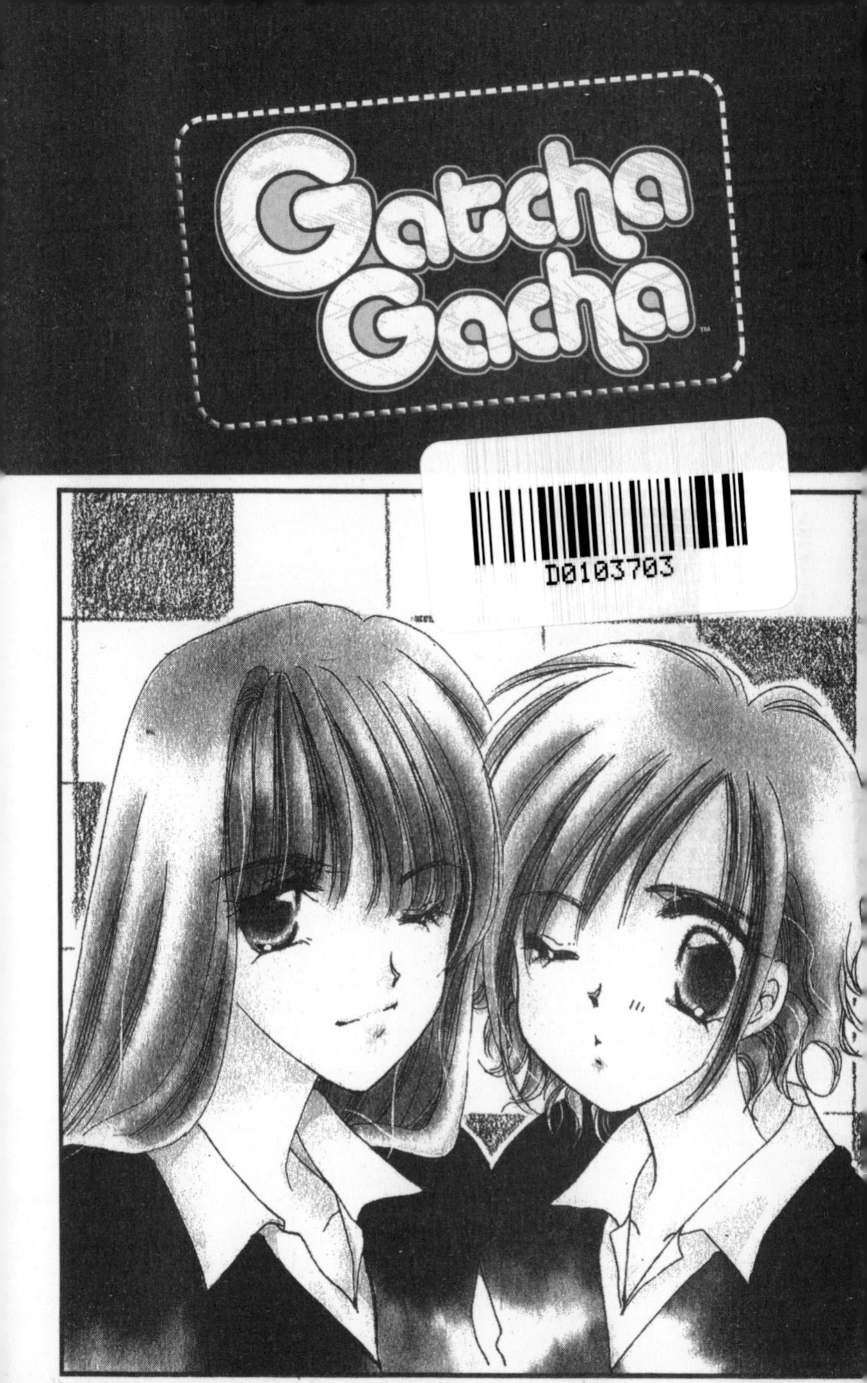

Gatcha Gacha Volume 1
Created by Yutaka Tachibana

Translation - Adrienne Beck
English Adaptation - Jamie S. Rich
Retouch and Lettering - Fawn Lau
Production Artist - Jose Macasocol, Jr.
Cover Design - Jorge Negrete

Editor - Rob Valois
Digital Imaging Manager - Chris Buford
Production Manager - Jennifer Miller
Managing Editor - Lindsey Johnston
VP of Production - Ron Klamert
Publisher and E.I.C. - Mike Kiley
President and C.O.O. - John Parker
C.E.O. and Chief Creative Officer - Stuart Levy

A 🔲 TOKYOPOP® Manga

TOKYOPOP Inc.
5900 Wilshire Blvd. Suite 2000
Los Angeles, CA 90036

E-mail: info@TOKYOPOP.com
Come visit us online at www.TOKYOPOP.com

ISBN: 1-59816-153-9

First TOKYOPOP printing: March 2006
10 9 8 7 6 5 4 3 2 1
Printed in Canada

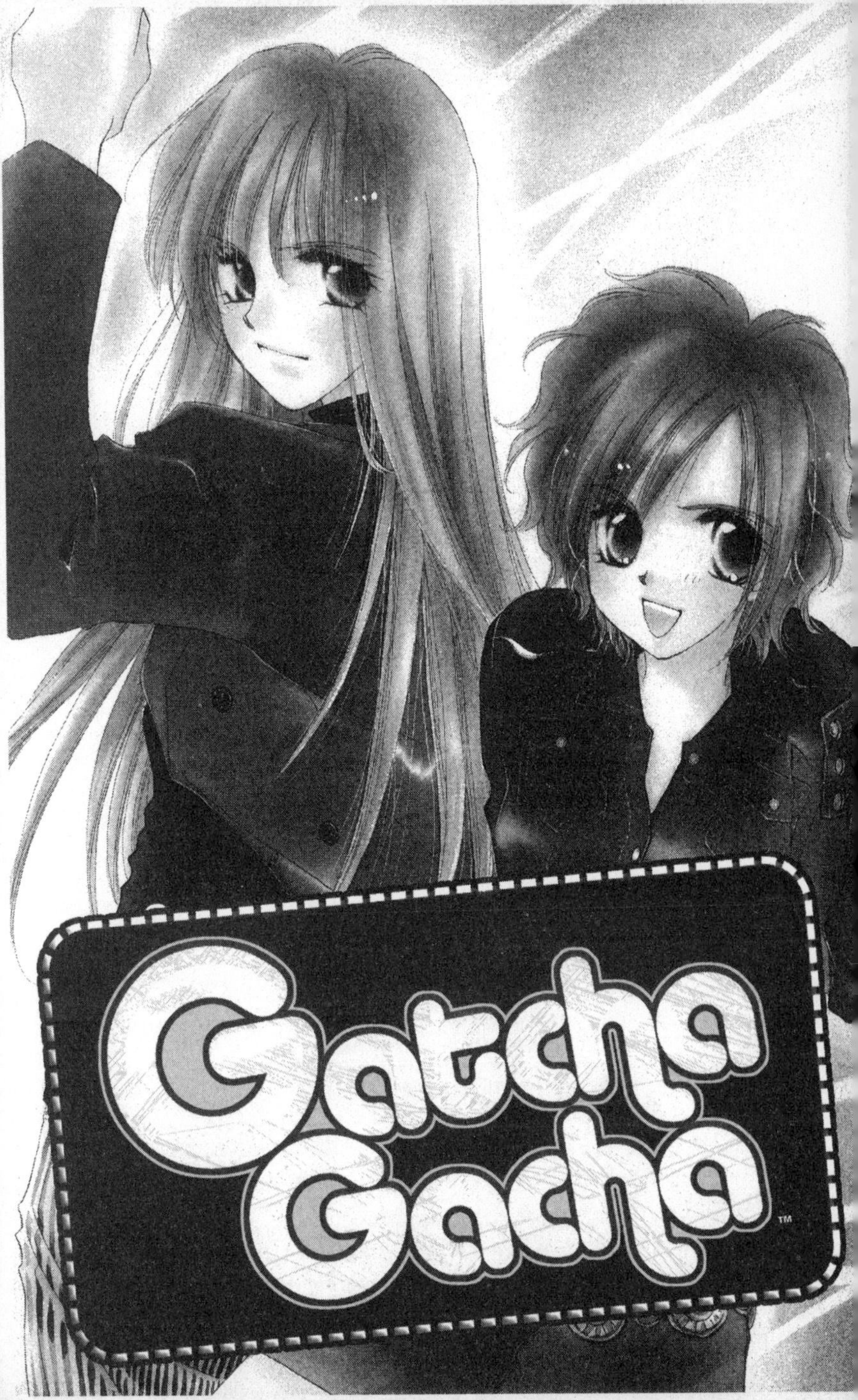
Gatcha
Gacha™

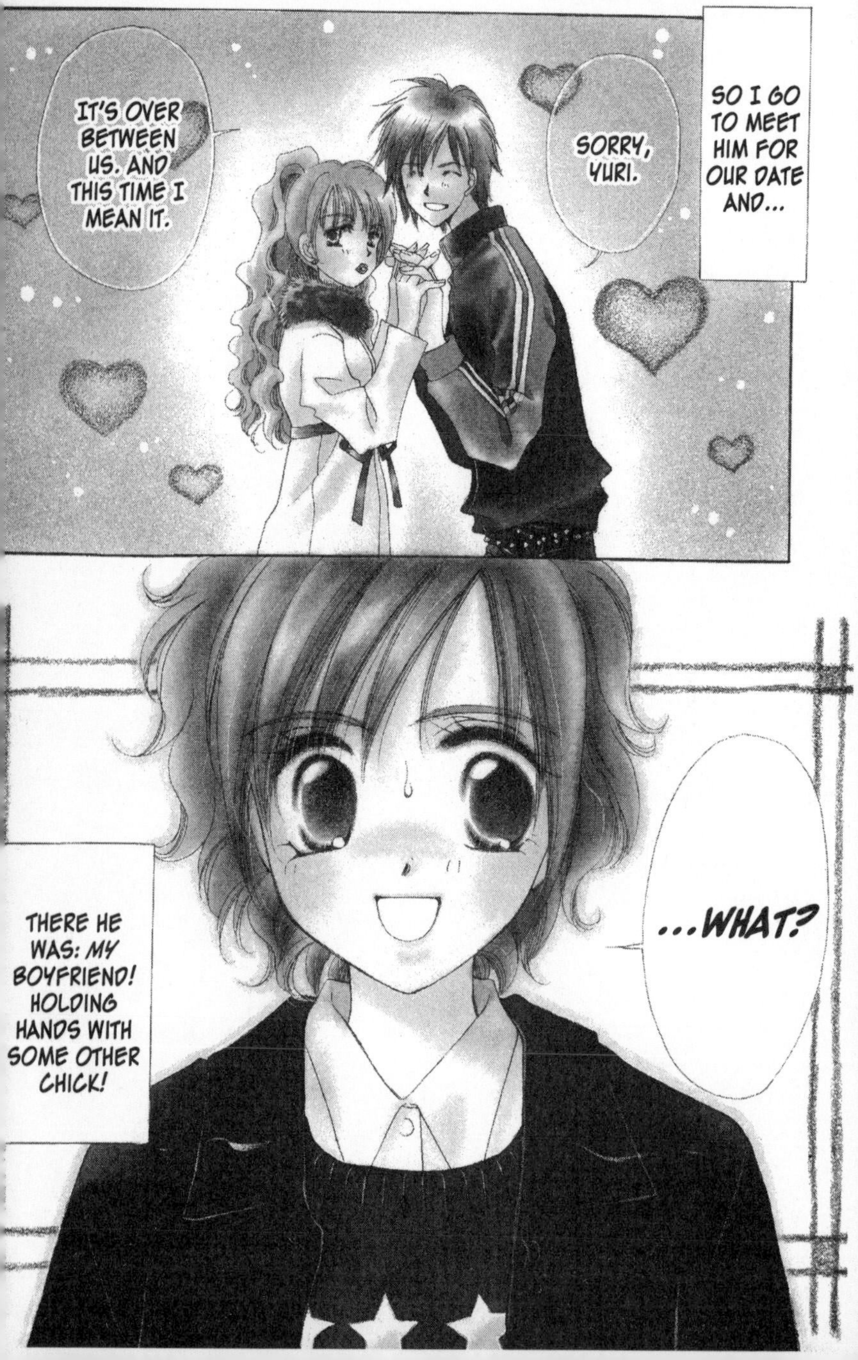
SO I GO TO MEET HIM FOR OUR DATE AND...
SORRY, YURI.
IT'S OVER BETWEEN US. AND THIS TIME I MEAN IT.
...WHAT?
THERE HE WAS: *MY* BOYFRIEND! HOLDING HANDS WITH SOME OTHER CHICK!

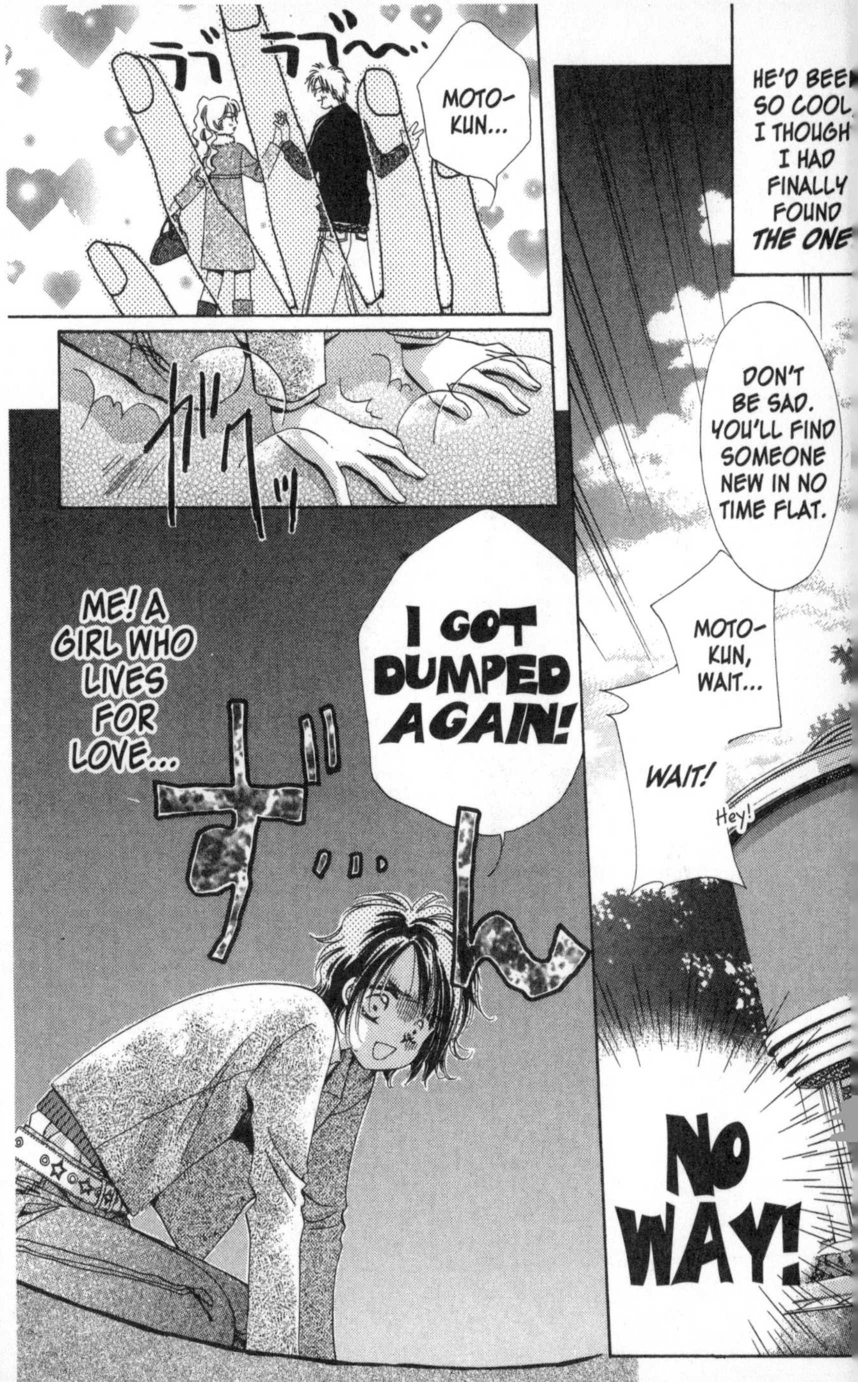
HE'D BEEN SO COOL, I THOUGH I HAD FINALLY FOUND THE ONE
DON'T BE SAD. YOU'LL FIND SOMEONE NEW IN NO TIME FLAT.
MOTO-KUN, WAIT...
WAIT!
Hey!
NO WAY!
ラブラブ〜
MOTO-KUN...
ガクッ
I GOT DUMPED AGAIN!
ME! A GIRL WHO LIVES FOR LOVE...

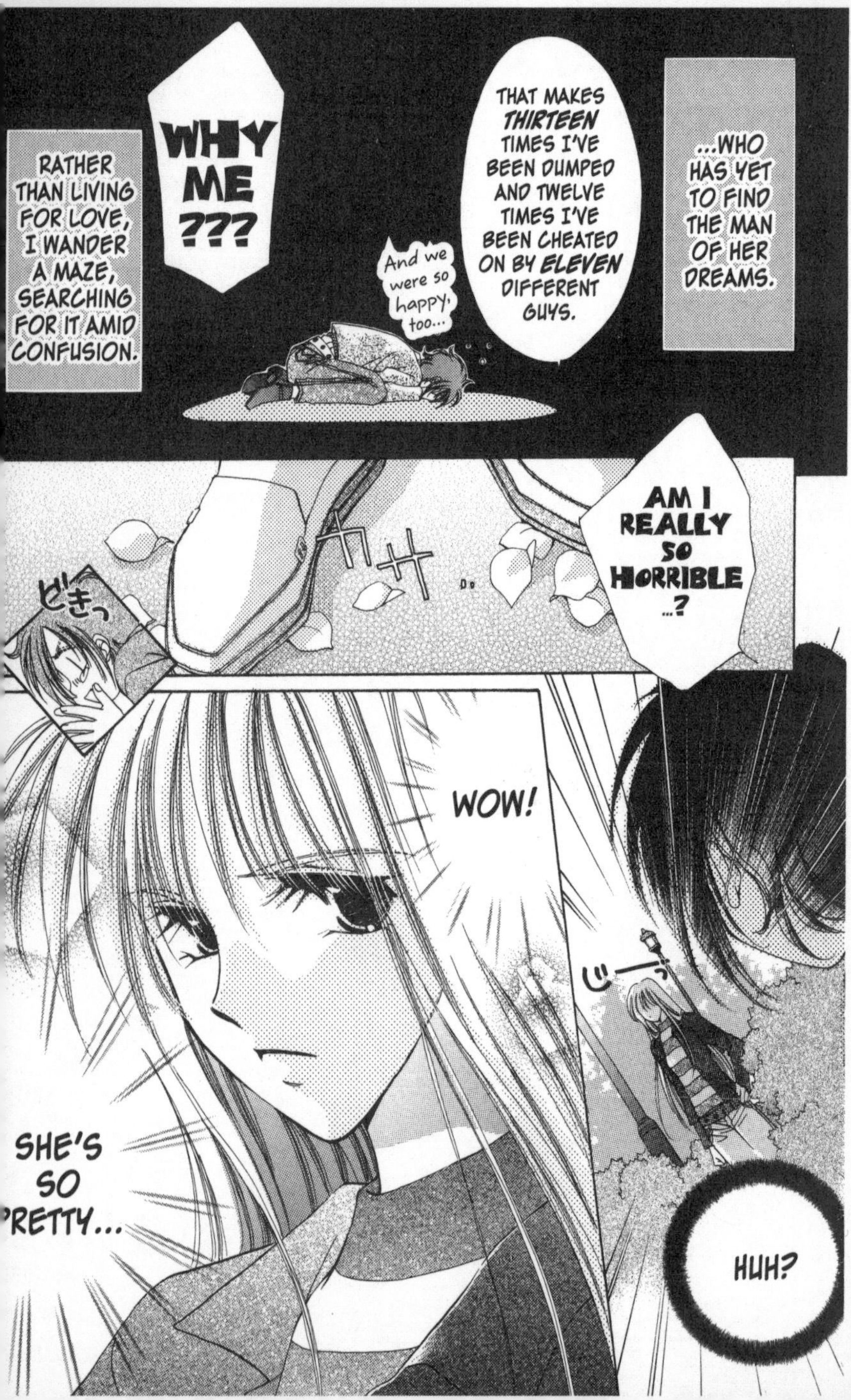
...WHO HAS YET TO FIND THE MAN OF HER DREAMS.
THAT MAKES THIRTEEN TIMES I'VE BEEN DUMPED AND TWELVE TIMES I'VE BEEN CHEATED ON BY ELEVEN DIFFERENT GUYS.
And we were so happy, too...
WHY ME ???
RATHER THAN LIVING FOR LOVE, I WANDER A MAZE, SEARCHING FOR IT AMID CONFUSION.
AM I REALLY SO HORRIBLE ...?
どきっ
WOW!
じーっ
HUH?
SHE'S SO PRETTY...

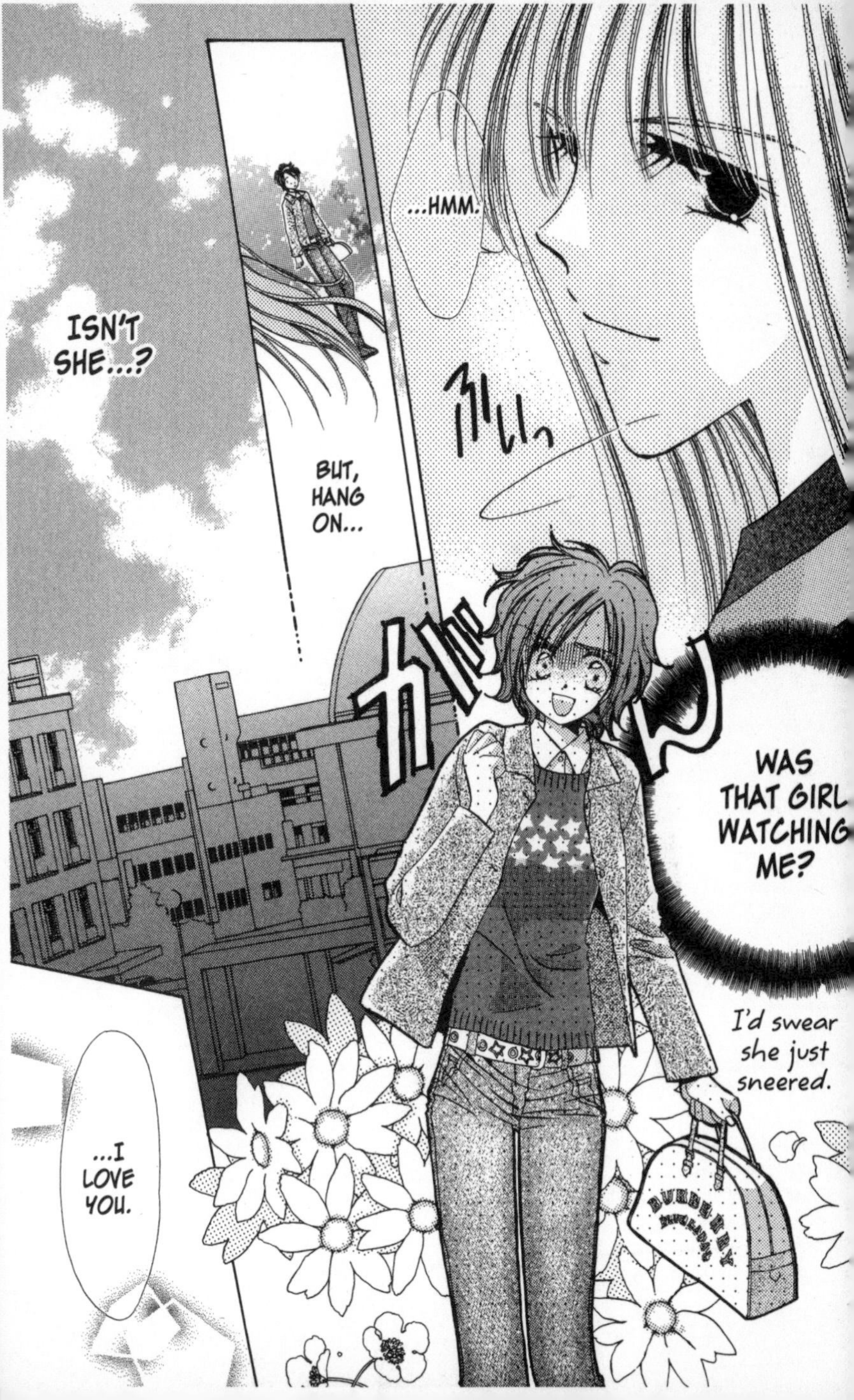
...HMM.
ふいっ
BUT, HANG ON...
ISN'T SHE...?
カチン
WAS THAT GIRL WATCHING ME?
I'd swear she just sneered.
...I LOVE YOU.

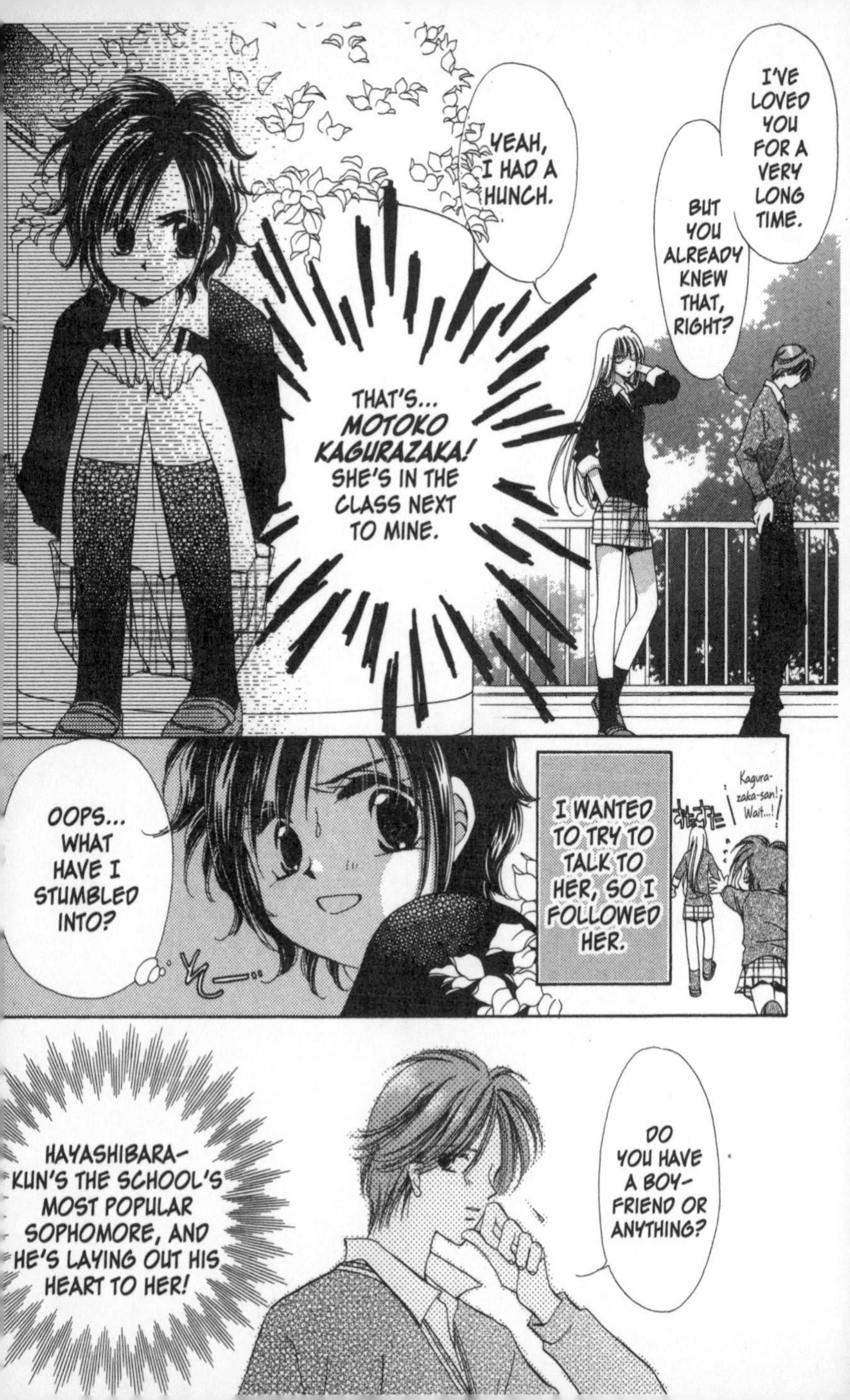
I'VE LOVED YOU FOR A VERY LONG TIME.
BUT YOU ALREADY KNEW THAT, RIGHT?
YEAH, I HAD A HUNCH.
THAT'S... *MOTOKO KAGURAZAKA!* SHE'S IN THE CLASS NEXT TO MINE.
Kagura-zaka-san! Wait...!
I WANTED TO TRY TO TALK TO HER, SO I FOLLOWED HER.
OOPS... WHAT HAVE I STUMBLED INTO?
DO YOU HAVE A BOY-FRIEND OR ANYTHING?
HAYASHIBARA-KUN'S THE SCHOOL'S MOST POPULAR SOPHOMORE, AND HE'S LAYING OUT HIS HEART TO HER!

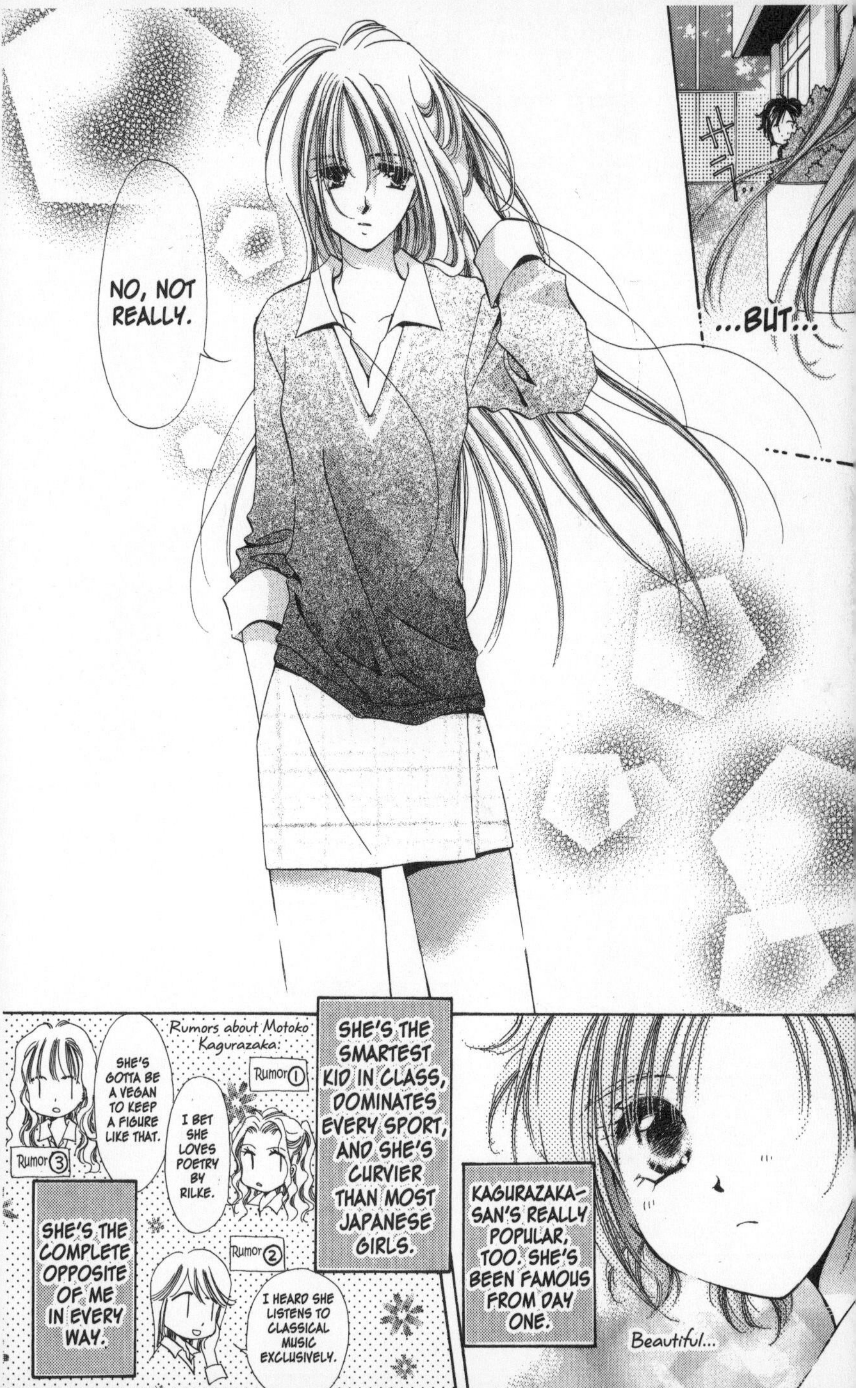
...BUT...
NO, NOT REALLY.
Beautiful...
KAGURAZAKA-SAN'S REALLY POPULAR, TOO. SHE'S BEEN FAMOUS FROM DAY ONE.
SHE'S THE SMARTEST KID IN CLASS, DOMINATES EVERY SPORT, AND SHE'S CURVIER THAN MOST JAPANESE GIRLS.
Rumors about Motoko Kagurazaka:
Rumor 1
I BET SHE LOVES POETRY BY RILKE.
Rumor 3
SHE'S GOTTA BE A VEGAN TO KEEP A FIGURE LIKE THAT.
Rumor 2
I HEARD SHE LISTENS TO CLASSICAL MUSIC EXCLUSIVELY.
SHE'S THE COMPLETE OPPOSITE OF ME IN EVERY WAY.

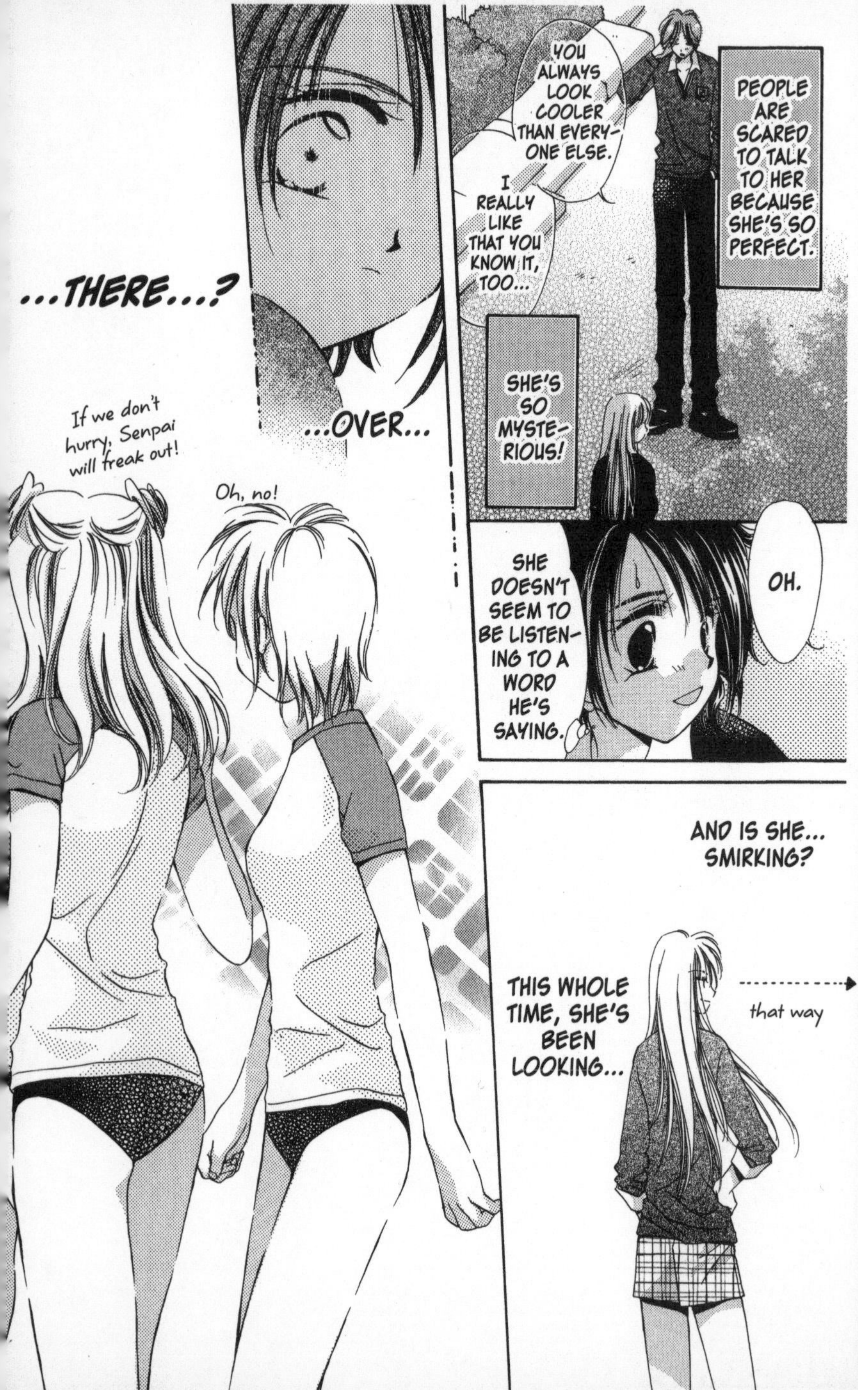
PEOPLE ARE SCARED TO TALK TO HER BECAUSE SHE'S SO PERFECT.
YOU ALWAYS LOOK COOLER THAN EVERY-ONE ELSE.
I REALLY LIKE THAT YOU KNOW IT, TOO...
SHE'S SO MYSTE-RIOUS!
OH.
SHE DOESN'T SEEM TO BE LISTEN-ING TO A WORD HE'S SAYING.
AND IS SHE... SMIRKING?
that way
THIS WHOLE TIME, SHE'S BEEN LOOKING...
...OVER...
...THERE...?
Oh, no!
If we don't hurry, Senpai will freak out!

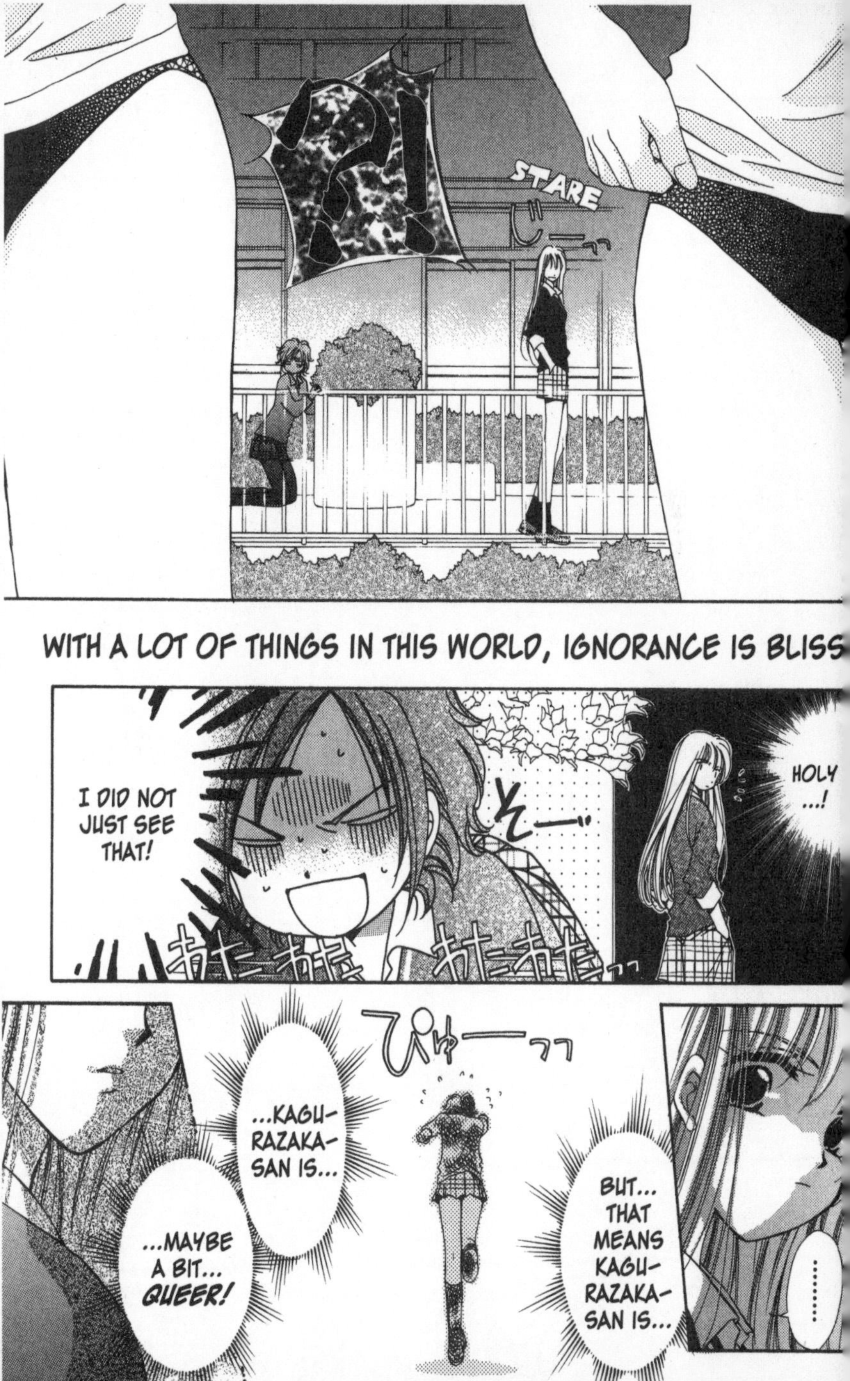
STARE
WITH A LOT OF THINGS IN THIS WORLD, IGNORANCE IS BLISS
HOLY ...!
I DID NOT JUST SEE THAT!
......
BUT... THAT MEANS KAGU-RAZAKA-SAN IS...
...KAGU-RAZAKA-SAN IS...
...MAYBE A BIT... QUEER!

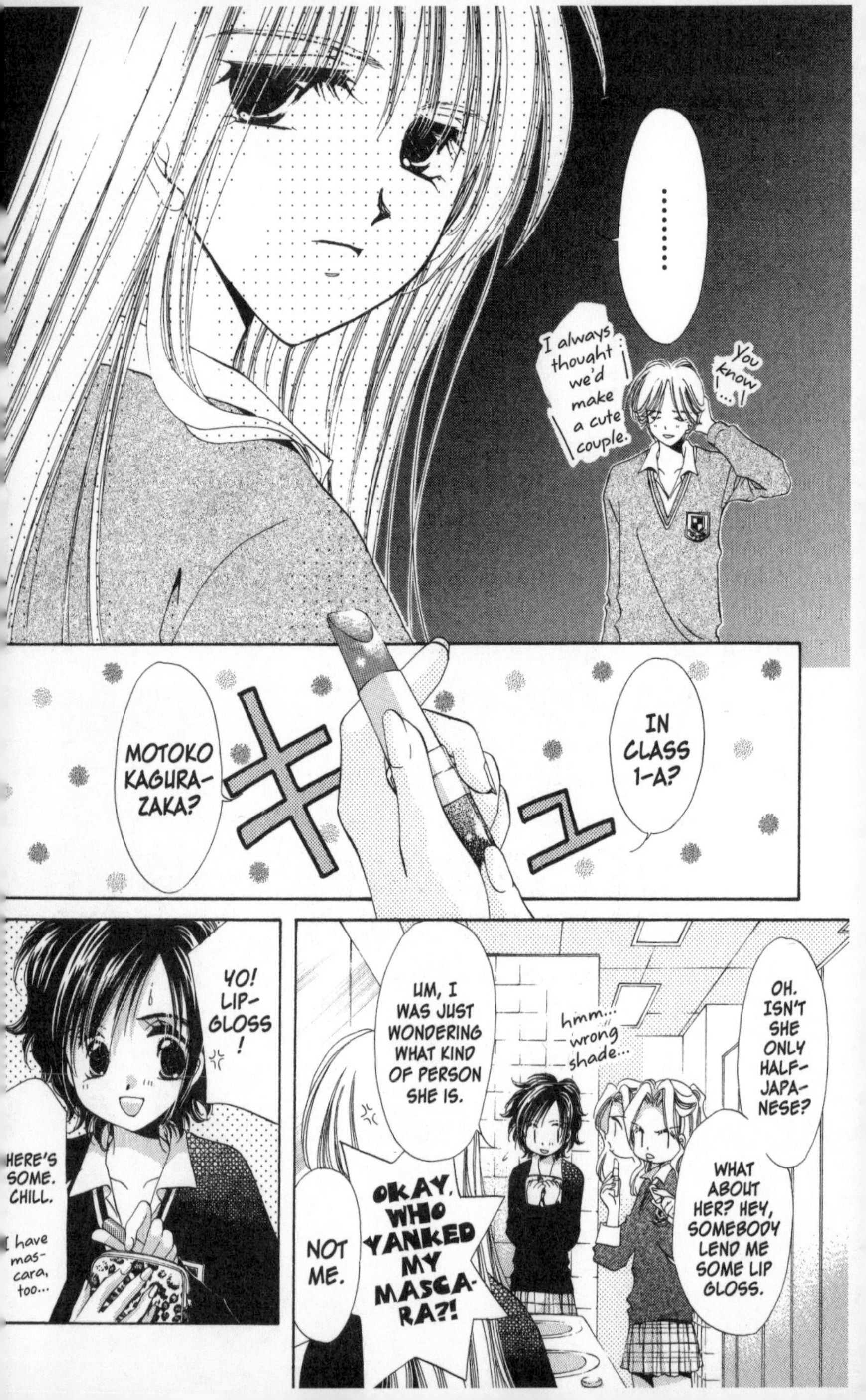
......
You know...!
I always thought we'd make a cute couple.
IN CLASS 1-A?
キュ
MOTOKO KAGURAZAKA?
OH. ISN'T SHE ONLY HALF-JAPANESE?
hmm... wrong shade...
UM, I WAS JUST WONDERING WHAT KIND OF PERSON SHE IS.
WHAT ABOUT HER? HEY, SOMEBODY LEND ME SOME LIP GLOSS.
OKAY, WHO YANKED MY MASCARA?!
NOT ME.
YO! LIP-GLOSS!
HERE'S SOME. CHILL.
I have mascara, too...

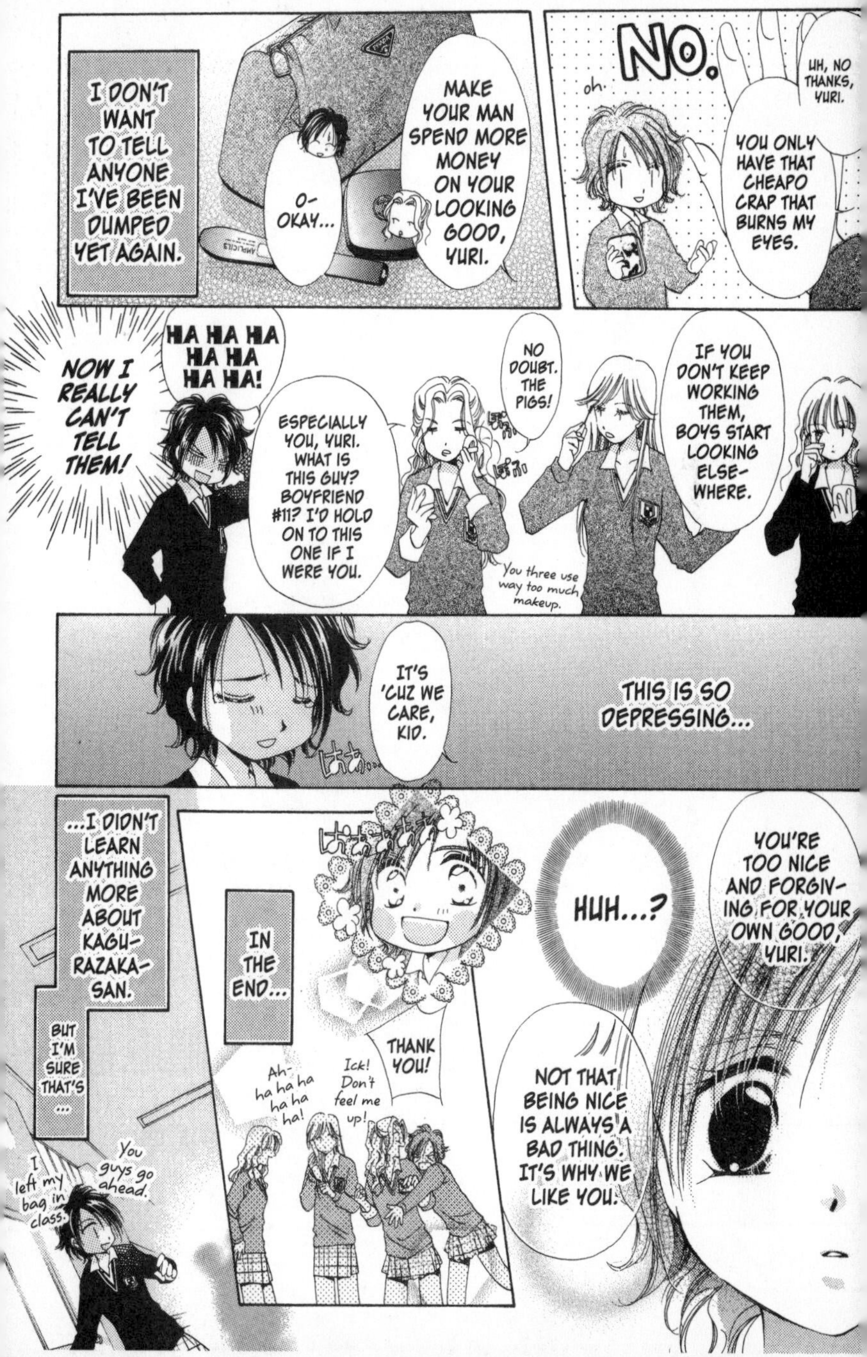
UH, NO THANKS, YURI.
YOU ONLY HAVE THAT CHEAPO CRAP THAT BURNS MY EYES.
NO.
oh.
MAKE YOUR MAN SPEND MORE MONEY ON YOUR LOOKING GOOD, YURI.
O-OKAY...
I DON'T WANT TO TELL ANYONE I'VE BEEN DUMPED YET AGAIN.
IF YOU DON'T KEEP WORKING THEM, BOYS START LOOKING ELSE-WHERE.
NO DOUBT. THE PIGS!
You three use way too much makeup.
ESPECIALLY YOU, YURI. WHAT IS THIS GUY? BOYFRIEND #11? I'D HOLD ON TO THIS ONE IF I WERE YOU.
HA HA HA HA HA HA HA!
NOW I REALLY CAN'T TELL THEM!
THIS IS SO DEPRESSING...
IT'S 'CUZ WE CARE, KID.
YOU'RE TOO NICE AND FORGIV-ING FOR YOUR OWN GOOD, YURI.
HUH...?
NOT THAT BEING NICE IS ALWAYS A BAD THING. IT'S WHY WE LIKE YOU.
IN THE END...
THANK YOU!
Ick! Don't feel me up!
Ah-ha ha ha ha ha ha!
...I DIDN'T LEARN ANYTHING MORE ABOUT KAGU-RAZAKA-SAN.
BUT I'M SURE THAT'S ...
You guys go ahead.
I left my bag in class.

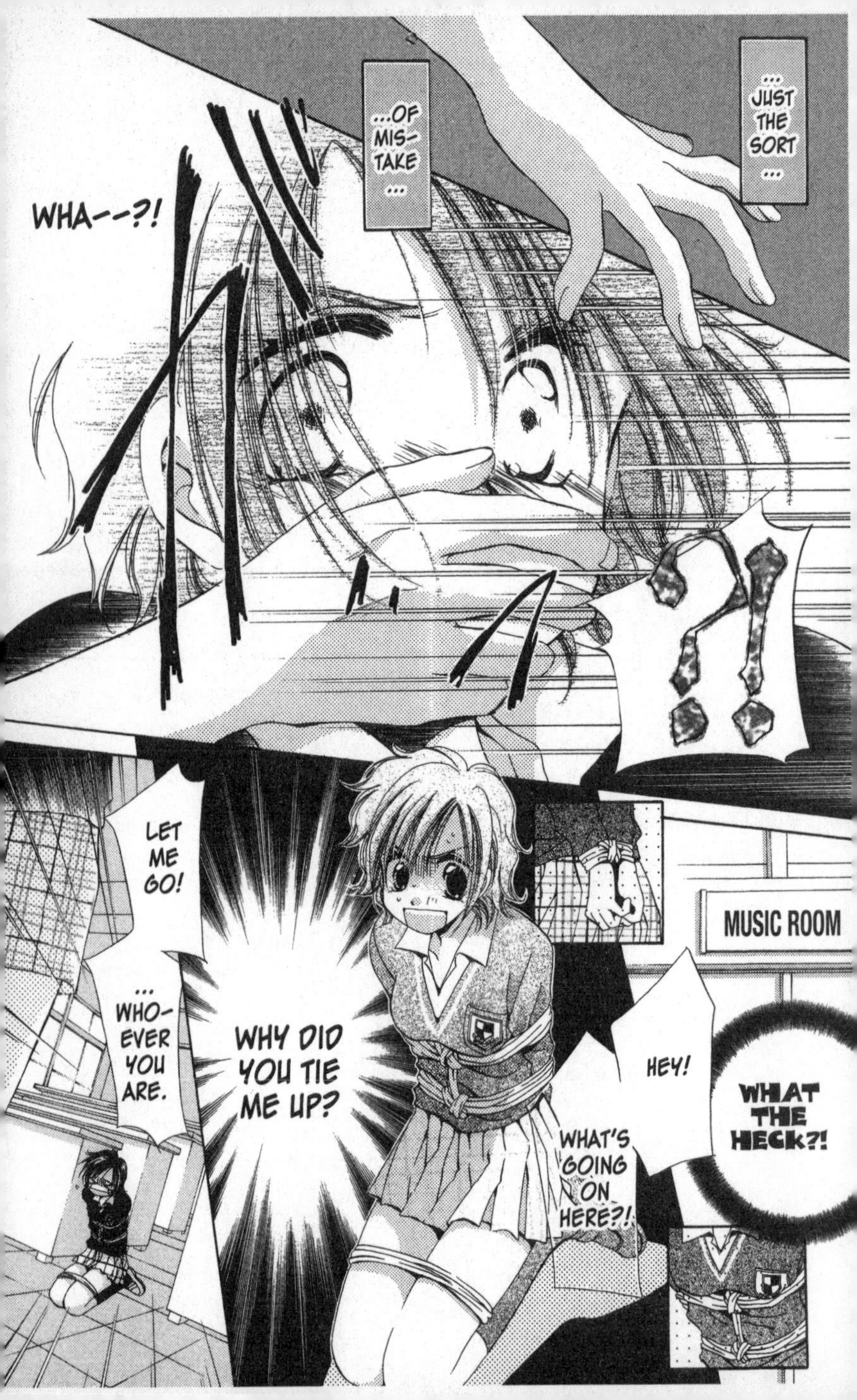
...JUST THE SORT...
...OF MISTAKE...
WHA--?!
?!
MUSIC ROOM
WHAT THE HECK?!
HEY!
WHAT'S GOING ON HERE?!
WHY DID YOU TIE ME UP?
LET ME GO!
...WHOEVER YOU ARE.

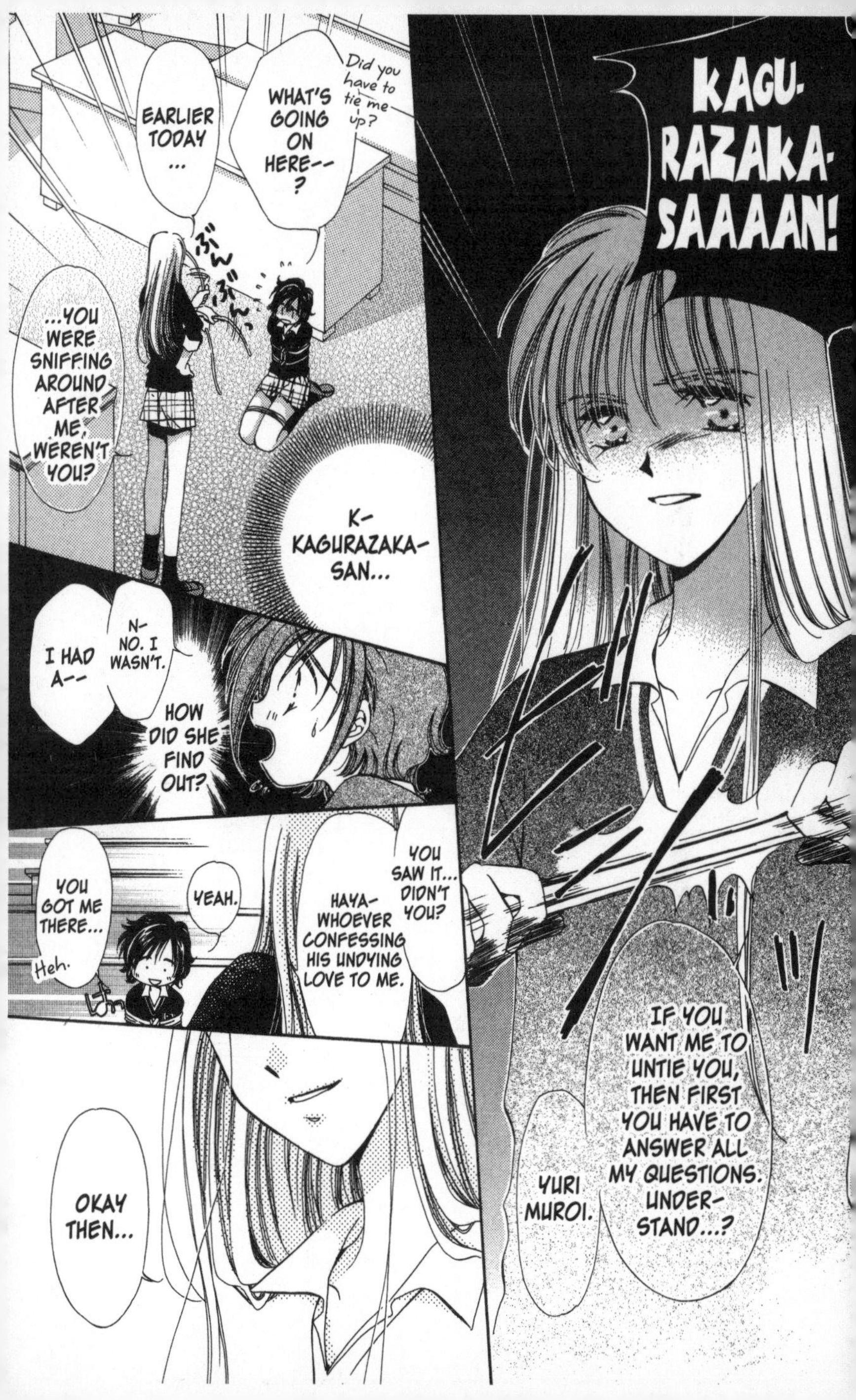
KAGU-RAZAKA-SAAAAN!
IF YOU WANT ME TO UNTIE YOU, THEN FIRST YOU HAVE TO ANSWER ALL MY QUESTIONS. UNDER-STAND...?
YURI MUROI.
Did you have to tie me up?
WHAT'S GOING ON HERE--?
EARLIER TODAY...
ぶんぶん
...YOU WERE SNIFFING AROUND AFTER ME, WEREN'T YOU?
K-KAGURAZAKA-SAN...
N-NO. I WASN'T.
I HAD A--
HOW DID SHE FIND OUT?
YOU SAW IT... DIDN'T YOU?
HAYA-WHOEVER CONFESSING HIS UNDYING LOVE TO ME.
YEAH.
YOU GOT ME THERE...
Heh.
OKAY THEN...

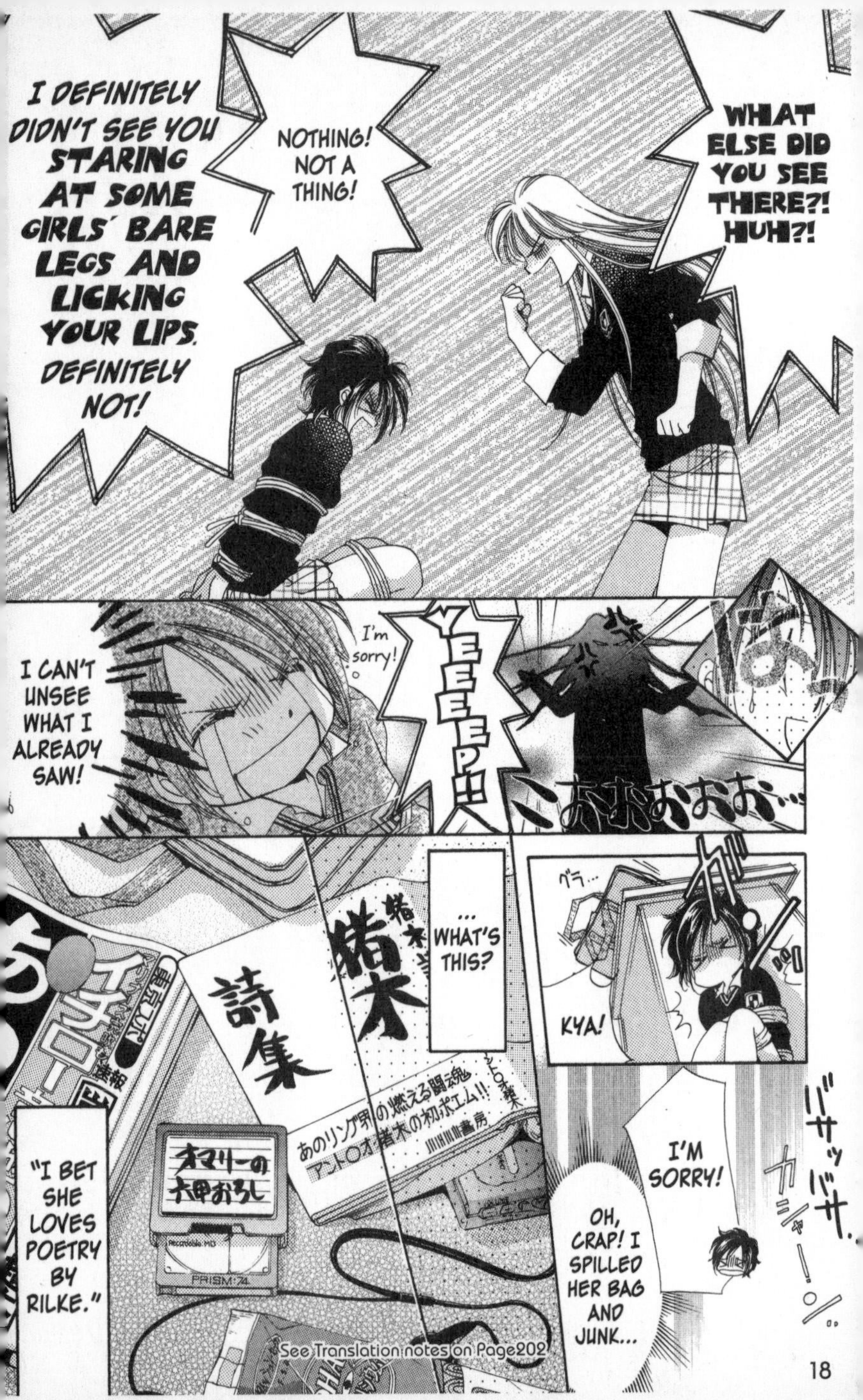
WHAT ELSE DID YOU SEE THERE?! HUH?!
NOTHING! NOT A THING!
I DEFINITELY DIDN'T SEE YOU STARING AT SOME GIRLS' BARE LEGS AND LICKING YOUR LIPS. DEFINITELY NOT!
YEEEEP!!
I'm sorry!
I CAN'T UNSEE WHAT I ALREADY SAW!
グラ…
KYA!
バサッバサ.
カシャー!
I'M SORRY!
OH, CRAP! I SPILLED HER BAG AND JUNK...
...WHAT'S THIS?
猪木
詩集
あのリング界の燃える闘魂
アント〇オ猪木の初ポエム!!
書房
オマリーの六甲おろし
PRISM:74
"I BET SHE LOVES POETRY BY RILKE."

See Translation notes on Page202

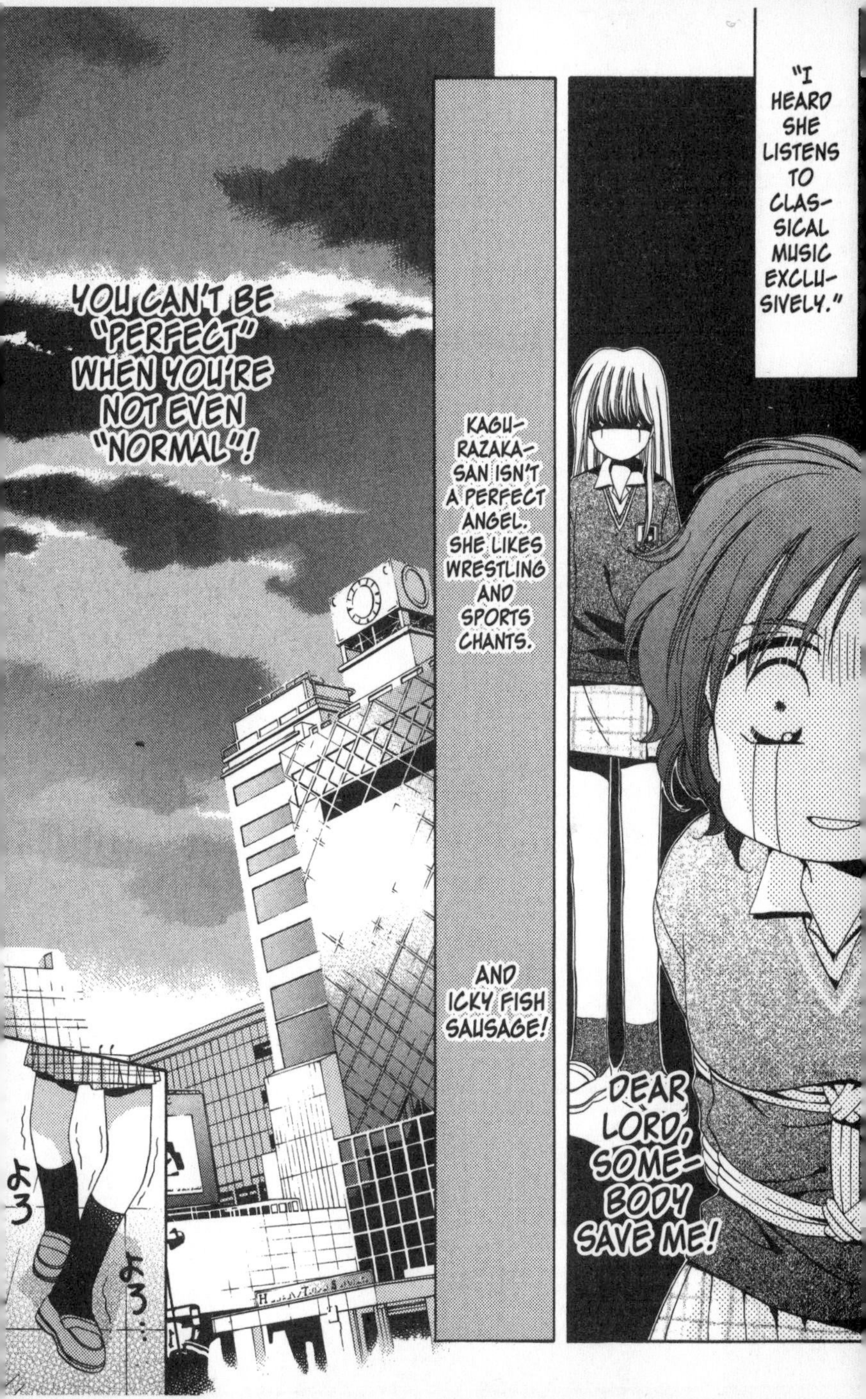
"I HEARD SHE LISTENS TO CLAS-SICAL MUSIC EXCLU-SIVELY."
DEAR LORD, SOME-BODY SAVE ME!
KAGU-RAZAKA-SAN ISN'T A PERFECT ANGEL. SHE LIKES WRESTLING AND SPORTS CHANTS.
AND ICKY FISH SAUSAGE!
YOU CAN'T BE "PERFECT" WHEN YOU'RE NOT EVEN "NORMAL"!

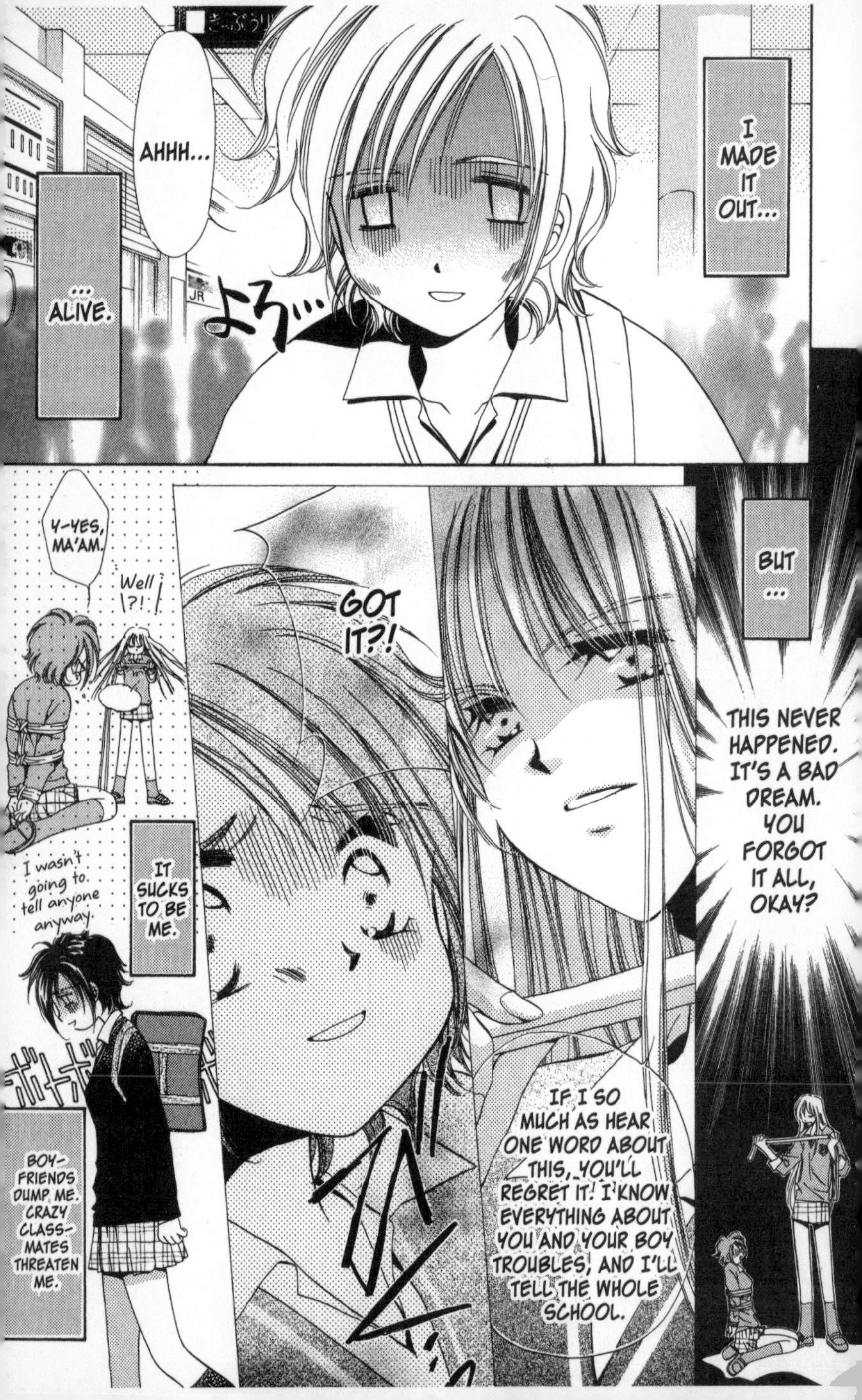
I MADE IT OUT...
AHHH...
...ALIVE.
よろ…
BUT ...
THIS NEVER HAPPENED. IT'S A BAD DREAM. YOU FORGOT IT ALL, OKAY?
GOT IT?!
IF I SO MUCH AS HEAR ONE WORD ABOUT THIS, YOU'LL REGRET IT. I KNOW EVERYTHING ABOUT YOU AND YOUR BOY TROUBLES, AND I'LL TELL THE WHOLE SCHOOL.
Y-YES, MA'AM.
Well I?!
IT SUCKS TO BE ME.
I wasn't going to tell anyone anyway.
BOY-FRIENDS DUMP ME. CRAZY CLASS-MATES THREATEN ME.

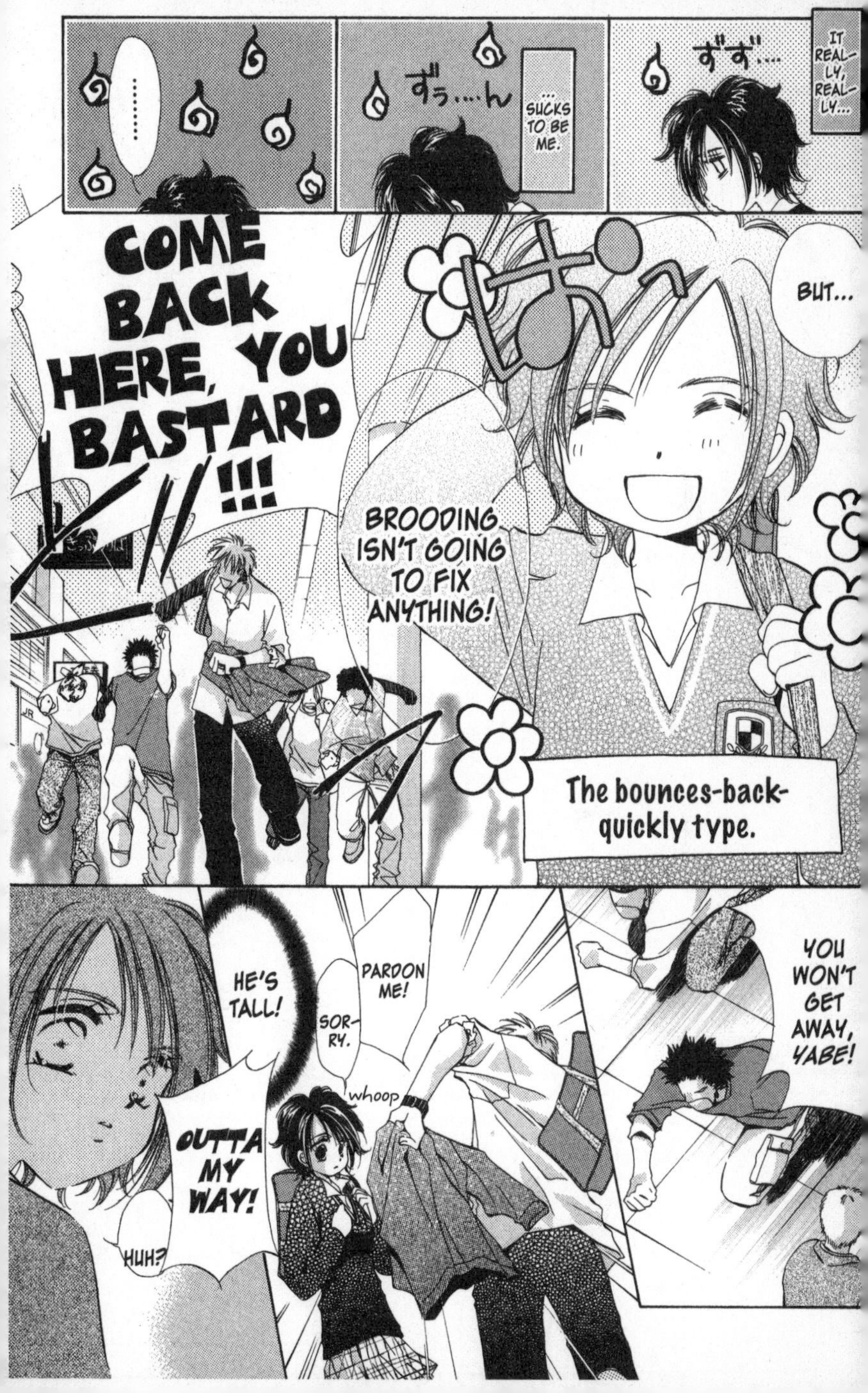
IT REALLY, REALLY...
ずず…
...SUCKS TO BE ME.
ずぅ…ん
……
BUT...
BROODING ISN'T GOING TO FIX ANYTHING!
The bounces-back-quickly type.
COME BACK HERE, YOU BASTARD!!!
YOU WON'T GET AWAY, YABE!
PARDON ME!
SORRY.
whoop
OUTTA MY WAY!
HE'S TALL!
HUH?

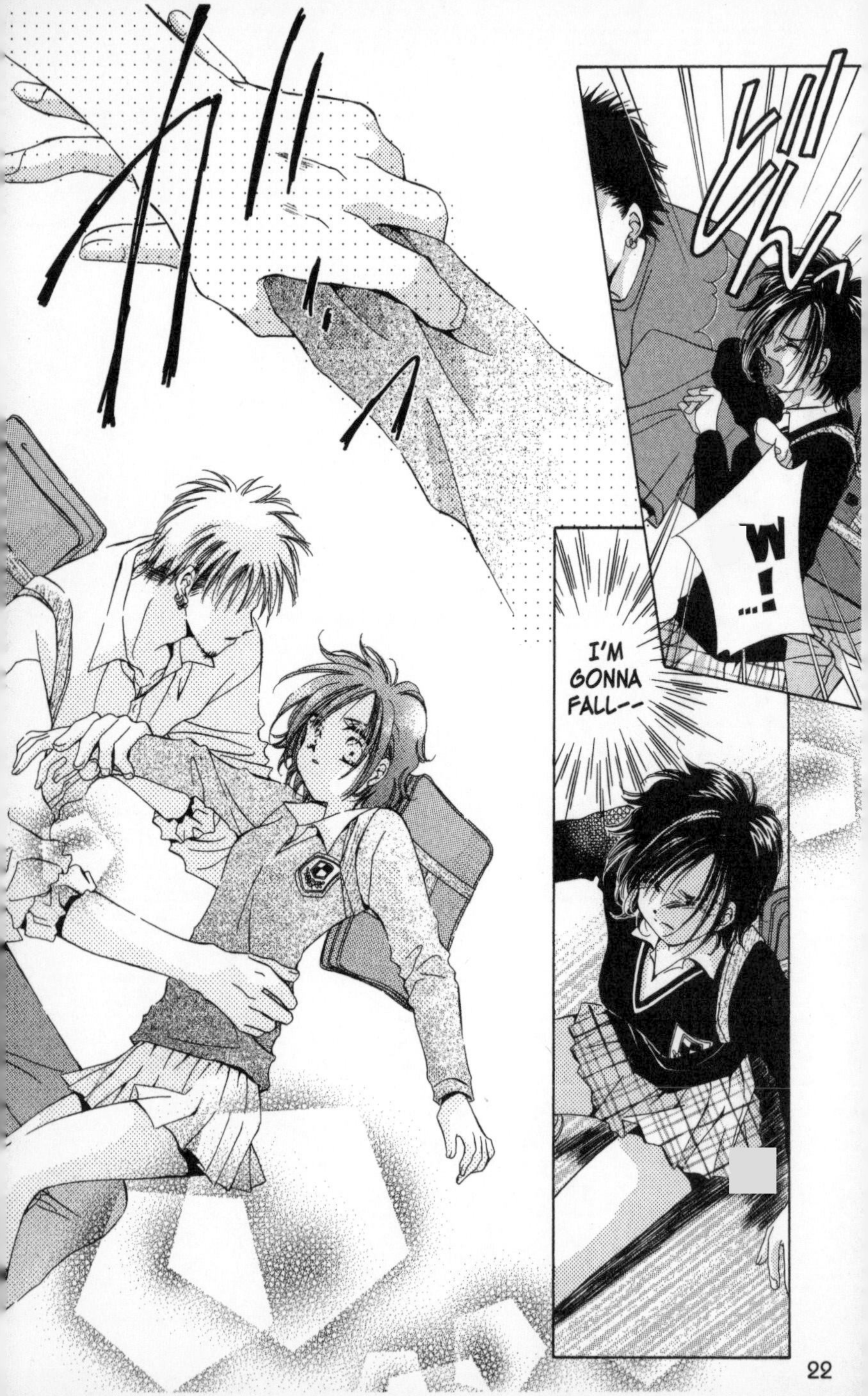
W!...!
I'M GONNA FALL--

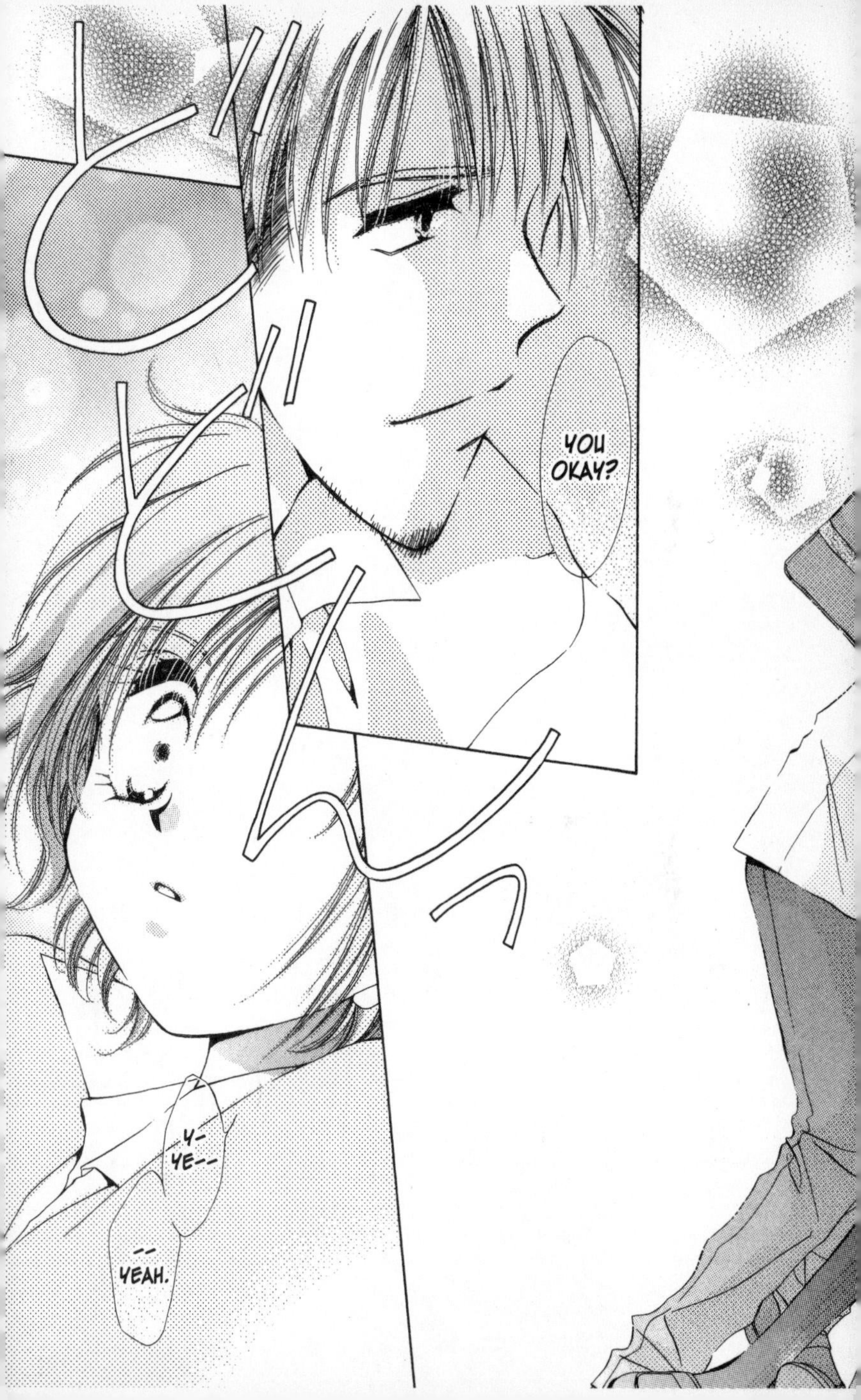
YOU OKAY?
Y-YE--
--YEAH.

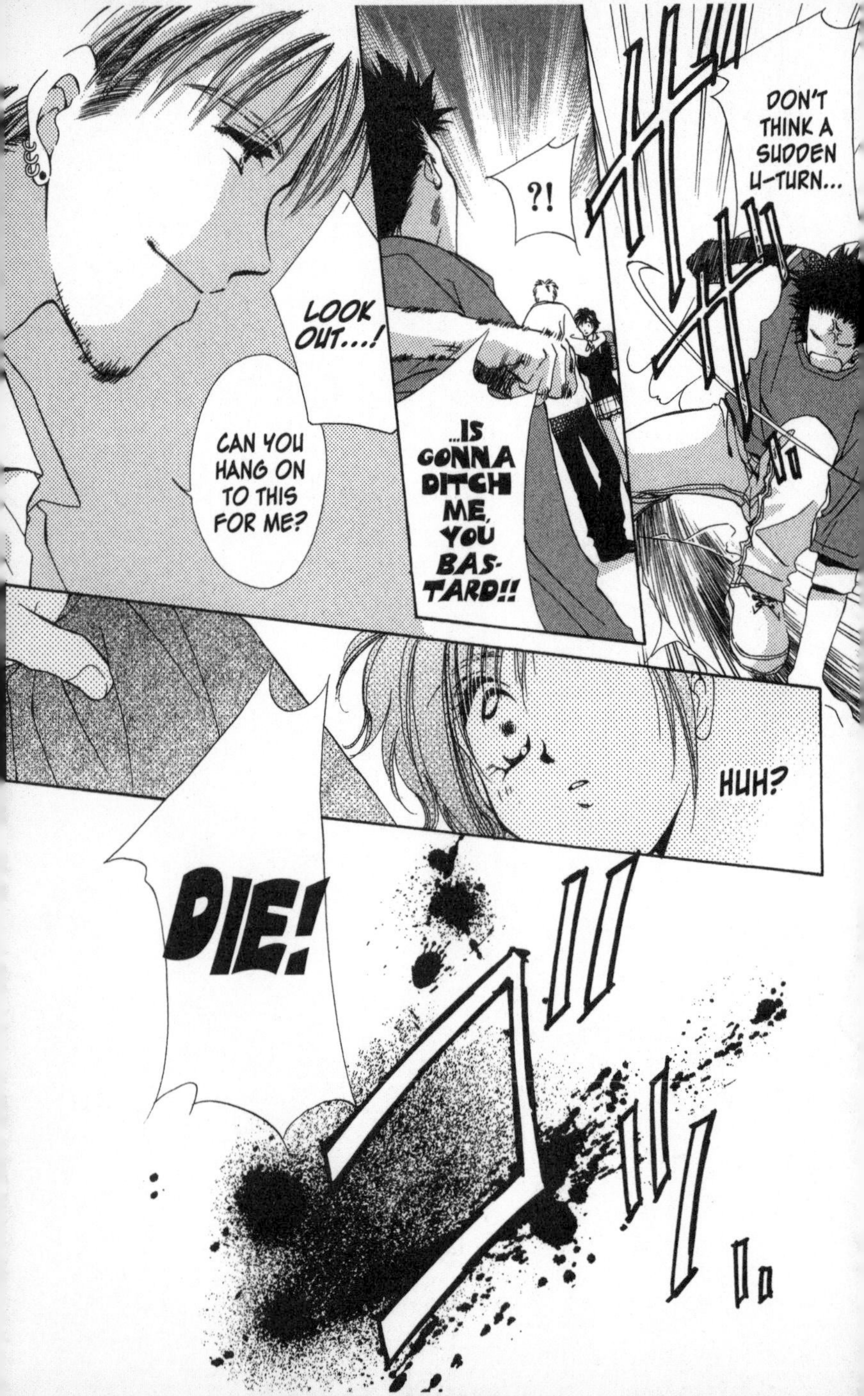
DON'T THINK A SUDDEN U-TURN...
?!
...IS GONNA DITCH ME, YOU BASTARD!!
LOOK OUT...!
CAN YOU HANG ON TO THIS FOR ME?
HUH?
DIE!

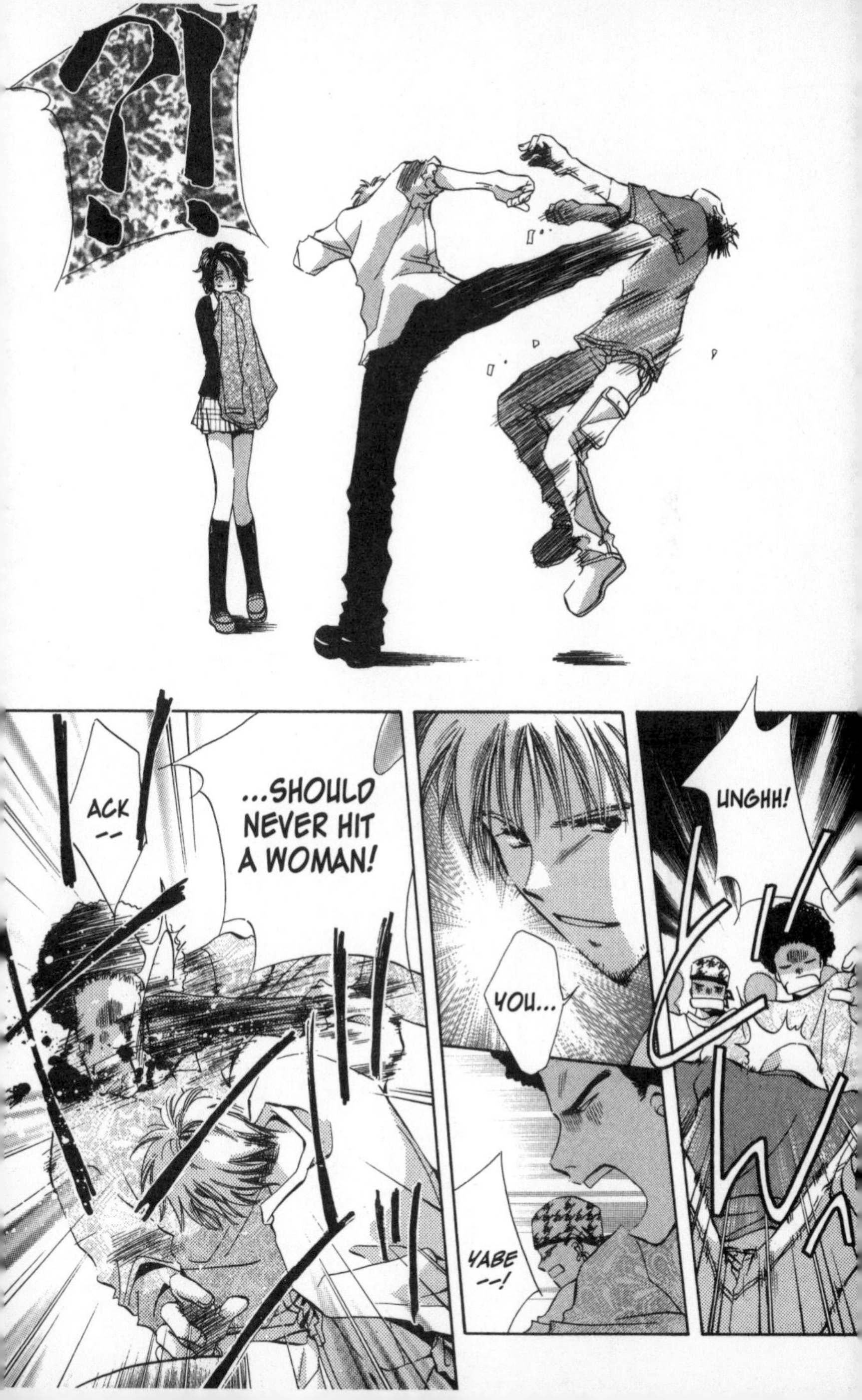
?!
UNGHH!
YOU...
YABE--!
...SHOULD NEVER HIT A WOMAN!
ACK--

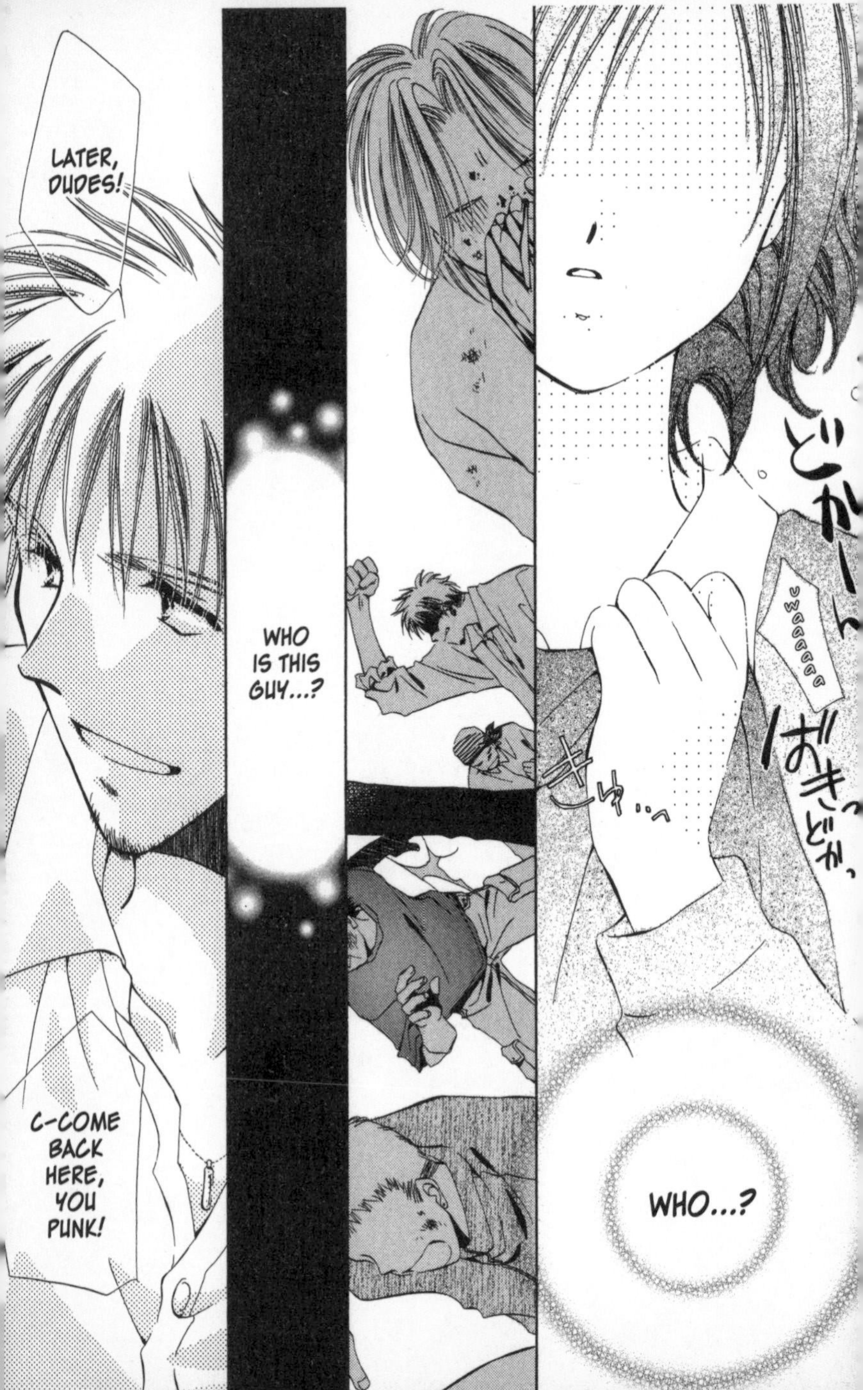
どかーん
UWAAAAAAA
ぼきっ どかっ
ギュ…
WHO...?
WHO IS THIS GUY...?
LATER, DUDES!
C-COME BACK HERE, YOU PUNK!

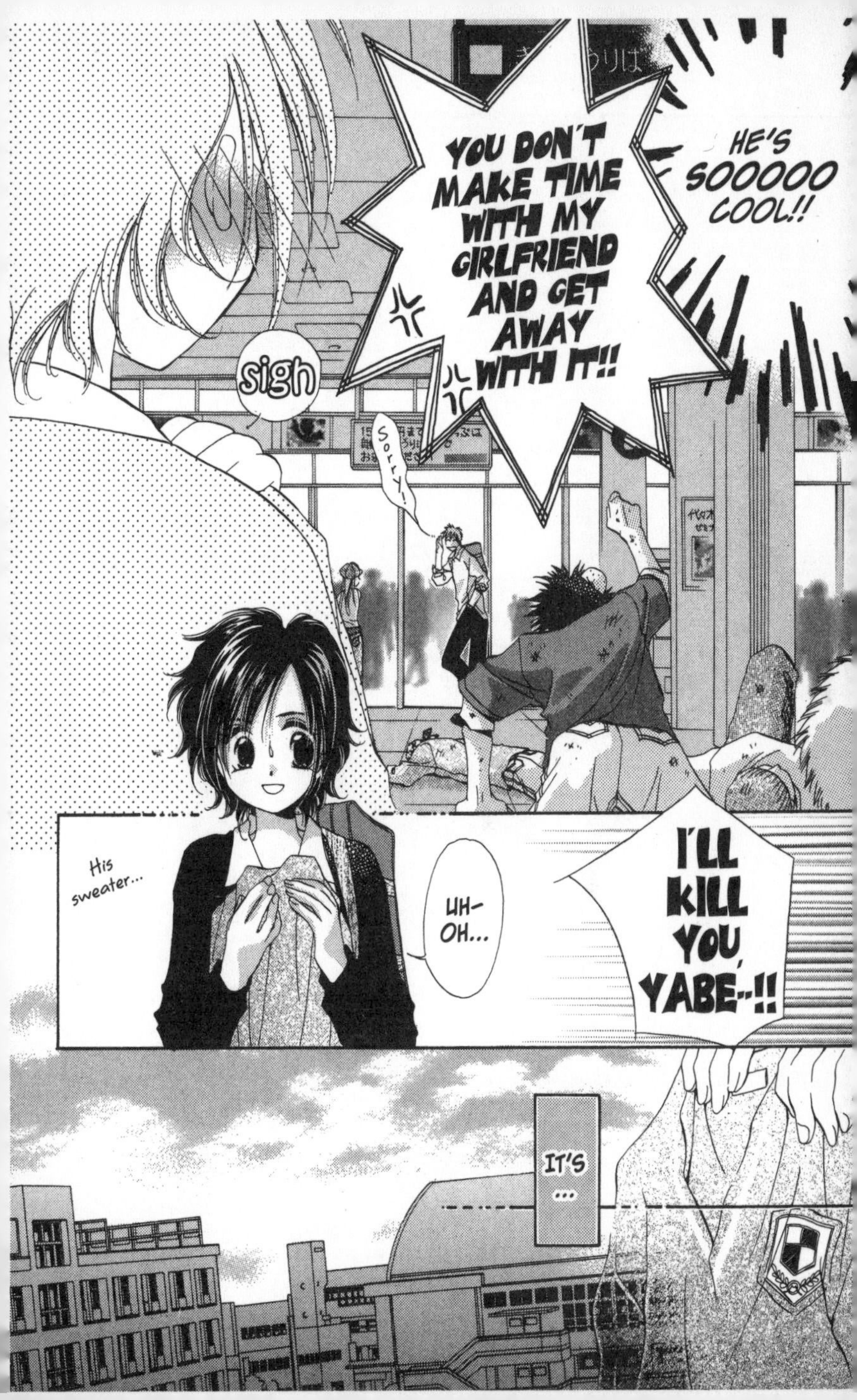
HE'S SOOOOO COOL!!
YOU DON'T MAKE TIME WITH MY GIRLFRIEND AND GET AWAY WITH IT!!
sigh
Sorry!
I'LL KILL YOU, YABE--!!
UH-OH...
His sweater...
IT'S ...

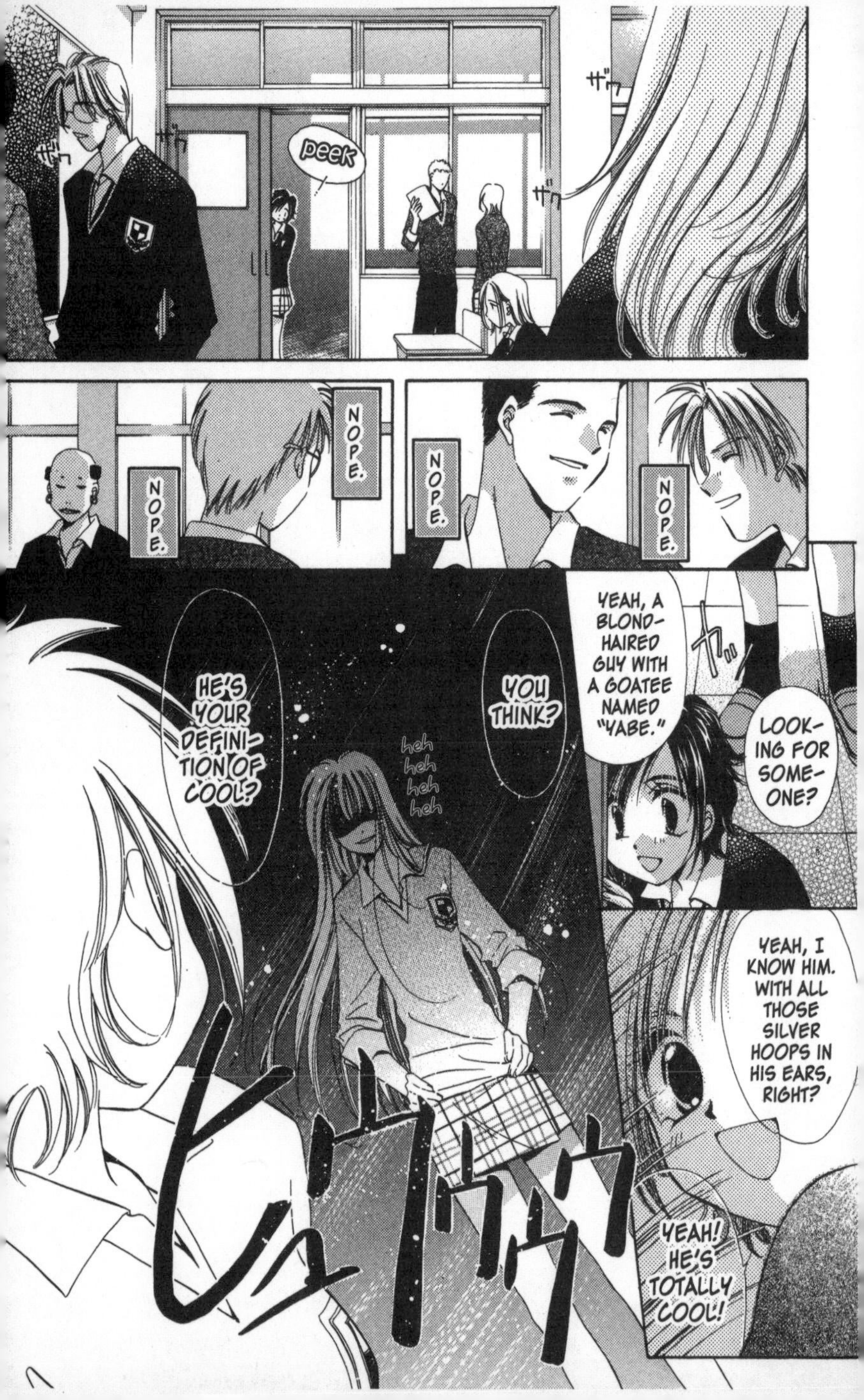
peek
NOPE.
NOPE.
NOPE.
NOPE.
LOOKING FOR SOMEONE?
YEAH, A BLOND-HAIRED GUY WITH A GOATEE NAMED "YABE."
YEAH, I KNOW HIM. WITH ALL THOSE SILVER HOOPS IN HIS EARS, RIGHT?
YEAH! HE'S TOTALLY COOL!
YOU THINK?
heh heh heh heh
HE'S YOUR DEFINITION OF COOL?

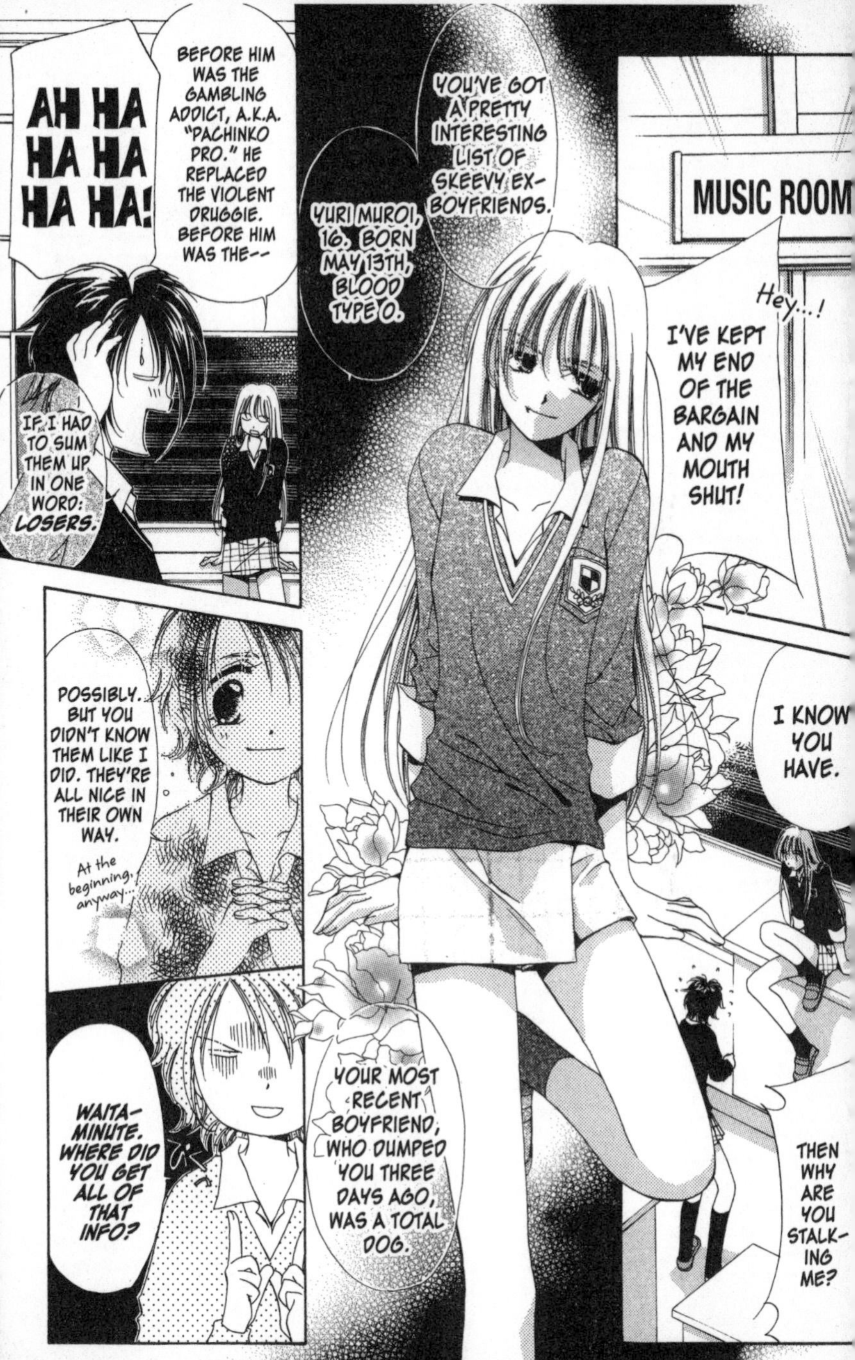
MUSIC ROOM
Hey...!
I'VE KEPT MY END OF THE BARGAIN AND MY MOUTH SHUT!
YOU'VE GOT A PRETTY INTERESTING LIST OF SKEEVY EX-BOYFRIENDS.
YURI MUROI, 16. BORN MAY 13TH, BLOOD TYPE O.
I KNOW YOU HAVE.
THEN WHY ARE YOU STALKING ME?
YOUR MOST RECENT BOYFRIEND, WHO DUMPED YOU THREE DAYS AGO, WAS A TOTAL DOG.
BEFORE HIM WAS THE GAMBLING ADDICT, A.K.A. "PACHINKO PRO." HE REPLACED THE VIOLENT DRUGGIE. BEFORE HIM WAS THE--
AH HA HA HA HA HA!
IF I HAD TO SUM THEM UP IN ONE WORD: LOSERS.
POSSIBLY. BUT YOU DIDN'T KNOW THEM LIKE I DID. THEY'RE ALL NICE IN THEIR OWN WAY.
At the beginning, anyway...
WAITA-MINUTE. WHERE DID YOU GET ALL OF THAT INFO?

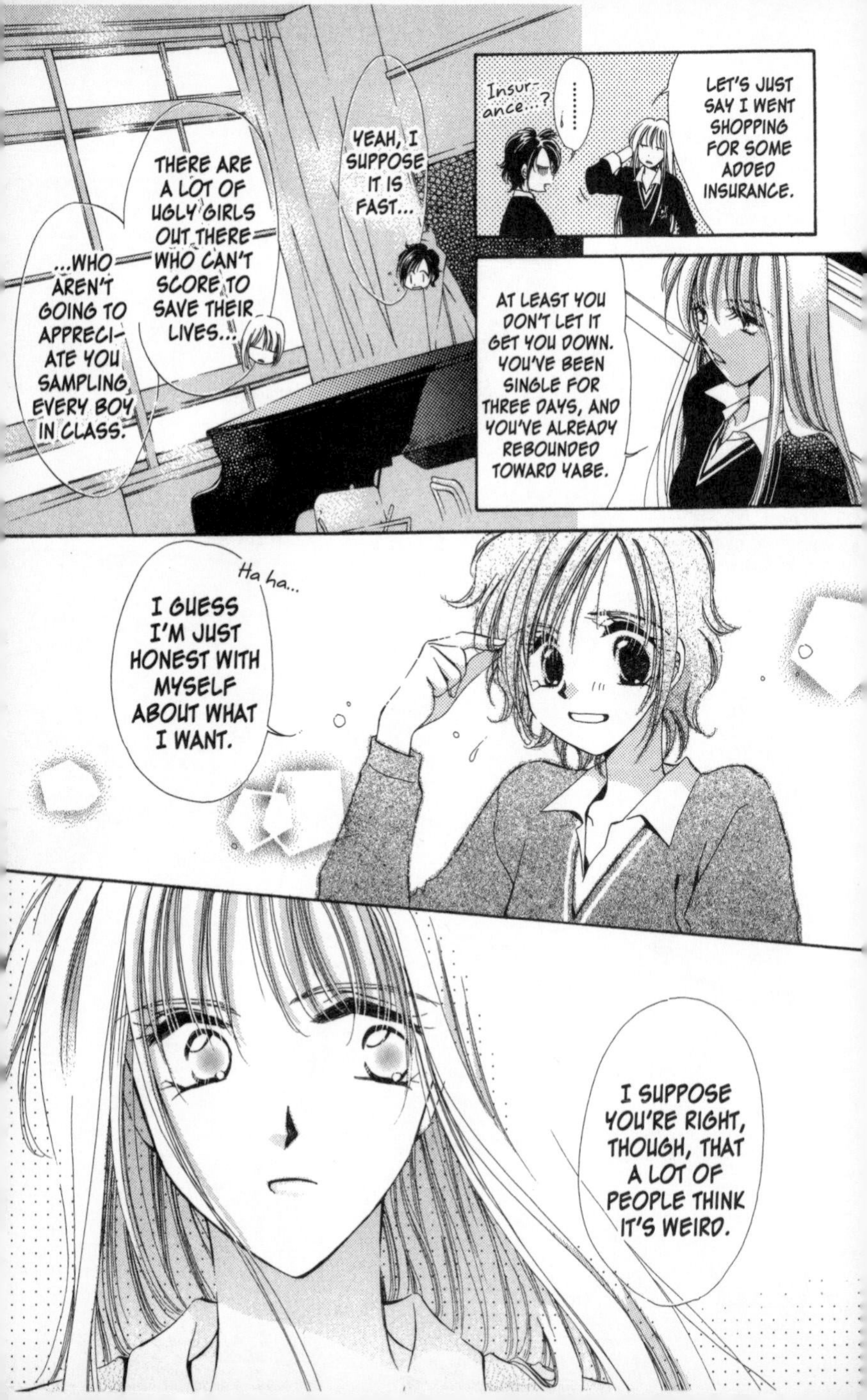
LET'S JUST SAY I WENT SHOPPING FOR SOME ADDED INSURANCE.
Insur-ance...?
......!
AT LEAST YOU DON'T LET IT GET YOU DOWN. YOU'VE BEEN SINGLE FOR THREE DAYS, AND YOU'VE ALREADY REBOUNDED TOWARD YABE.
YEAH, I SUPPOSE IT IS FAST...
THERE ARE A LOT OF UGLY GIRLS OUT THERE WHO CAN'T SCORE TO SAVE THEIR LIVES...
...WHO AREN'T GOING TO APPRECI-ATE YOU SAMPLING EVERY BOY IN CLASS.
Ha ha...
I GUESS I'M JUST HONEST WITH MYSELF ABOUT WHAT I WANT.
I SUPPOSE YOU'RE RIGHT, THOUGH, THAT A LOT OF PEOPLE THINK IT'S WEIRD.

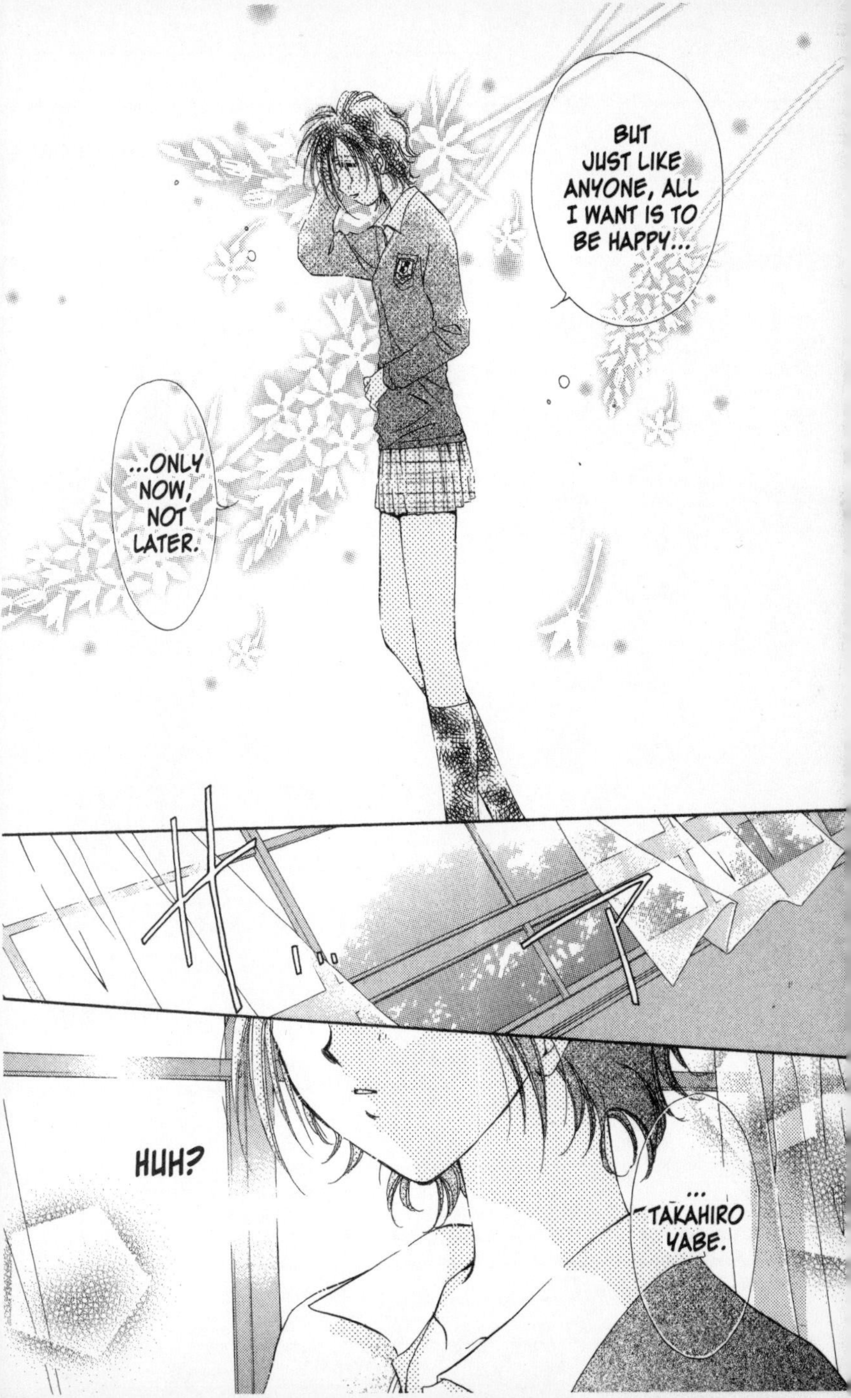
BUT JUST LIKE ANYONE, ALL I WANT IS TO BE HAPPY...
...ONLY NOW, NOT LATER.
...TAKAHIRO YABE.
HUH?

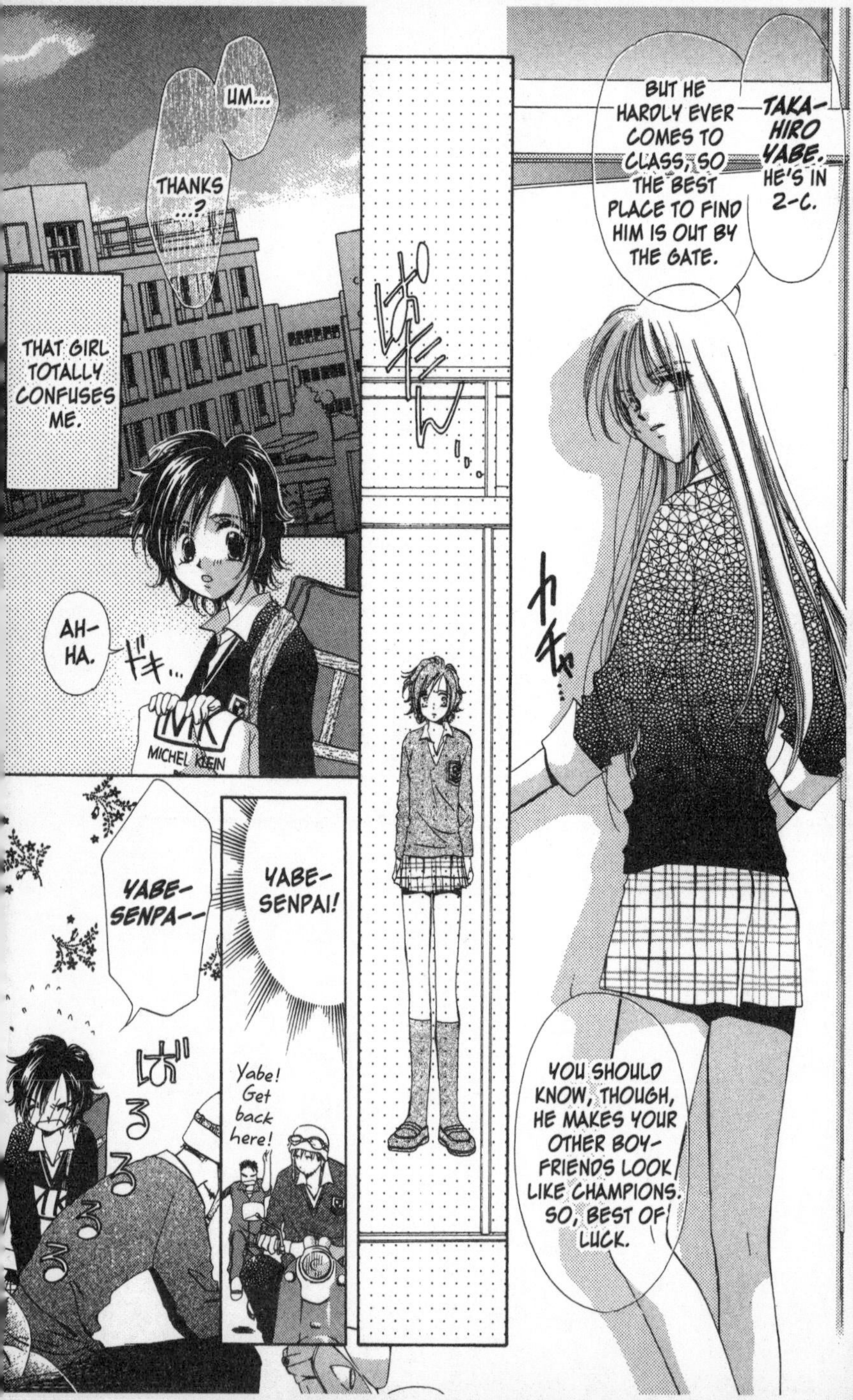
TAKA-HIRO YABE. HE'S IN 2-C.
BUT HE HARDLY EVER COMES TO CLASS, SO THE BEST PLACE TO FIND HIM IS OUT BY THE GATE.
カチャ…
YOU SHOULD KNOW, THOUGH, HE MAKES YOUR OTHER BOY-FRIENDS LOOK LIKE CHAMPIONS. SO, BEST OF LUCK.
UM...
THANKS ...?
THAT GIRL TOTALLY CONFUSES ME.
AH-HA.
ドキ…
MK
MICHEL KLEIN
YABE-SENPAI!
Yabe! Get back here!
YABE-SENPA--

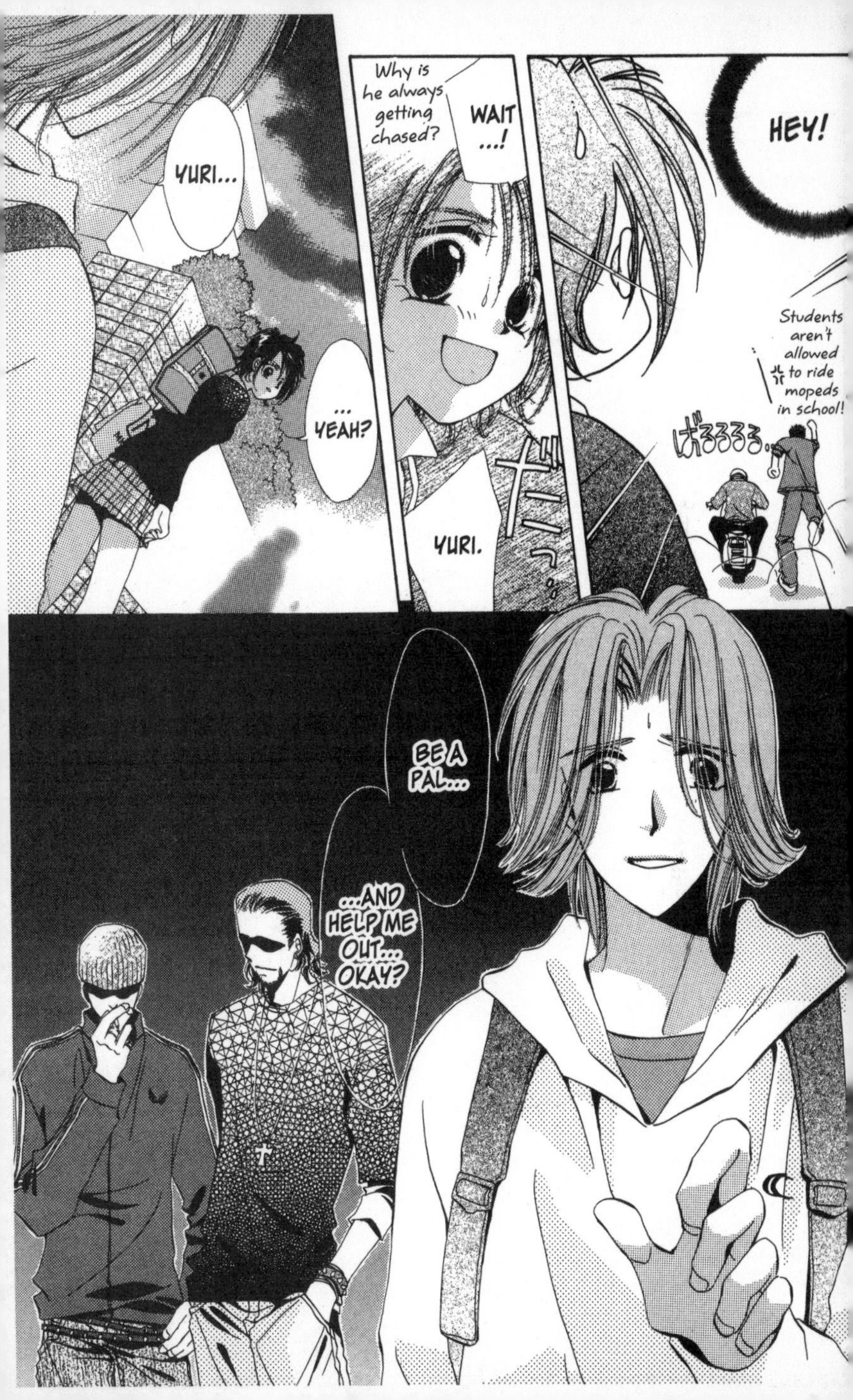
HEY!
Students aren't allowed to ride mopeds in school!
ぶるるるる
Why is he always getting chased?
WAIT ...!
YURI.
YURI...
... YEAH?
BE A PAL...
...AND HELP ME OUT... OKAY?

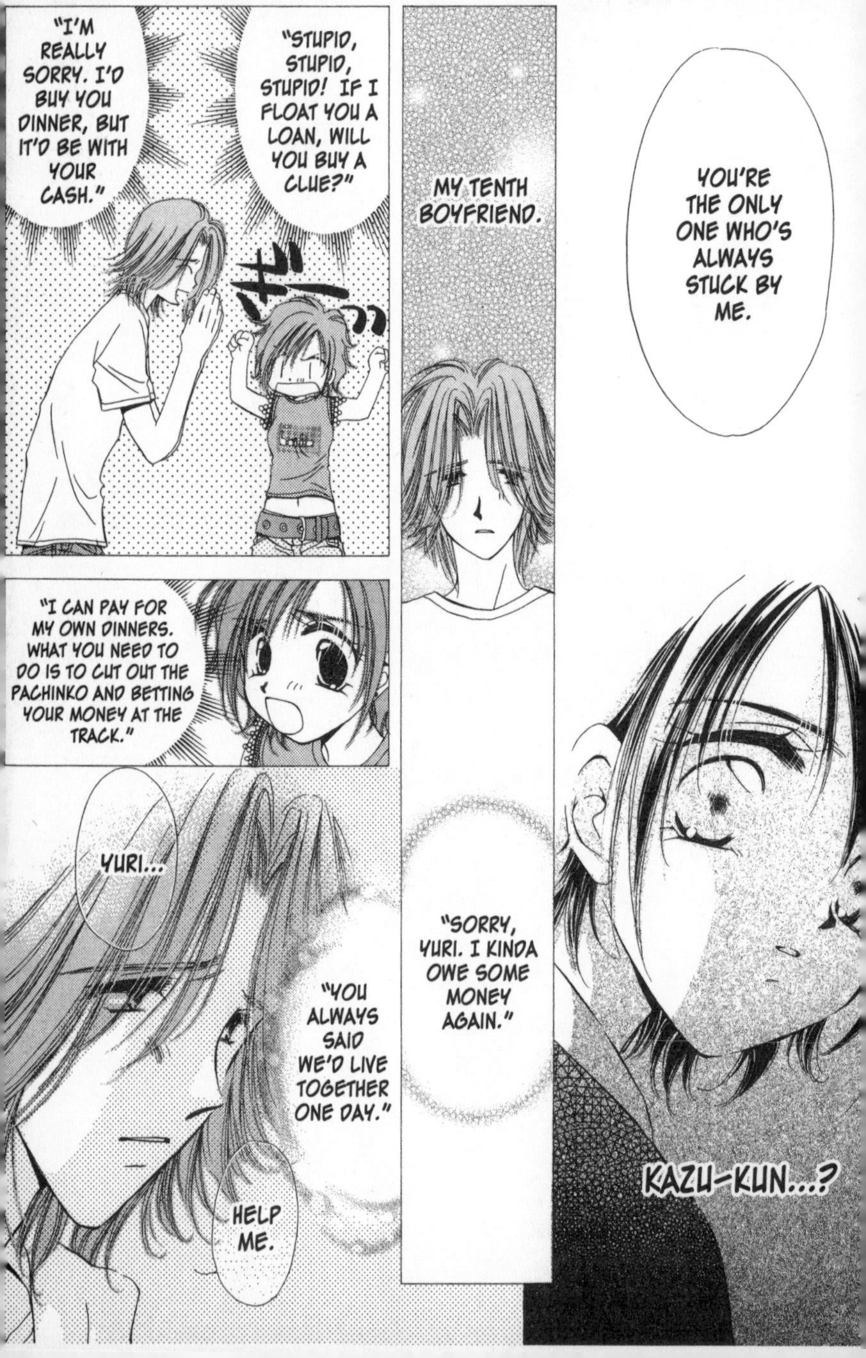
YOU'RE THE ONLY ONE WHO'S ALWAYS STUCK BY ME.
KAZU-KUN...?
MY TENTH BOYFRIEND.
"SORRY, YURI. I KINDA OWE SOME MONEY AGAIN."
"STUPID, STUPID, STUPID! IF I FLOAT YOU A LOAN, WILL YOU BUY A CLUE?"
"I'M REALLY SORRY. I'D BUY YOU DINNER, BUT IT'D BE WITH YOUR CASH."
"I CAN PAY FOR MY OWN DINNERS. WHAT YOU NEED TO DO IS TO CUT OUT THE PACHINKO AND BETTING YOUR MONEY AT THE TRACK."
YURI...
"YOU ALWAYS SAID WE'D LIVE TOGETHER ONE DAY."
HELP ME.

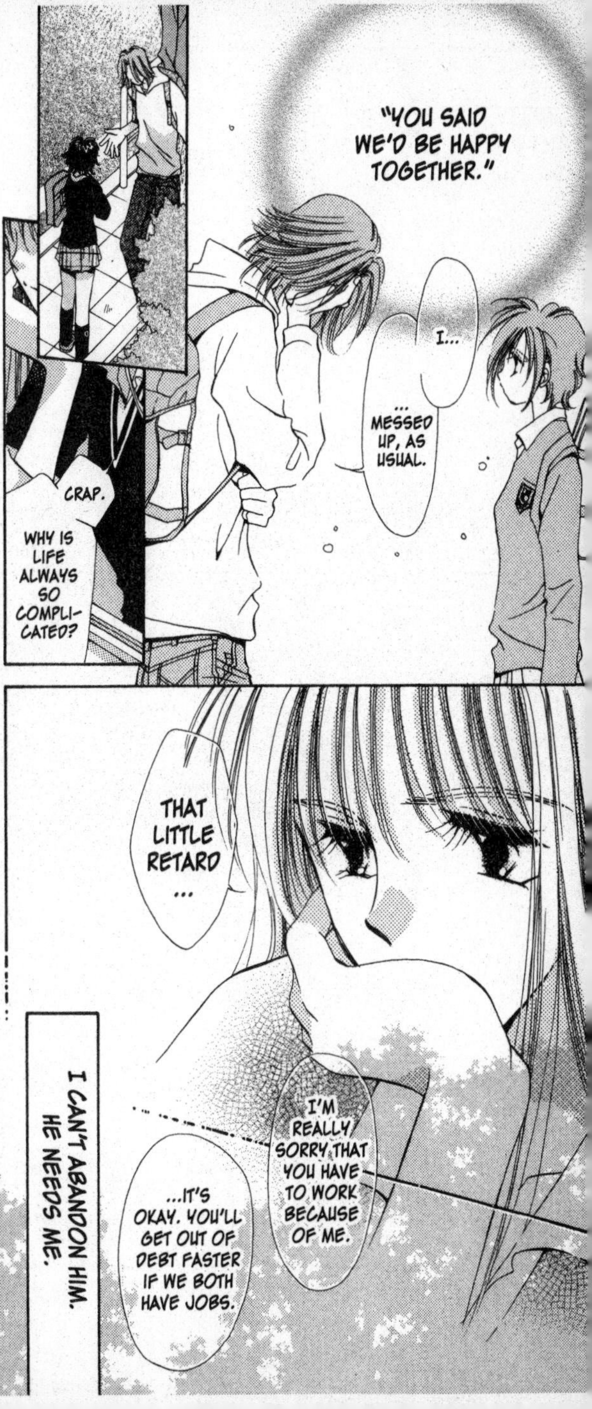
"YOU SAID WE'D BE HAPPY TOGETHER."
I...
...MESSED UP, AS USUAL.
CRAP.
WHY IS LIFE ALWAYS SO COMPLICATED?
THAT LITTLE RETARD...
I'M REALLY SORRY THAT YOU HAVE TO WORK BECAUSE OF ME.
...IT'S OKAY. YOU'LL GET OUT OF DEBT FASTER IF WE BOTH HAVE JOBS.
I CAN'T ABANDON HIM. HE NEEDS ME.

Konnichiwa! This is my 28th (yes, I started counting again) manga collection. Thank you very much for picking it up.

Well, I finally started it: *Gatcha Gacha*. The story is full of suspense and twists and turns, so I'm having a lot of fun drawing it. At first, I'd only intended to make it a one-volume book, but then I received a whole lot of encouraging fan letters and I decided to make it a little bit longer. Thank you!

Gatcha Gacha is being serialized in the *Melody* anthology. I have another title (Honey, please read it!) running in the *LaLa DX* anthology, too. That means I'm drawing two different comics at the same time, so my free time is pretty much, well, you know...I want to keep going as long as I can manage it, though.

Though it's getting kinda frightening, wondering when my assistants are going to snap...

So, that's how it is! I patiently await your adoring fanmail.

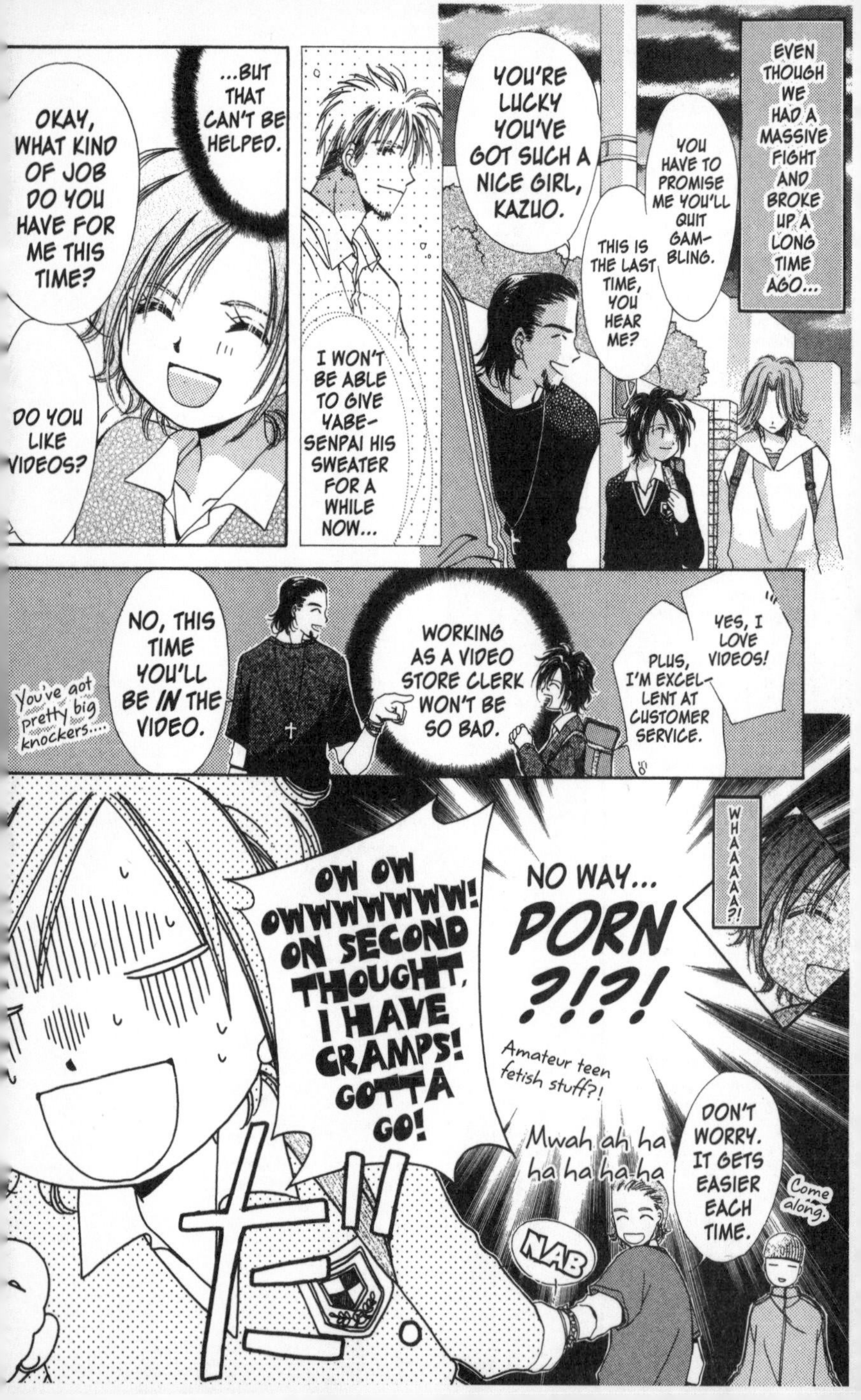
EVEN THOUGH WE HAD A MASSIVE FIGHT AND BROKE UP A LONG TIME AGO...
YOU HAVE TO PROMISE ME YOU'LL QUIT GAM-BLING.
THIS IS THE LAST TIME, YOU HEAR ME?
YOU'RE LUCKY YOU'VE GOT SUCH A NICE GIRL, KAZUO.
...BUT THAT CAN'T BE HELPED.
I WON'T BE ABLE TO GIVE YABE-SENPAI HIS SWEATER FOR A WHILE NOW...
OKAY, WHAT KIND OF JOB DO YOU HAVE FOR ME THIS TIME?
DO YOU LIKE VIDEOS?
YES, I LOVE VIDEOS!
PLUS, I'M EXCEL-LENT AT CUSTOMER SERVICE.
WORKING AS A VIDEO STORE CLERK WON'T BE SO BAD.
NO, THIS TIME YOU'LL BE *IN* THE VIDEO.
You've got pretty big knockers....
WHAAAAA?!
NO WAY... PORN?!?!
Amateur teen fetish stuff?!
OW OW OWWWWWWW! ON SECOND THOUGHT, I HAVE CRAMPS! GOTTA GO!
DON'T WORRY. IT GETS EASIER EACH TIME.
Come along.
Mwah ah ha ha ha ha ha
NAB

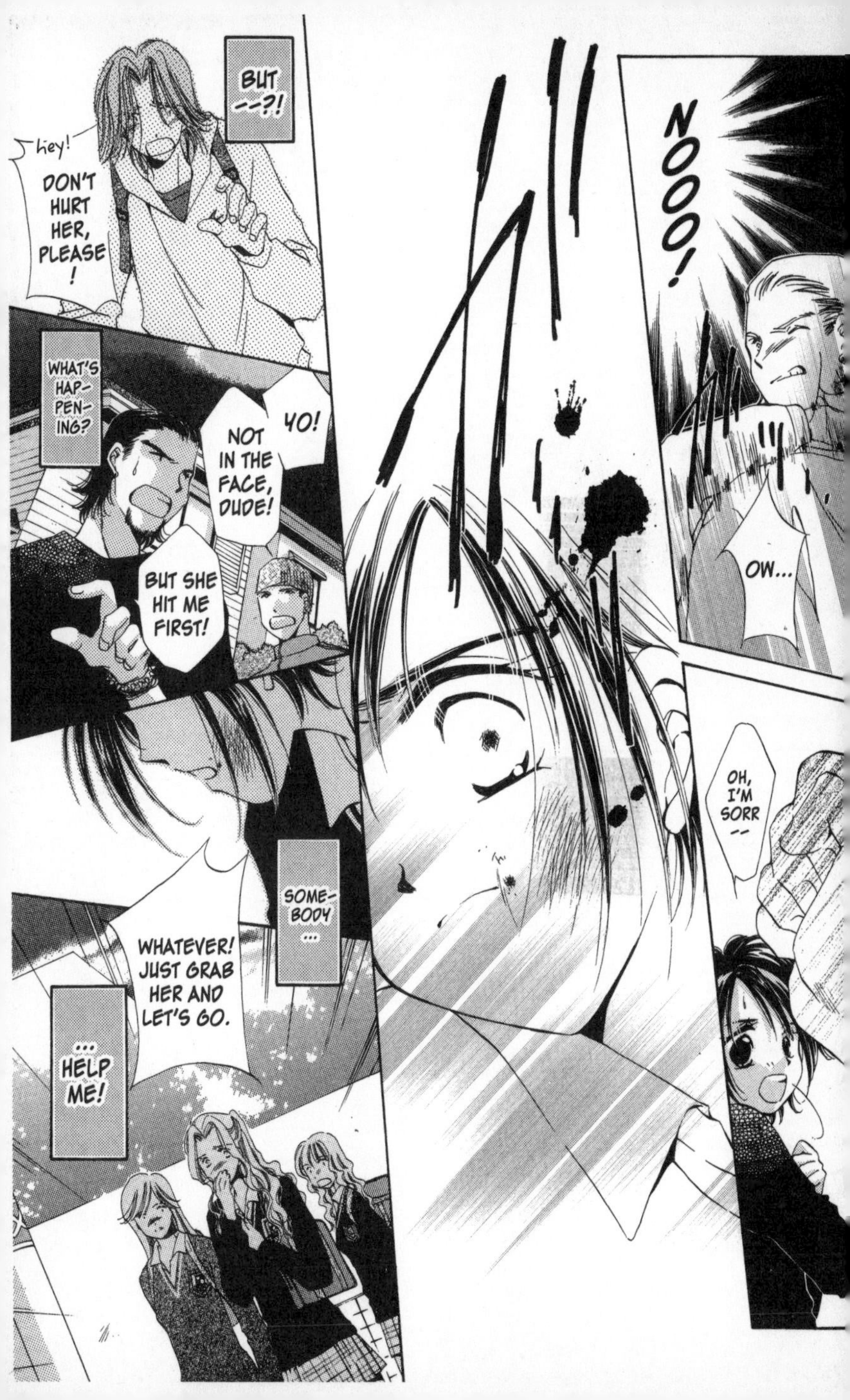
NOOOO!
OW...
OH, I'M SORR--
BUT--?!
hey!
DON'T HURT HER, PLEASE!
YO!
NOT IN THE FACE, DUDE!
WHAT'S HAP-PEN-ING?
BUT SHE HIT ME FIRST!
SOME-BODY...
WHATEVER! JUST GRAB HER AND LET'S GO.
...HELP ME!

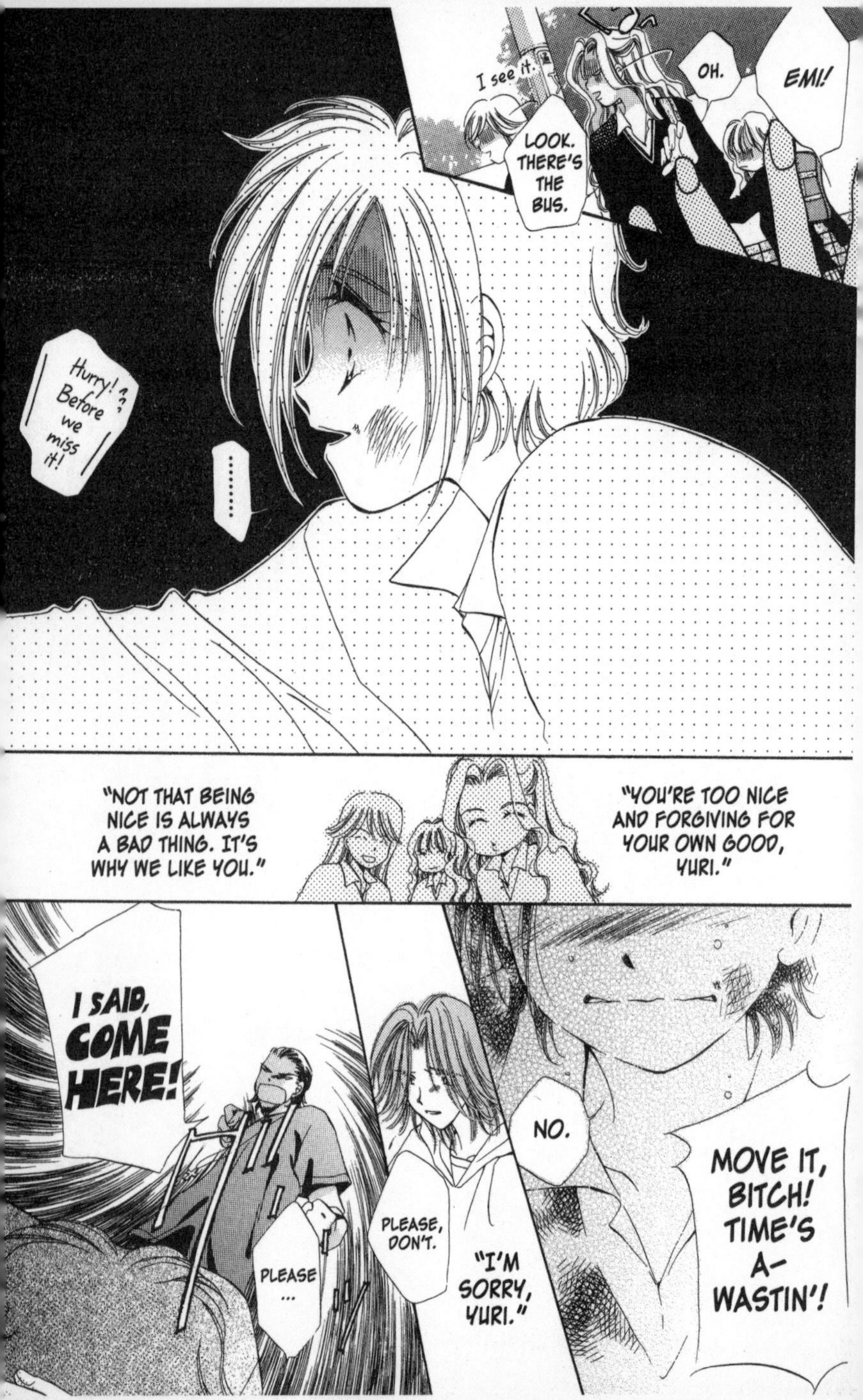
EMI!
OH.
LOOK. THERE'S THE BUS.
I see it.
......
Hurry! ?? Before we miss it!
"YOU'RE TOO NICE AND FORGIVING FOR YOUR OWN GOOD, YURI."
"NOT THAT BEING NICE IS ALWAYS A BAD THING. IT'S WHY WE LIKE YOU."
MOVE IT, BITCH! TIME'S A-WASTIN'!
NO.
"I'M SORRY, YURI."
PLEASE, DON'T.
I SAID, COME HERE!
PLEASE ...

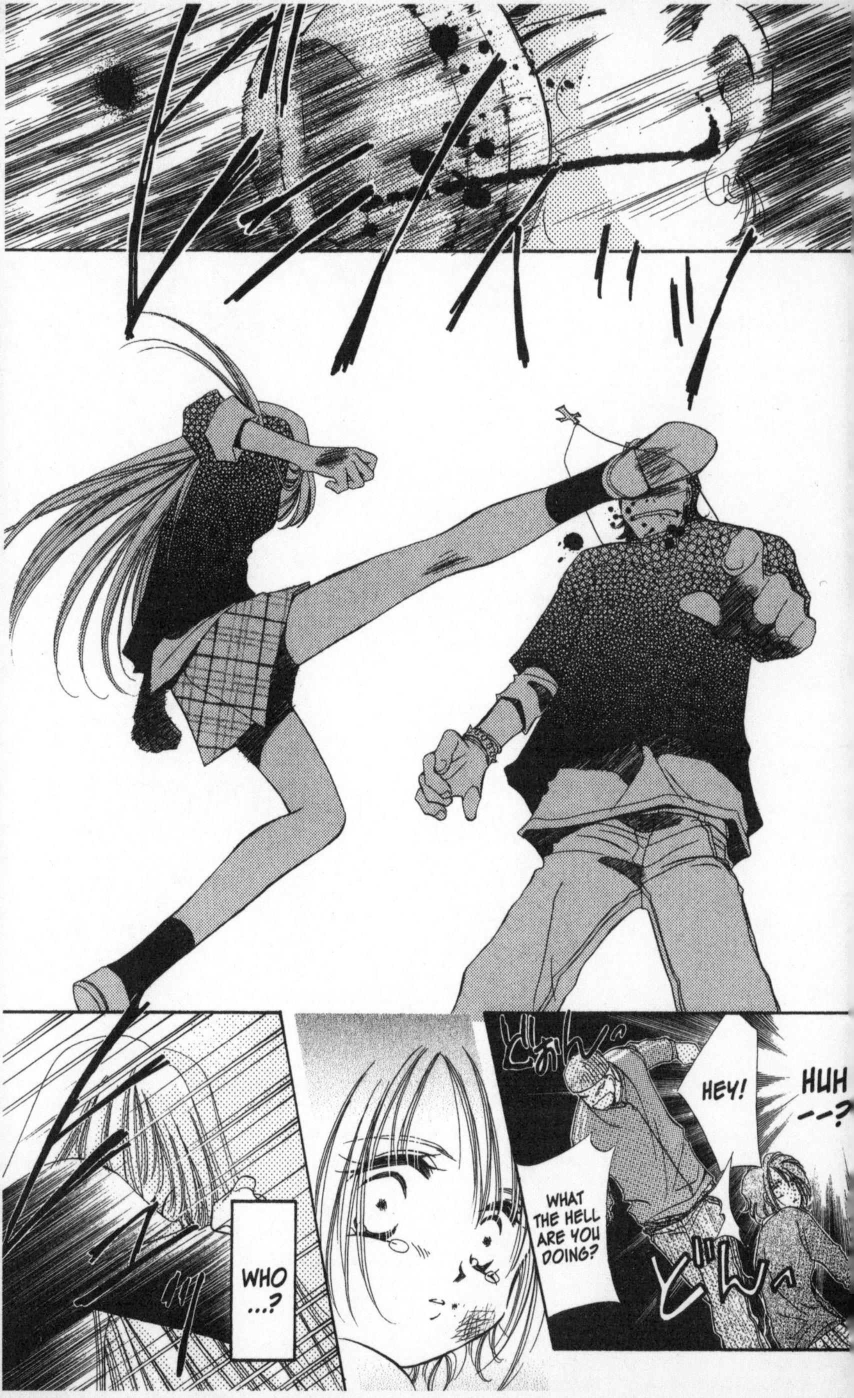
HUH --?
HEY!
WHAT THE HELL ARE YOU DOING?
WHO ...?

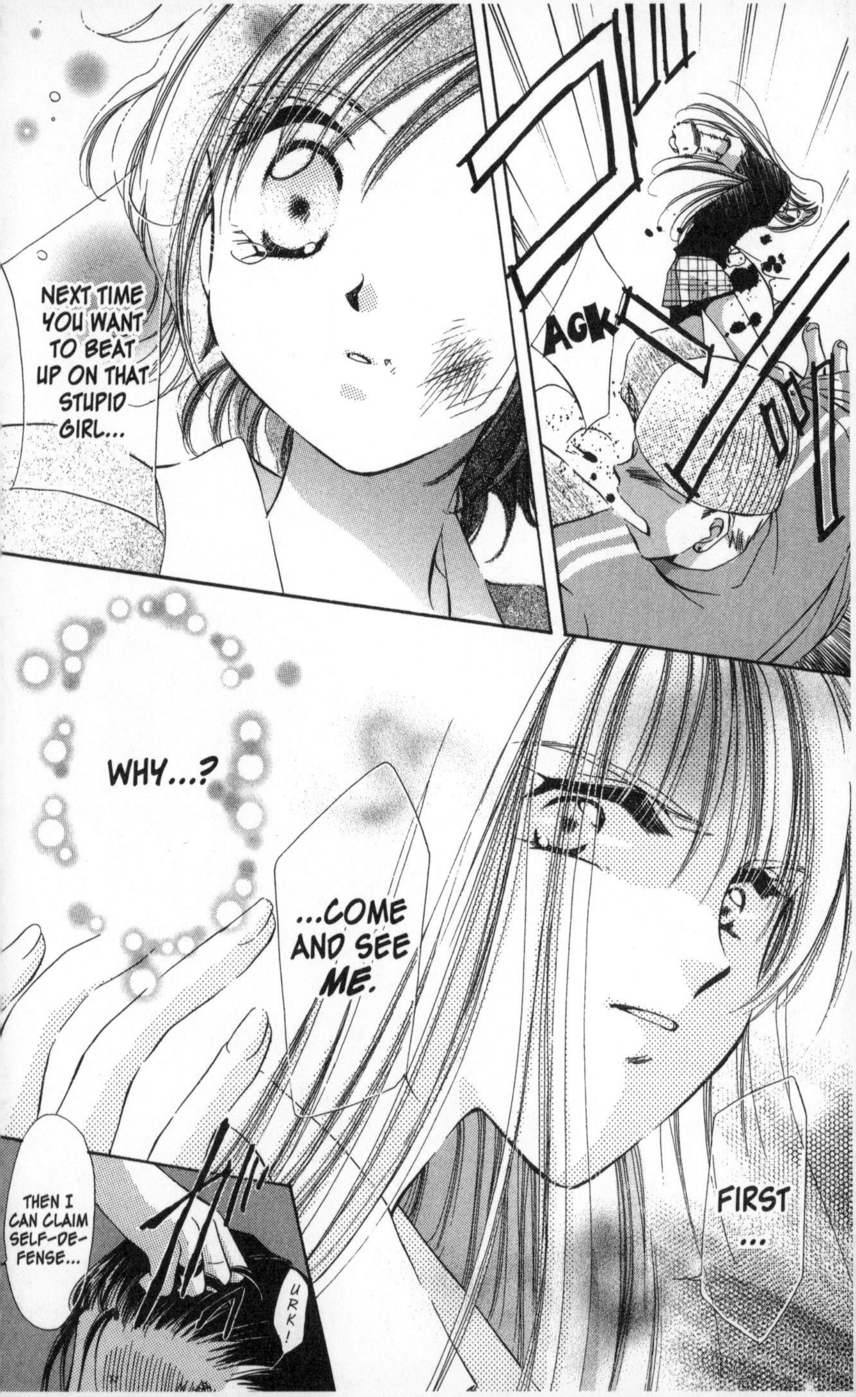
AGK
NEXT TIME YOU WANT TO BEAT UP ON THAT STUPID GIRL...
FIRST ...
...COME AND SEE ME.
THEN I CAN CLAIM SELF-DE-FENSE...
URK!
WHY...?

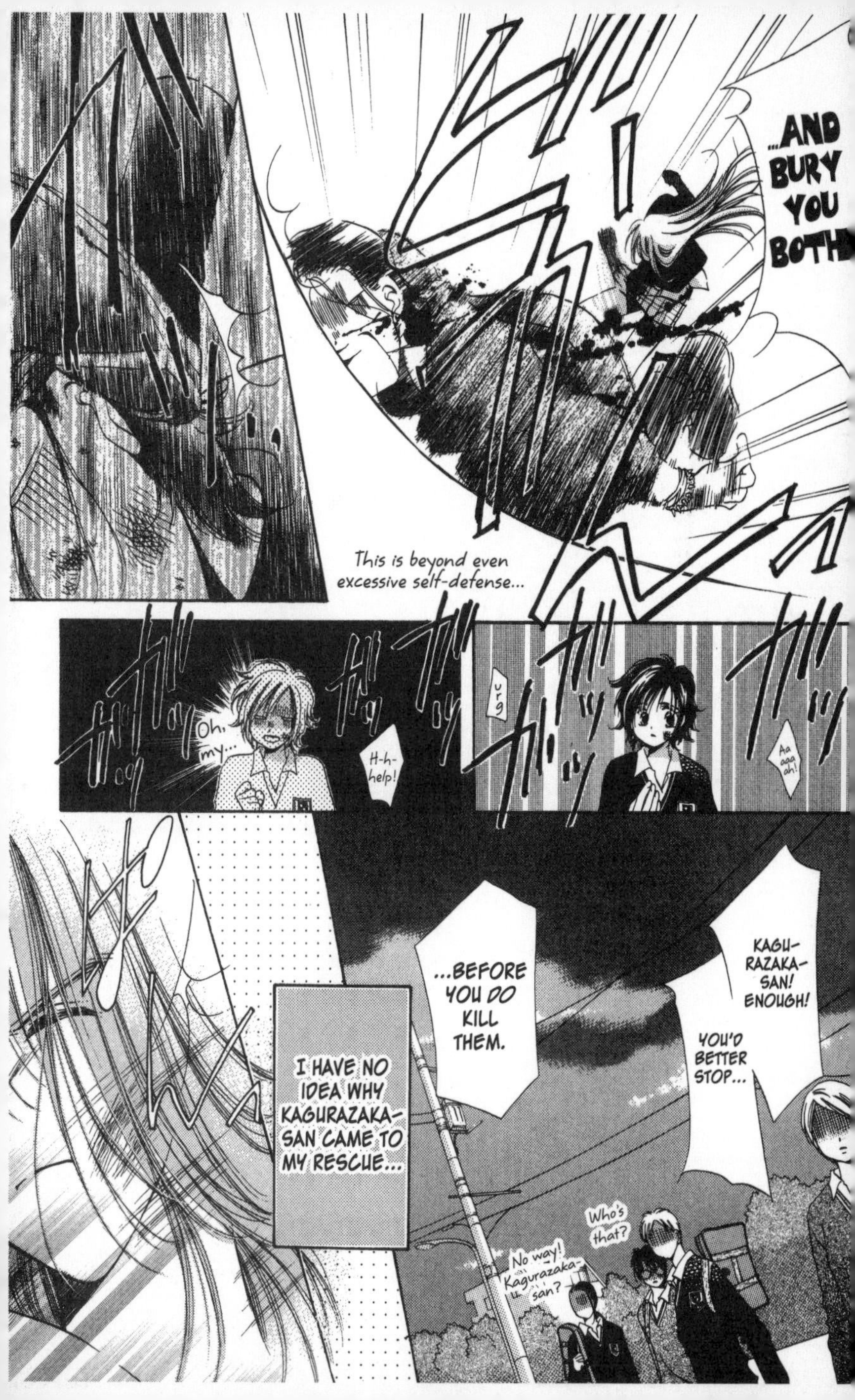
...AND BURY YOU BOTH
This is beyond even excessive self-defense...
urg
Aa aaa ah!
H-h-help!
Oh, my...
KAGURAZAKA-SAN! ENOUGH!
YOU'D BETTER STOP...
...BEFORE YOU DO KILL THEM.
I HAVE NO IDEA WHY KAGURAZAKA-SAN CAME TO MY RESCUE...
Who's that?
No way! Kagurazaka-san?

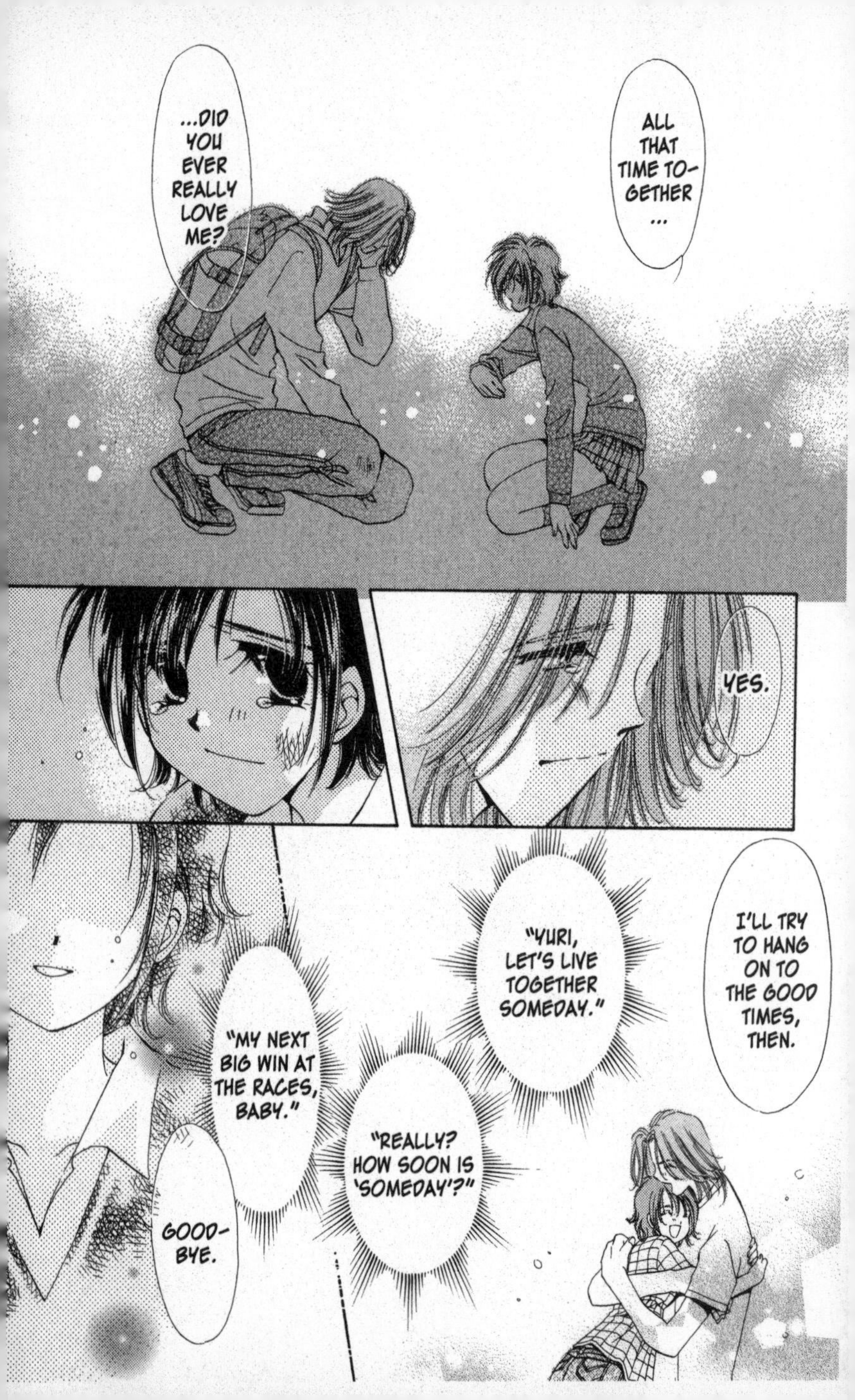
ALL THAT TIME TO-GETHER...
...DID YOU EVER REALLY LOVE ME?
YES.
I'LL TRY TO HANG ON TO THE GOOD TIMES, THEN.
"YURI, LET'S LIVE TOGETHER SOMEDAY."
"REALLY? HOW SOON IS 'SOMEDAY'?"
"MY NEXT BIG WIN AT THE RACES, BABY."
GOOD-BYE.

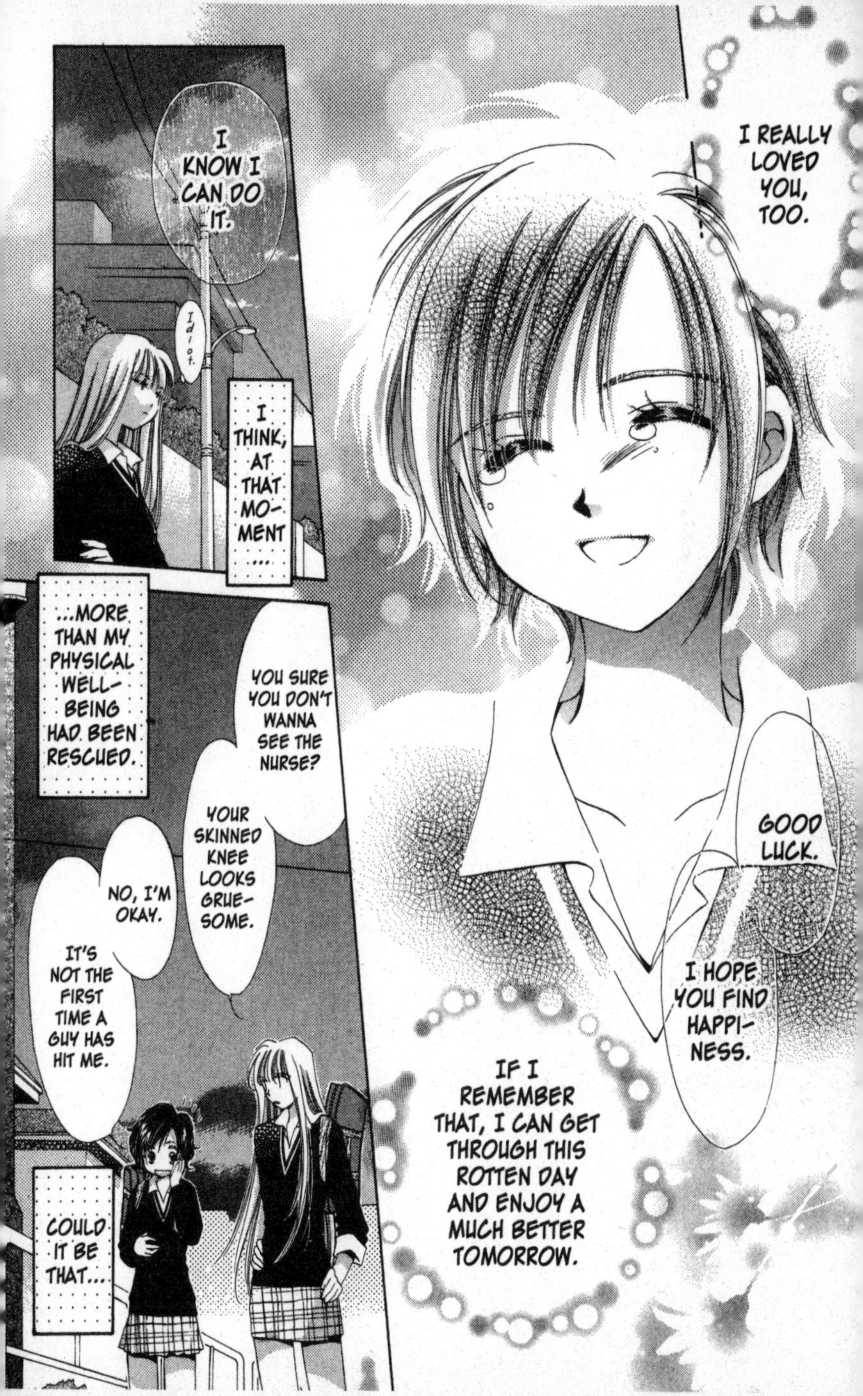
I REALLY LOVED YOU, TOO.
GOOD LUCK.
I HOPE YOU FIND HAPPI-NESS.
IF I REMEMBER THAT, I CAN GET THROUGH THIS ROTTEN DAY AND ENJOY A MUCH BETTER TOMORROW.
I KNOW I CAN DO IT.
Idiot.
I THINK, AT THAT MO-MENT....
...MORE THAN MY PHYSICAL WELL-BEING HAD BEEN RESCUED.
YOU SURE YOU DON'T WANNA SEE THE NURSE?
YOUR SKINNED KNEE LOOKS GRUE-SOME.
NO, I'M OKAY.
IT'S NOT THE FIRST TIME A GUY HAS HIT ME.
COULD IT BE THAT...

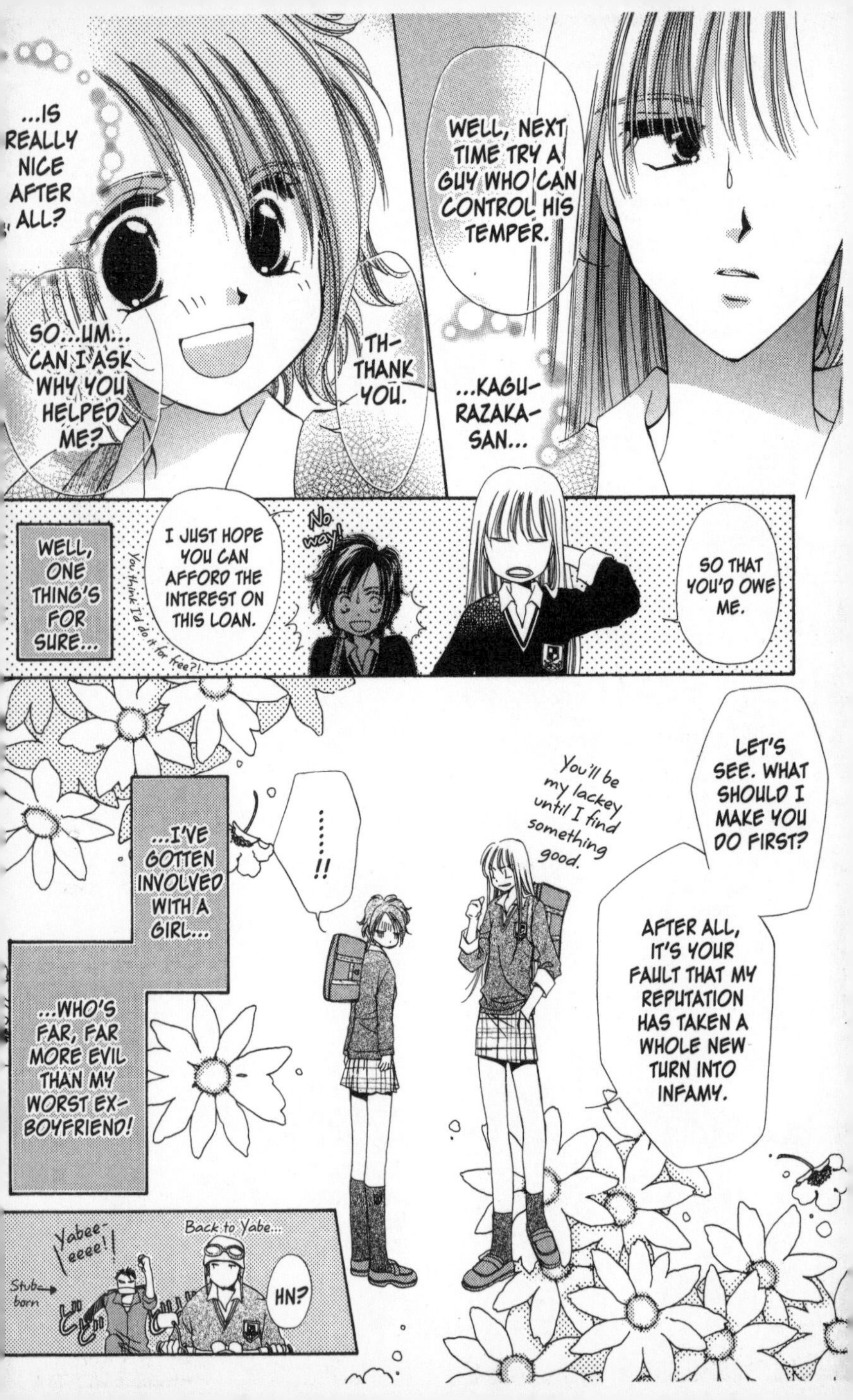
WELL, NEXT TIME TRY A GUY WHO CAN CONTROL HIS TEMPER.
...KAGU-RAZAKA-SAN...
...IS REALLY NICE AFTER ALL?
TH-THANK YOU.
SO...UM... CAN I ASK WHY YOU HELPED ME?
SO THAT YOU'D OWE ME.
No way!
I JUST HOPE YOU CAN AFFORD THE INTEREST ON THIS LOAN.
You think I'd do it for free?!
WELL, ONE THING'S FOR SURE...
LET'S SEE. WHAT SHOULD I MAKE YOU DO FIRST?
AFTER ALL, IT'S YOUR FAULT THAT MY REPUTATION HAS TAKEN A WHOLE NEW TURN INTO INFAMY.
You'll be my lackey until I find something good.
......!!
...I'VE GOTTEN INVOLVED WITH A GIRL...
...WHO'S FAR, FAR MORE EVIL THAN MY WORST EX-BOYFRIEND!
HN?
Back to Yabe...
Yabee-eeee!
Stubborn

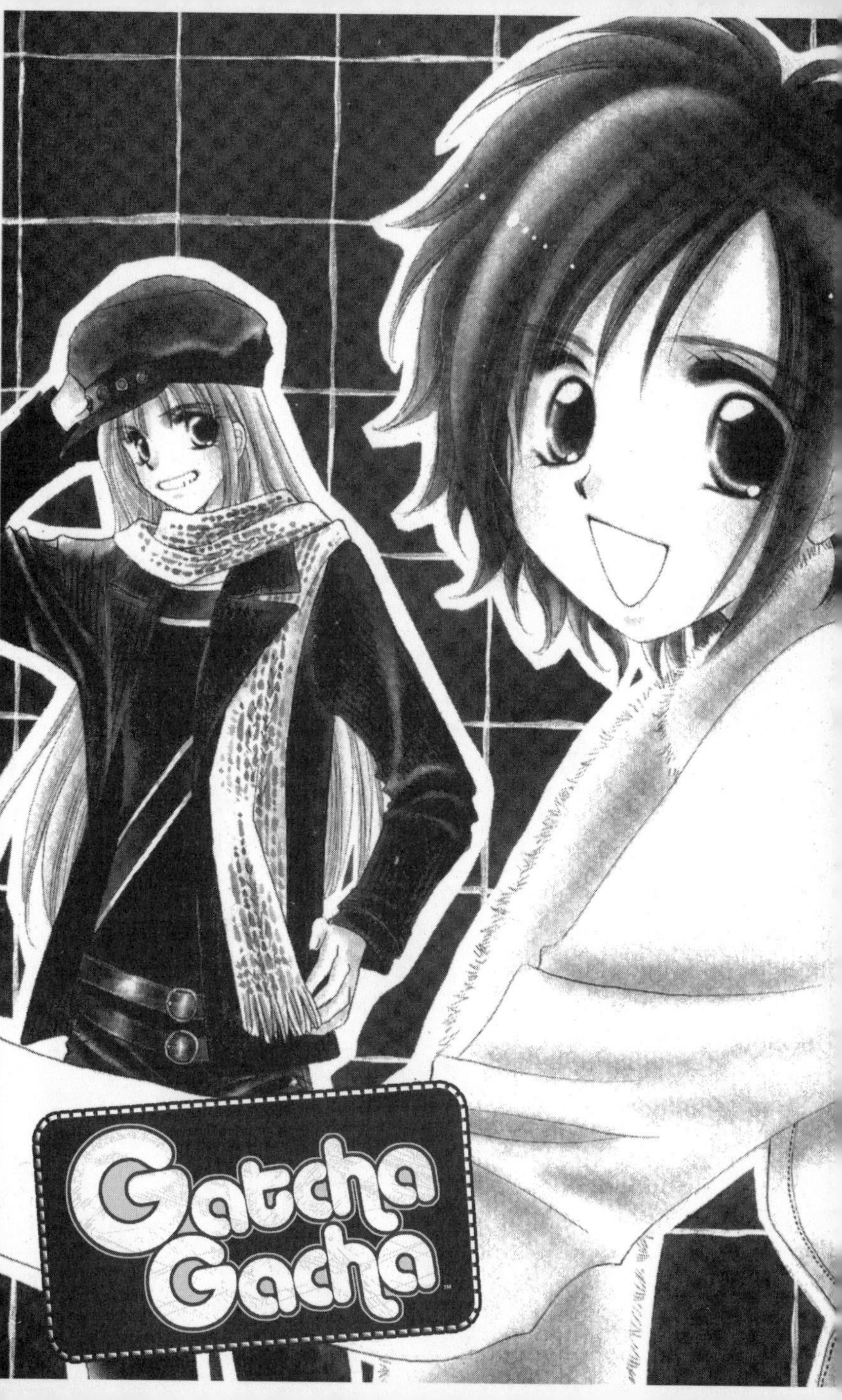
Gatcha Gacha™

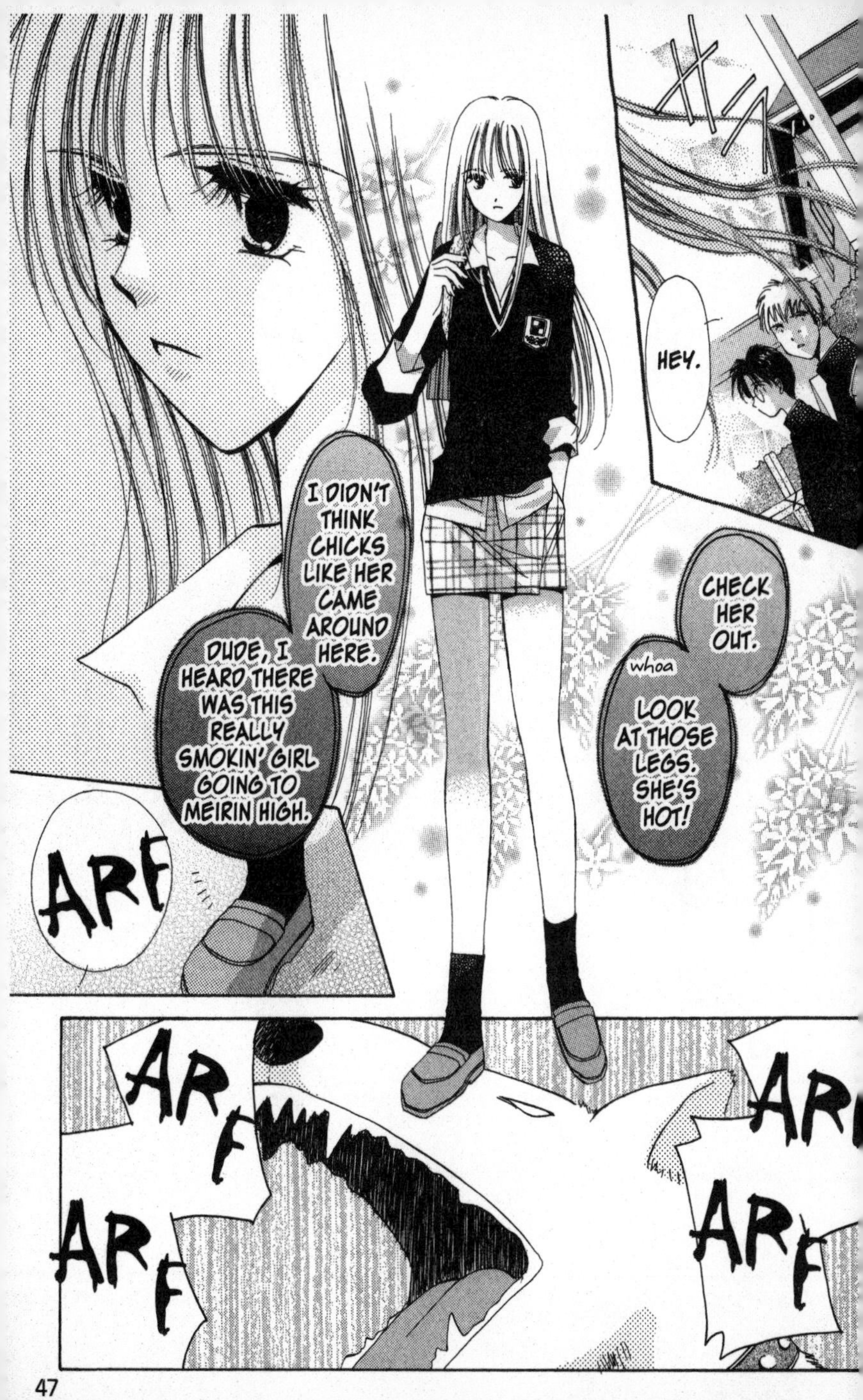
HEY.
CHECK HER OUT.
whoa
LOOK AT THOSE LEGS. SHE'S HOT!
I DIDN'T THINK CHICKS LIKE HER CAME AROUND HERE.
DUDE, I HEARD THERE WAS THIS REALLY SMOKIN' GIRL GOING TO MEIRIN HIGH.
ARF
AR
ARF
ARF
ARF

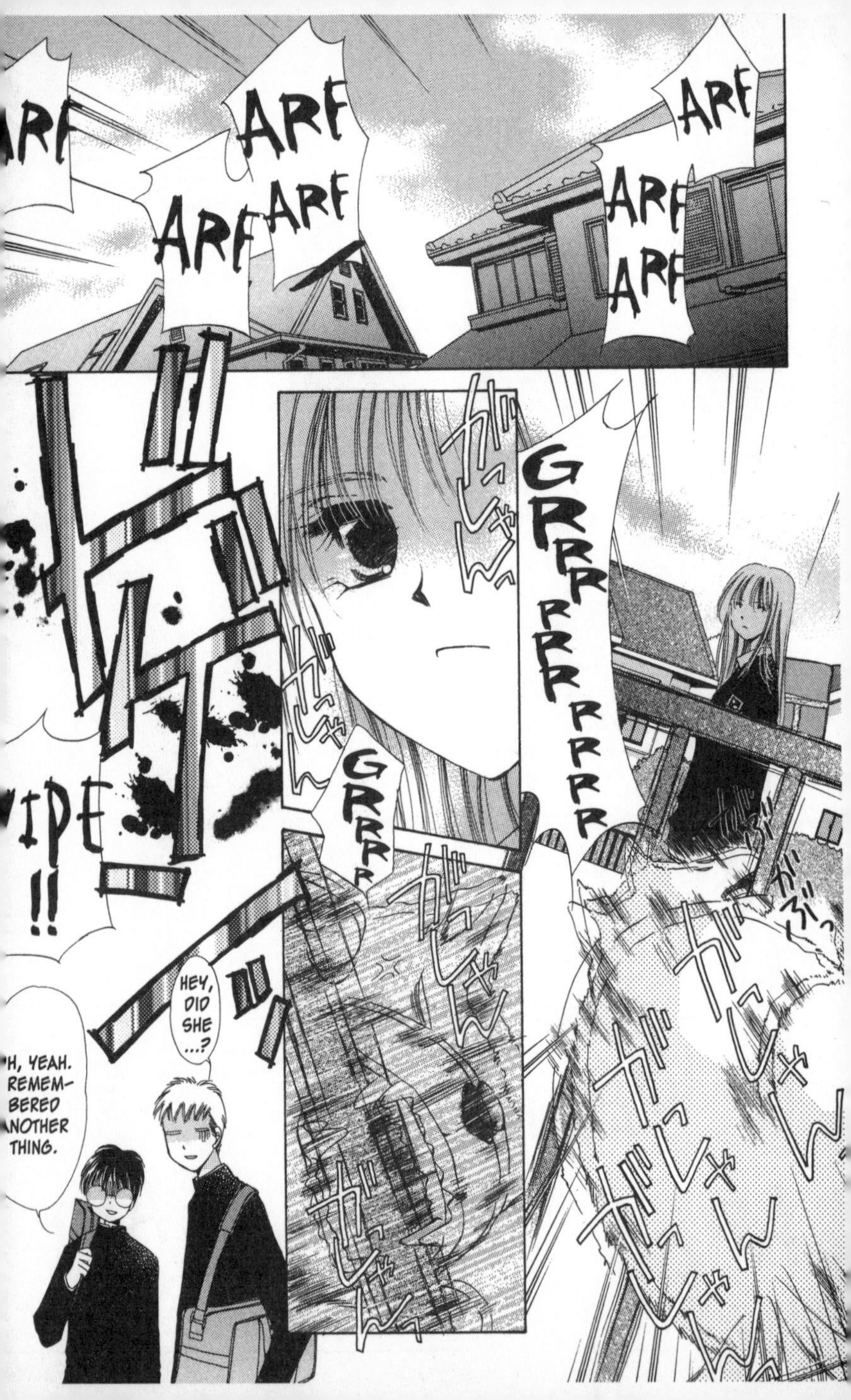
ARF
ARF
ARF
ARF
ARF
ARF
ARF
ARF
GRRRRRRRRRRRRR
GRRRR
IPE !!
HEY, DID SHE ...?
H, YEAH. REMEMBERED ANOTHER THING.

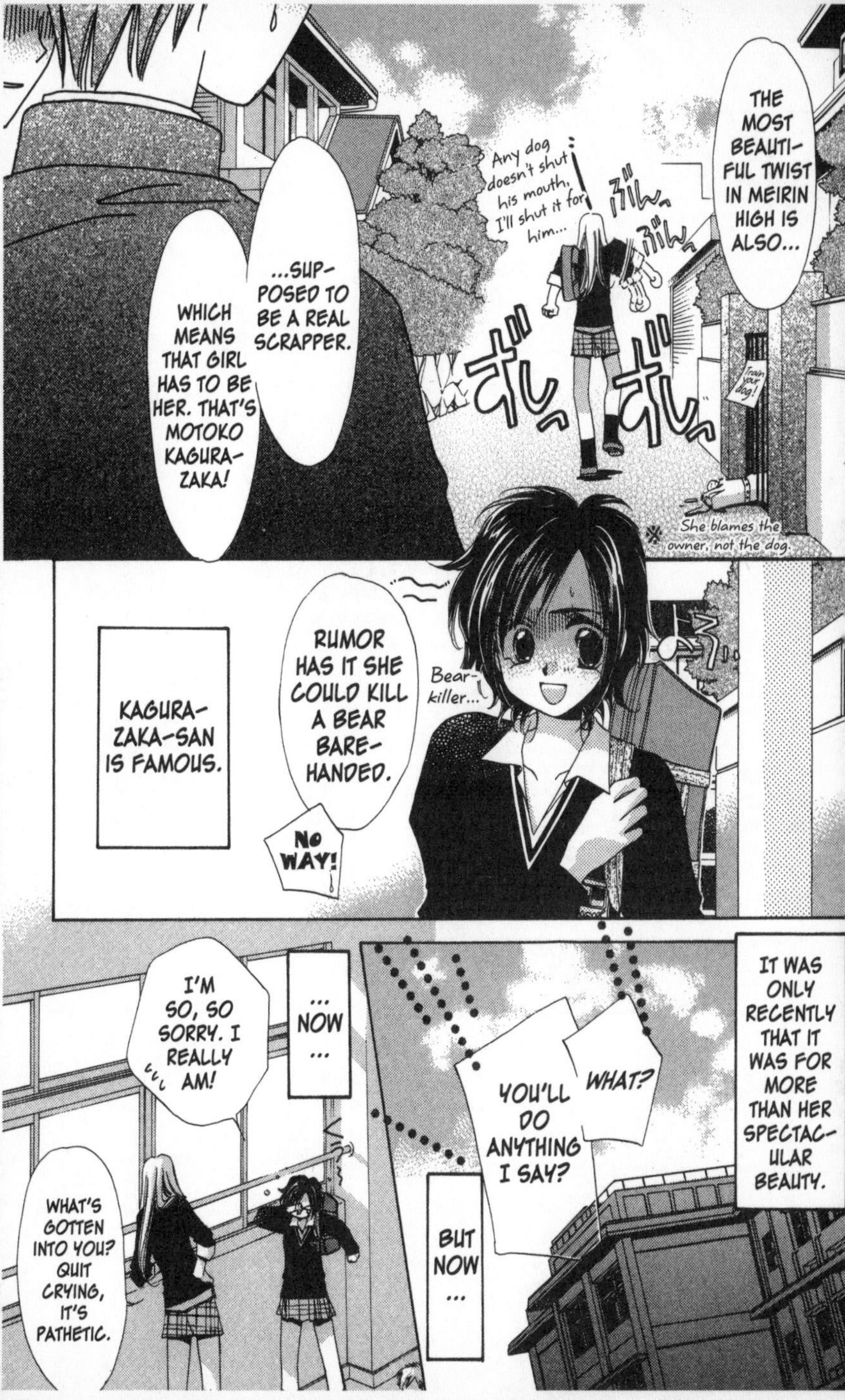
THE MOST BEAUTIFUL TWIST IN MEIRIN HIGH IS ALSO...
Any dog doesn't shut his mouth, I'll shut it for him...
Train your dog!
※She blames the owner, not the dog.
...SUPPOSED TO BE A REAL SCRAPPER.
WHICH MEANS THAT GIRL HAS TO BE HER. THAT'S MOTOKO KAGURAZAKA!
RUMOR HAS IT SHE COULD KILL A BEAR BAREHANDED.
Bear-killer...
NO WAY!
KAGURAZAKA-SAN IS FAMOUS.
IT WAS ONLY RECENTLY THAT IT WAS FOR MORE THAN HER SPECTACULAR BEAUTY.
WHAT?
YOU'LL DO ANYTHING I SAY?
BUT NOW...
...NOW...
I'M SO, SO SORRY. I REALLY AM!
WHAT'S GOTTEN INTO YOU? QUIT CRYING, IT'S PATHETIC.

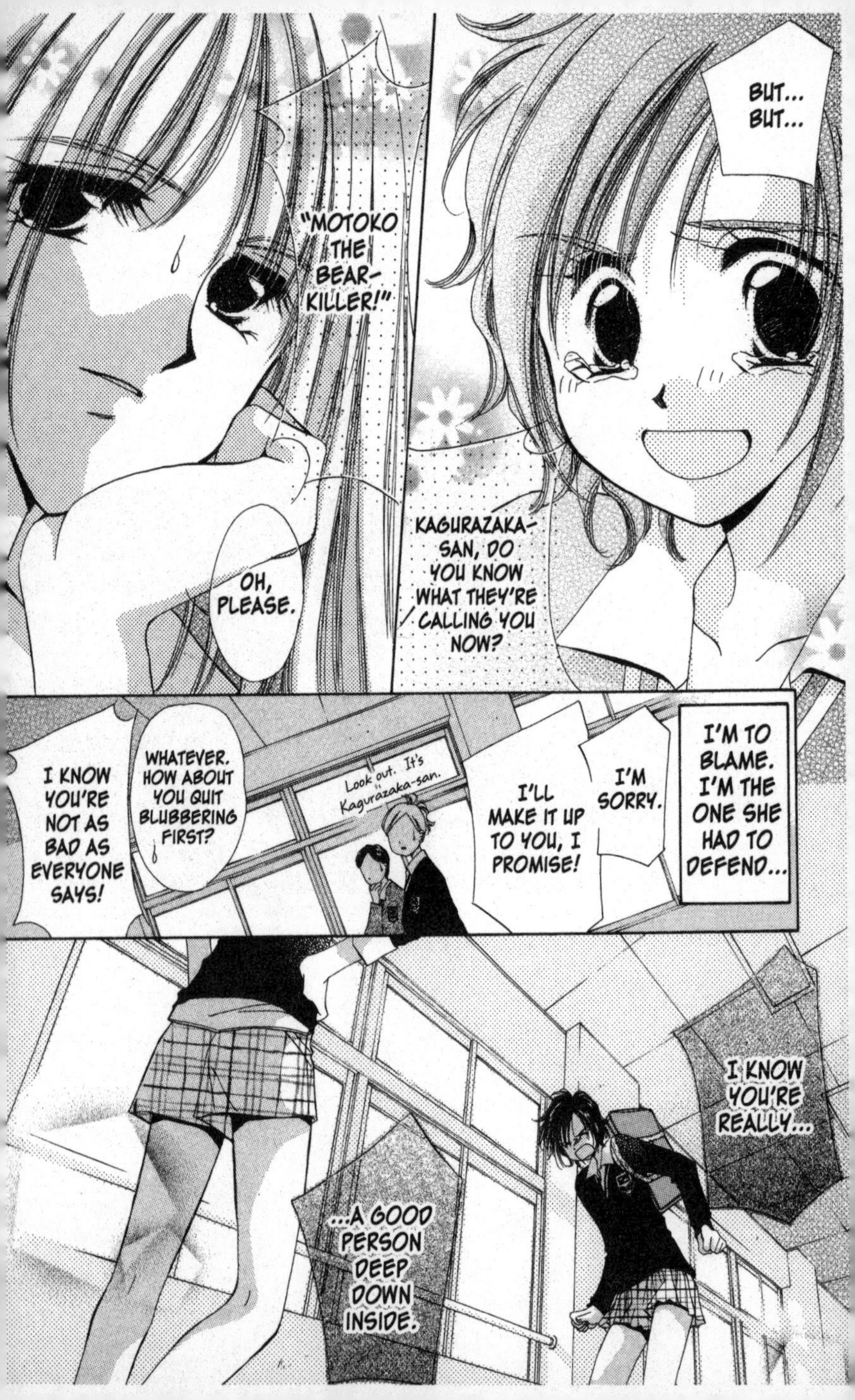
BUT... BUT...
KAGURAZAKA-SAN, DO YOU KNOW WHAT THEY'RE CALLING YOU NOW?
"MOTOKO THE BEAR-KILLER!"
OH, PLEASE.
I'M TO BLAME. I'M THE ONE SHE HAD TO DEFEND...
I'M SORRY.
I'LL MAKE IT UP TO YOU, I PROMISE!
Look out. It's Kagurazaka-san.
WHATEVER. HOW ABOUT YOU QUIT BLUBBERING FIRST?
I KNOW YOU'RE NOT AS BAD AS EVERYONE SAYS!
I KNOW YOU'RE REALLY...
...A GOOD PERSON DEEP DOWN INSIDE.

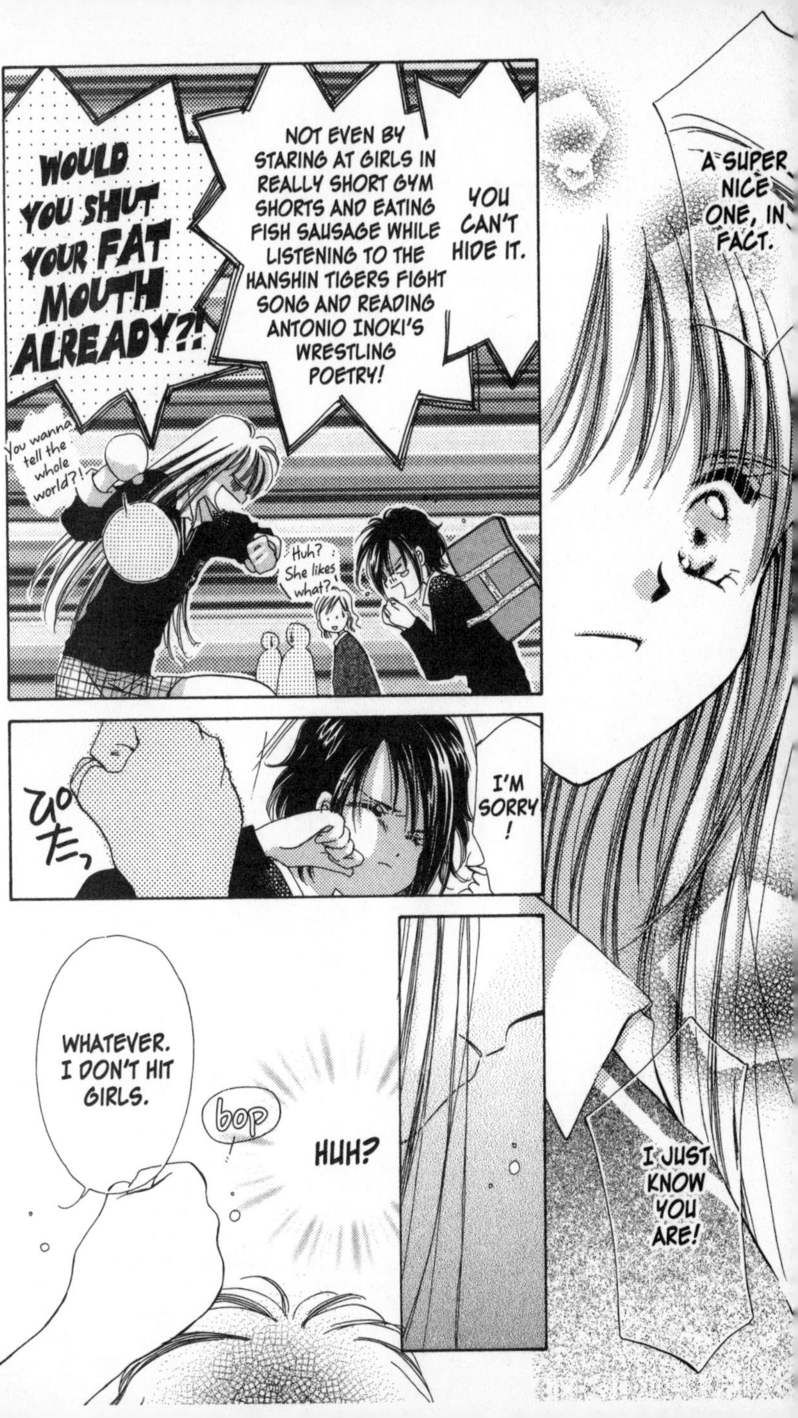
A SUPER NICE ONE, IN FACT.
I JUST KNOW YOU ARE!
YOU CAN'T HIDE IT.
NOT EVEN BY STARING AT GIRLS IN REALLY SHORT GYM SHORTS AND EATING FISH SAUSAGE WHILE LISTENING TO THE HANSHIN TIGERS FIGHT SONG AND READING ANTONIO INOKI'S WRESTLING POETRY!
WOULD YOU SHUT YOUR FAT MOUTH ALREADY?!
Huh? She likes what?
You wanna tell the whole world?!
I'M SORRY!
ぴたっ
HUH?
bop
WHATEVER. I DON'T HIT GIRLS.

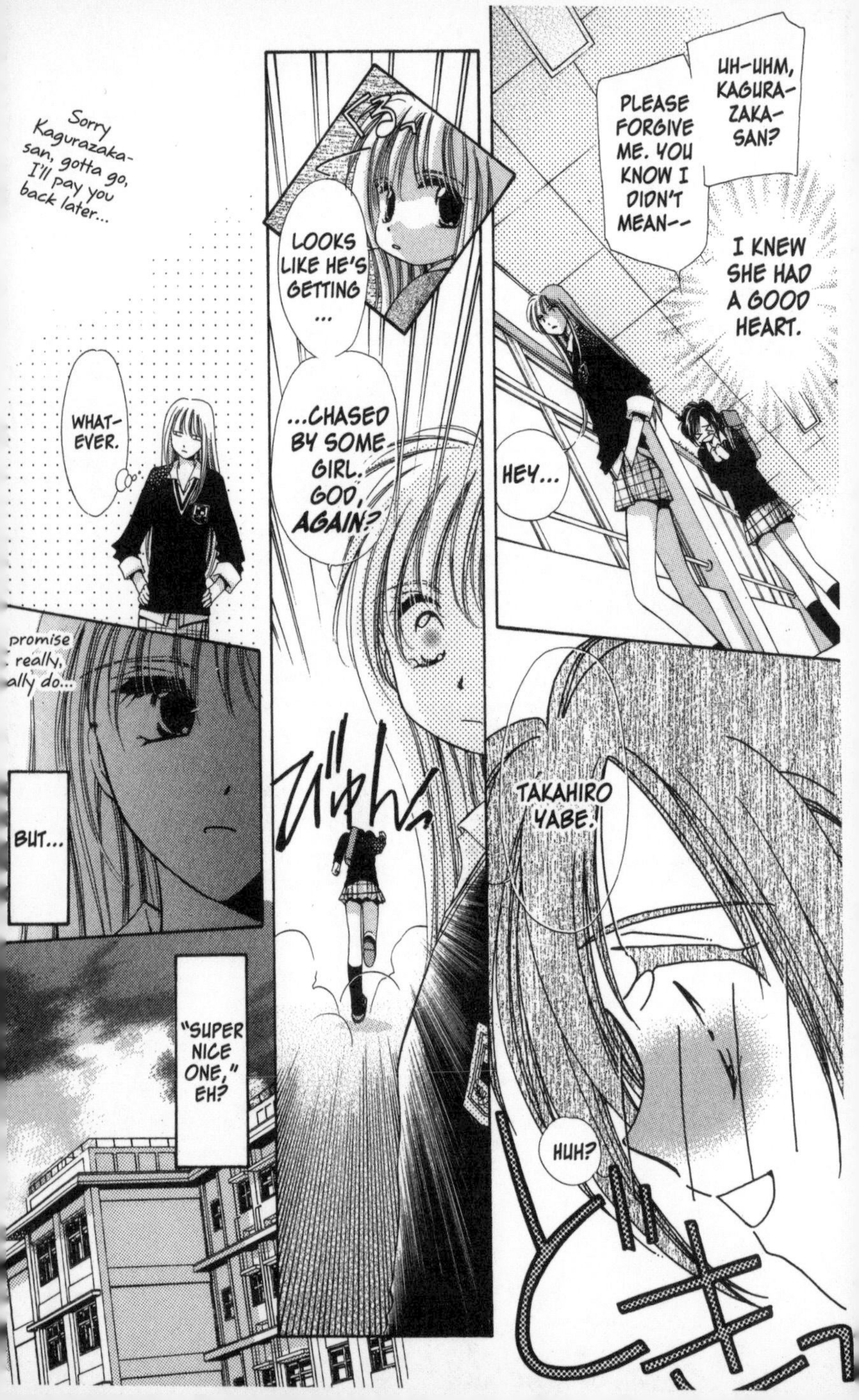
UH-UHM, KAGURA-ZAKA-SAN?
PLEASE FORGIVE ME. YOU KNOW I DIDN'T MEAN--
I KNEW SHE HAD A GOOD HEART.
HEY...
TAKAHIRO YABE.
HUH?
LOOKS LIKE HE'S GETTING ...
...CHASED BY SOME GIRL. GOD, AGAIN?
Sorry Kagurazaka-san, gotta go, I'll pay you back later...
WHAT-EVER.
promise really, ally do...
BUT...
"SUPER NICE ONE," EH?

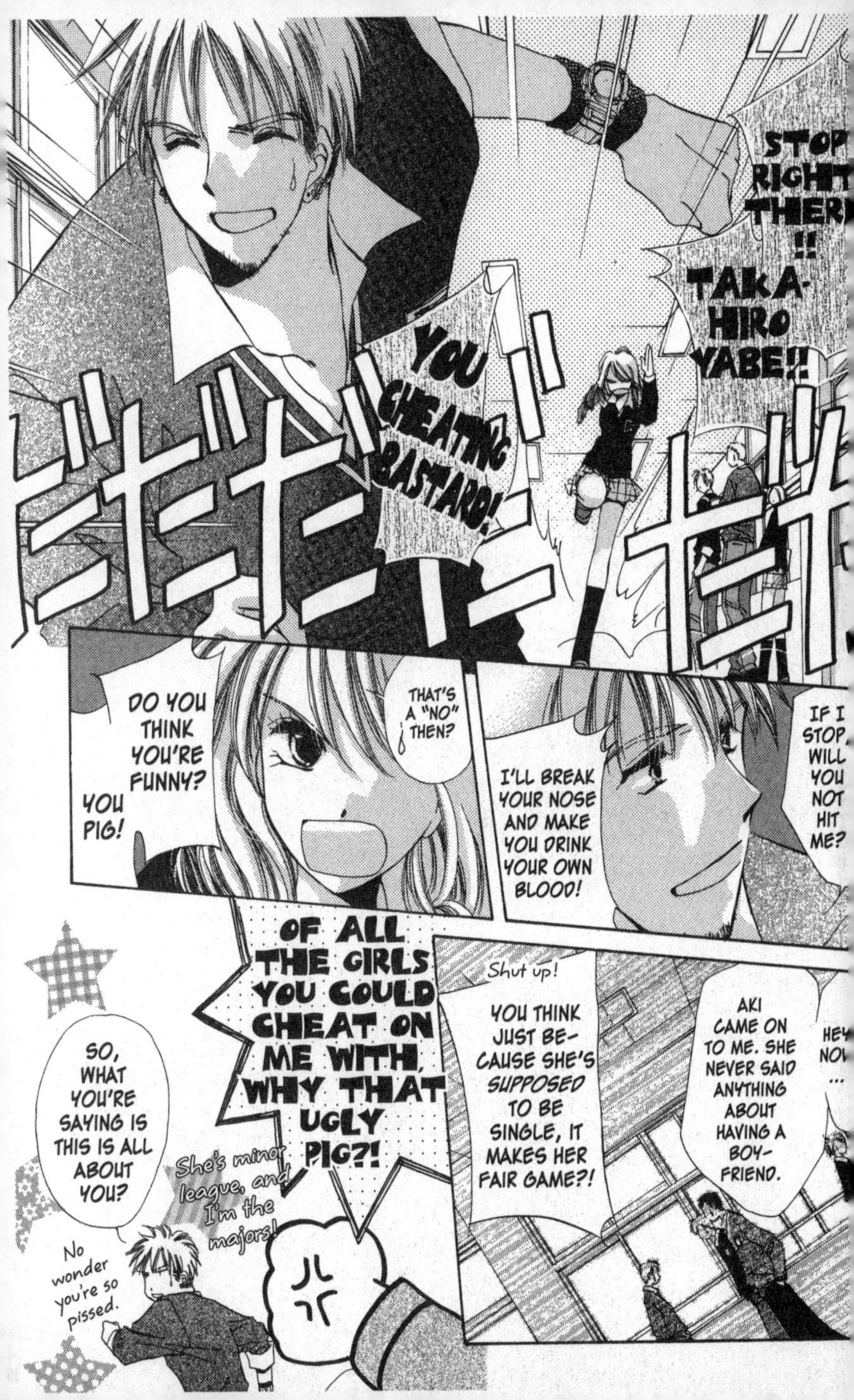
STOP RIGHT THERE!! TAKA-HIRO YABE!!
YOU CHEATING BASTARD!
IF I STOP, WILL YOU NOT HIT ME?
I'LL BREAK YOUR NOSE AND MAKE YOU DRINK YOUR OWN BLOOD!
THAT'S A "NO" THEN?
DO YOU THINK YOU'RE FUNNY?
YOU PIG!
HEY NOW ...
AKI CAME ON TO ME. SHE NEVER SAID ANYTHING ABOUT HAVING A BOY-FRIEND.
Shut up!
YOU THINK JUST BE-CAUSE SHE'S SUPPOSED TO BE SINGLE, IT MAKES HER FAIR GAME?!
OF ALL THE GIRLS YOU COULD CHEAT ON ME WITH, WHY THAT UGLY PIG?!
SO, WHAT YOU'RE SAYING IS THIS IS ALL ABOUT YOU?
She's minor league, and I'm the majors!
No wonder you're so pissed.

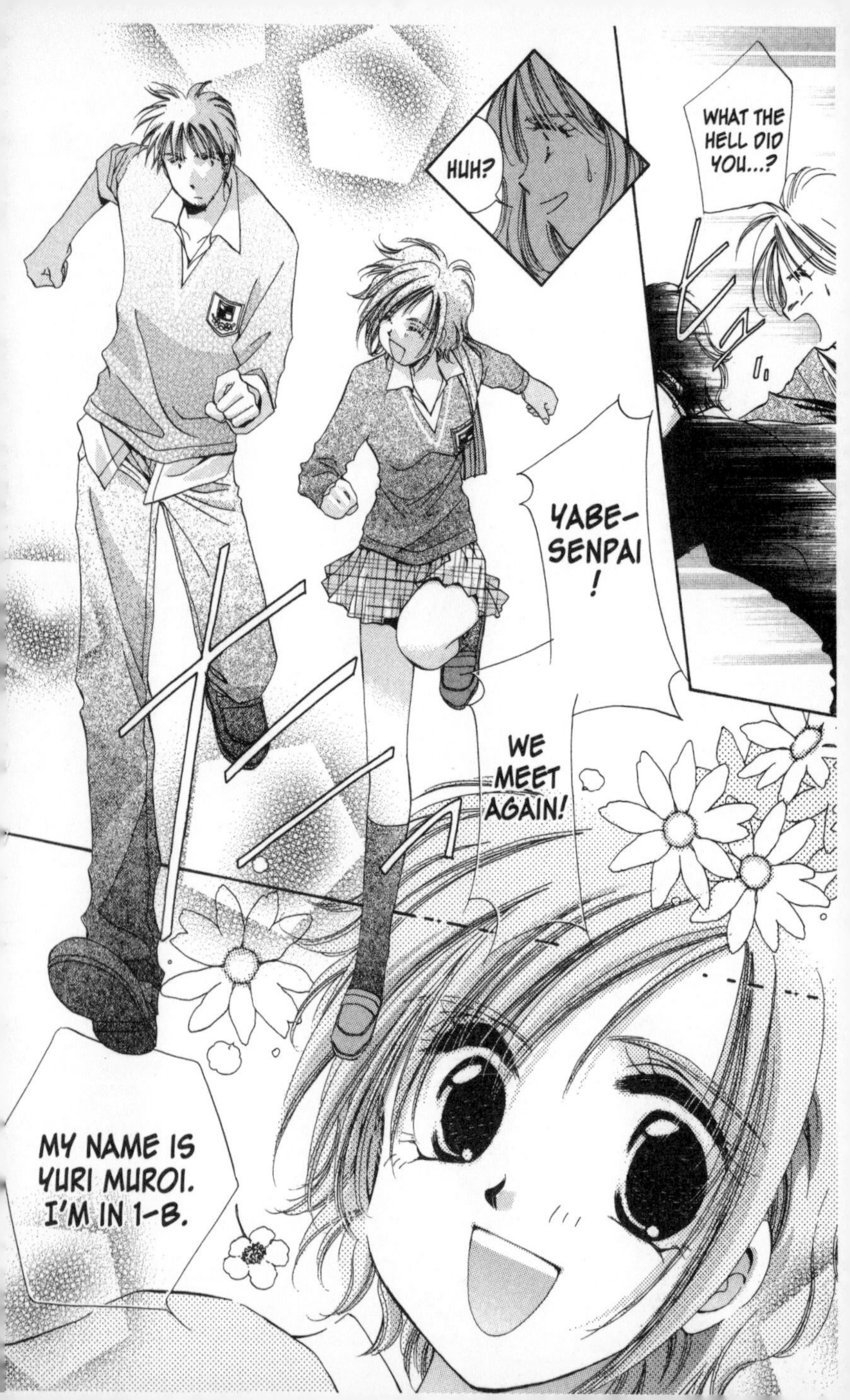
WHAT THE HELL DID YOU...?
HUH?
YABE-SENPAI!
WE MEET AGAIN!
MY NAME IS YURI MUROI. I'M IN 1-B.

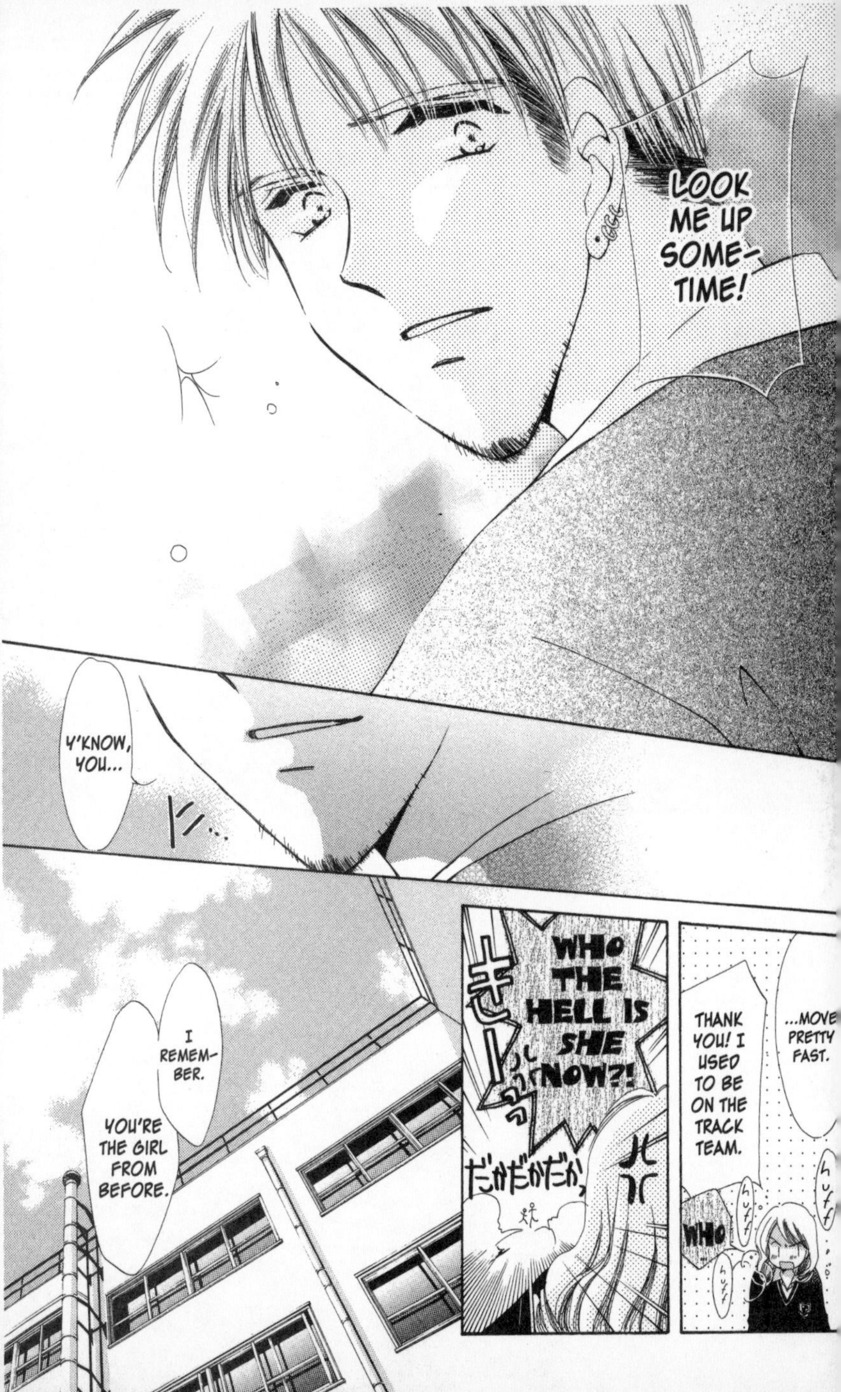
LOOK ME UP SOME-TIME!
Y'KNOW, YOU...
...MOVE PRETTY FAST.
THANK YOU! I USED TO BE ON THE TRACK TEAM.
huff
huff
huff
WHO
WHO THE HELL IS SHE NOW?!
キーッ
だかだかだか
I REMEM-BER.
YOU'RE THE GIRL FROM BEFORE.

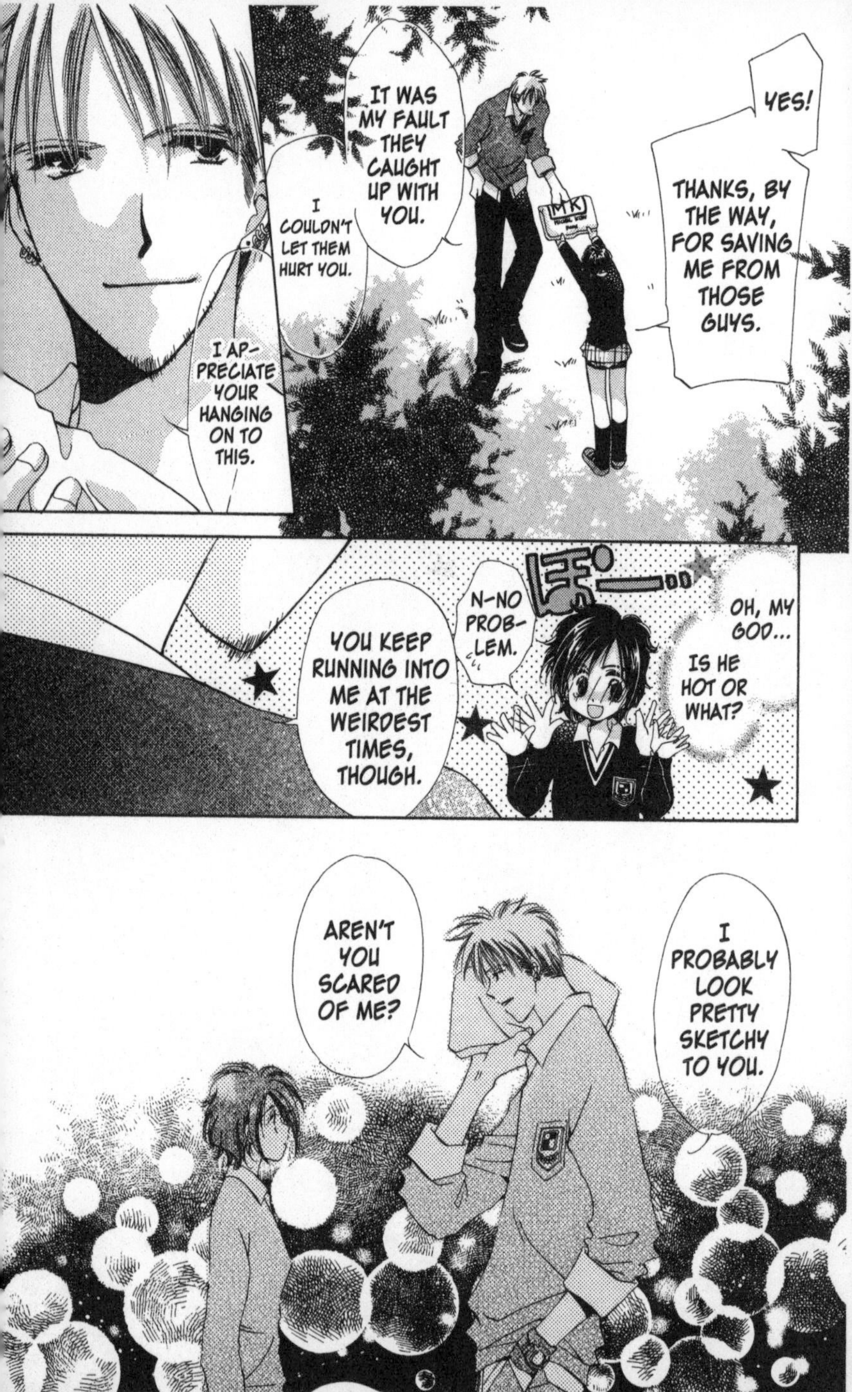
YES!
THANKS, BY THE WAY, FOR SAVING ME FROM THOSE GUYS.
IT WAS MY FAULT THEY CAUGHT UP WITH YOU.
I COULDN'T LET THEM HURT YOU.
I AP-PRECIATE YOUR HANGING ON TO THIS.
OH, MY GOD...
IS HE HOT OR WHAT?
ぽー
N-NO PROB-LEM.
YOU KEEP RUNNING INTO ME AT THE WEIRDEST TIMES, THOUGH.
I PROBABLY LOOK PRETTY SKETCHY TO YOU.
AREN'T YOU SCARED OF ME?

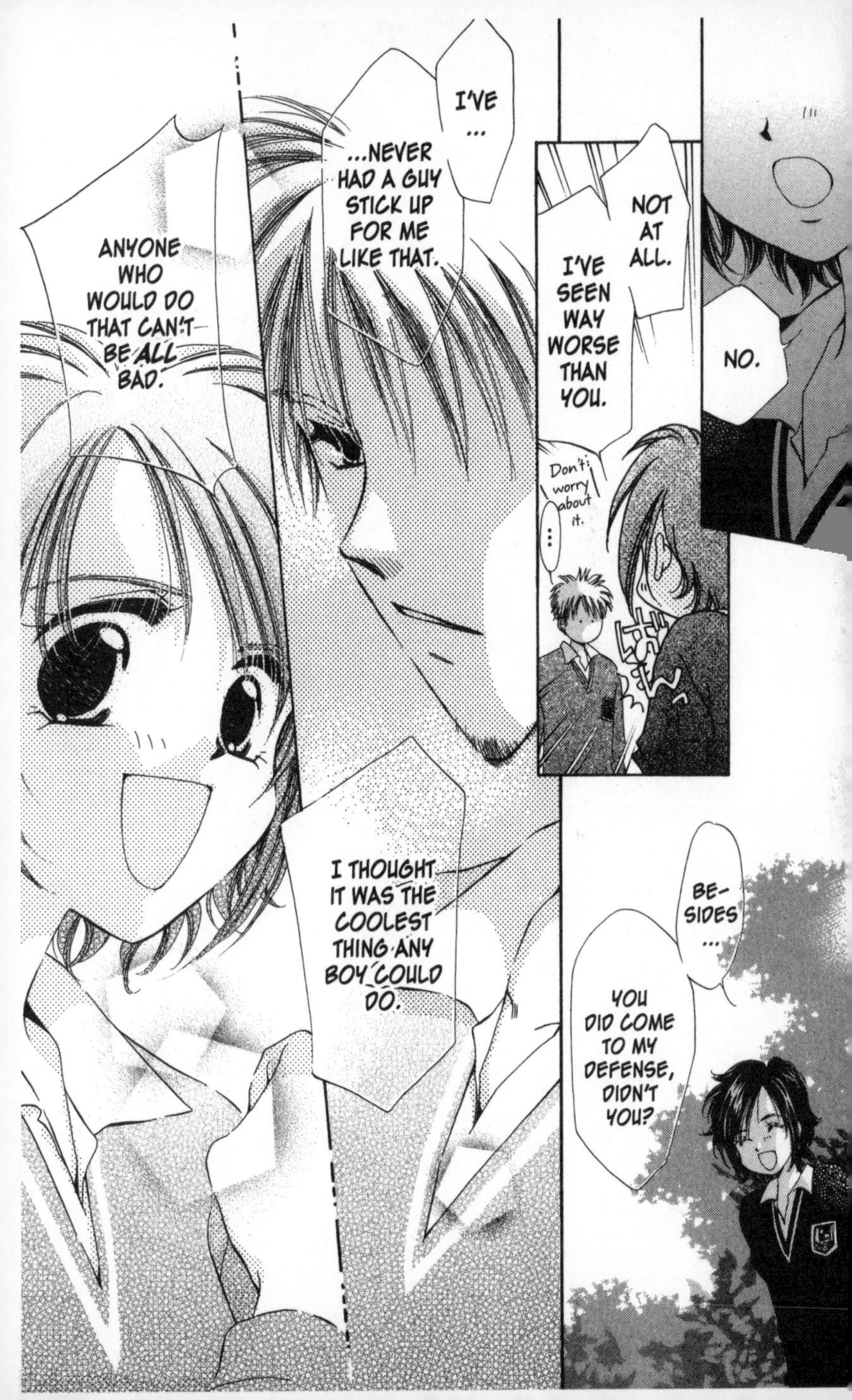
NO.
NOT AT ALL.
I'VE SEEN WAY WORSE THAN YOU.
Don't worry about it.
...
BE-SIDES...
YOU DID COME TO MY DEFENSE, DIDN'T YOU?
I'VE...
...NEVER HAD A GUY STICK UP FOR ME LIKE THAT.
I THOUGHT IT WAS THE COOLEST THING ANY BOY COULD DO.
ANYONE WHO WOULD DO THAT CAN'T BE ALL BAD.

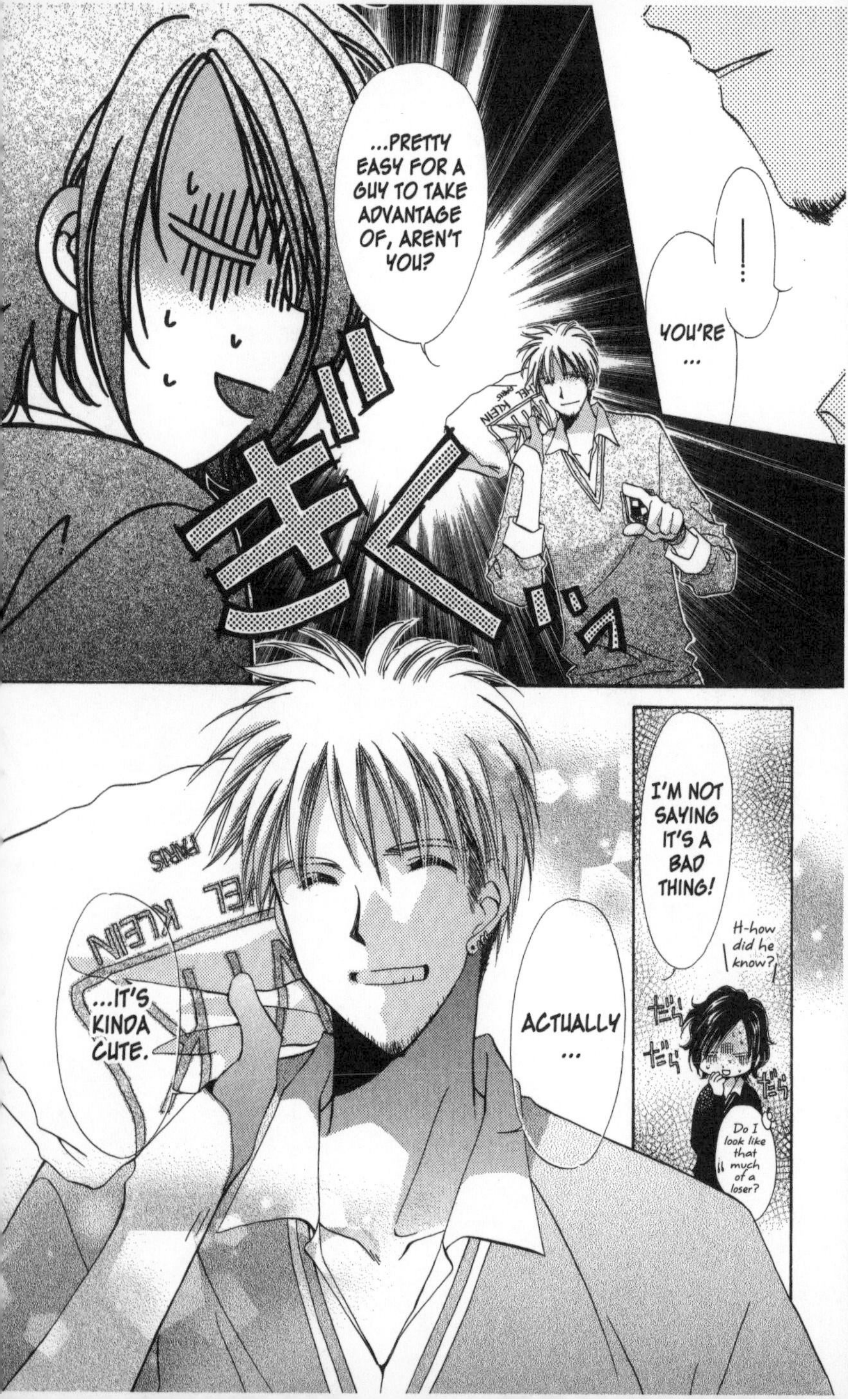
—!
YOU'RE ...
...PRETTY EASY FOR A GUY TO TAKE ADVANTAGE OF, AREN'T YOU?
ギクッ
I'M NOT SAYING IT'S A BAD THING!
H-how did he know?
だら だら だら
Do I look like that much of a loser?
ACTUALLY ...
...IT'S KINDA CUTE.

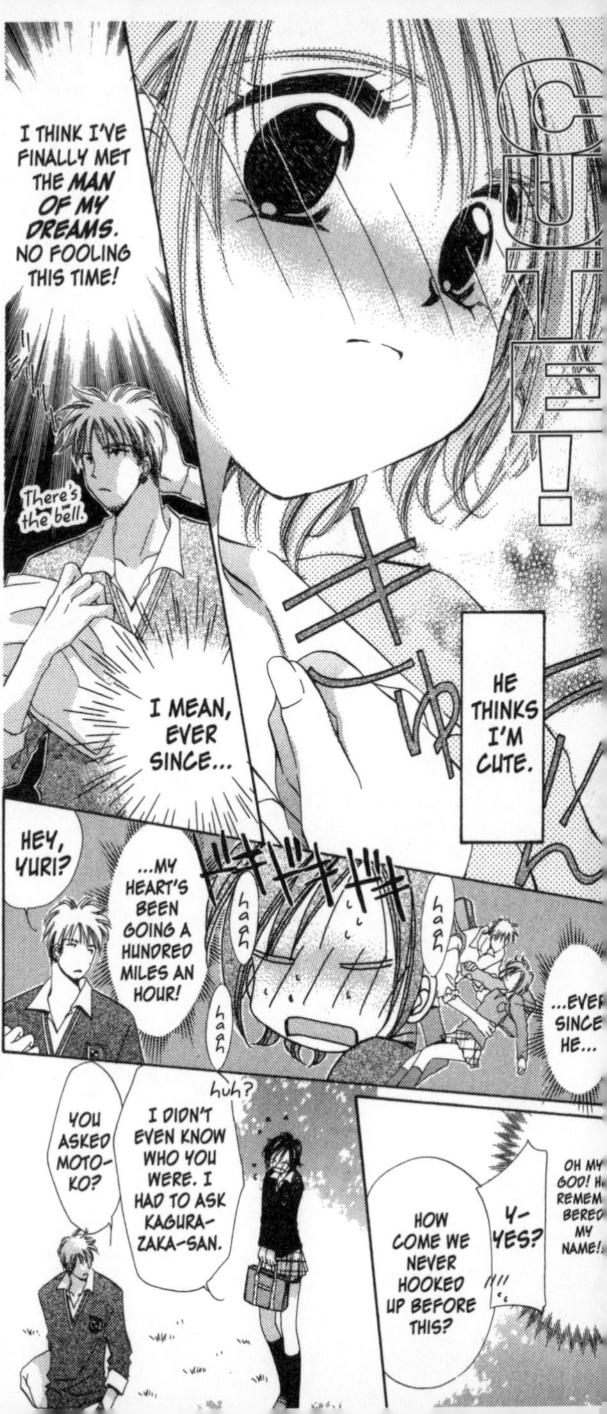
CUTE!
HE THINKS I'M CUTE.
I THINK I'VE FINALLY MET THE MAN OF MY DREAMS. NO FOOLING THIS TIME!
There's the bell.
I MEAN, EVER SINCE...
...EVER SINCE HE...
haah
haah
haah
...MY HEART'S BEEN GOING A HUNDRED MILES AN HOUR!
HEY, YURI?
OH MY GOD! H REMEMBERED MY NAME!!
Y-YES?
HOW COME WE NEVER HOOKED UP BEFORE THIS?
huh?
I DIDN'T EVEN KNOW WHO YOU WERE. I HAD TO ASK KAGURA-ZAKA-SAN.
YOU ASKED MOTO-KO?

Yuri Muroi

Yuri is a little bit different from the other heroines I've drawn. Y'see, there's this unwritten rule in shojo manga that goes: "heroines are better off being innocent girls." I decided to be daring and ignore that, so I made Yuri an "impure" heroine. (Though now that I look at her, she doesn't seem all that impure, does she?)

At the same time, I was a little nervous about the whole thing. If Yuri wasn't the traditional heroine, what if nobody liked her? Fortunately, it looks like I have a lot of broad-minded, mature readers, so Yuri turned out to be pretty popular. Thank goodness. I can rest easy.

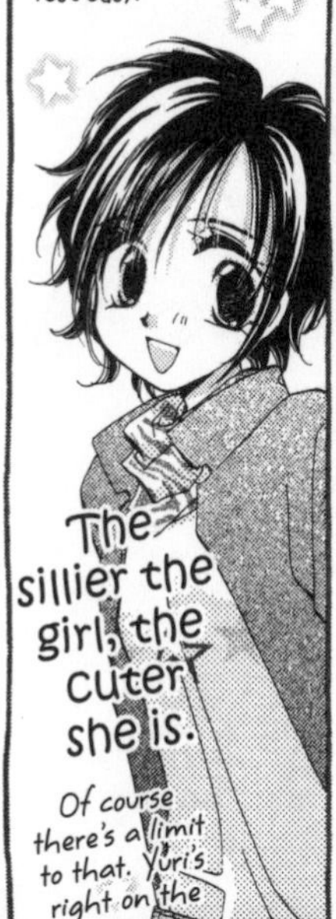
The sillier the girl, the cuter she is.
Of course there's a limit to that. Yuri's right on the line.

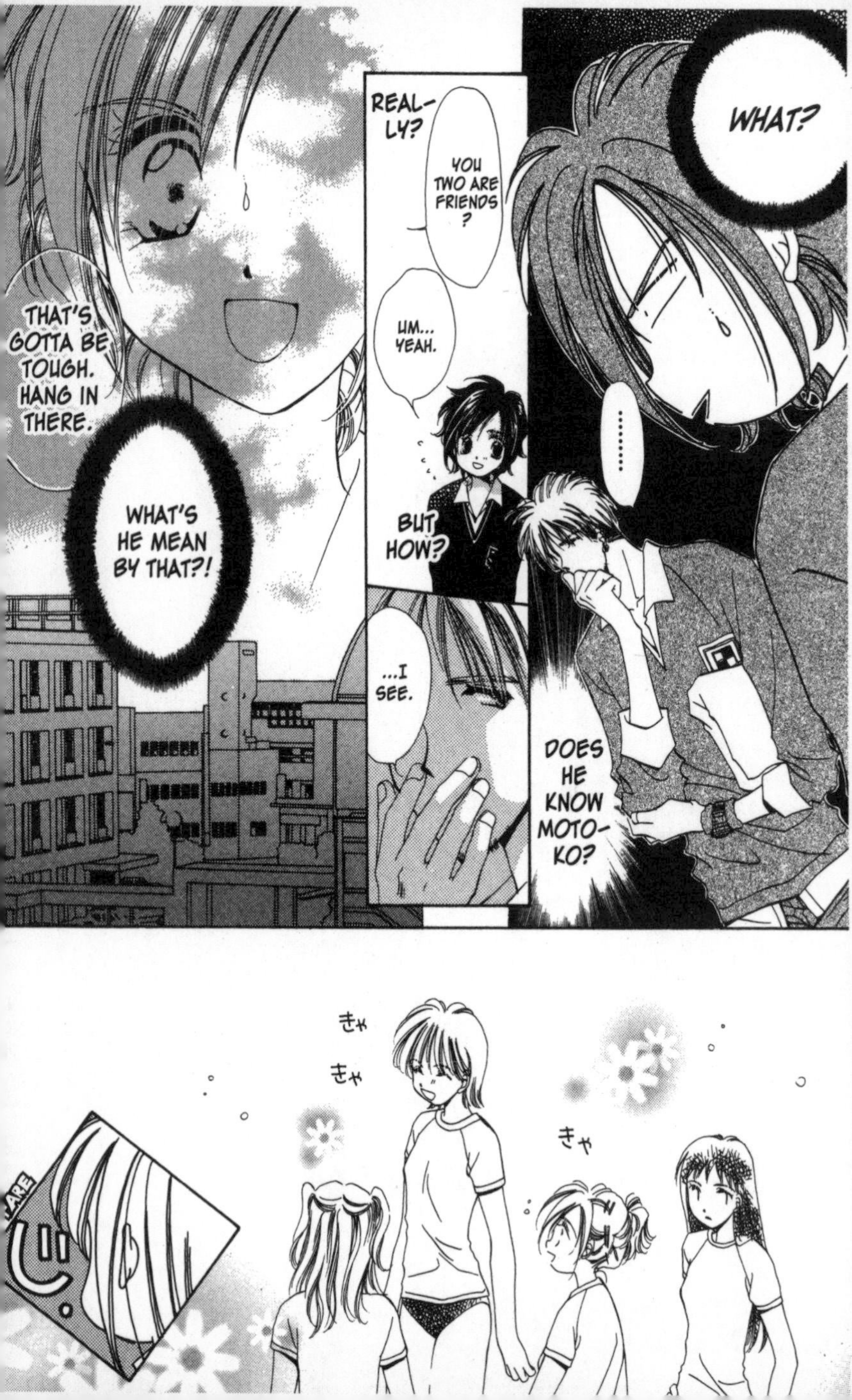
WHAT?
......
REAL-LY?
YOU TWO ARE FRIENDS?
UM... YEAH.
BUT HOW?
...I SEE.
DOES HE KNOW MOTO-KO?
THAT'S GOTTA BE TOUGH. HANG IN THERE.
WHAT'S HE MEAN BY THAT?!
きゃ
きゃ
きゃ
じー

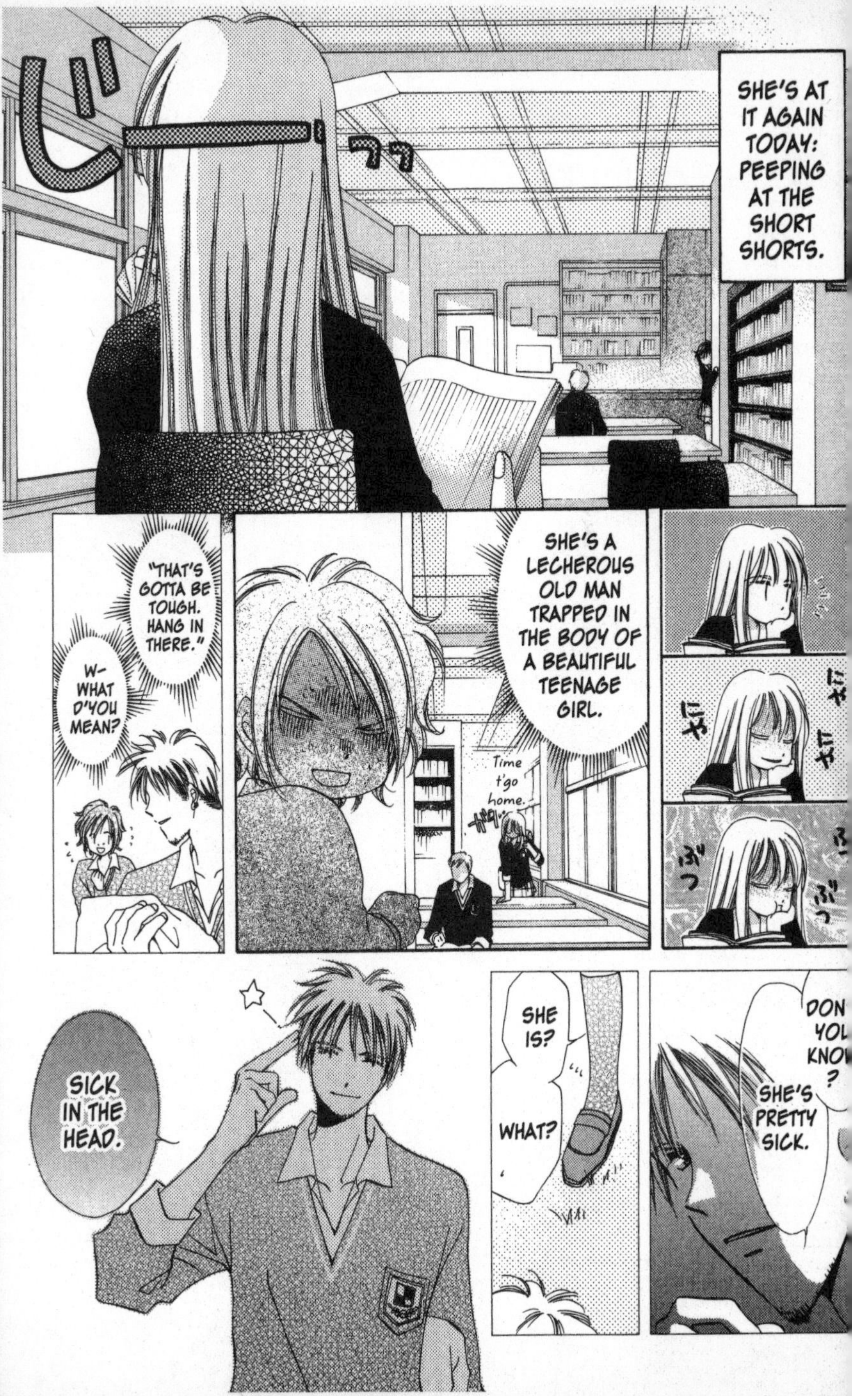
じーーっ
SHE'S AT IT AGAIN TODAY: PEEPING AT THE SHORT SHORTS.
にやにや
ぶつぶつ
SHE'S A LECHEROUS OLD MAN TRAPPED IN THE BODY OF A BEAUTIFUL TEENAGE GIRL.
Time t'go home.
"THAT'S GOTTA BE TOUGH. HANG IN THERE."
W-WHAT D'YOU MEAN?
SHE'S PRETTY SICK.
SHE IS?
WHAT?
SICK IN THE HEAD.

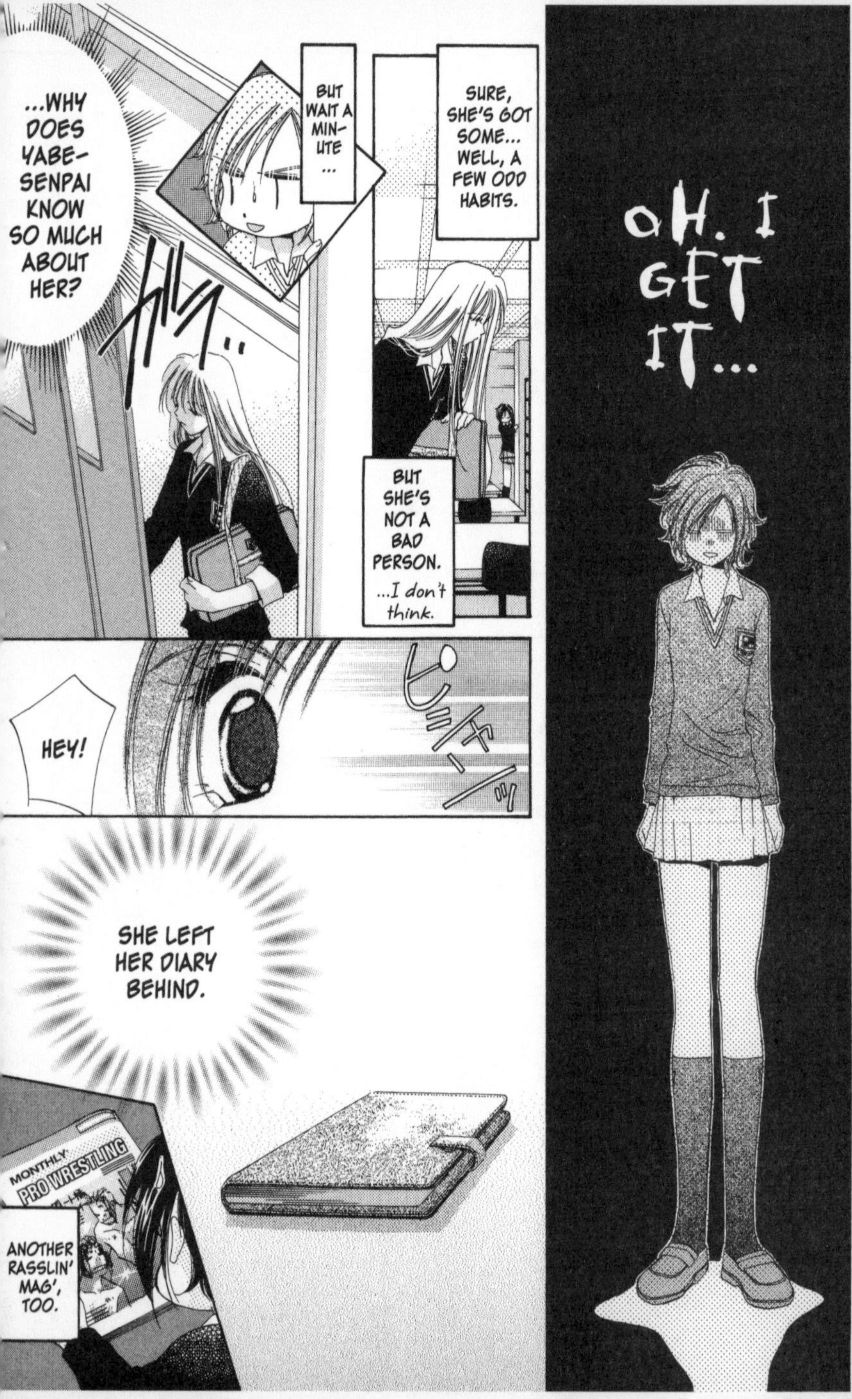
OH. I GET IT...
SURE, SHE'S GOT SOME... WELL, A FEW ODD HABITS.
BUT SHE'S NOT A BAD PERSON.
...I don't think.
BUT WAIT A MIN-UTE ...
...WHY DOES YABE-SENPAI KNOW SO MUCH ABOUT HER?
ピシャーンッ
HEY!
SHE LEFT HER DIARY BEHIND.
MONTHLY PRO WRESTLING
ANOTHER RASSLIN' MAG', TOO.

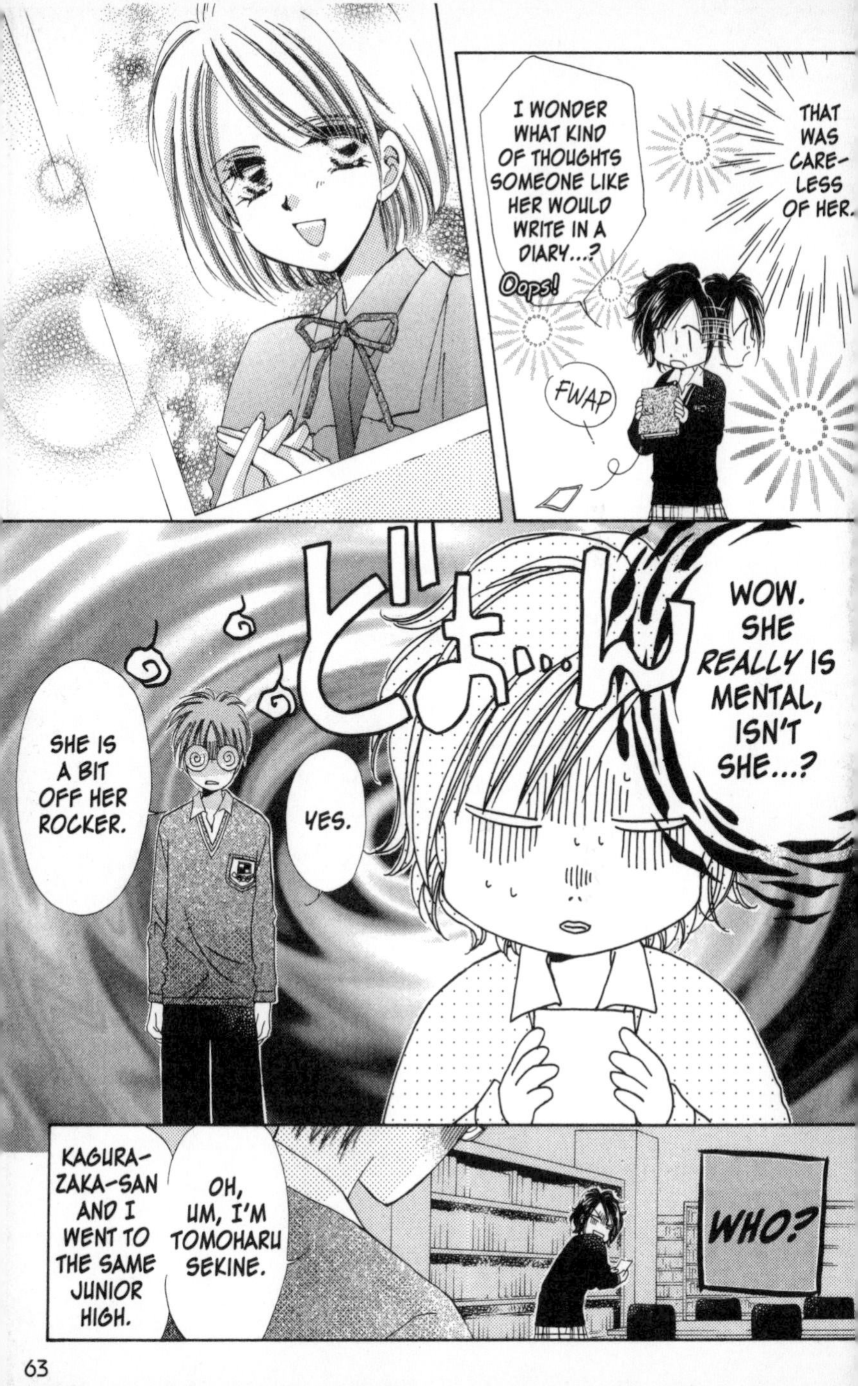
THAT WAS CARE-LESS OF HER.
I WONDER WHAT KIND OF THOUGHTS SOMEONE LIKE HER WOULD WRITE IN A DIARY...?
Oops!
FWAP
WOW. SHE *REALLY* IS MENTAL, ISN'T SHE...?
どお…ん
YES.
SHE IS A BIT OFF HER ROCKER.
WHO?
OH, UM, I'M TOMOHARU SEKINE.
KAGURA-ZAKA-SAN AND I WENT TO THE SAME JUNIOR HIGH.

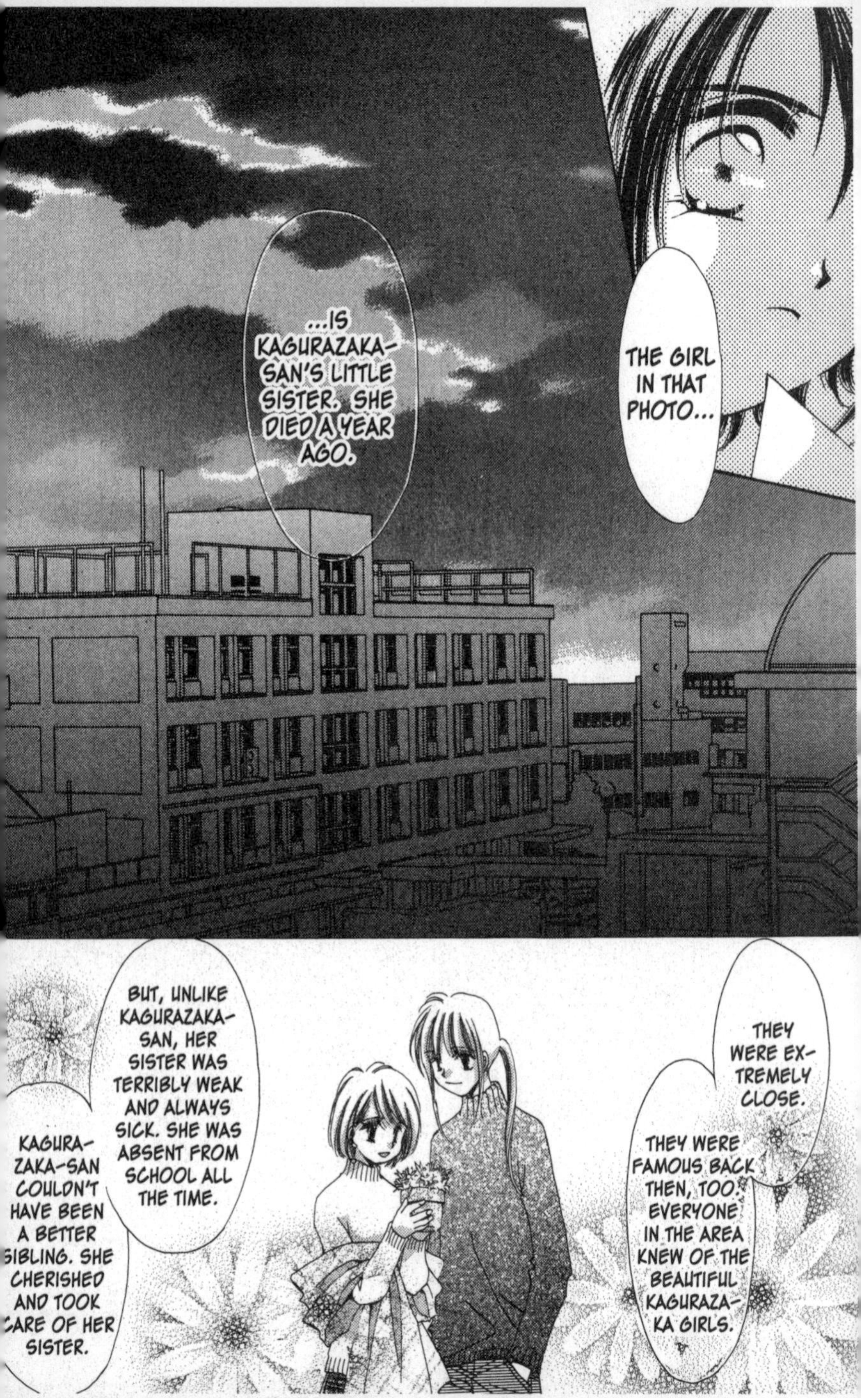
THE GIRL IN THAT PHOTO...
...IS KAGURAZAKA-SAN'S LITTLE SISTER. SHE DIED A YEAR AGO.
THEY WERE EX-TREMELY CLOSE.
THEY WERE FAMOUS BACK THEN, TOO. EVERYONE IN THE AREA KNEW OF THE BEAUTIFUL KAGURAZA-KA GIRLS.
BUT, UNLIKE KAGURAZAKA-SAN, HER SISTER WAS TERRIBLY WEAK AND ALWAYS SICK. SHE WAS ABSENT FROM SCHOOL ALL THE TIME.
KAGURA-ZAKA-SAN COULDN'T HAVE BEEN A BETTER SIBLING. SHE CHERISHED AND TOOK CARE OF HER SISTER.

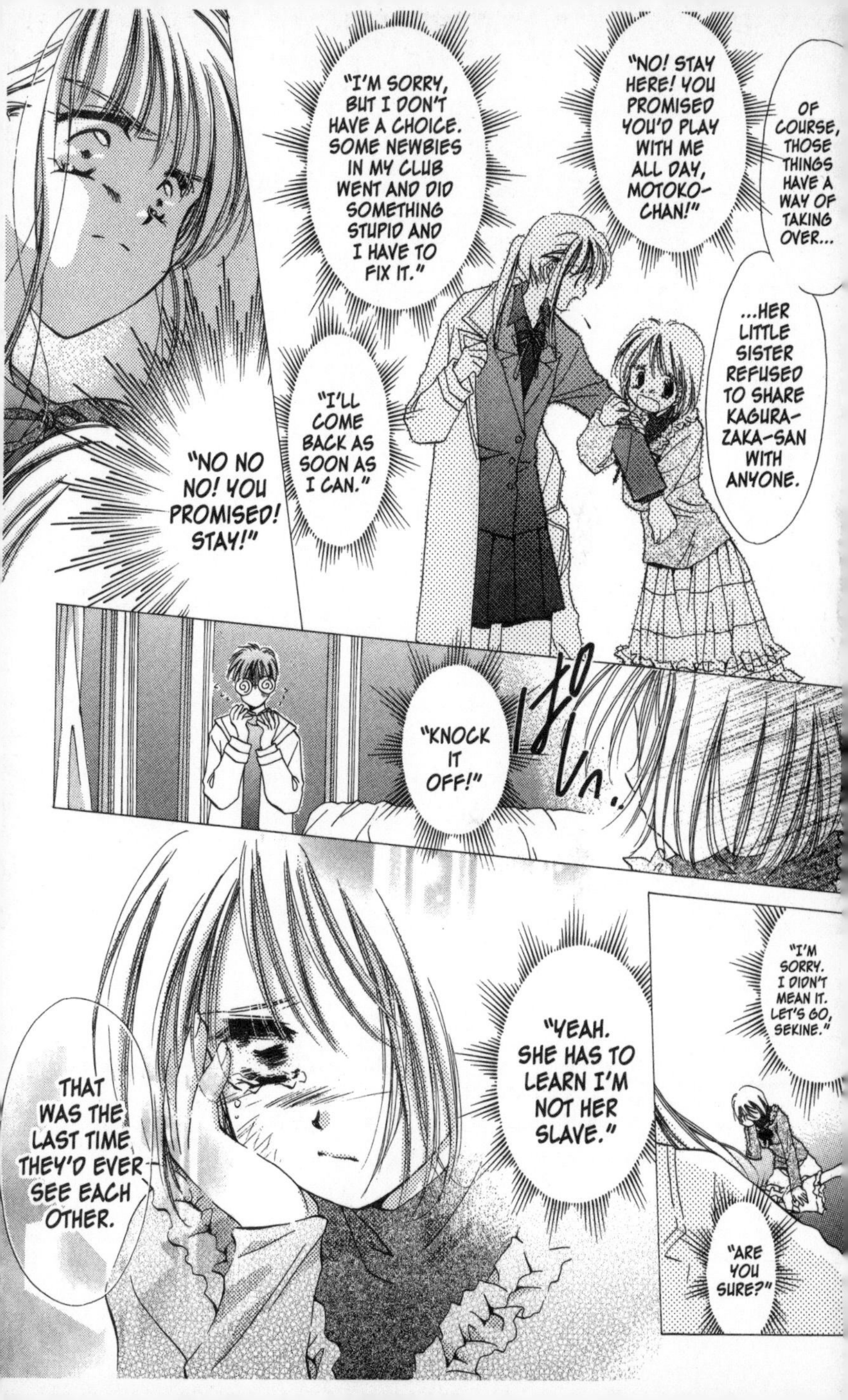
OF COURSE, THOSE THINGS HAVE A WAY OF TAKING OVER...
...HER LITTLE SISTER REFUSED TO SHARE KAGURAZAKA-SAN WITH ANYONE.
"NO! STAY HERE! YOU PROMISED YOU'D PLAY WITH ME ALL DAY, MOTOKO-CHAN!"
"I'M SORRY, BUT I DON'T HAVE A CHOICE. SOME NEWBIES IN MY CLUB WENT AND DID SOMETHING STUPID AND I HAVE TO FIX IT."
"I'LL COME BACK AS SOON AS I CAN."
"NO NO NO! YOU PROMISED! STAY!"
"KNOCK IT OFF!"
"I'M SORRY. I DIDN'T MEAN IT. LET'S GO, SEKINE."
"ARE YOU SURE?"
"YEAH. SHE HAS TO LEARN I'M NOT HER SLAVE."
THAT WAS THE LAST TIME THEY'D EVER SEE EACH OTHER.

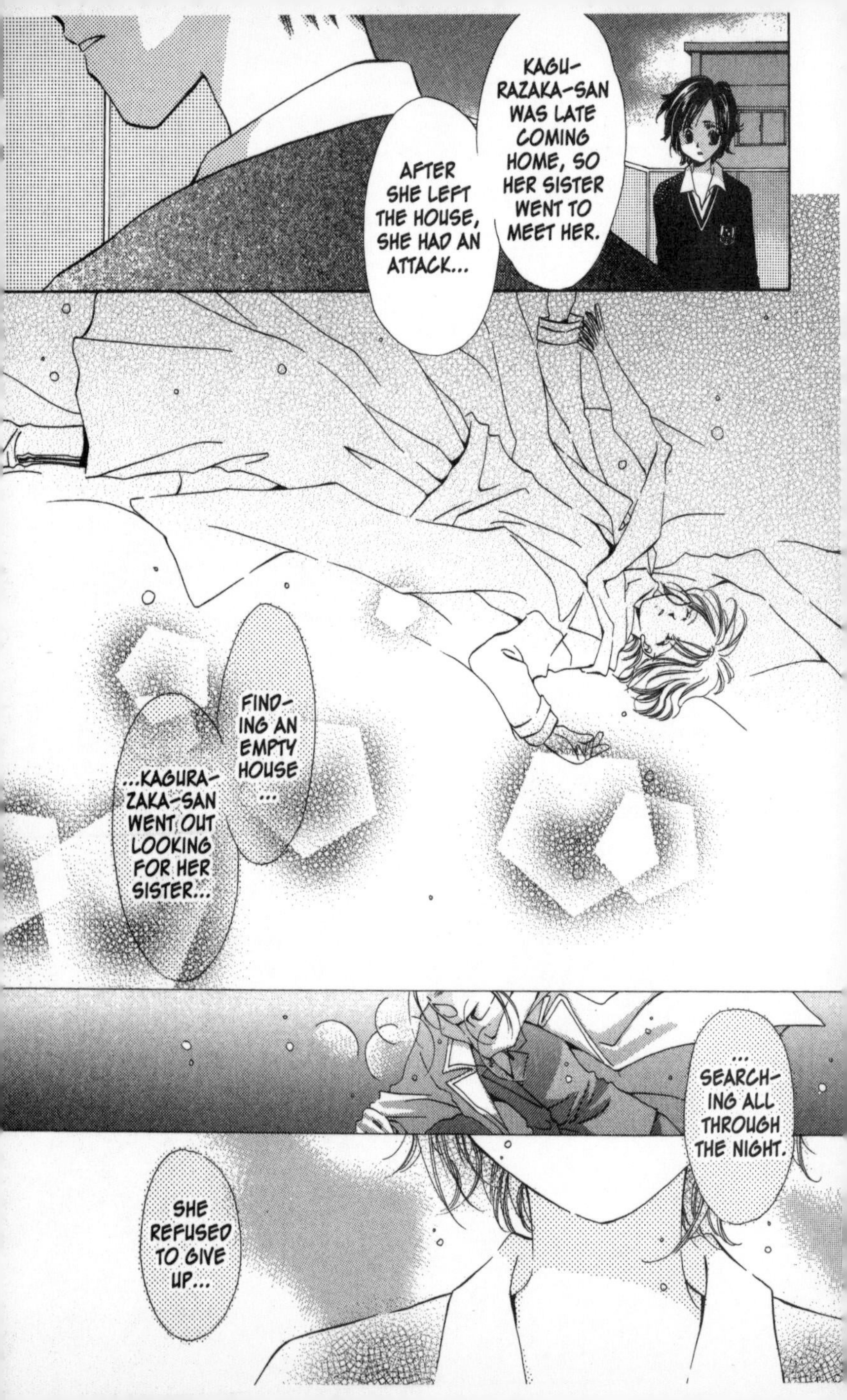
KAGURAZAKA-SAN WAS LATE COMING HOME, SO HER SISTER WENT TO MEET HER.
AFTER SHE LEFT THE HOUSE, SHE HAD AN ATTACK...
FINDING AN EMPTY HOUSE...
...KAGURAZAKA-SAN WENT OUT LOOKING FOR HER SISTER...
...SEARCHING ALL THROUGH THE NIGHT.
SHE REFUSED TO GIVE UP...

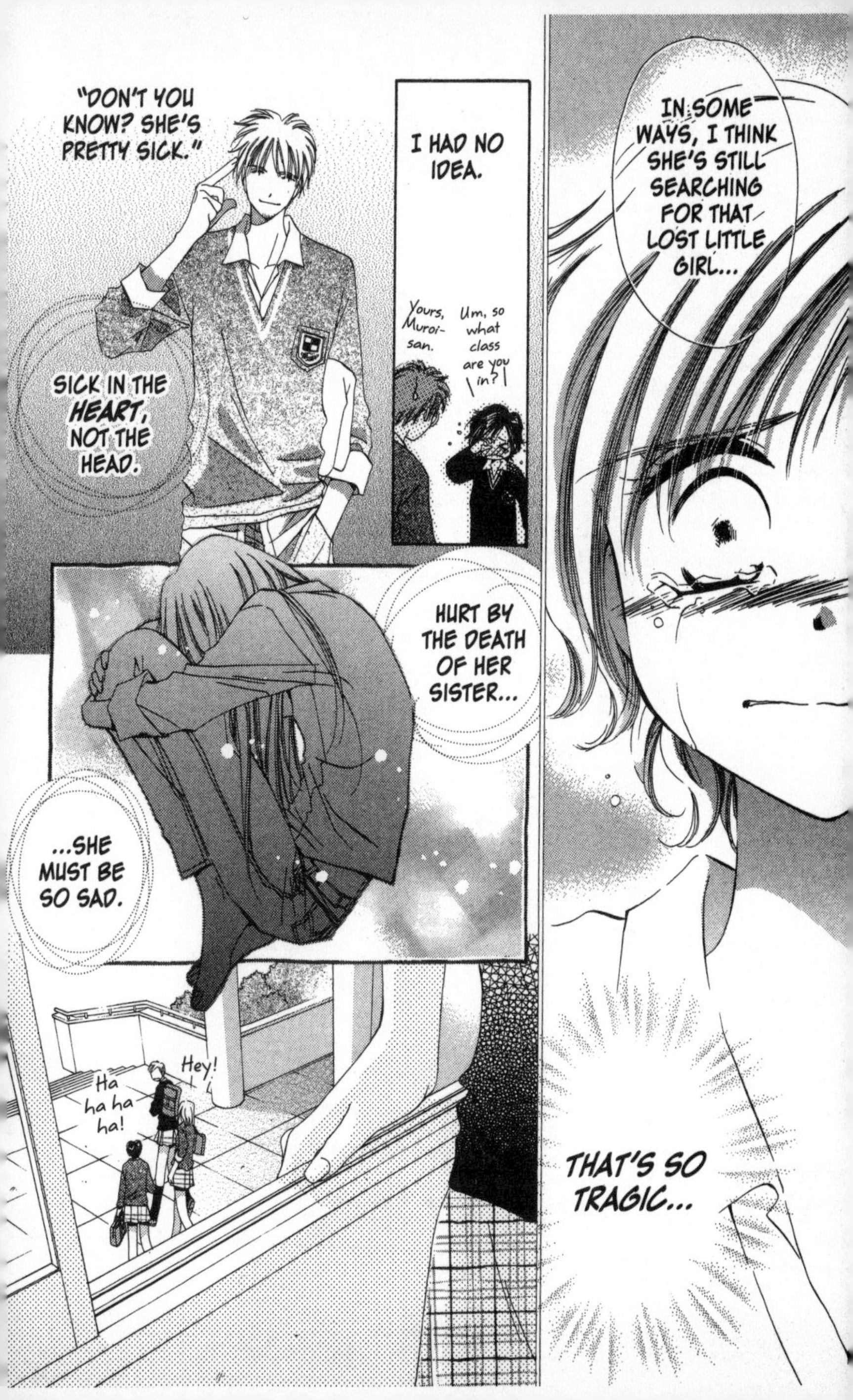
IN SOME WAYS, I THINK SHE'S STILL SEARCHING FOR THAT LOST LITTLE GIRL...
THAT'S SO TRAGIC...
I HAD NO IDEA.
Um, so what class are you in?
Yours, Muroi-san.
"DON'T YOU KNOW? SHE'S PRETTY SICK."
SICK IN THE *HEART*, NOT THE HEAD.
HURT BY THE DEATH OF HER SISTER...
...SHE MUST BE SO SAD.
Hey!
Ha ha ha ha!

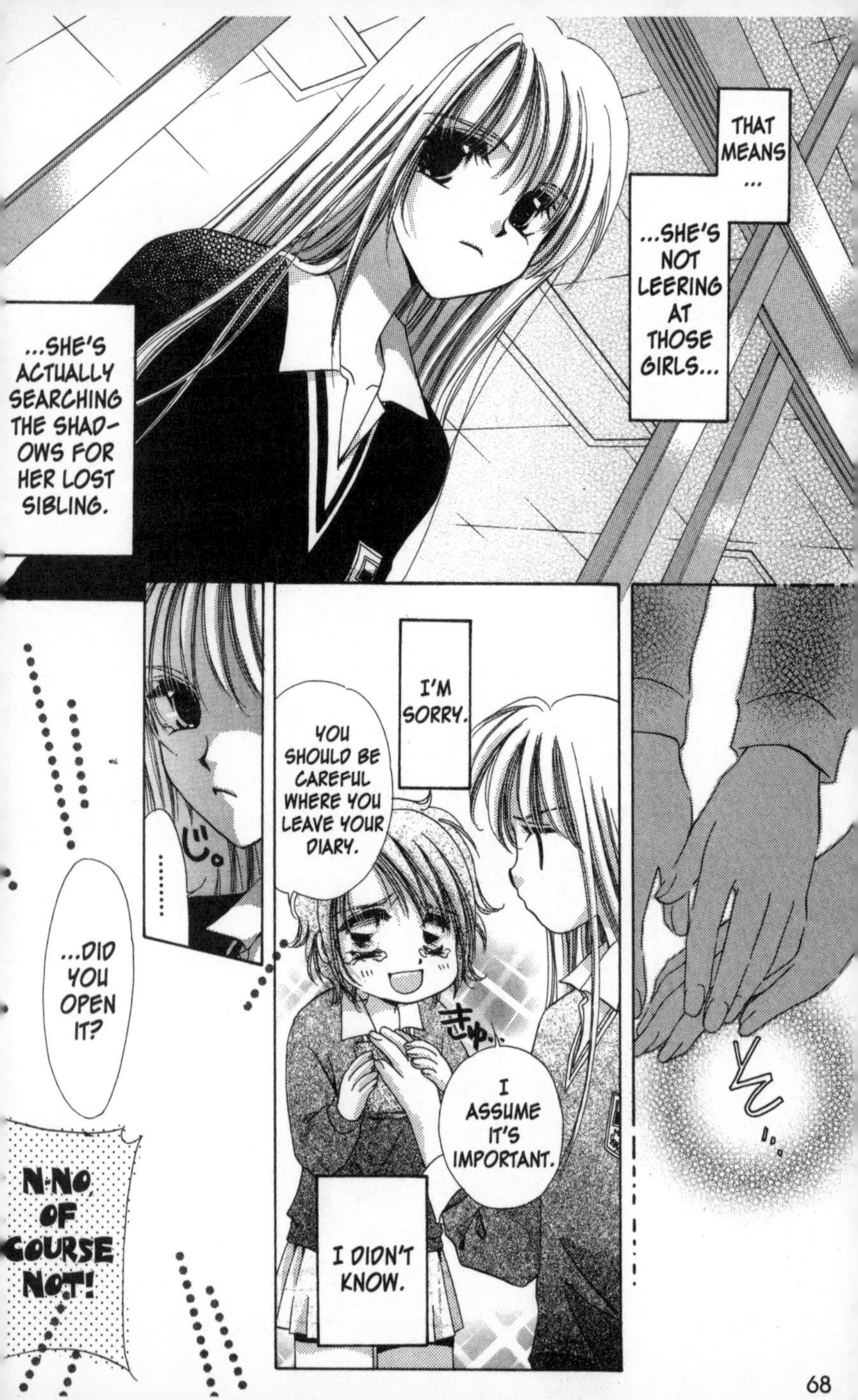
THAT MEANS...
...SHE'S NOT LEERING AT THOSE GIRLS...
...SHE'S ACTUALLY SEARCHING THE SHADOWS FOR HER LOST SIBLING.
I'M SORRY.
YOU SHOULD BE CAREFUL WHERE YOU LEAVE YOUR DIARY.
きゅ.
I ASSUME IT'S IMPORTANT.
I DIDN'T KNOW.
じ。
......
...DID YOU OPEN IT?
N-NO, OF COURSE NOT!

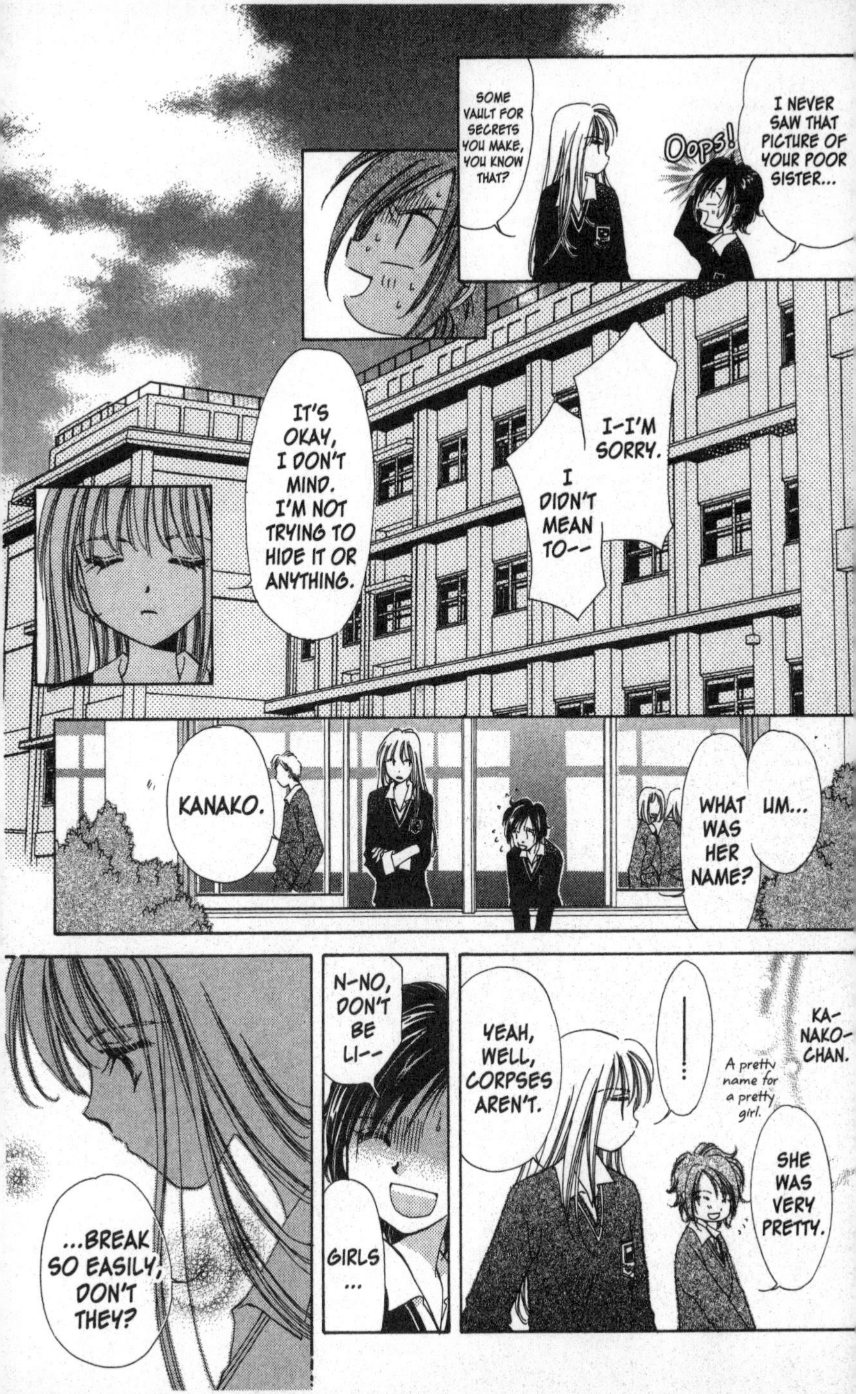
I NEVER SAW THAT PICTURE OF YOUR POOR SISTER...
Oops!
SOME VAULT FOR SECRETS YOU MAKE, YOU KNOW THAT?
I-I'M SORRY.
I DIDN'T MEAN TO--
IT'S OKAY, I DON'T MIND. I'M NOT TRYING TO HIDE IT OR ANYTHING.
UM...
WHAT WAS HER NAME?
KANAKO.
KA-NAKO-CHAN.
A pretty name for a pretty girl.
SHE WAS VERY PRETTY.
—!
YEAH, WELL, CORPSES AREN'T.
N-NO, DON'T BE LI--
GIRLS...
...BREAK SO EASILY, DON'T THEY?

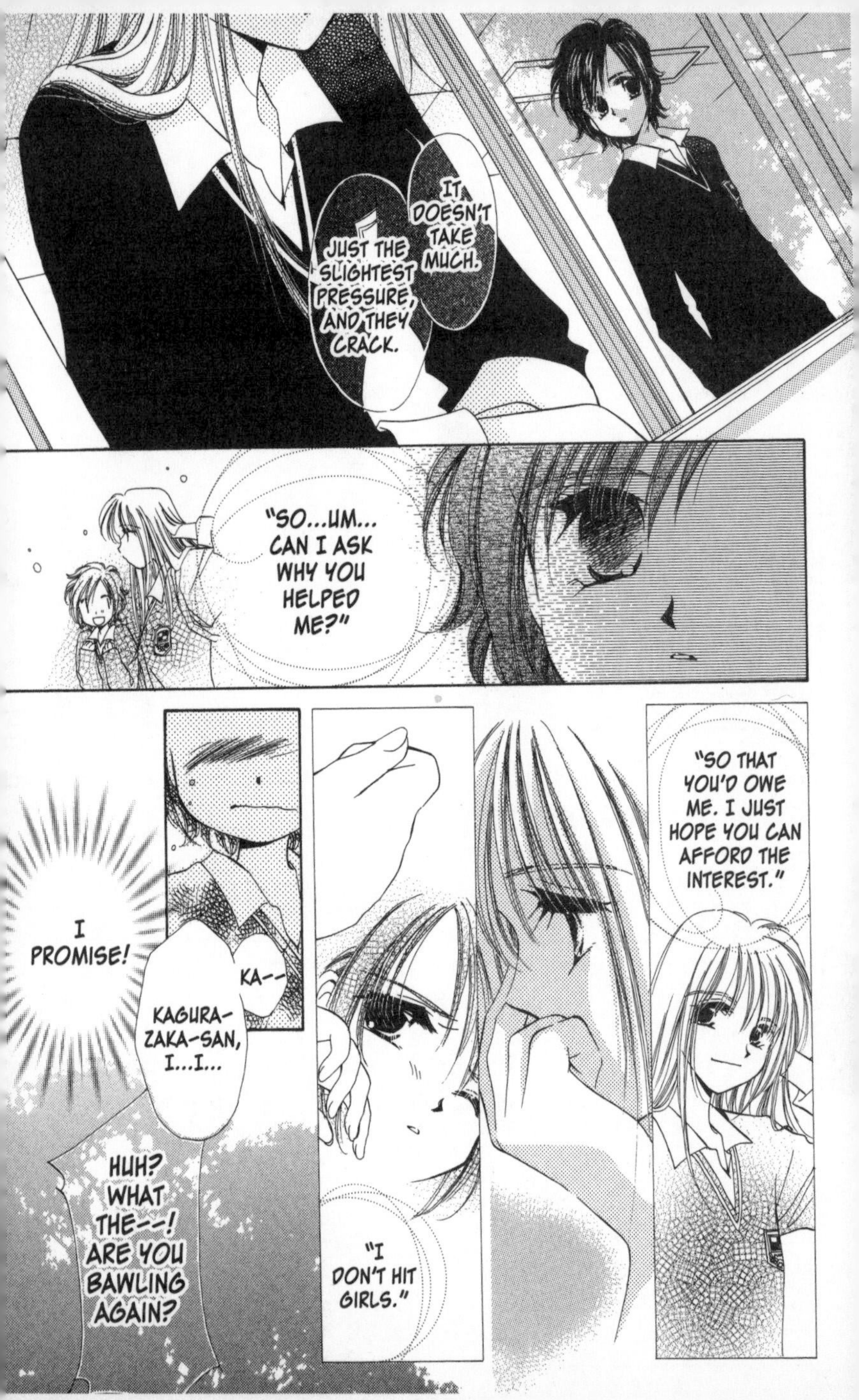
IT DOESN'T TAKE MUCH.
JUST THE SLIGHTEST PRESSURE, AND THEY CRACK.
"SO...UM... CAN I ASK WHY YOU HELPED ME?"
"SO THAT YOU'D OWE ME. I JUST HOPE YOU CAN AFFORD THE INTEREST."
"I DON'T HIT GIRLS."
KA--
KAGURA-ZAKA-SAN, I...I...
I PROMISE!
HUH? WHAT THE--! ARE YOU BAWLING AGAIN?

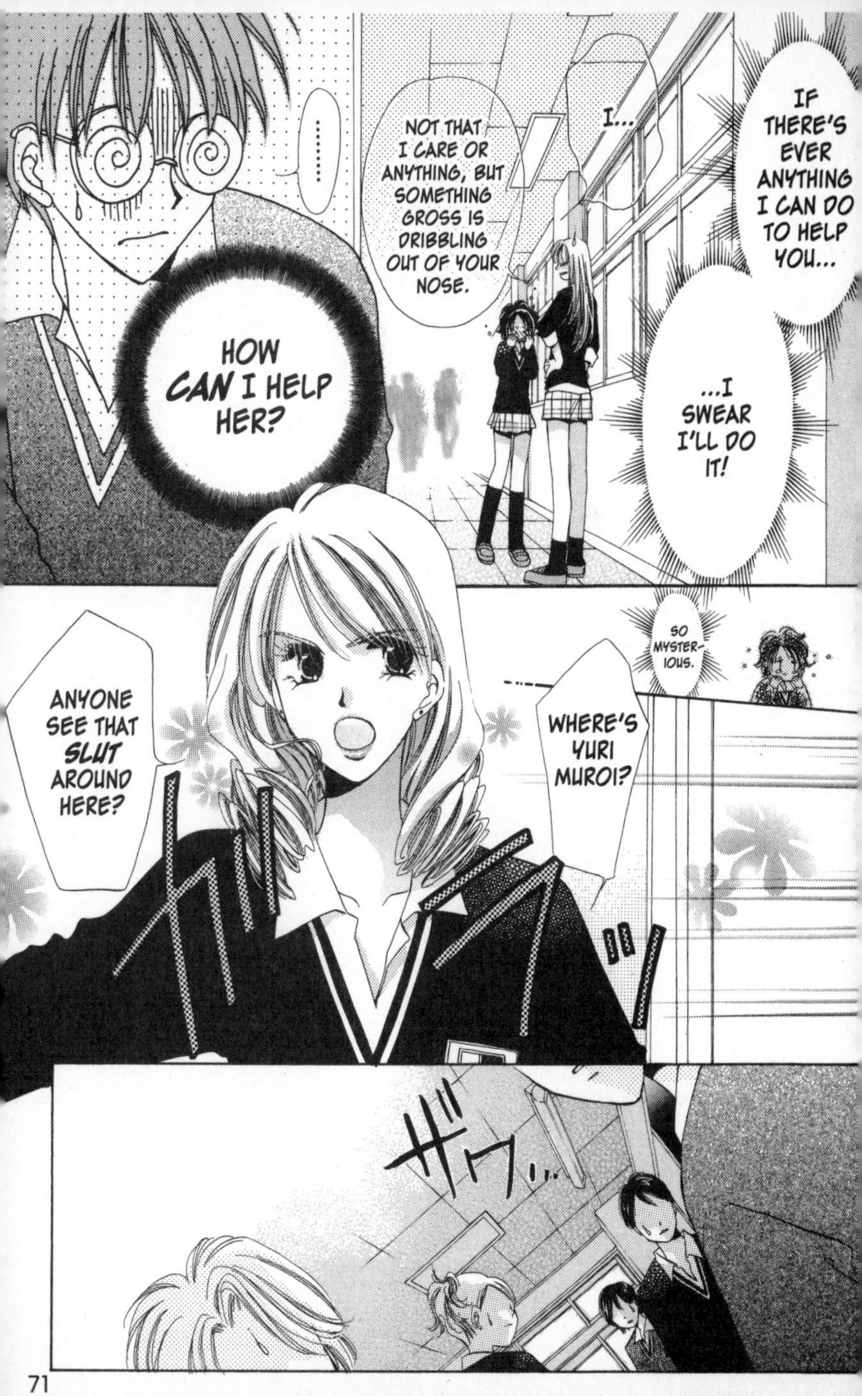
I...
IF THERE'S EVER ANYTHING I CAN DO TO HELP YOU...
...I SWEAR I'LL DO IT!
NOT THAT I CARE OR ANYTHING, BUT SOMETHING GROSS IS DRIBBLING OUT OF YOUR NOSE.
......
HOW CAN I HELP HER?
SO MYSTERIOUS.
WHERE'S YURI MUROI?
ANYONE SEE THAT SLUT AROUND HERE?
ザワ..

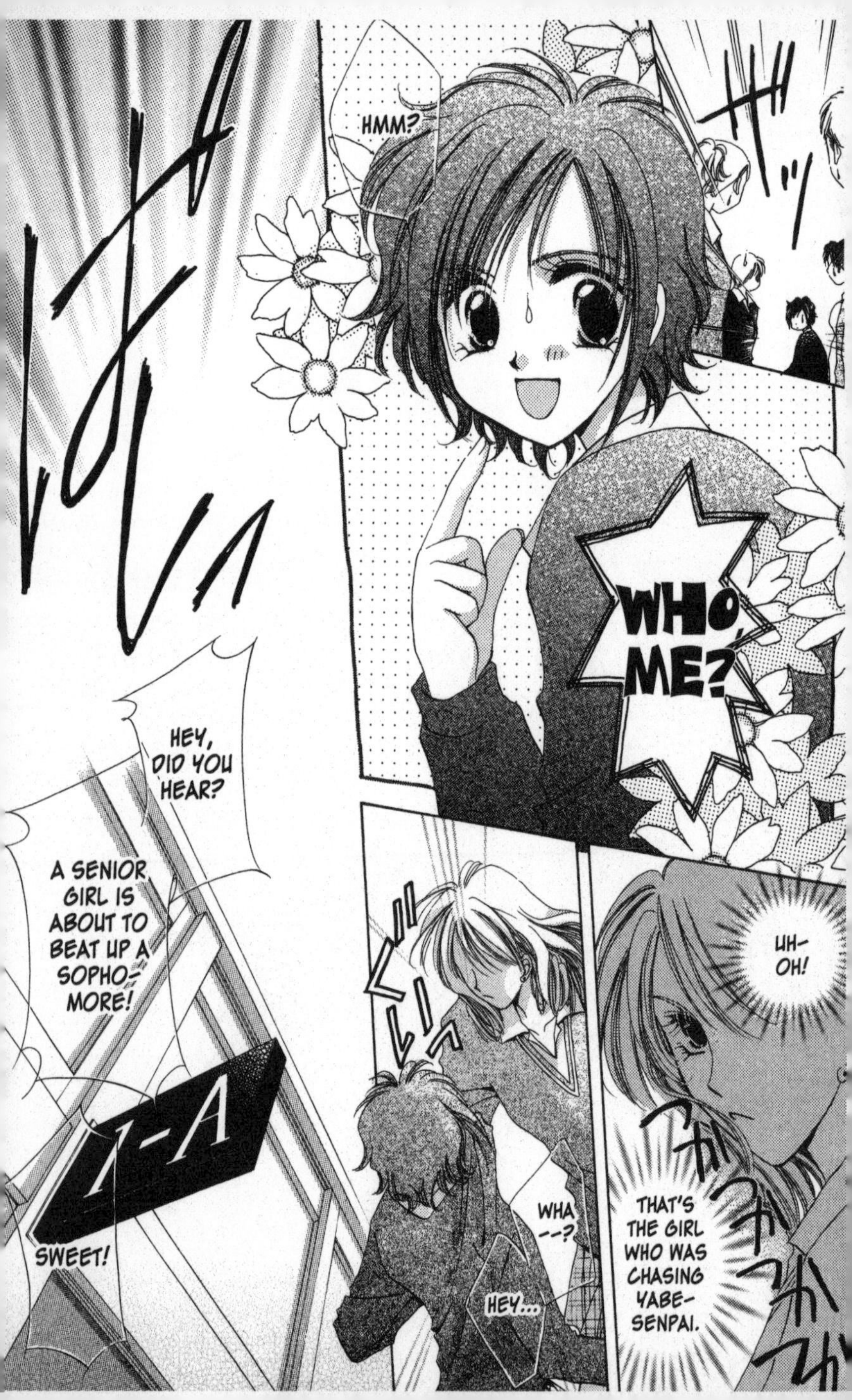

HMM?
WHO, ME?
UH-OH!
THAT'S THE GIRL WHO WAS CHASING YABE-SENPAI.
WHA--?
HEY...
HEY, DID YOU HEAR?
A SENIOR GIRL IS ABOUT TO BEAT UP A SOPHOMORE!
1-A
SWEET!

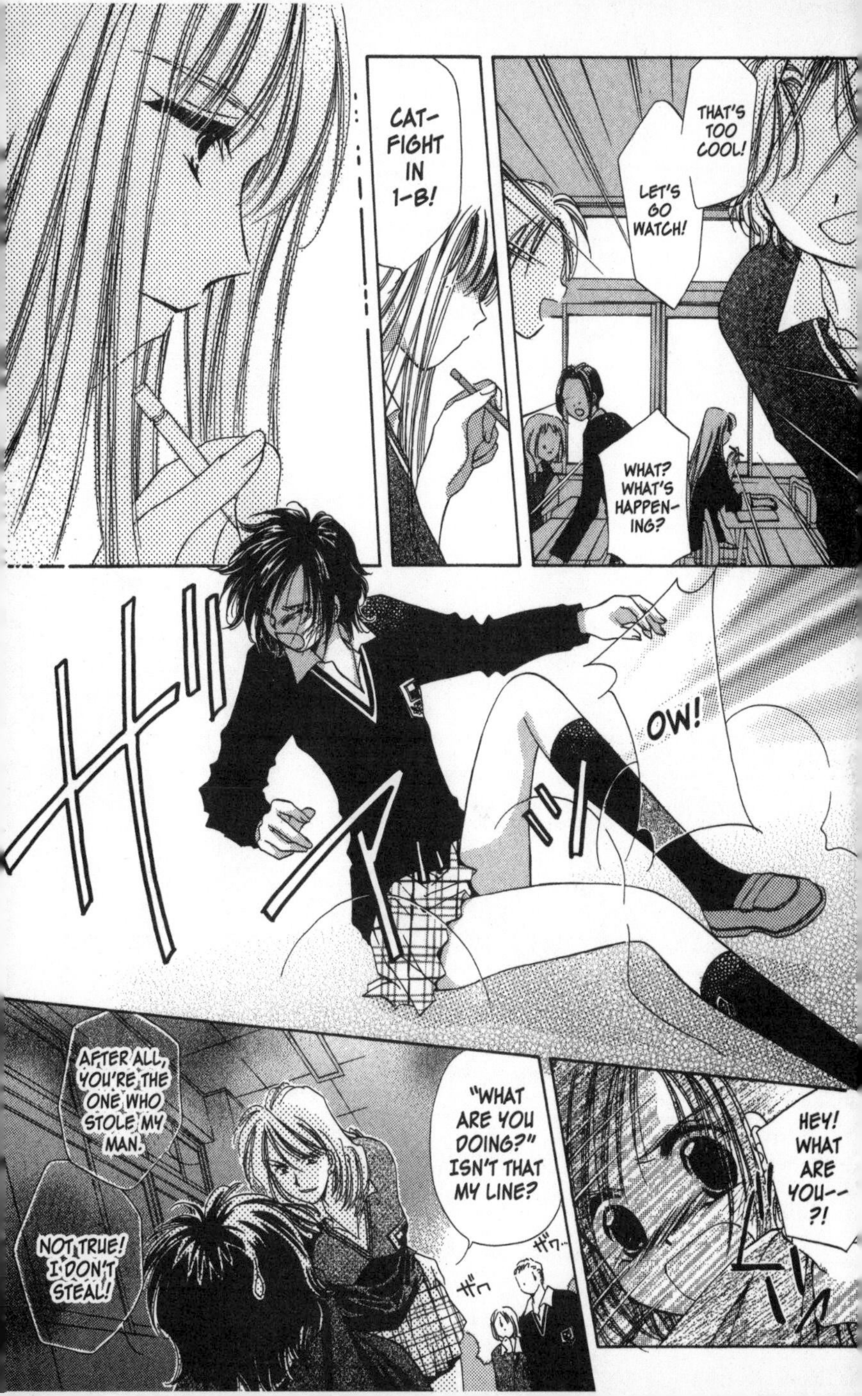
THAT'S TOO COOL!
LET'S GO WATCH!
WHAT? WHAT'S HAPPENING?
CAT-FIGHT IN 1-B!
OW!
HEY! WHAT ARE YOU--?!
"WHAT ARE YOU DOING?" ISN'T THAT MY LINE?
AFTER ALL, YOU'RE THE ONE WHO STOLE MY MAN.
NOT TRUE! I DON'T STEAL!

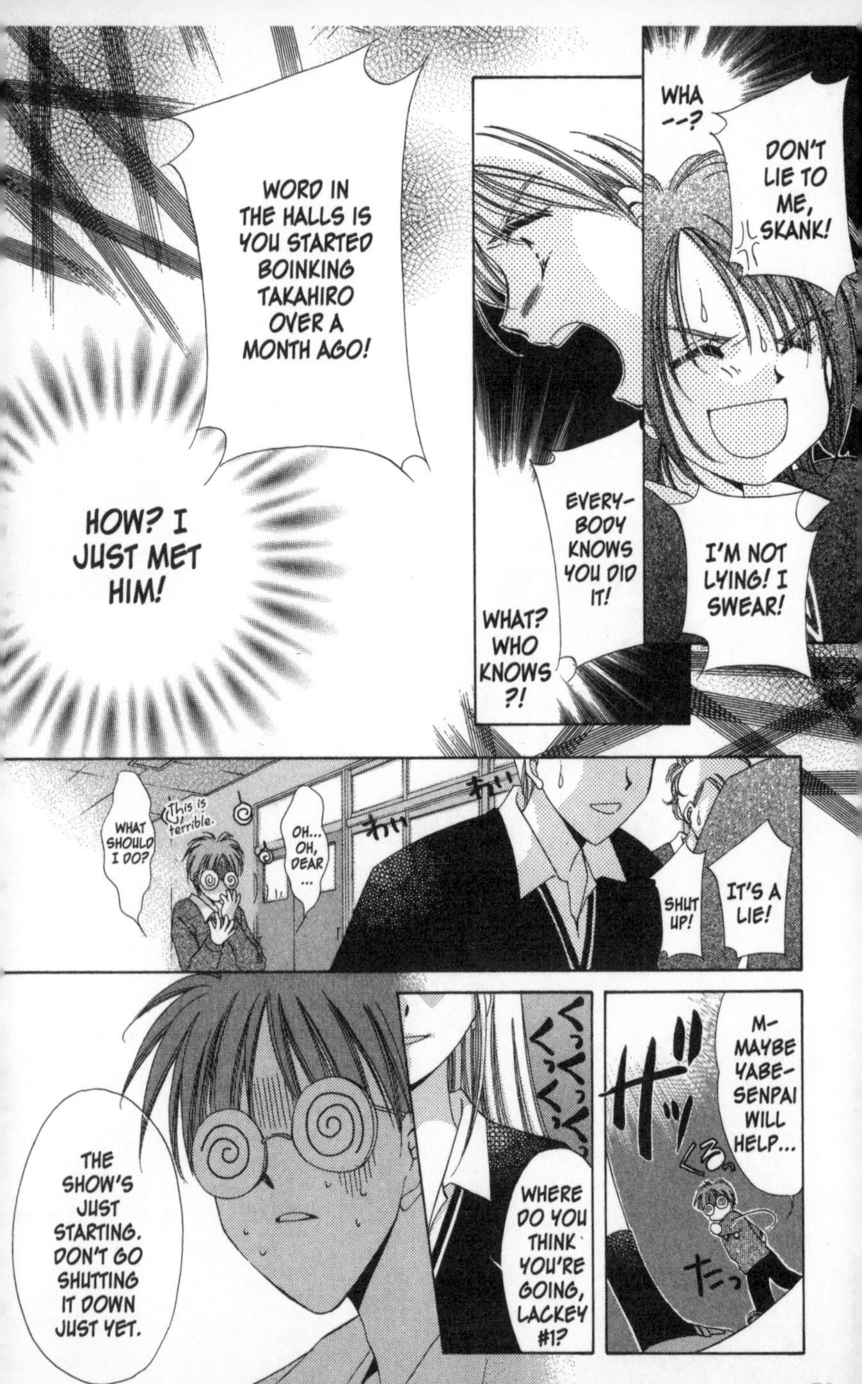
WHA--?
DON'T LIE TO ME, SKANK!
I'M NOT LYING! I SWEAR!
EVERY-BODY KNOWS YOU DID IT!
WHAT? WHO KNOWS?!
WORD IN THE HALLS IS YOU STARTED BOINKING TAKAHIRO OVER A MONTH AGO!
HOW? I JUST MET HIM!
IT'S A LIE!
SHUT UP!
OH... OH, DEAR...
This is terrible.
WHAT SHOULD I DO?
M-MAYBE YABE-SENPAI WILL HELP...
WHERE DO YOU THINK YOU'RE GOING, LACKEY #1?
THE SHOW'S JUST STARTING. DON'T GO SHUTTING IT DOWN JUST YET.

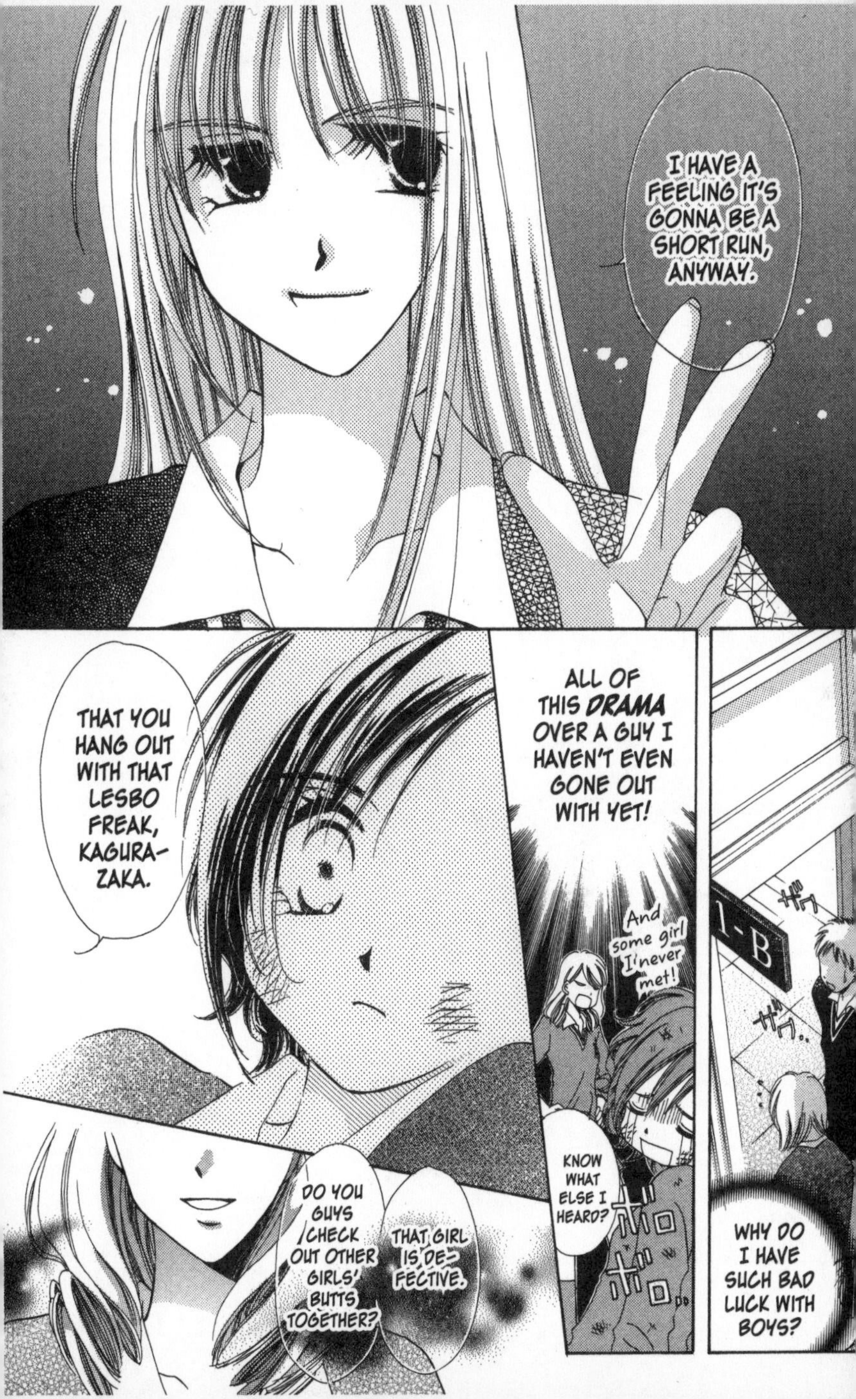
I HAVE A FEELING IT'S GONNA BE A SHORT RUN, ANYWAY.
WHY DO I HAVE SUCH BAD LUCK WITH BOYS?
ALL OF THIS *DRAMA* OVER A GUY I HAVEN'T EVEN GONE OUT WITH YET!
And some girl I'never met!
KNOW WHAT ELSE I HEARD?
THAT YOU HANG OUT WITH THAT LESBO FREAK, KAGURA-ZAKA.
THAT GIRL IS DE-FECTIVE.
DO YOU GUYS CHECK OUT OTHER GIRLS' BUTTS TOGETHER?

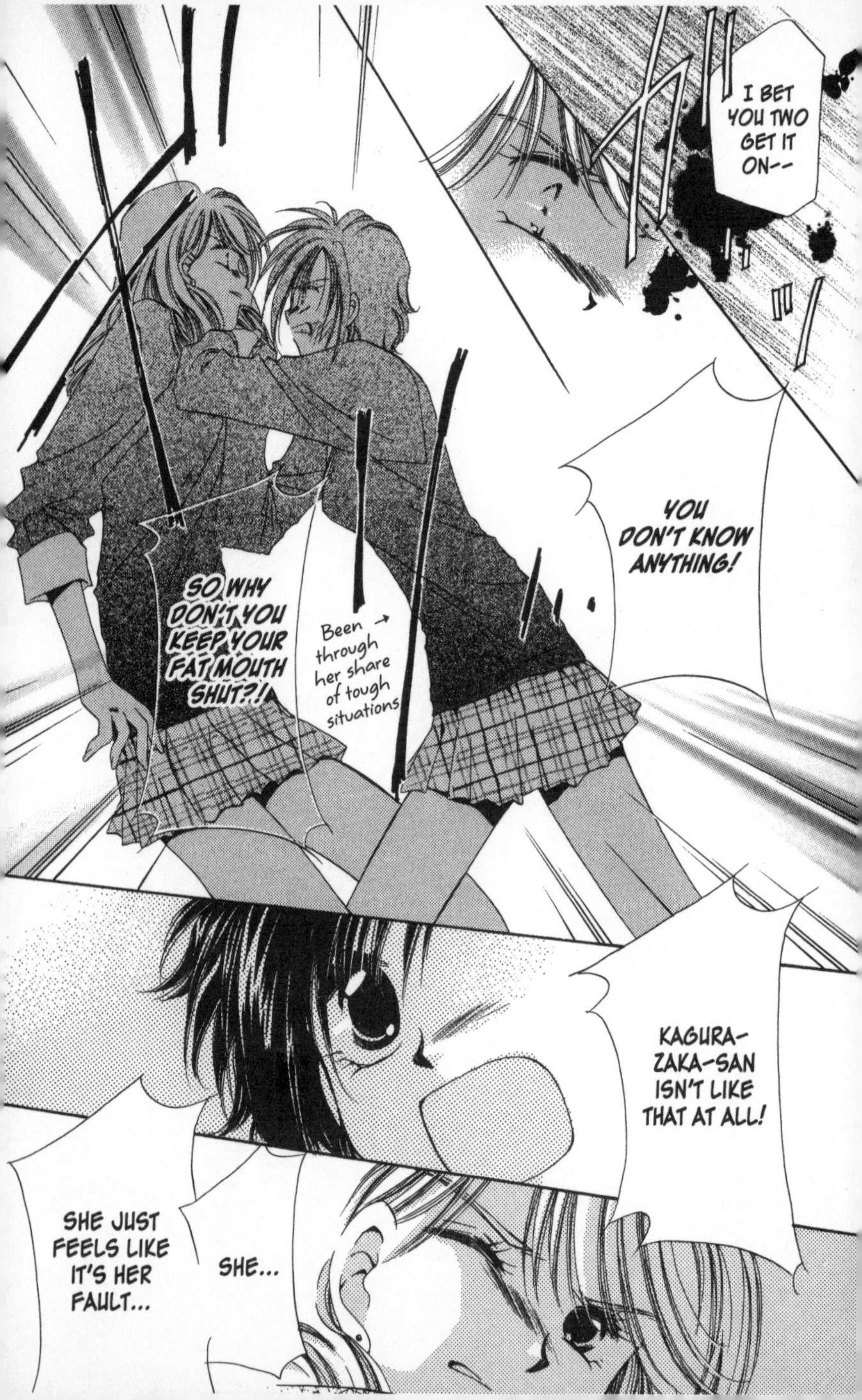
I BET YOU TWO GET IT ON--
YOU DON'T KNOW ANYTHING!
Been through her share of tough situations
SO WHY DON'T YOU KEEP YOUR FAT MOUTH SHUT?!
KAGURA-ZAKA-SAN ISN'T LIKE THAT AT ALL!
SHE...
SHE JUST FEELS LIKE IT'S HER FAULT...

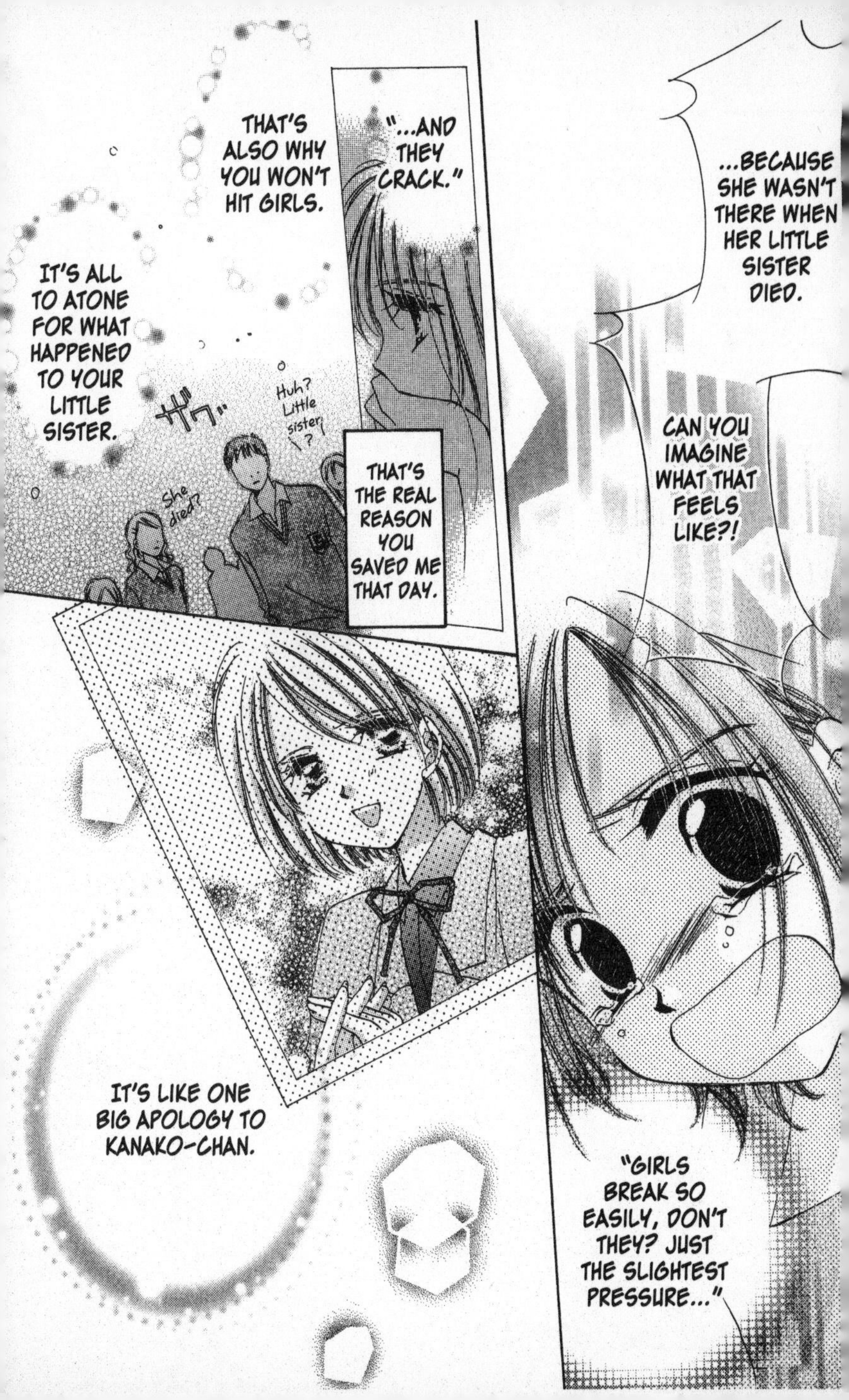
...BECAUSE SHE WASN'T THERE WHEN HER LITTLE SISTER DIED.
CAN YOU IMAGINE WHAT THAT FEELS LIKE?!
"GIRLS BREAK SO EASILY, DON'T THEY? JUST THE SLIGHTEST PRESSURE..."
"...AND THEY CRACK."
THAT'S ALSO WHY YOU WON'T HIT GIRLS.
IT'S ALL TO ATONE FOR WHAT HAPPENED TO YOUR LITTLE SISTER.
Huh? Little sister?
She died?
THAT'S THE REAL REASON YOU SAVED ME THAT DAY.
IT'S LIKE ONE BIG APOLOGY TO KANAKO-CHAN.

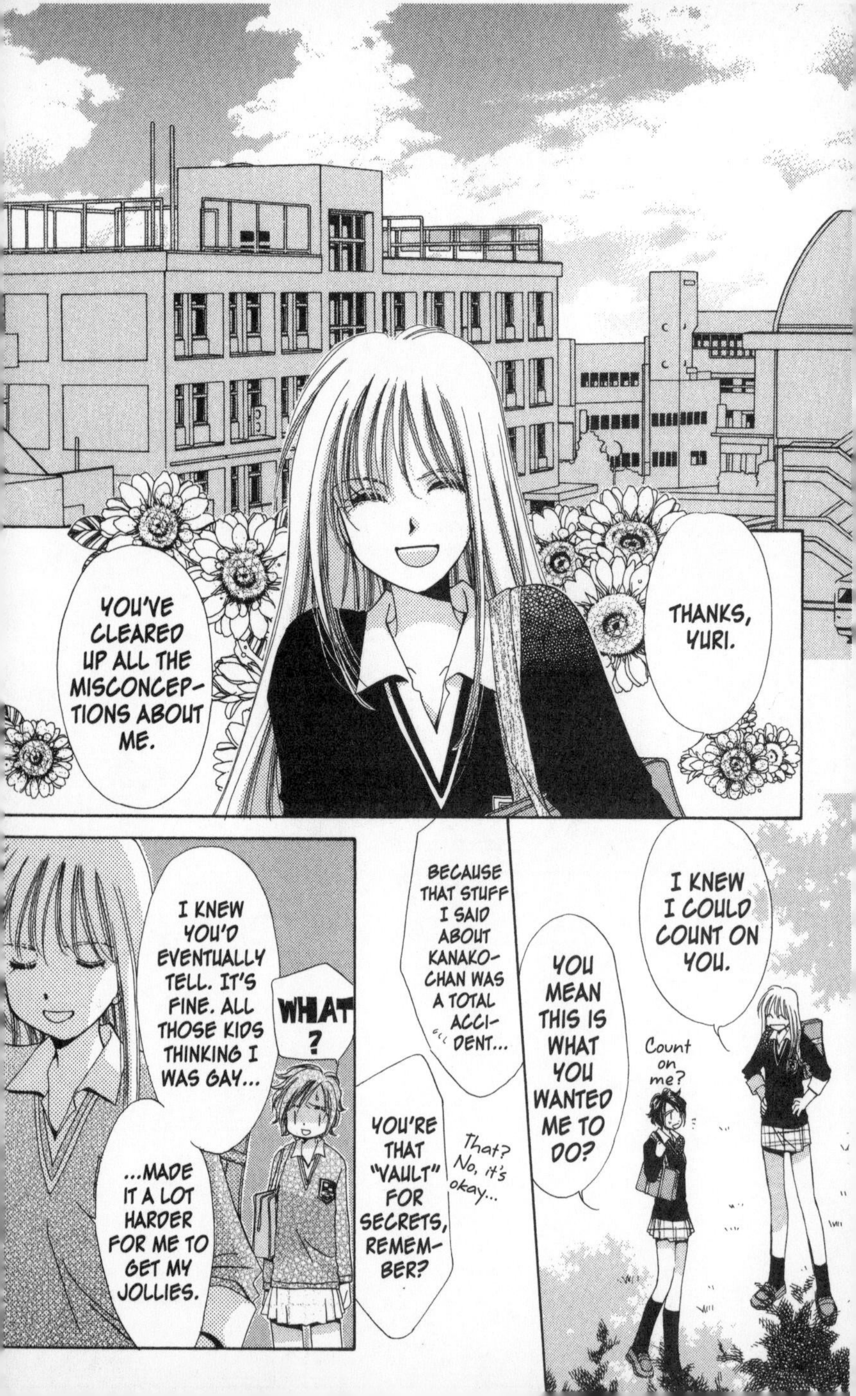
THANKS, YURI.
YOU'VE CLEARED UP ALL THE MISCONCEPTIONS ABOUT ME.
I KNEW I COULD COUNT ON YOU.
Count on me?
YOU MEAN THIS IS WHAT YOU WANTED ME TO DO?
BECAUSE THAT STUFF I SAID ABOUT KANAKO-CHAN WAS A TOTAL ACCIDENT...
YOU'RE THAT "VAULT" FOR SECRETS, REMEMBER?
That? No, it's okay...
I KNEW YOU'D EVENTUALLY TELL. IT'S FINE. ALL THOSE KIDS THINKING I WAS GAY...
WHAT?
...MADE IT A LOT HARDER FOR ME TO GET MY JOLLIES.

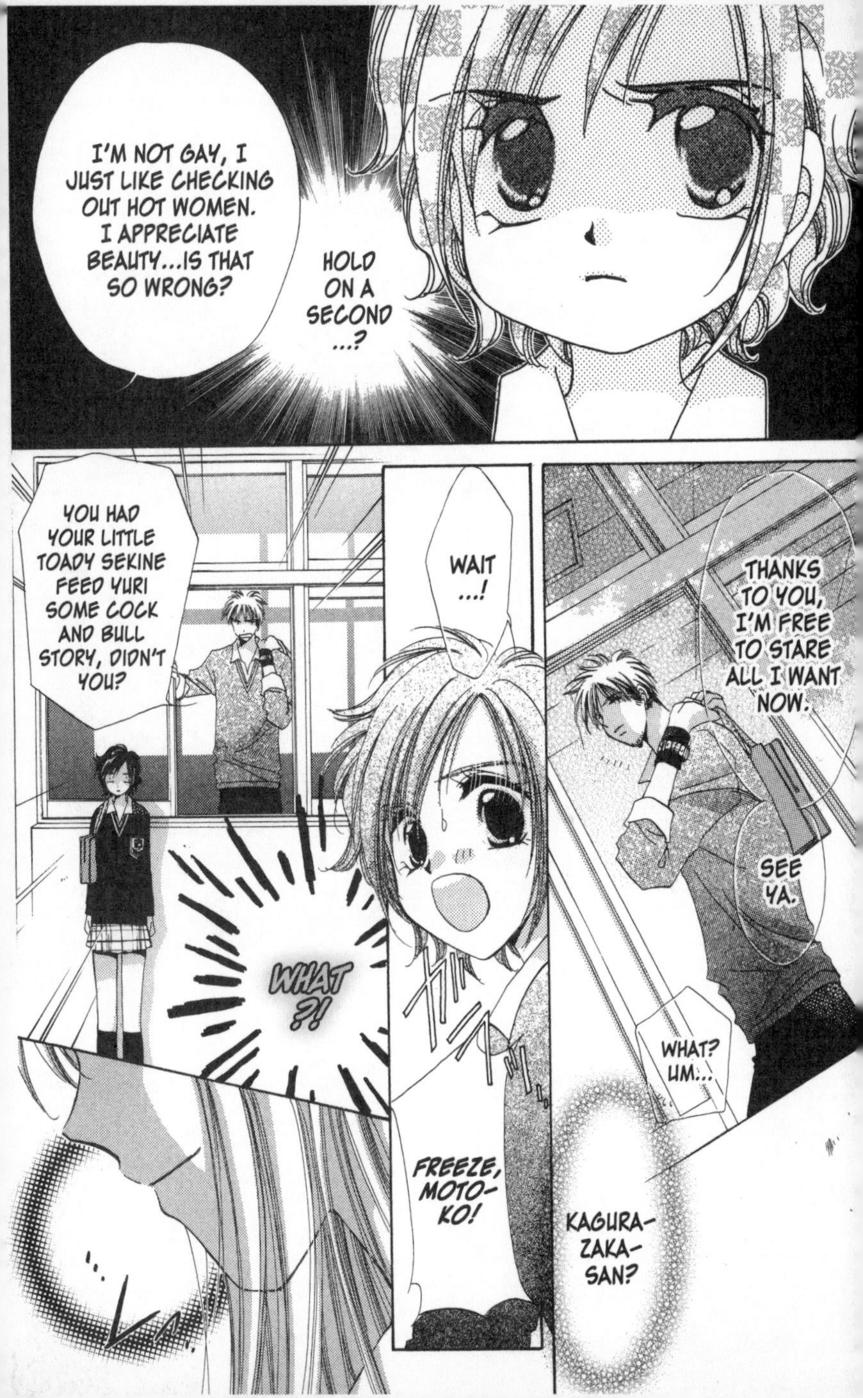

I'M NOT GAY, I JUST LIKE CHECKING OUT HOT WOMEN. I APPRECIATE BEAUTY...IS THAT SO WRONG?
HOLD ON A SECOND ...?
THANKS TO YOU, I'M FREE TO STARE ALL I WANT NOW.
SEE YA.
WHAT? UM...
KAGURA-ZAKA-SAN?
WAIT ...!
FREEZE, MOTO-KO!
YOU HAD YOUR LITTLE TOADY SEKINE FEED YURI SOME COCK AND BULL STORY, DIDN'T YOU?
WHAT ?!

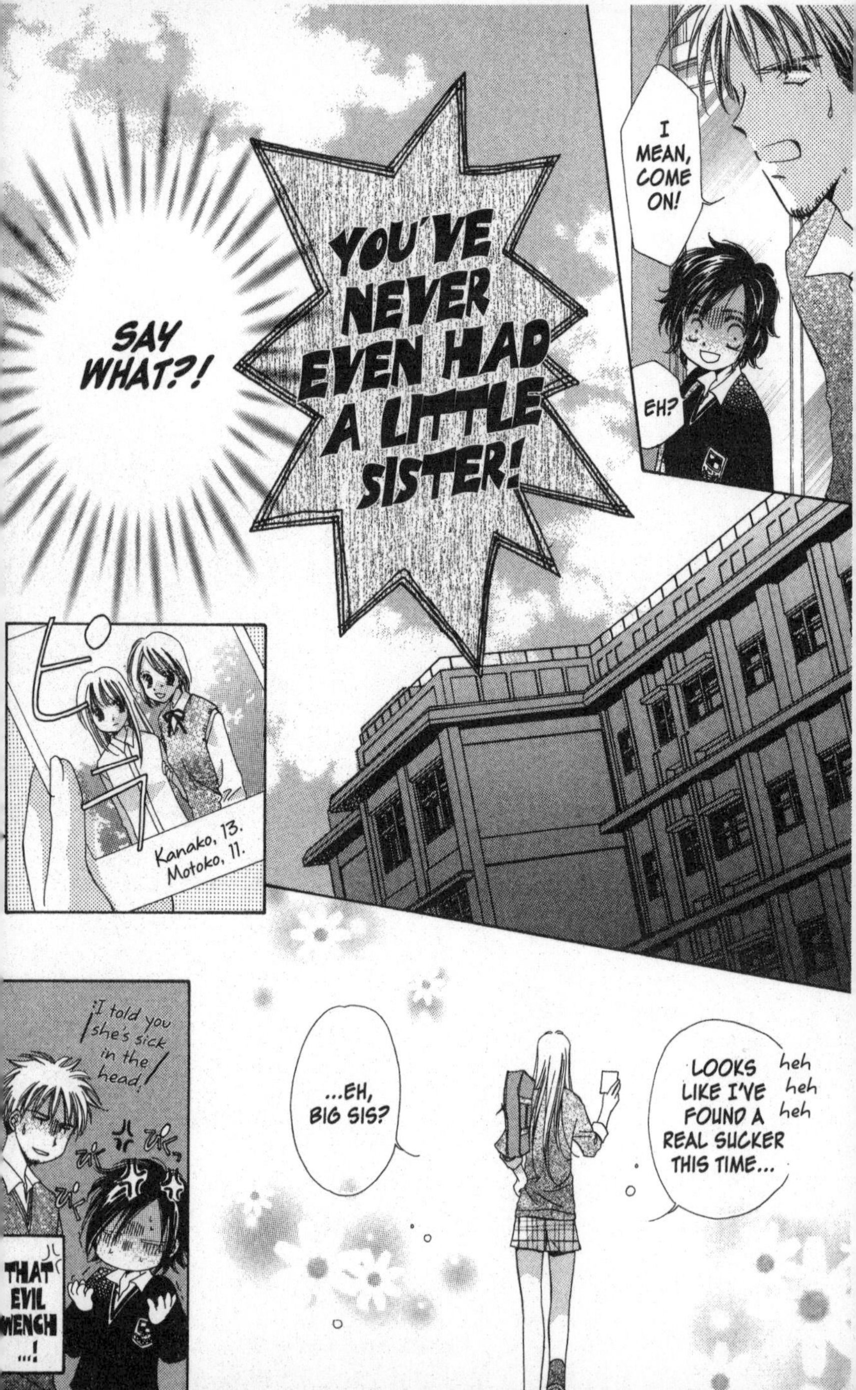
I MEAN, COME ON!
EH?
YOU'VE NEVER EVEN HAD A LITTLE SISTER!
SAY WHAT?!
Kanako, 13.
Motoko, 11.
LOOKS LIKE I'VE FOUND A REAL SUCKER THIS TIME...
heh heh heh
...EH, BIG SIS?
I told you she's sick in the head.
THAT EVIL WENCH ...!

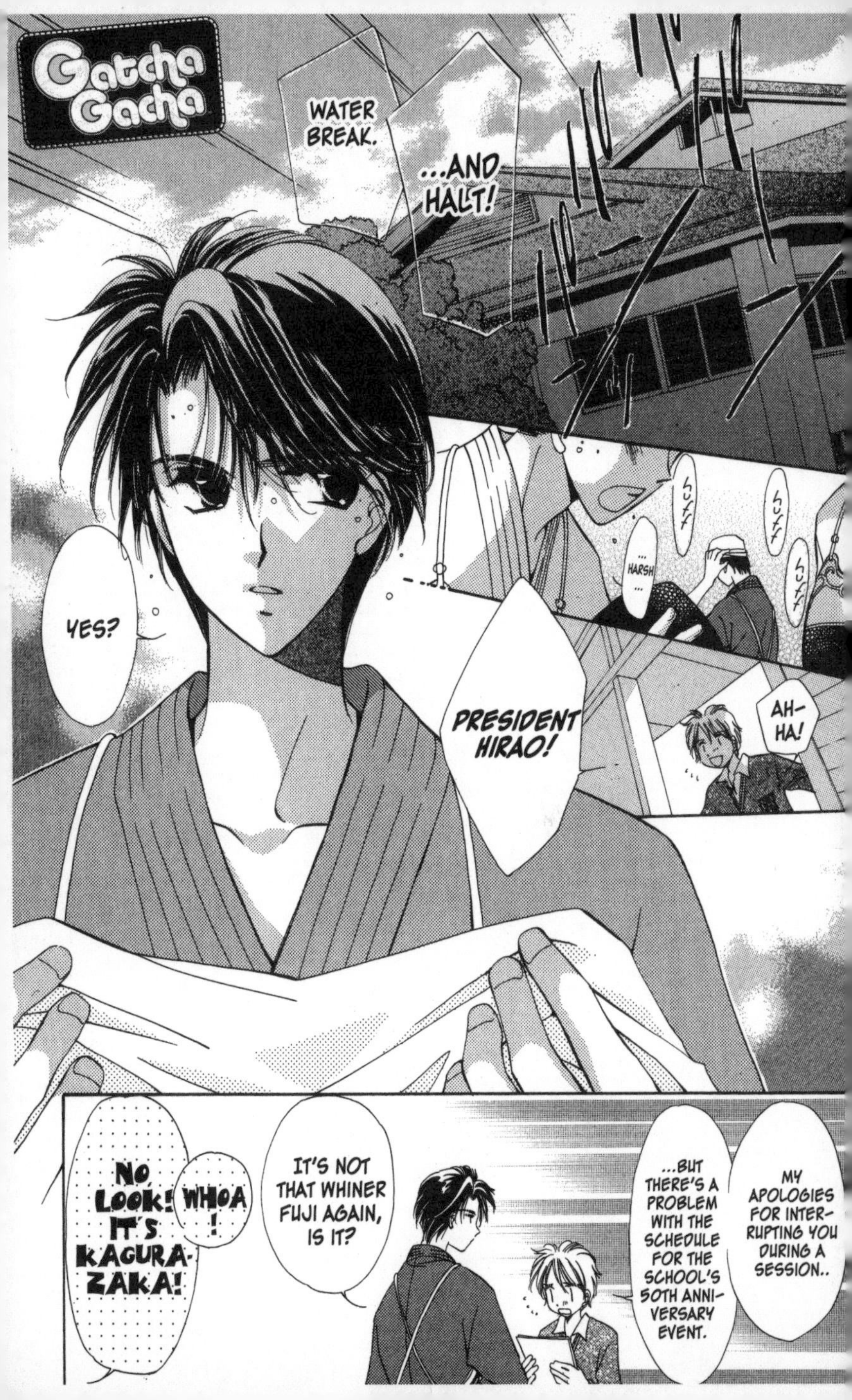
Gatcha Gacha
WATER BREAK.
...AND HALT!
huff
huff
huff
...HARSH...
PRESIDENT HIRAO!
AH-HA!
YES?
MY APOLOGIES FOR INTER-RUPTING YOU DURING A SESSION..
...BUT THERE'S A PROBLEM WITH THE SCHEDULE FOR THE SCHOOL'S 50TH ANNI-VERSARY EVENT.
IT'S NOT THAT WHINER FUJI AGAIN, IS IT?
WHOA!
NO, LOOK! IT'S KAGURA-ZAKA!

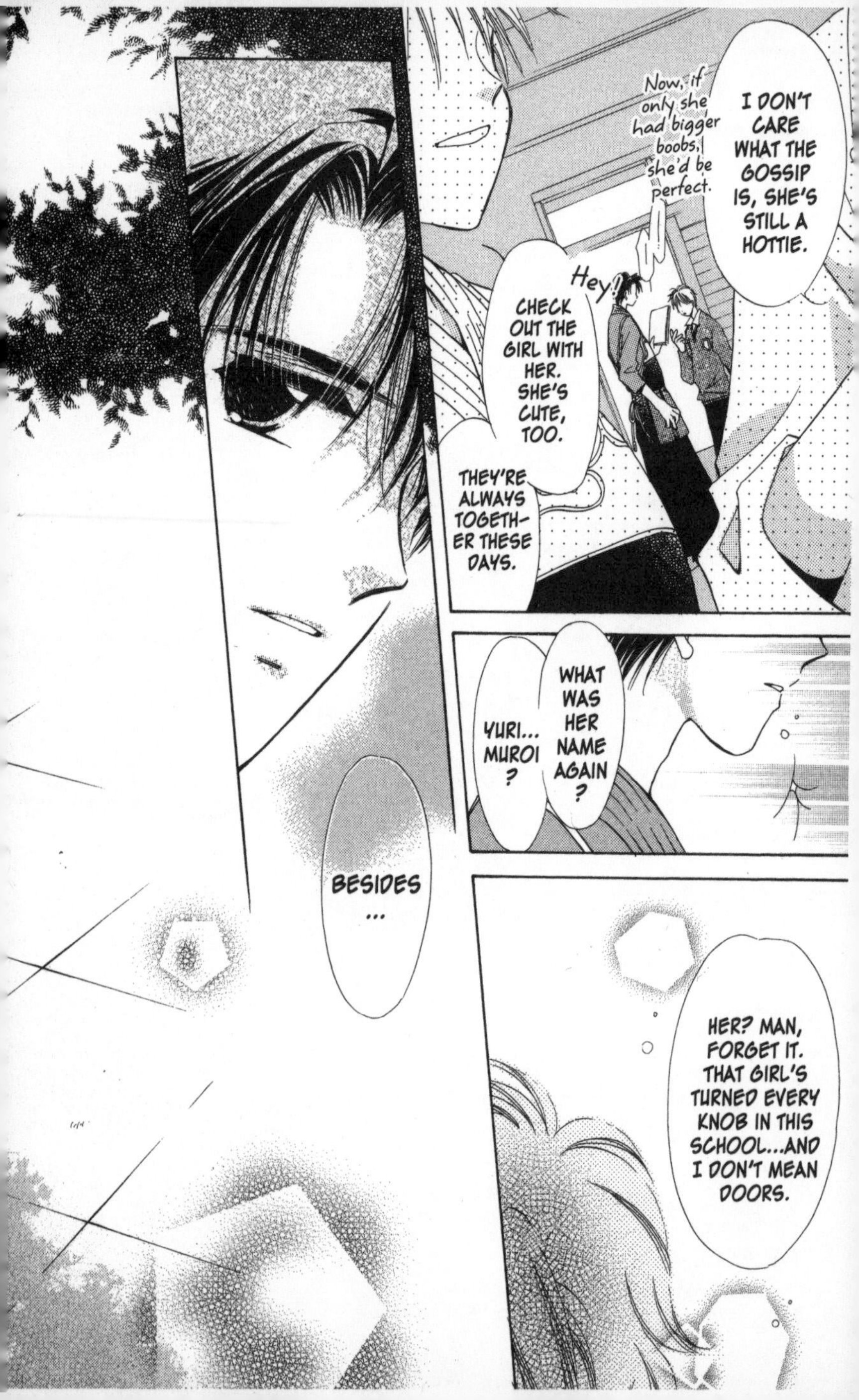
I DON'T CARE WHAT THE GOSSIP IS, SHE'S STILL A HOTTIE.
Now, if only she had bigger boobs, she'd be perfect.
Hey!
CHECK OUT THE GIRL WITH HER. SHE'S CUTE, TOO.
THEY'RE ALWAYS TOGETHER THESE DAYS.
WHAT WAS HER NAME AGAIN?
YURI... MUROI?
HER? MAN, FORGET IT. THAT GIRL'S TURNED EVERY KNOB IN THIS SCHOOL...AND I DON'T MEAN DOORS.
BESIDES...

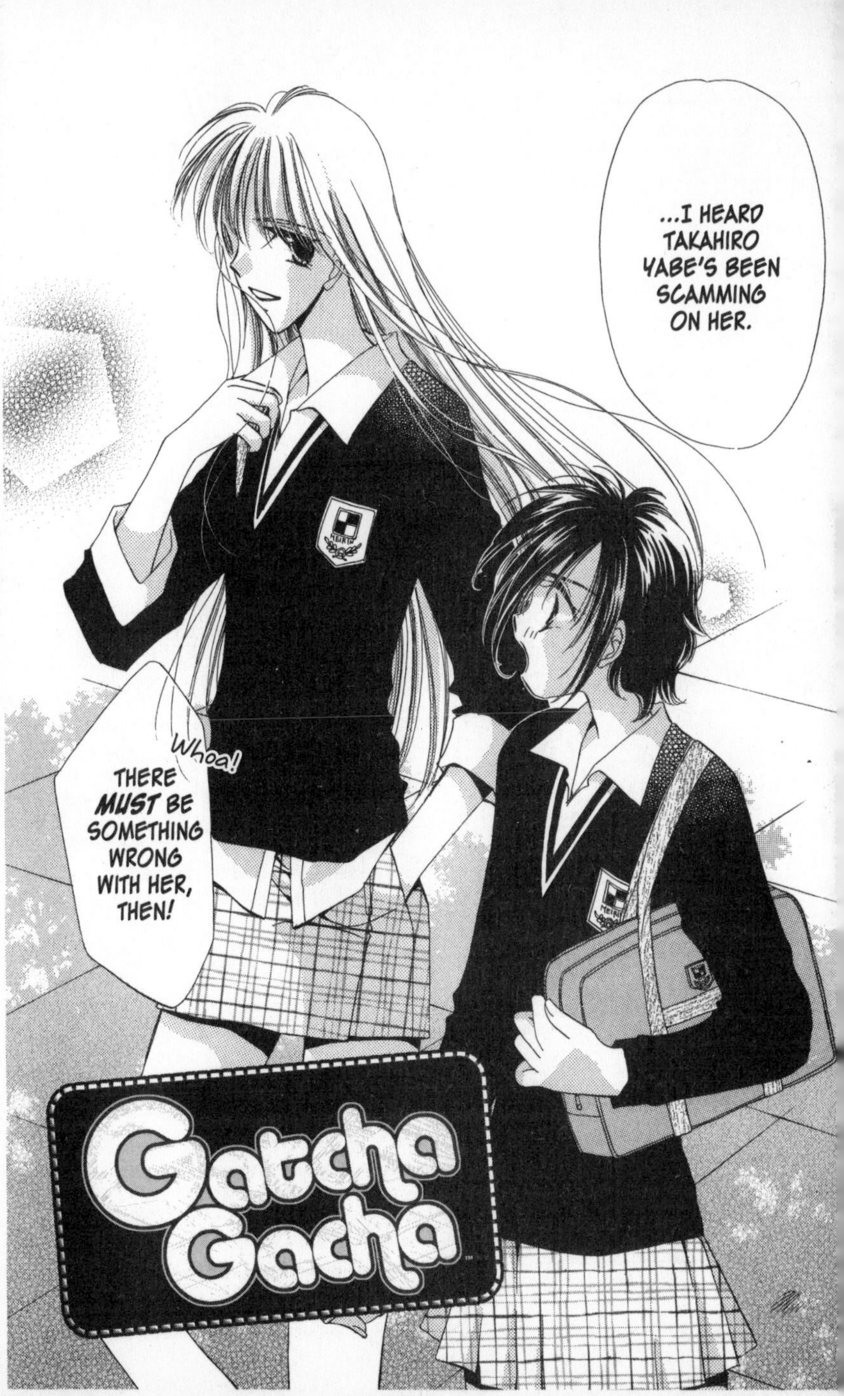
...I HEARD TAKAHIRO YABE'S BEEN SCAMMING ON HER.
Whoa!
THERE *MUST* BE SOMETHING WRONG WITH HER, THEN!
Gatcha Gacha

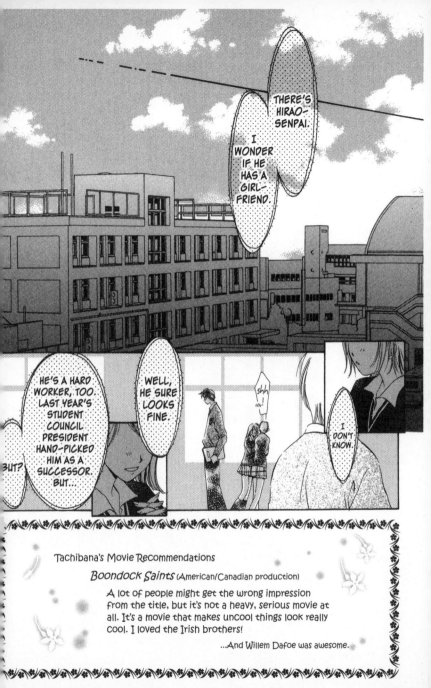

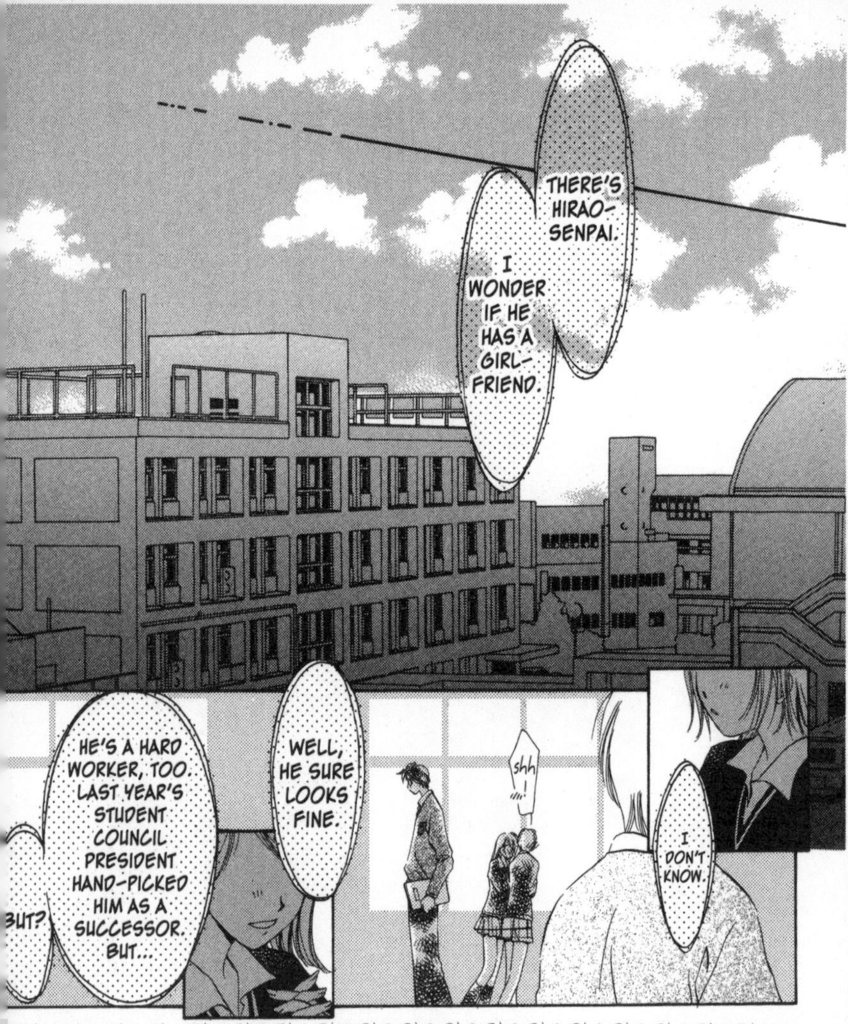
THERE'S HIRAO-SENPAI.
I WONDER IF HE HAS A GIRL-FRIEND.
I DON'T KNOW.
shh!
WELL, HE SURE LOOKS FINE.
HE'S A HARD WORKER, TOO. LAST YEAR'S STUDENT COUNCIL PRESIDENT HAND-PICKED HIM AS A SUCCESSOR. BUT...
BUT?

Tachibana's Movie Recommendations

Boondock Saints (American/Canadian production)

A lot of people might get the wrong impression from the title, but it's not a heavy, serious movie at all. It's a movie that makes uncool things look really cool. I loved the Irish brothers!

...And Willem Dafoe was awesome.

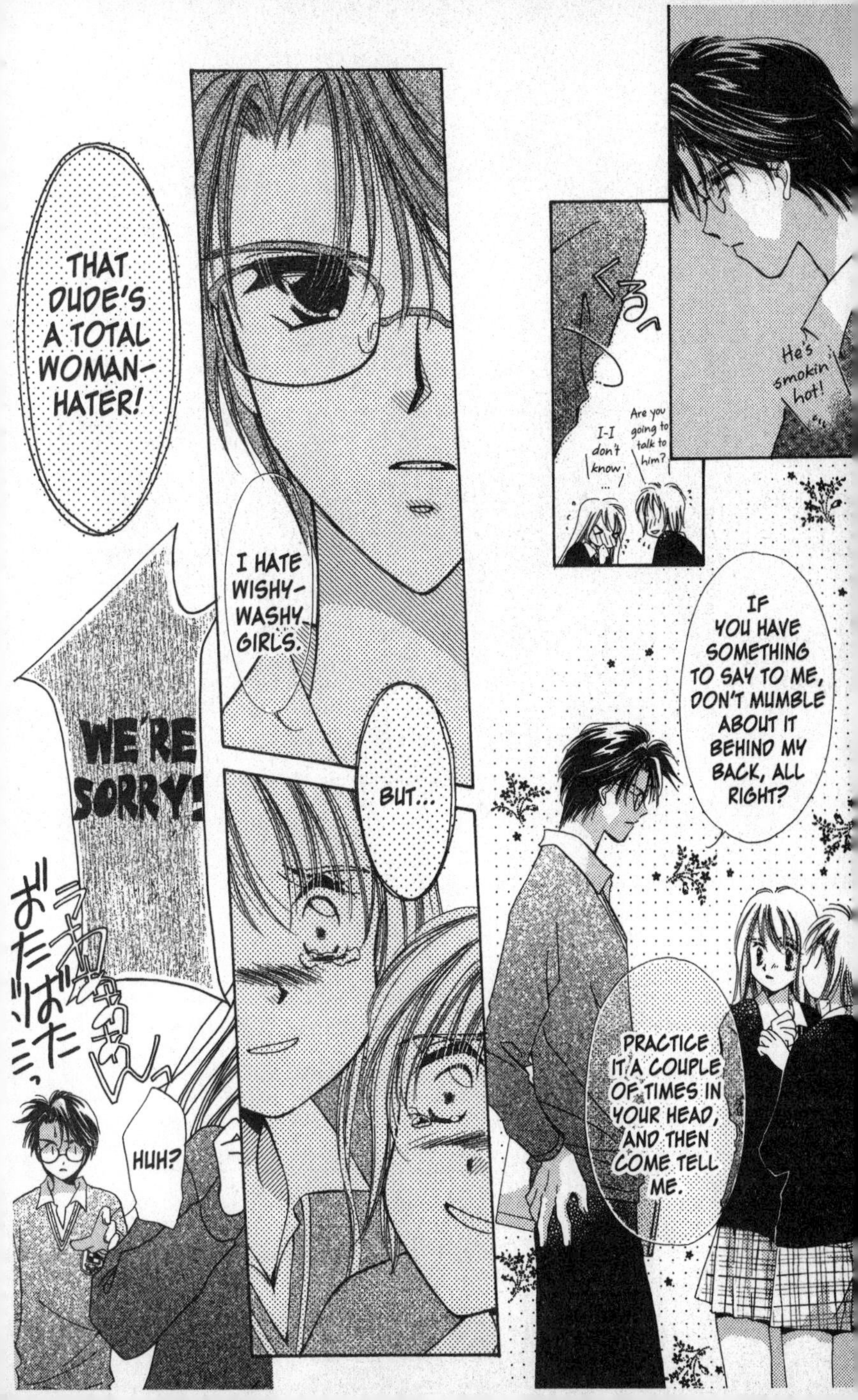
He's smokin hot!
Are you going to talk to him?
I-I don't know...
IF YOU HAVE SOMETHING TO SAY TO ME, DON'T MUMBLE ABOUT IT BEHIND MY BACK, ALL RIGHT?
PRACTICE IT A COUPLE OF TIMES IN YOUR HEAD, AND THEN COME TELL ME.
I HATE WISHY-WASHY GIRLS.
BUT...
THAT DUDE'S A TOTAL WOMAN-HATER!
WE'RE SORRY!
HUH?

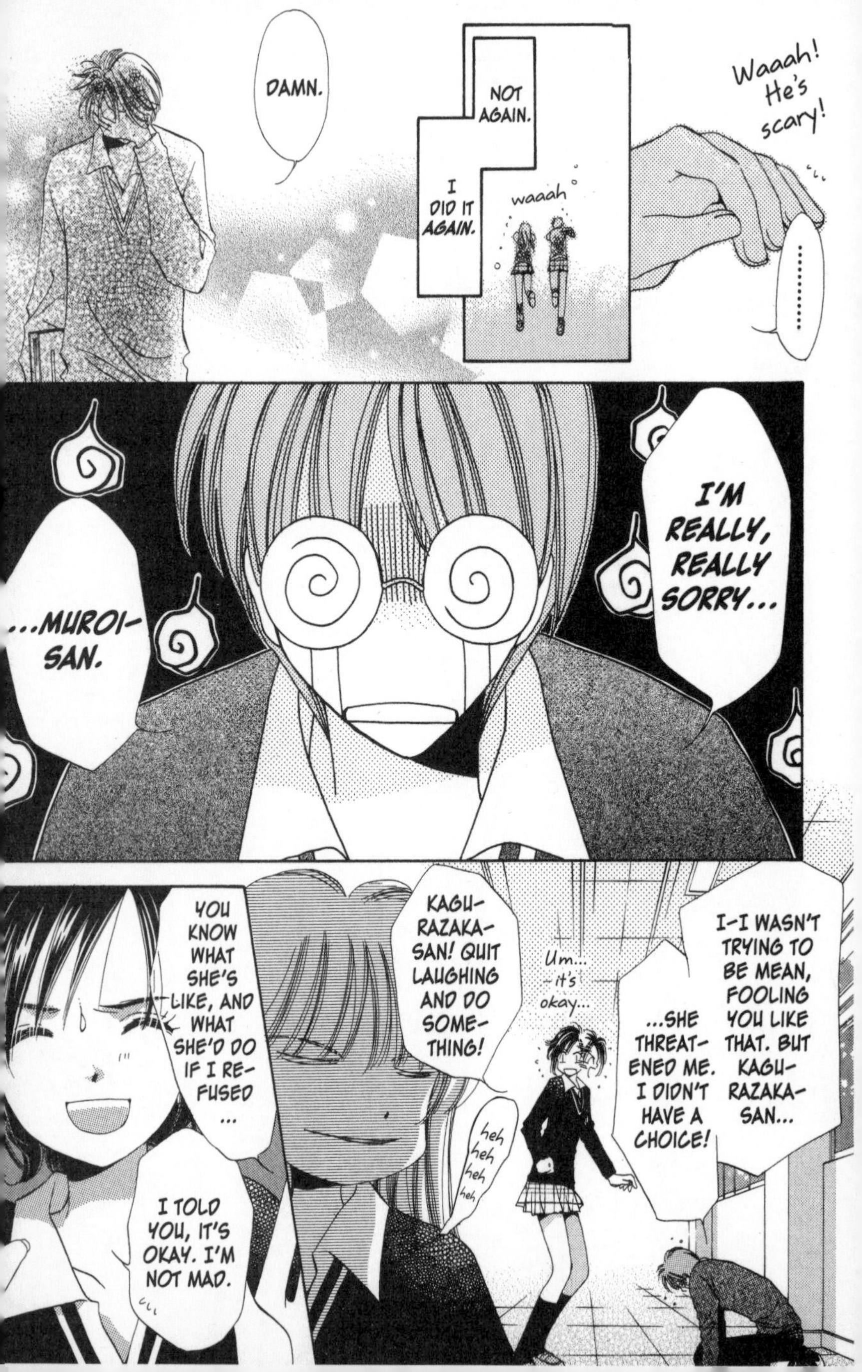
Waaah! He's scary!
......
NOT AGAIN.
I DID IT AGAIN.
waaah
DAMN.
I'M REALLY, REALLY SORRY...
...MUROI-SAN.
I-I WASN'T TRYING TO BE MEAN, FOOLING YOU LIKE THAT. BUT KAGURAZAKA-SAN...
...SHE THREAT-ENED ME. I DIDN'T HAVE A CHOICE!
Um... it's okay...
KAGU-RAZAKA-SAN! QUIT LAUGHING AND DO SOME-THING!
heh heh heh heh
YOU KNOW WHAT SHE'S LIKE, AND WHAT SHE'D DO IF I RE-FUSED ...
I TOLD YOU, IT'S OKAY. I'M NOT MAD.

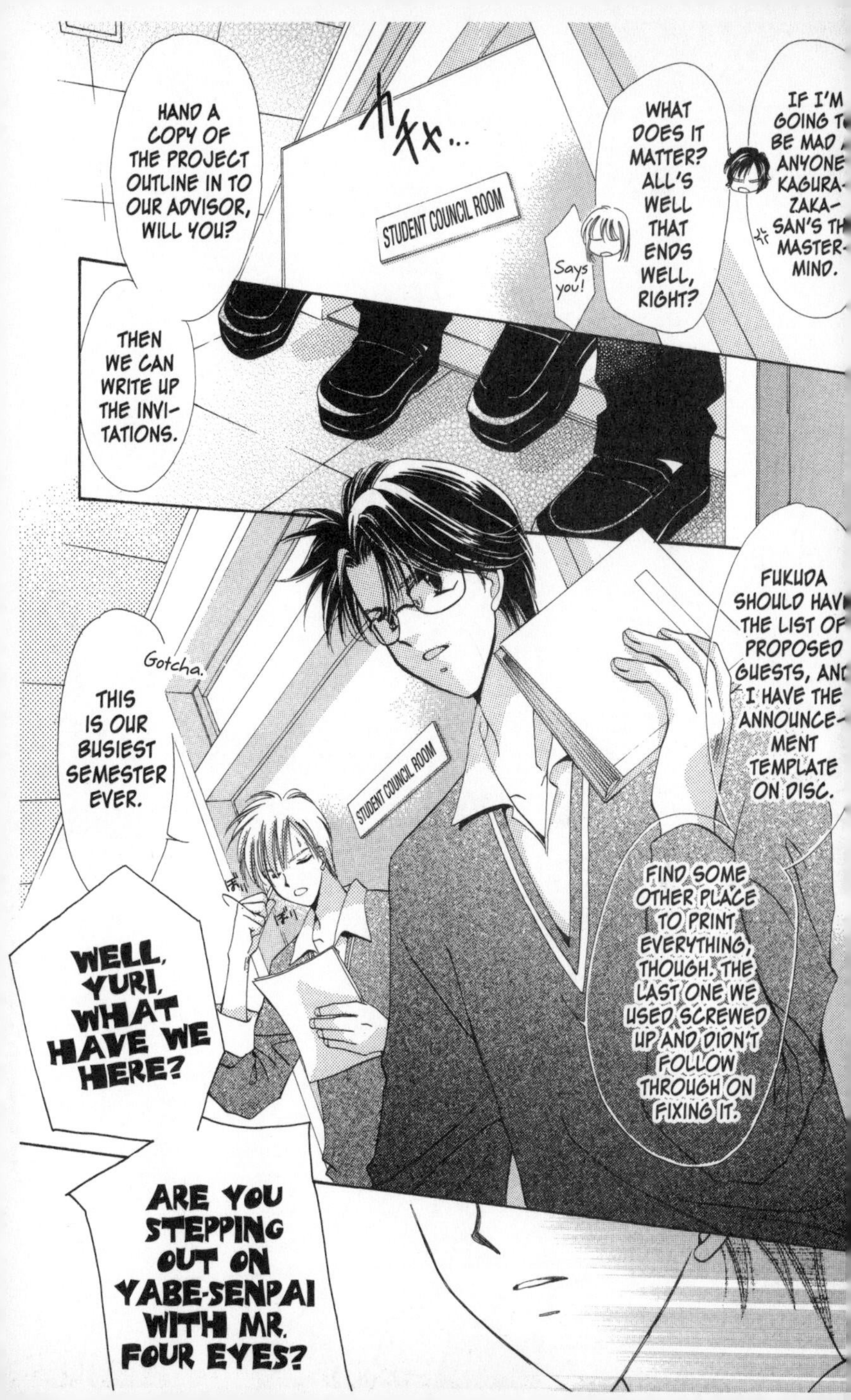

IF I'M GOING T BE MAD ANYONE KAGURA-ZAKA-SAN'S TH MASTER-MIND.
WHAT DOES IT MATTER? ALL'S WELL THAT ENDS WELL, RIGHT?
Says you!
STUDENT COUNCIL ROOM
カチャ...
HAND A COPY OF THE PROJECT OUTLINE IN TO OUR ADVISOR, WILL YOU?
THEN WE CAN WRITE UP THE INVI-TATIONS.
FUKUDA SHOULD HAV THE LIST OF PROPOSED GUESTS, AN I HAVE THE ANNOUNCE-MENT TEMPLATE ON DISC.
FIND SOME OTHER PLACE TO PRINT EVERYTHING, THOUGH. THE LAST ONE WE USED SCREWED UP AND DIDN'T FOLLOW THROUGH ON FIXING IT.
Gotcha.
THIS IS OUR BUSIEST SEMESTER EVER.
STUDENT COUNCIL ROOM
WELL, YURI, WHAT HAVE WE HERE?
ARE YOU STEPPING OUT ON YABE-SENPAI WITH MR. FOUR EYES?

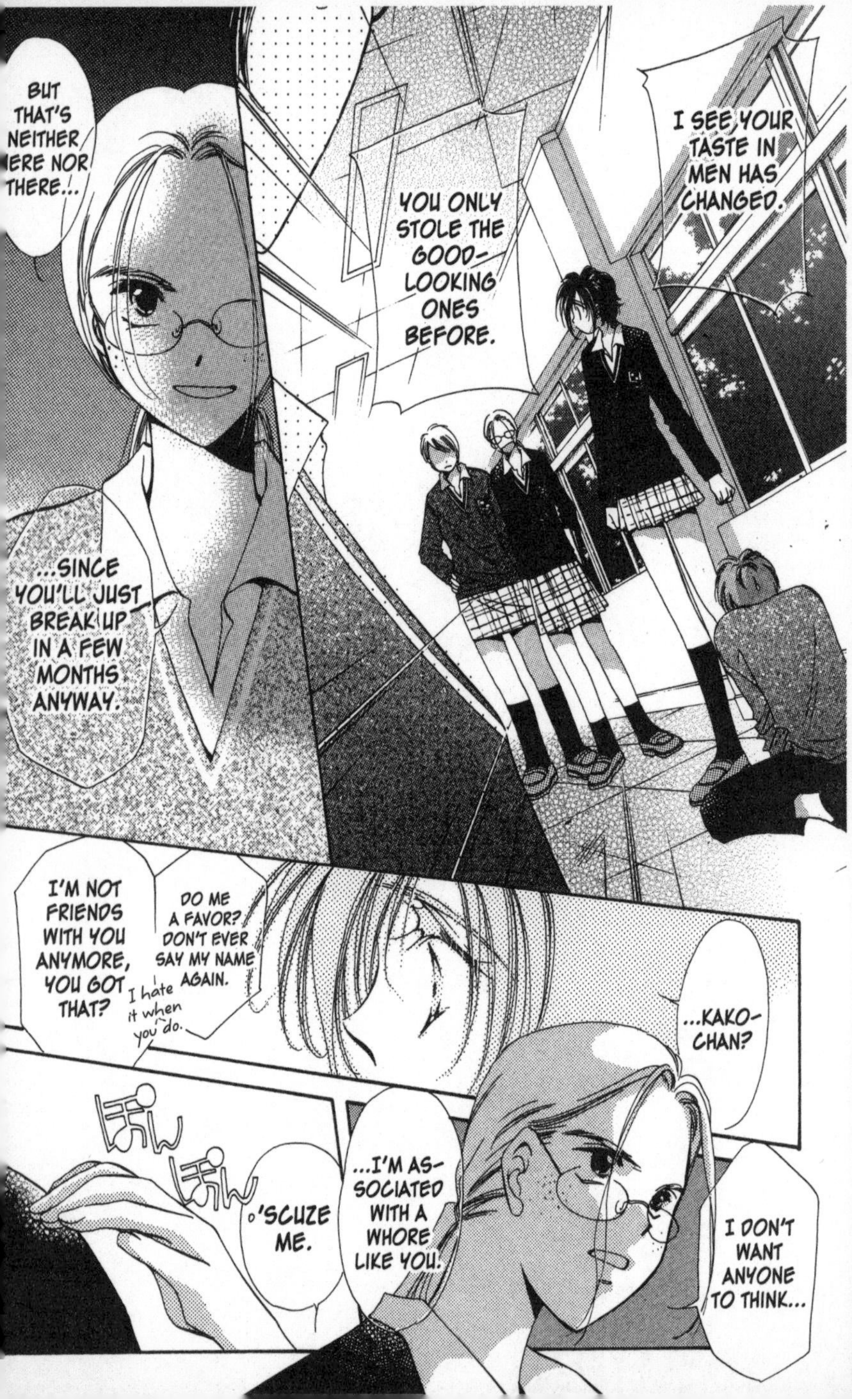
I SEE YOUR TASTE IN MEN HAS CHANGED.
YOU ONLY STOLE THE GOOD-LOOKING ONES BEFORE.
BUT THAT'S NEITHER ERE NOR THERE...
...SINCE YOU'LL JUST BREAK UP IN A FEW MONTHS ANYWAY.
...KAKO-CHAN?
DO ME A FAVOR? DON'T EVER SAY MY NAME AGAIN.
I hate it when you do.
I'M NOT FRIENDS WITH YOU ANYMORE, YOU GOT THAT?
I DON'T WANT ANYONE TO THINK...
...I'M ASSOCIATED WITH A WHORE LIKE YOU.
ぽん
ぽん
'SCUZE ME.

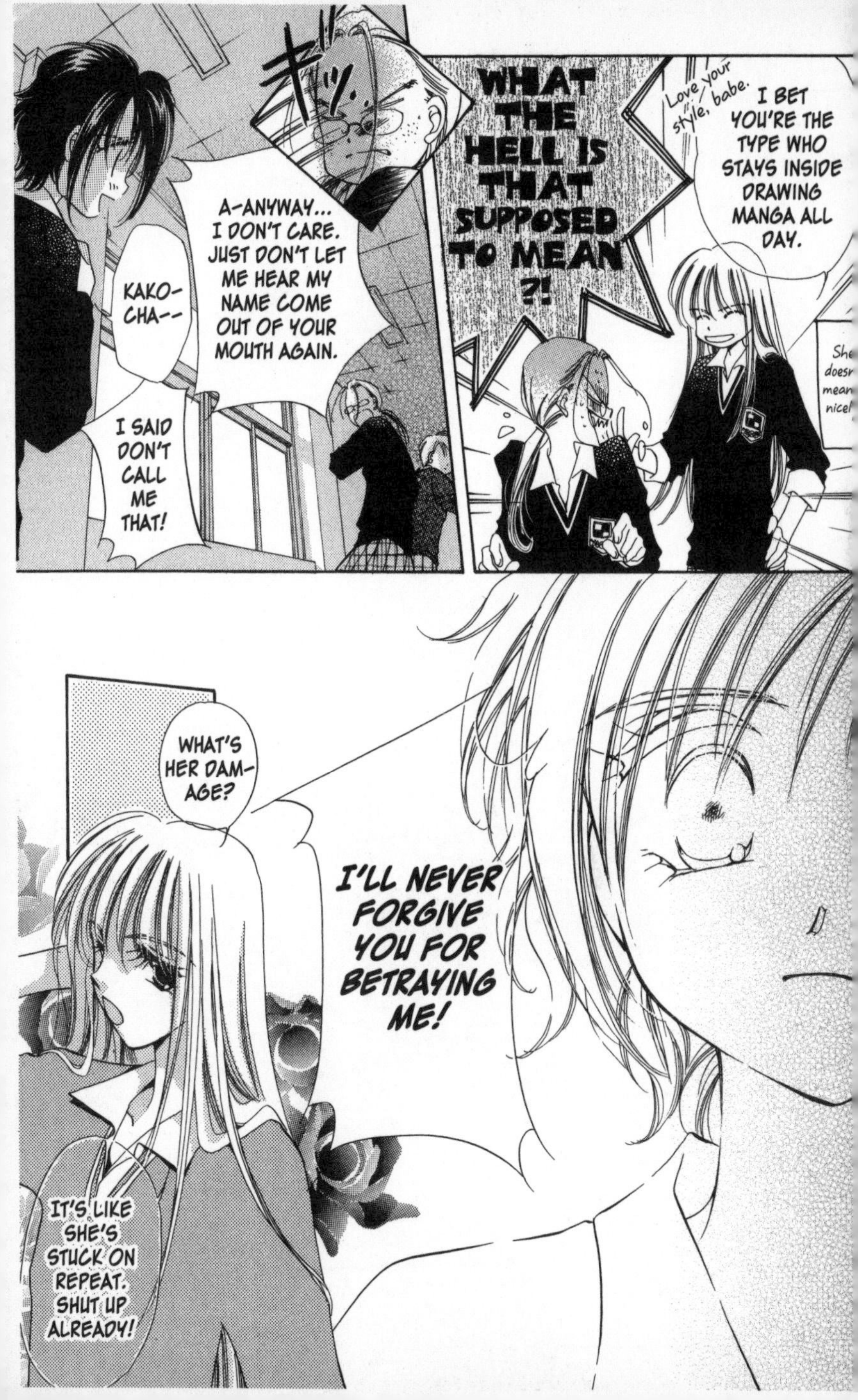
Love your style, babe.
I BET YOU'RE THE TYPE WHO STAYS INSIDE DRAWING MANGA ALL DAY.
WHAT THE HELL IS THAT SUPPOSED TO MEAN ?!
A-ANYWAY... I DON'T CARE. JUST DON'T LET ME HEAR MY NAME COME OUT OF YOUR MOUTH AGAIN.
KAKO-CHA--
I SAID DON'T CALL ME THAT!
I'LL NEVER FORGIVE YOU FOR BETRAYING ME!
WHAT'S HER DAMAGE?
IT'S LIKE SHE'S STUCK ON REPEAT. SHUT UP ALREADY!

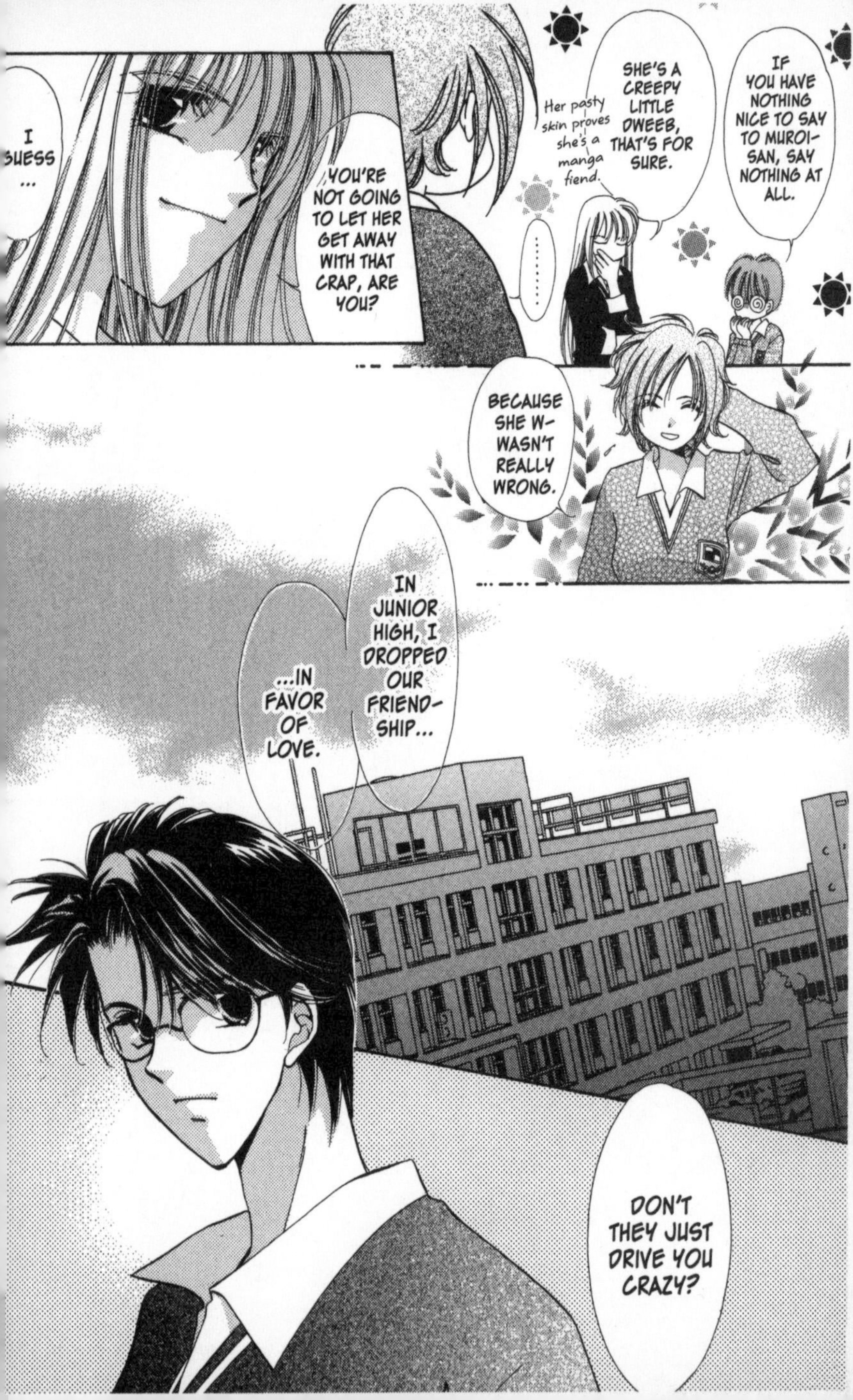
IF YOU HAVE NOTHING NICE TO SAY TO MUROI-SAN, SAY NOTHING AT ALL.
SHE'S A CREEPY LITTLE DWEEB, THAT'S FOR SURE.
Her pasty skin proves she's a manga fiend.
......
YOU'RE NOT GOING TO LET HER GET AWAY WITH THAT CRAP, ARE YOU?
I GUESS ...
BECAUSE SHE W-WASN'T REALLY WRONG.
IN JUNIOR HIGH, I DROPPED OUR FRIENDSHIP...
...IN FAVOR OF LOVE.
DON'T THEY JUST DRIVE YOU CRAZY?

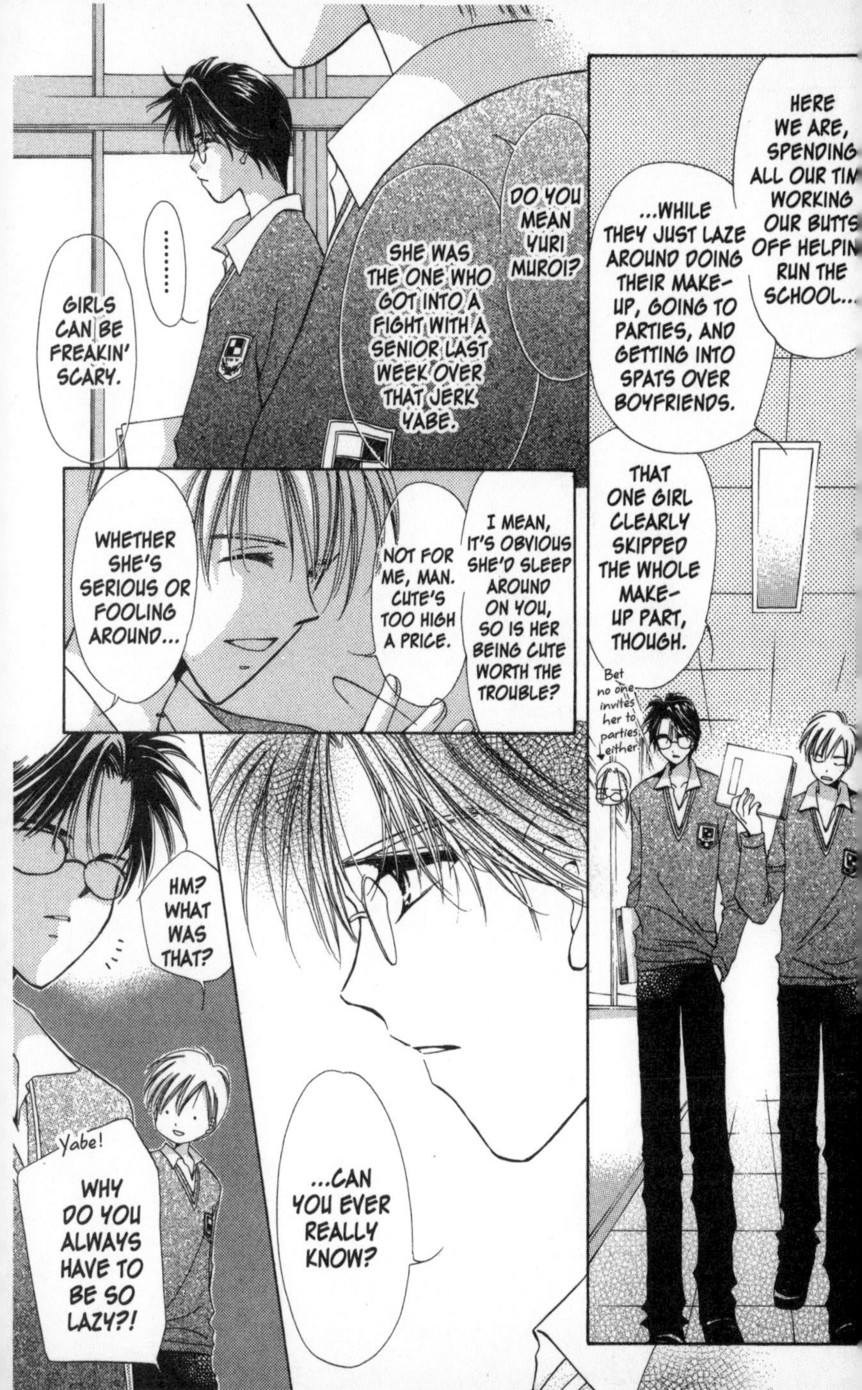
HERE WE ARE, SPENDING ALL OUR TIM WORKING OUR BUTTS OFF HELPIN RUN THE SCHOOL...
...WHILE THEY JUST LAZE AROUND DOING THEIR MAKE-UP, GOING TO PARTIES, AND GETTING INTO SPATS OVER BOYFRIENDS.
THAT ONE GIRL CLEARLY SKIPPED THE WHOLE MAKE-UP PART, THOUGH.
Bet no one invites her to parties, either.
DO YOU MEAN YURI MUROI?
SHE WAS THE ONE WHO GOT INTO A FIGHT WITH A SENIOR LAST WEEK OVER THAT JERK YABE.
....
GIRLS CAN BE FREAKIN' SCARY.
I MEAN, IT'S OBVIOUS SHE'D SLEEP AROUND ON YOU, SO IS HER BEING CUTE WORTH THE TROUBLE?
NOT FOR ME, MAN. CUTE'S TOO HIGH A PRICE.
WHETHER SHE'S SERIOUS OR FOOLING AROUND...
...CAN YOU EVER REALLY KNOW?
HM? WHAT WAS THAT?
Yabe!
WHY DO YOU ALWAYS HAVE TO BE SO LAZY?!

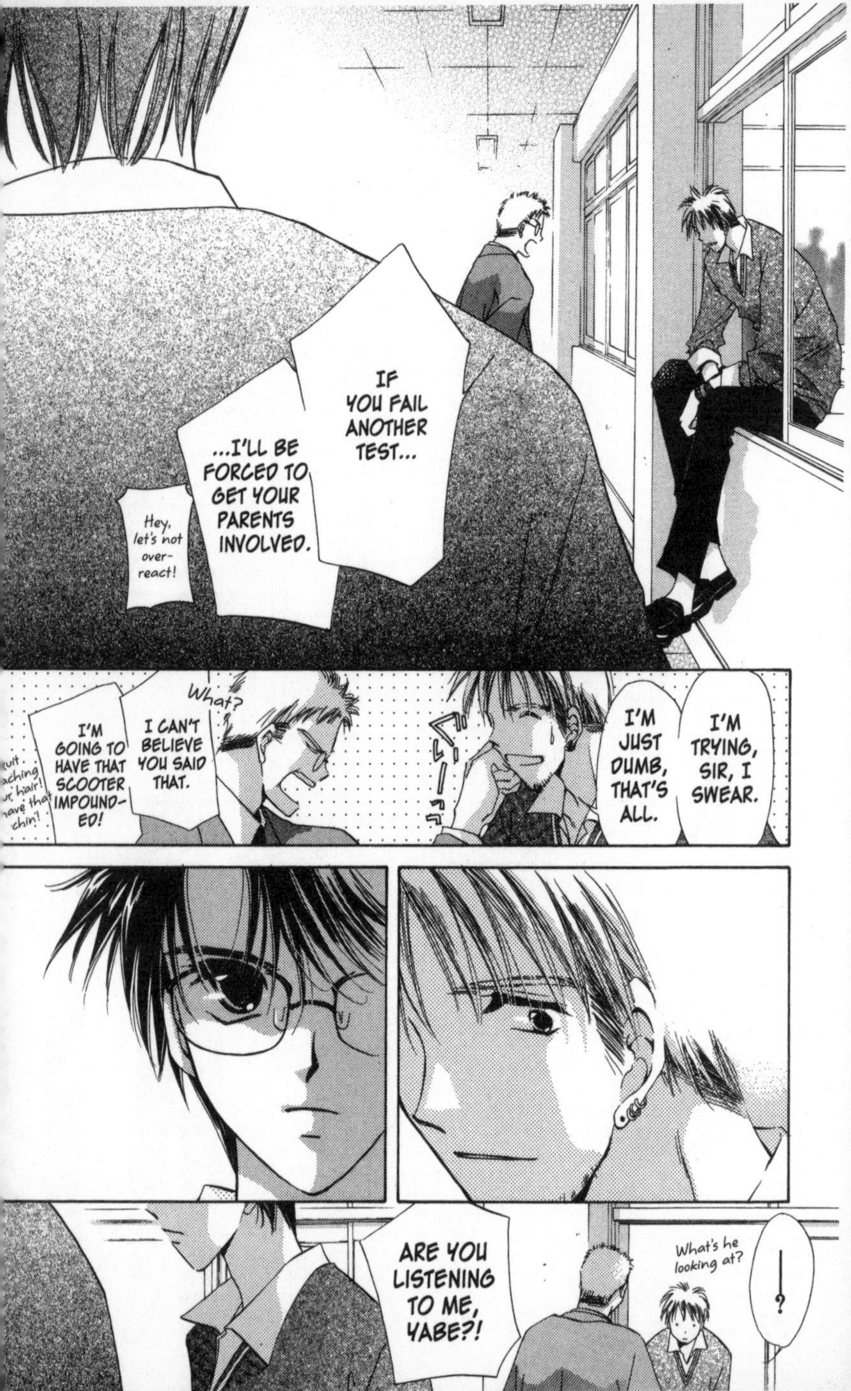
IF YOU FAIL ANOTHER TEST...
...I'LL BE FORCED TO GET YOUR PARENTS INVOLVED.
Hey, let's not over-react!
I'M TRYING, SIR, I SWEAR.
I'M JUST DUMB, THAT'S ALL.
What?
I CAN'T BELIEVE YOU SAID THAT.
I'M GOING TO HAVE THAT SCOOTER IMPOUND-ED!
?
What's he looking at?
ARE YOU LISTENING TO ME, YABE?!

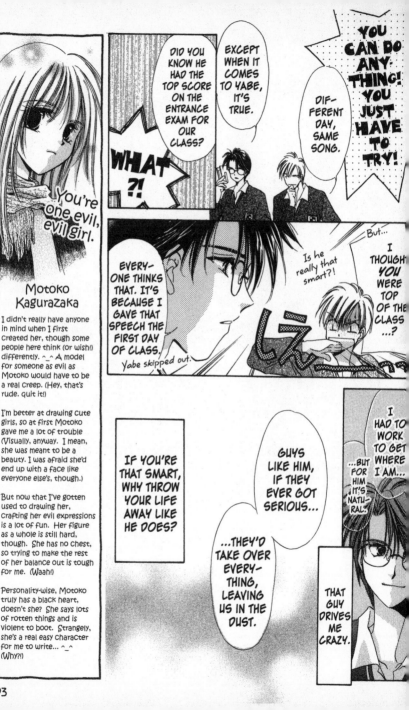

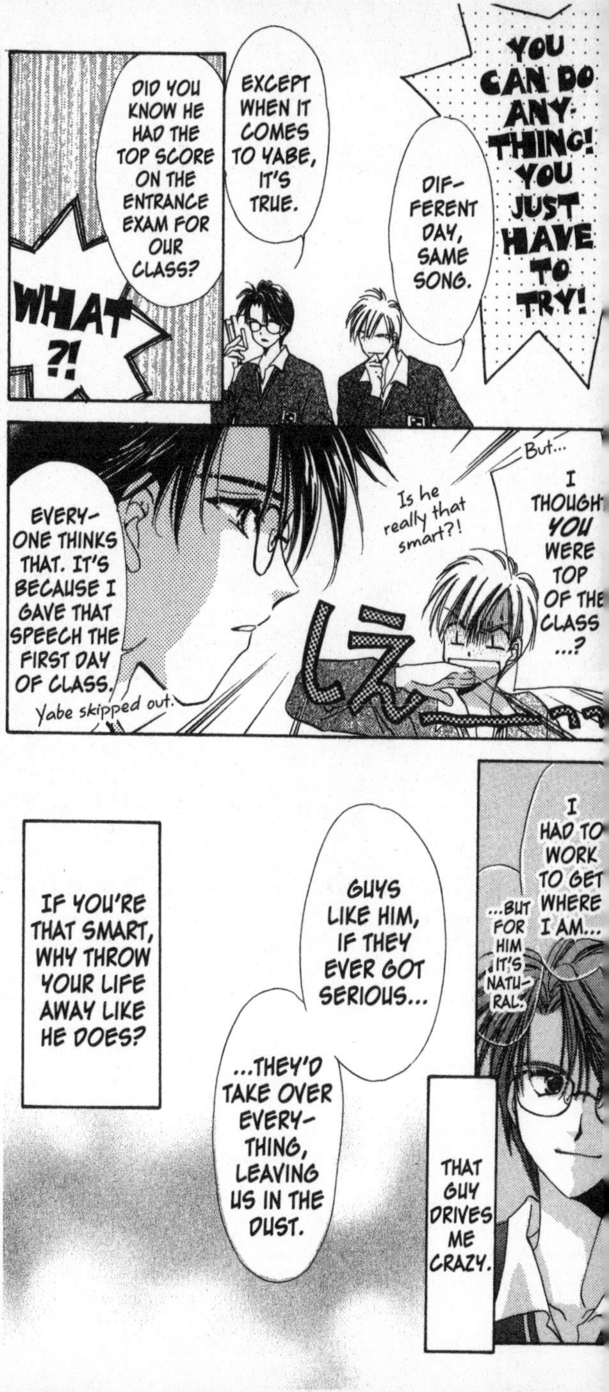
YOU CAN DO ANYTHING! YOU JUST HAVE TO TRY!
DIF-FERENT DAY, SAME SONG.
EXCEPT WHEN IT COMES TO YABE, IT'S TRUE.
DID YOU KNOW HE HAD THE TOP SCORE ON THE ENTRANCE EXAM FOR OUR CLASS?
WHAT ?!
I THOUGHT YOU WERE TOP OF THE CLASS ...?
But...
Is he really that smart?!
EVERY-ONE THINKS THAT. IT'S BECAUSE I GAVE THAT SPEECH THE FIRST DAY OF CLASS.
Yabe skipped out.
I HAD TO WORK TO GET WHERE I AM...
...BUT FOR HIM IT'S NATU-RAL.
THAT GUY DRIVES ME CRAZY.
GUYS LIKE HIM, IF THEY EVER GOT SERIOUS...
...THEY'D TAKE OVER EVERY-THING, LEAVING US IN THE DUST.
IF YOU'RE THAT SMART, WHY THROW YOUR LIFE AWAY LIKE HE DOES?

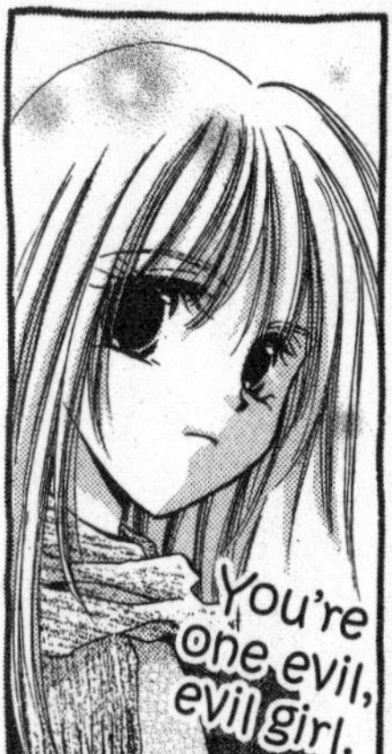
You're one evil, evil girl.

Motoko Kagurazaka

I didn't really have anyone in mind when I first created her, though some people here think (or wish!) differently. ^_^ A model for someone as evil as Motoko would have to be a real creep. (Hey, that's rude. quit it!)

I'm better at drawing cute girls, so at first Motoko gave me a lot of trouble (Visually, anyway. I mean, she was meant to be a beauty. I was afraid she'd end up with a face like everyone else's, though.)

But now that I've gotten used to drawing her, crafting her evil expressions is a lot of fun. Her figure as a whole is still hard, though. She has no chest, so trying to make the rest of her balance out is tough for me. (Waah!)

Personality-wise, Motoko truly has a black heart, doesn't she? She says lots of rotten things and is violent to boot. Strangely, she's a real easy character for me to write... ^_^ (Why?!)

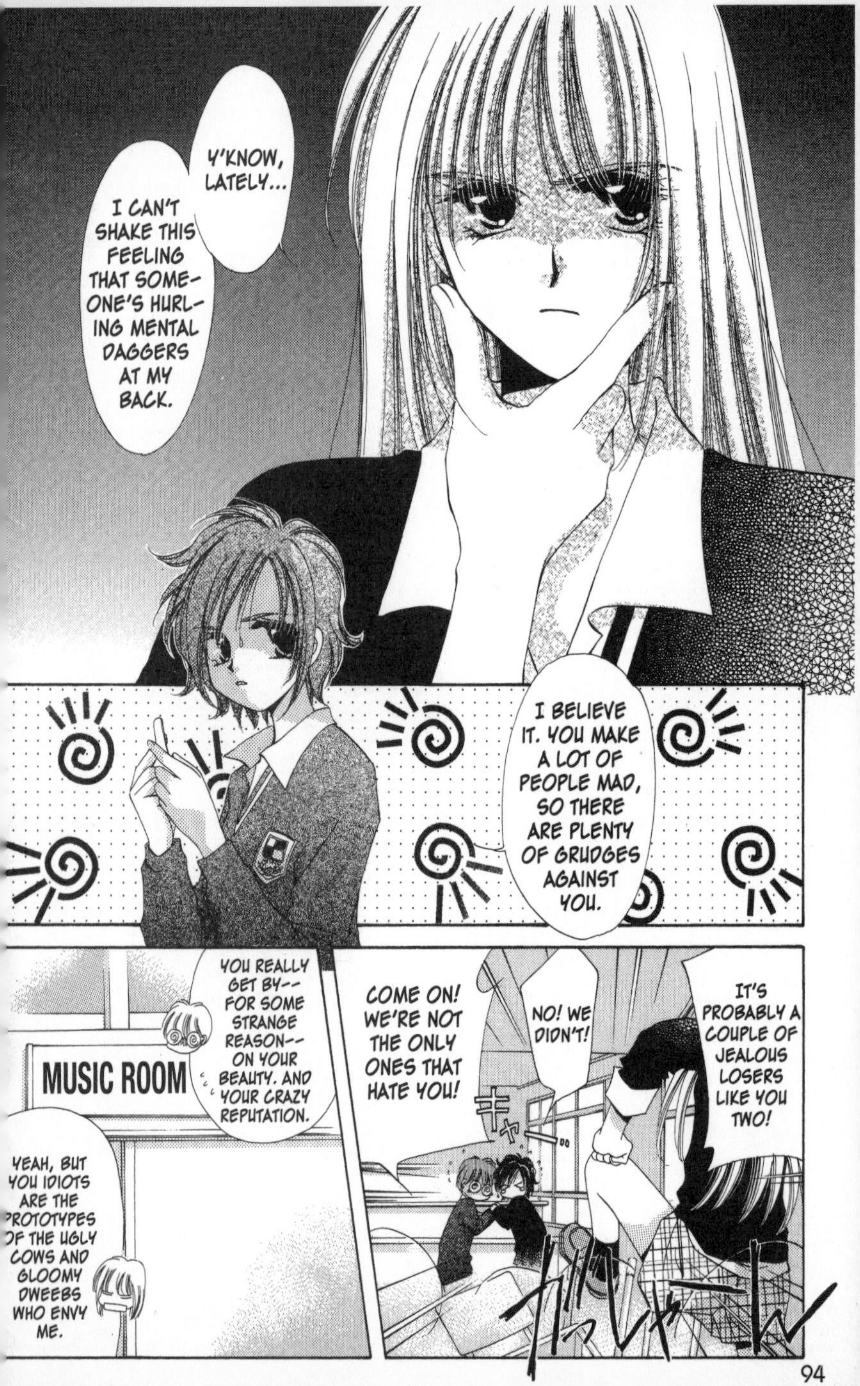
Y'KNOW, LATELY...
I CAN'T SHAKE THIS FEELING THAT SOME-ONE'S HURL-ING MENTAL DAGGERS AT MY BACK.
I BELIEVE IT. YOU MAKE A LOT OF PEOPLE MAD, SO THERE ARE PLENTY OF GRUDGES AGAINST YOU.
IT'S PROBABLY A COUPLE OF JEALOUS LOSERS LIKE YOU TWO!
NO! WE DIDN'T!
COME ON! WE'RE NOT THE ONLY ONES THAT HATE YOU!
YOU REALLY GET BY-- FOR SOME STRANGE REASON-- ON YOUR BEAUTY. AND YOUR CRAZY REPUTATION.
MUSIC ROOM
YEAH, BUT YOU IDIOTS ARE THE PROTOTYPES OF THE UGLY COWS AND GLOOMY DWEEBS WHO ENVY ME.

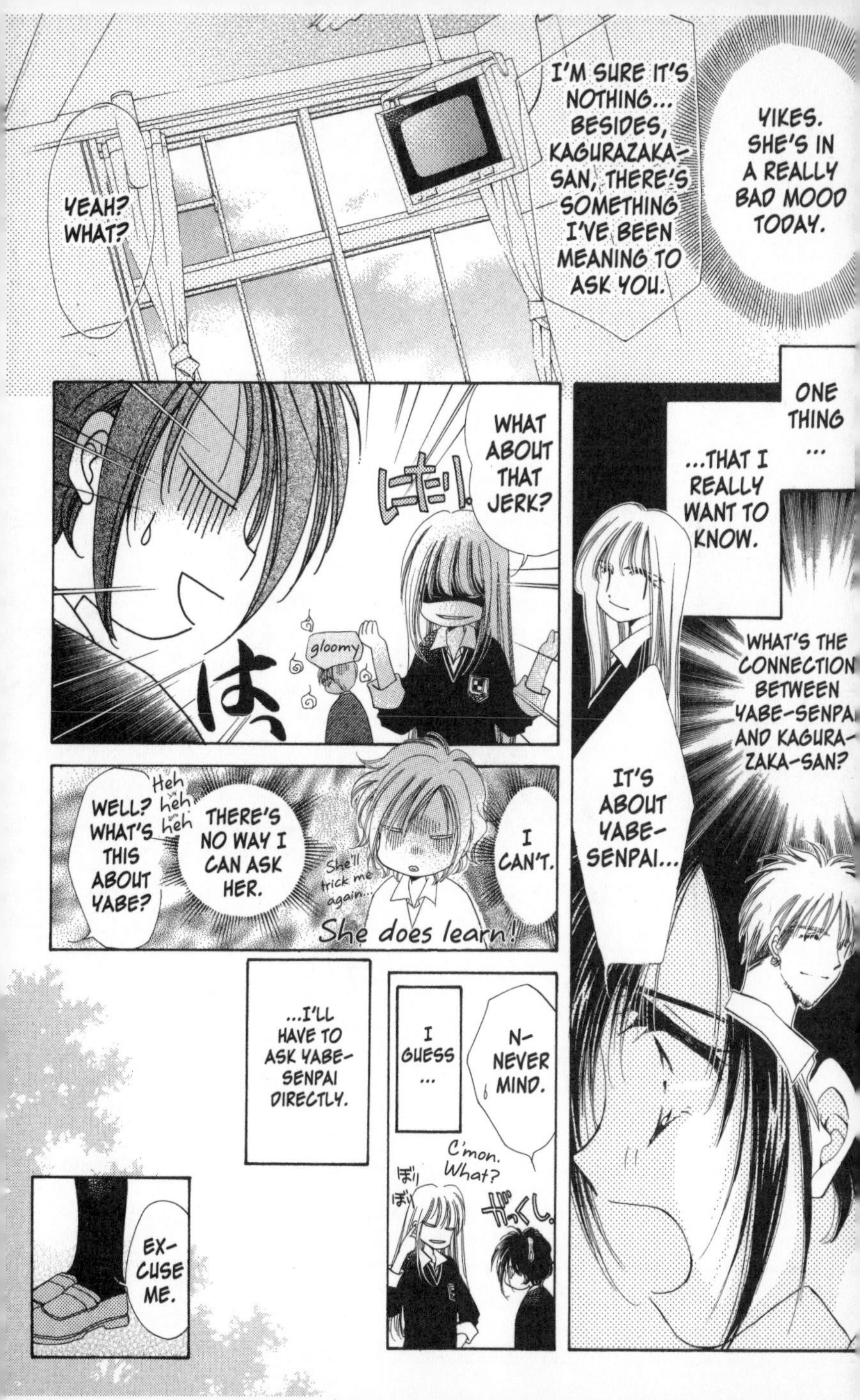
YIKES. SHE'S IN A REALLY BAD MOOD TODAY.
I'M SURE IT'S NOTHING... BESIDES, KAGURAZAKA-SAN, THERE'S SOMETHING I'VE BEEN MEANING TO ASK YOU.
YEAH? WHAT?
ONE THING ...
...THAT I REALLY WANT TO KNOW.
WHAT'S THE CONNECTION BETWEEN YABE-SENPAI AND KAGURAZAKA-SAN?
IT'S ABOUT YABE-SENPAI...
WHAT ABOUT THAT JERK?
gloomy
は
I CAN'T.
Heh heh heh
WELL? WHAT'S THIS ABOUT YABE?
THERE'S NO WAY I CAN ASK HER.
She'll trick me again...
She does learn!
N-NEVER MIND.
I GUESS ...
C'mon. What?
ぼり ぼり
がっくし。
...I'LL HAVE TO ASK YABE-SENPAI DIRECTLY.
EX-CUSE ME.

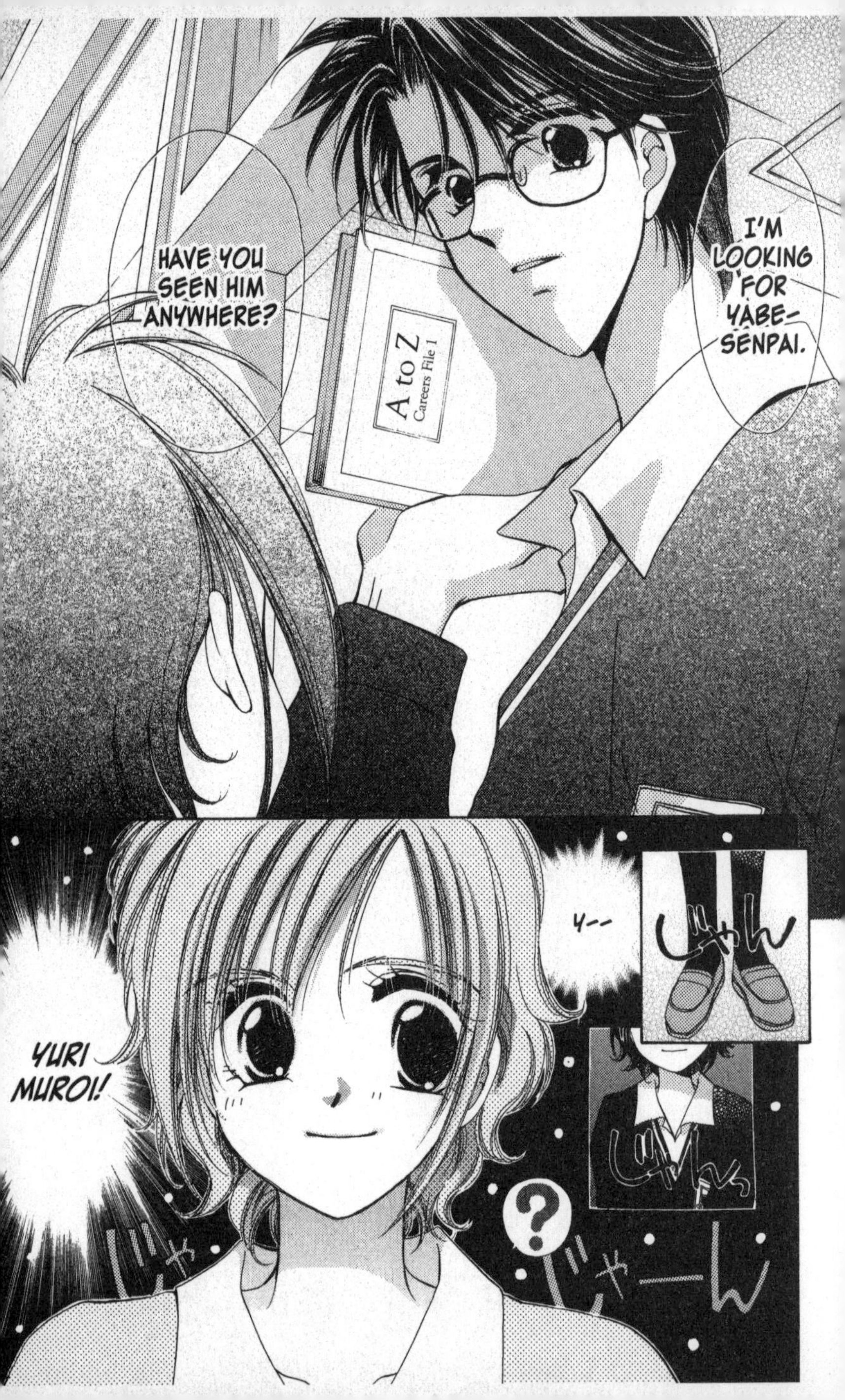
I'M LOOKING FOR YABE-SENPAI.
HAVE YOU SEEN HIM ANYWHERE?
A to Z
Careers File 1
Y--
YURI MUROI!

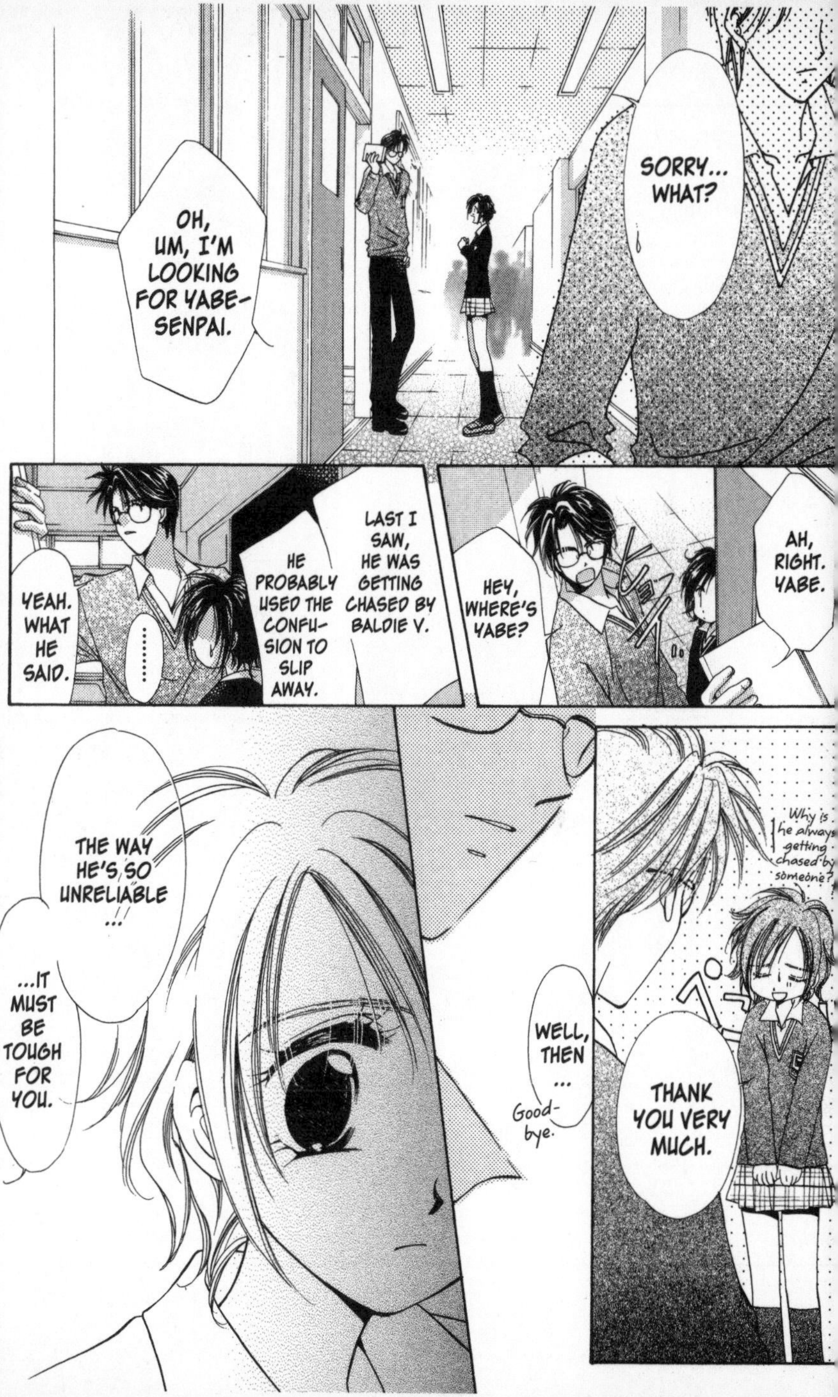
SORRY... WHAT?
OH, UM, I'M LOOKING FOR YABE-SENPAI.
AH, RIGHT. YABE.
HEY, WHERE'S YABE?
LAST I SAW, HE WAS GETTING CHASED BY BALDIE V.
HE PROBABLY USED THE CONFUSION TO SLIP AWAY.
YEAH. WHAT HE SAID.
....
Why is he always getting chased by someone?
THANK YOU VERY MUCH.
WELL, THEN ...
Good-bye.
THE WAY HE'S SO UNRELIABLE ...
...IT MUST BE TOUGH FOR YOU.

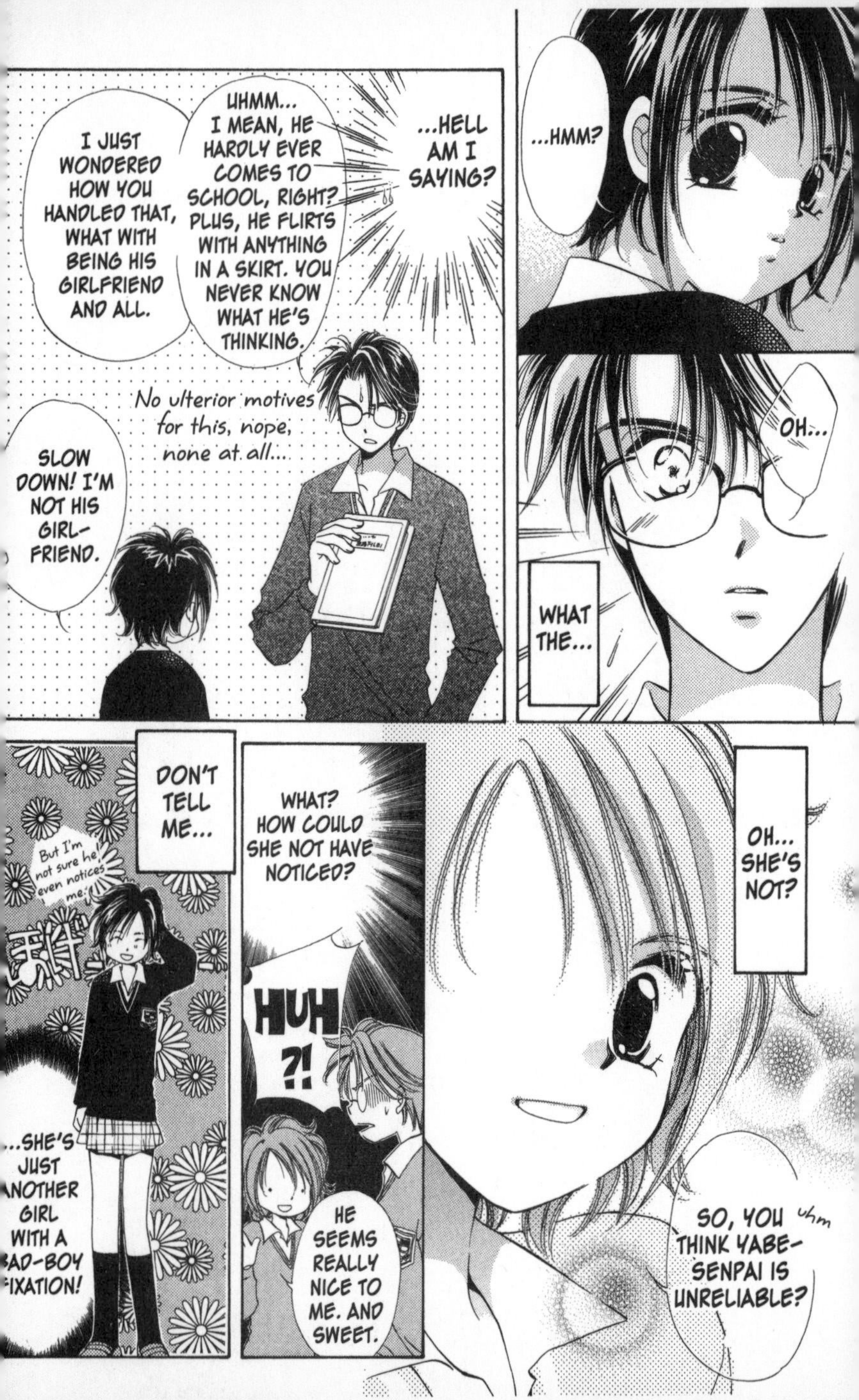
...HMM?
OH...
WHAT THE...
...HELL AM I SAYING?
UHMM... I MEAN, HE HARDLY EVER COMES TO SCHOOL, RIGHT? PLUS, HE FLIRTS WITH ANYTHING IN A SKIRT. YOU NEVER KNOW WHAT HE'S THINKING.
I JUST WONDERED HOW YOU HANDLED THAT, WHAT WITH BEING HIS GIRLFRIEND AND ALL.
No ulterior motives for this, nope, none at all...
SLOW DOWN! I'M NOT HIS GIRL-FRIEND.
OH... SHE'S NOT?
uhm
SO, YOU THINK YABE-SENPAI IS UNRELIABLE?
WHAT? HOW COULD SHE NOT HAVE NOTICED?
HUH ?!
HE SEEMS REALLY NICE TO ME. AND SWEET.
DON'T TELL ME...
But I'm not sure he even notices me.
...SHE'S JUST NOTHER GIRL WITH A AD-BOY IXATION!

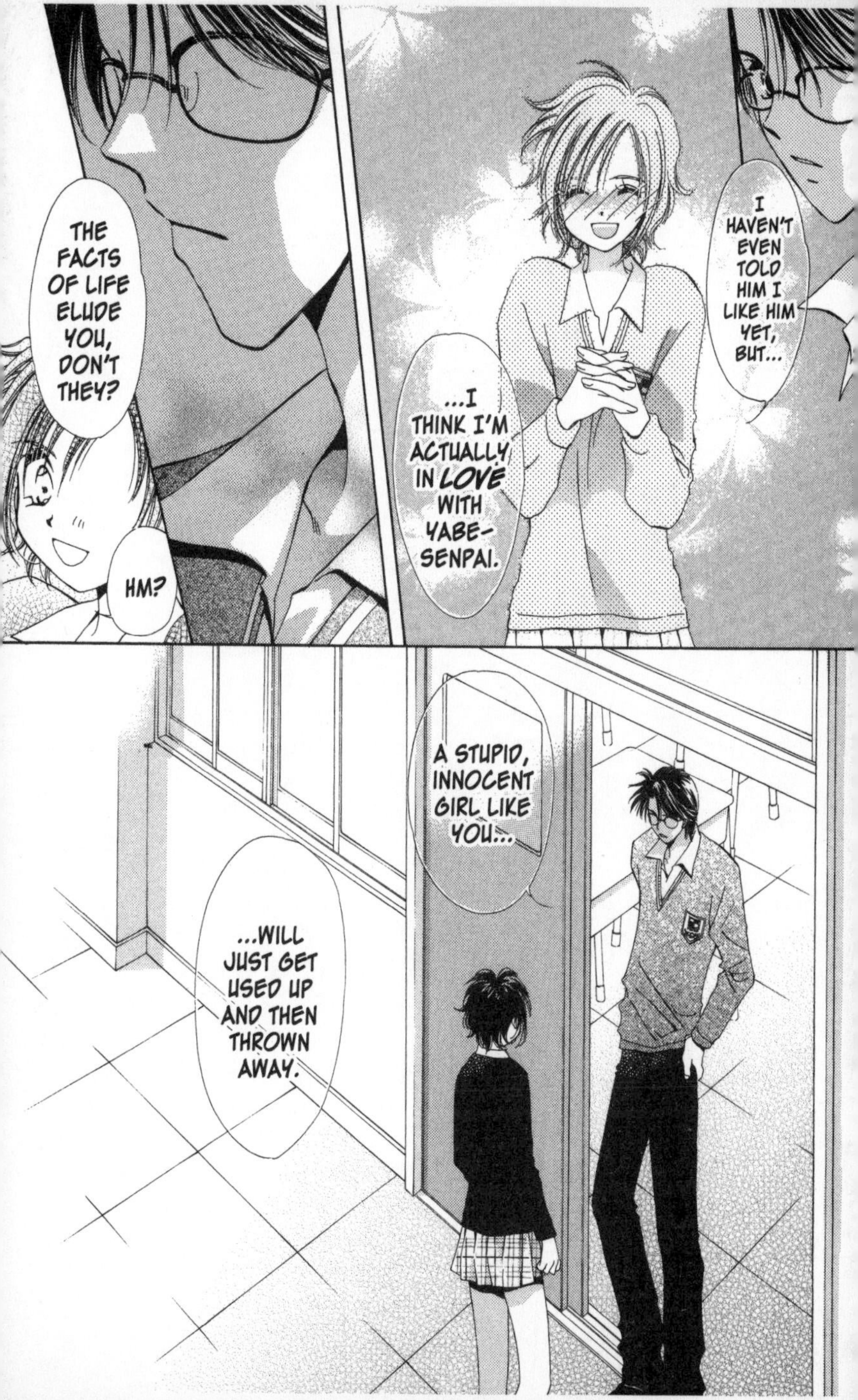
I HAVEN'T EVEN TOLD HIM I LIKE HIM YET, BUT...
...I THINK I'M ACTUALLY IN *LOVE* WITH YABE-SENPAI.
THE FACTS OF LIFE ELUDE YOU, DON'T THEY?
HM?
A STUPID, INNOCENT GIRL LIKE YOU...
...WILL JUST GET USED UP AND THEN THROWN AWAY.

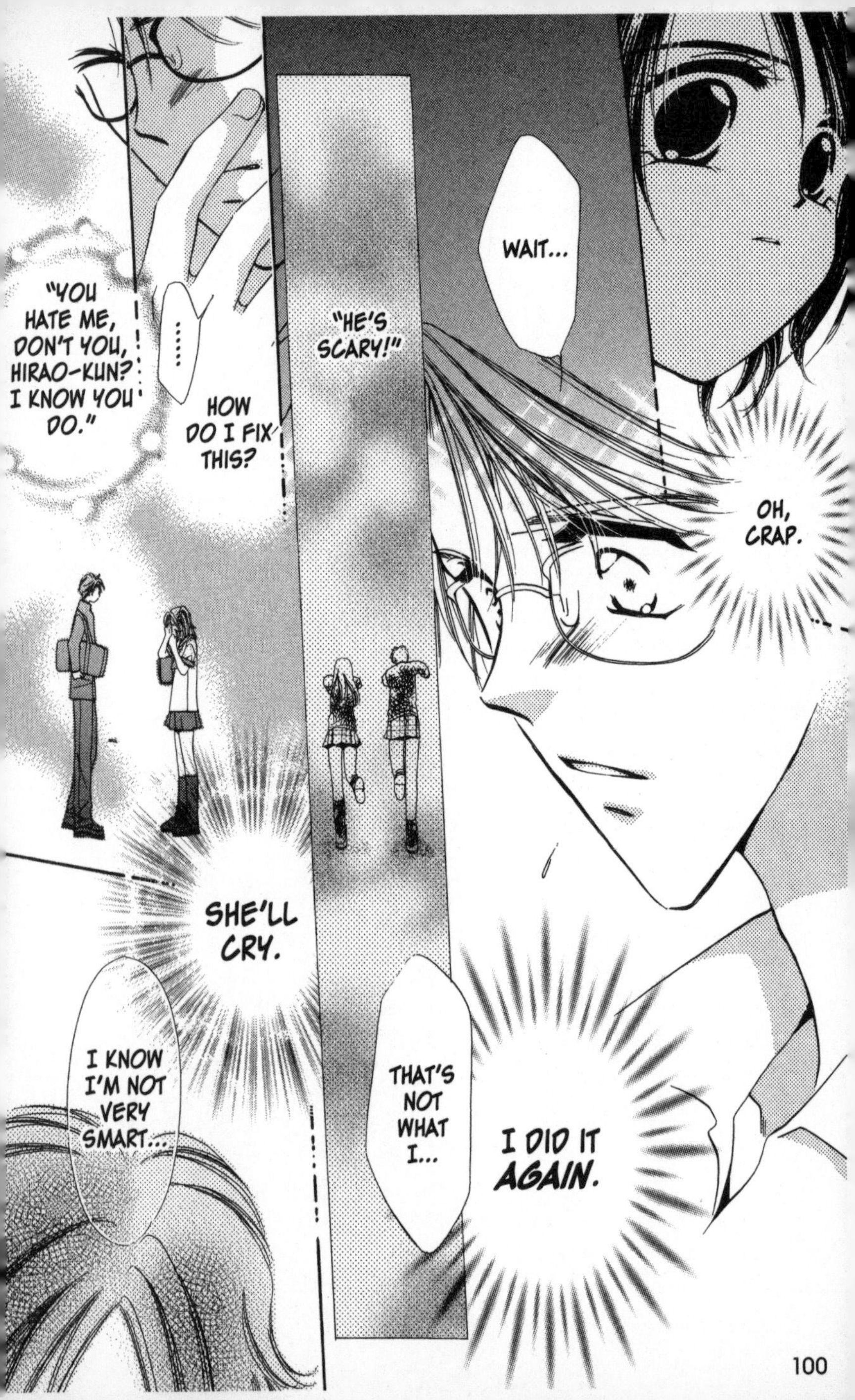
WAIT...
OH, CRAP.
THAT'S NOT WHAT I...
I DID IT AGAIN.
"HE'S SCARY!"
......
HOW DO I FIX THIS?
"YOU HATE ME, DON'T YOU, HIRAO-KUN? I KNOW YOU DO."
SHE'LL CRY.
I KNOW I'M NOT VERY SMART...

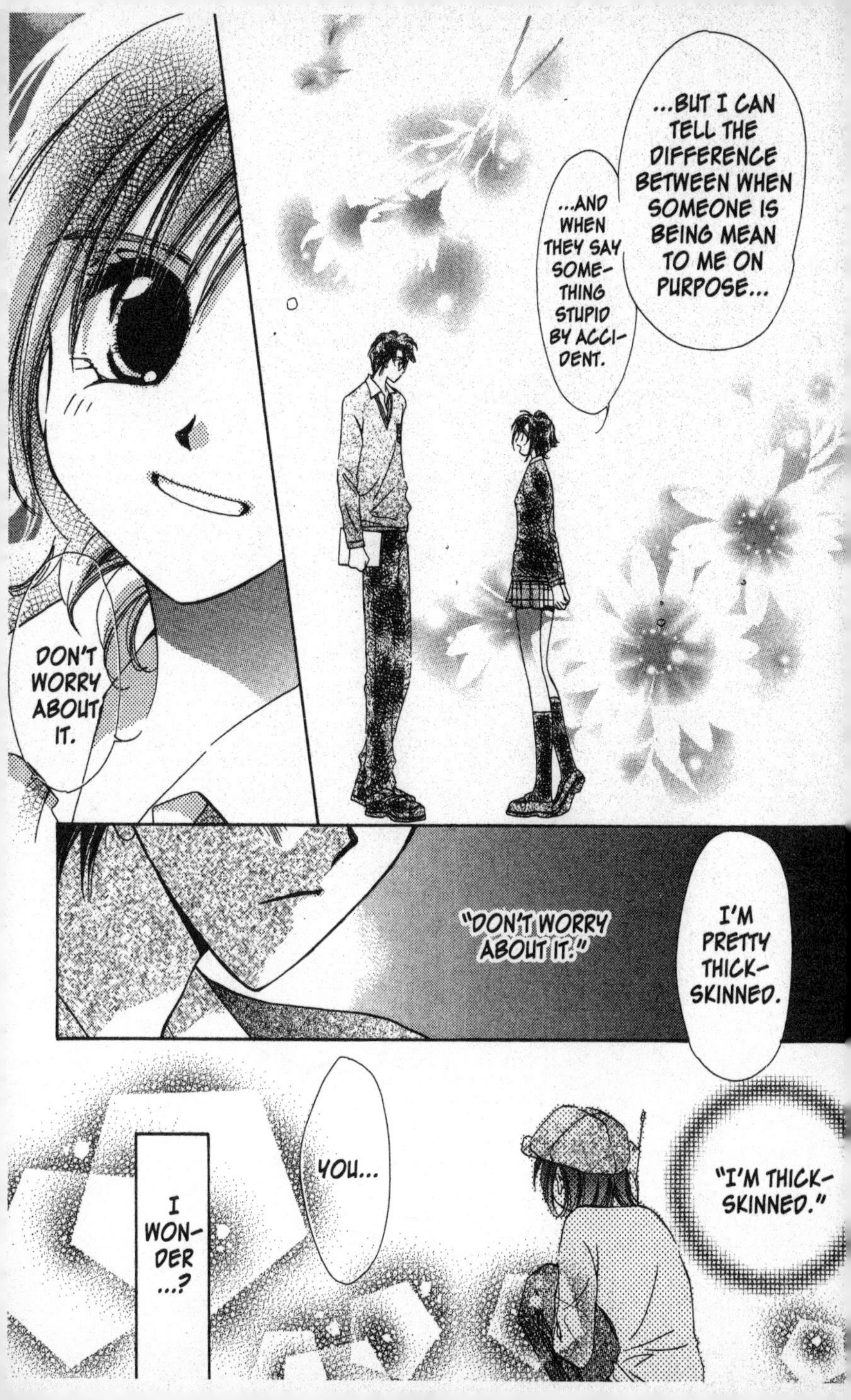
...BUT I CAN TELL THE DIFFERENCE BETWEEN WHEN SOMEONE IS BEING MEAN TO ME ON PURPOSE...
...AND WHEN THEY SAY SOME-THING STUPID BY ACCI-DENT.
DON'T WORRY ABOUT IT.
I'M PRETTY THICK-SKINNED.
"DON'T WORRY ABOUT IT."
"I'M THICK-SKINNED."
YOU...
I WON-DER ...?

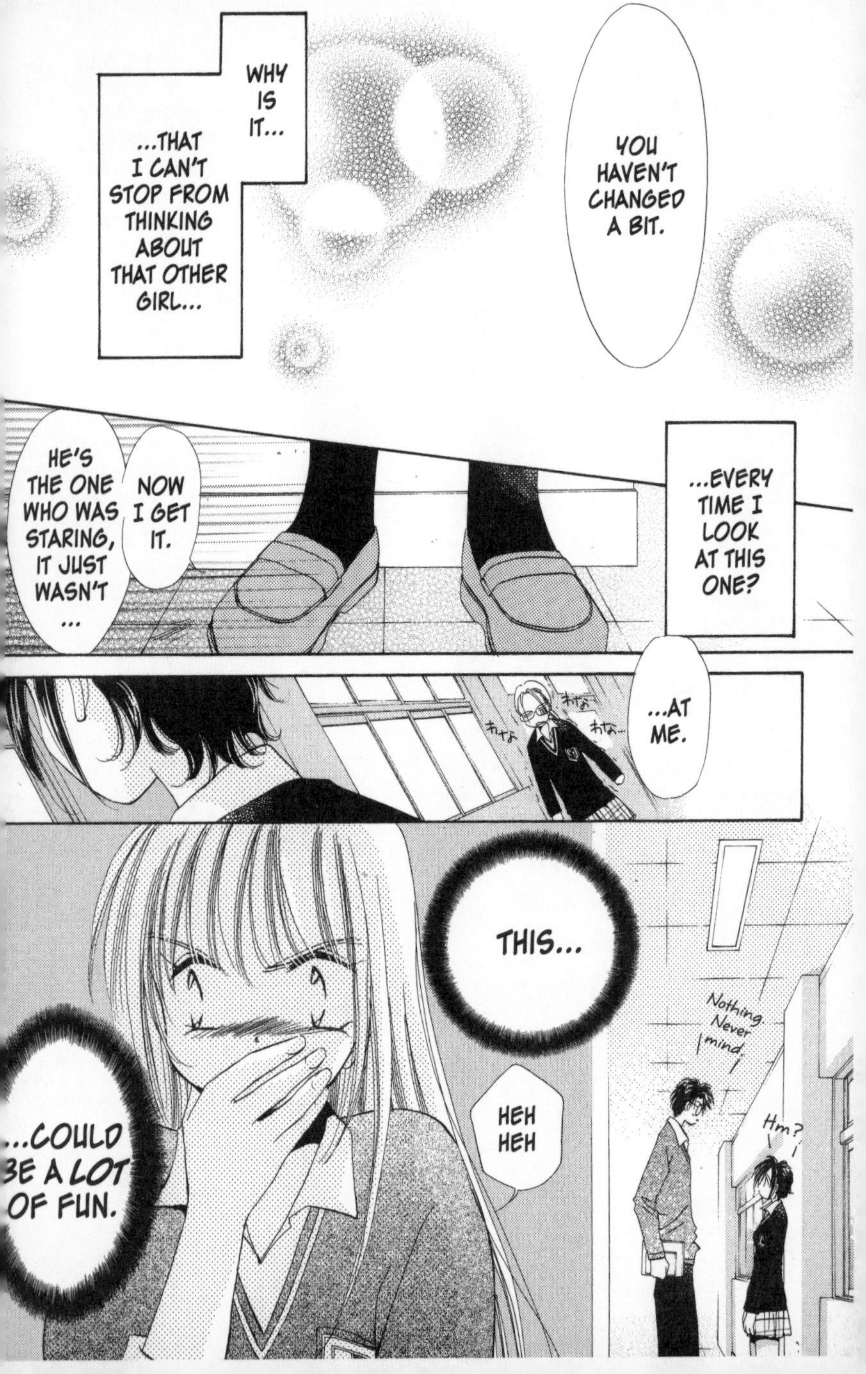
YOU HAVEN'T CHANGED A BIT.
WHY IS IT...
...THAT I CAN'T STOP FROM THINKING ABOUT THAT OTHER GIRL...
...EVERY TIME I LOOK AT THIS ONE?
NOW I GET IT.
HE'S THE ONE WHO WAS STARING, IT JUST WASN'T ...
...AT ME.
Nothing. Never mind.
Hm?
THIS...
HEH HEH
...COULD BE A *LOT* OF FUN.

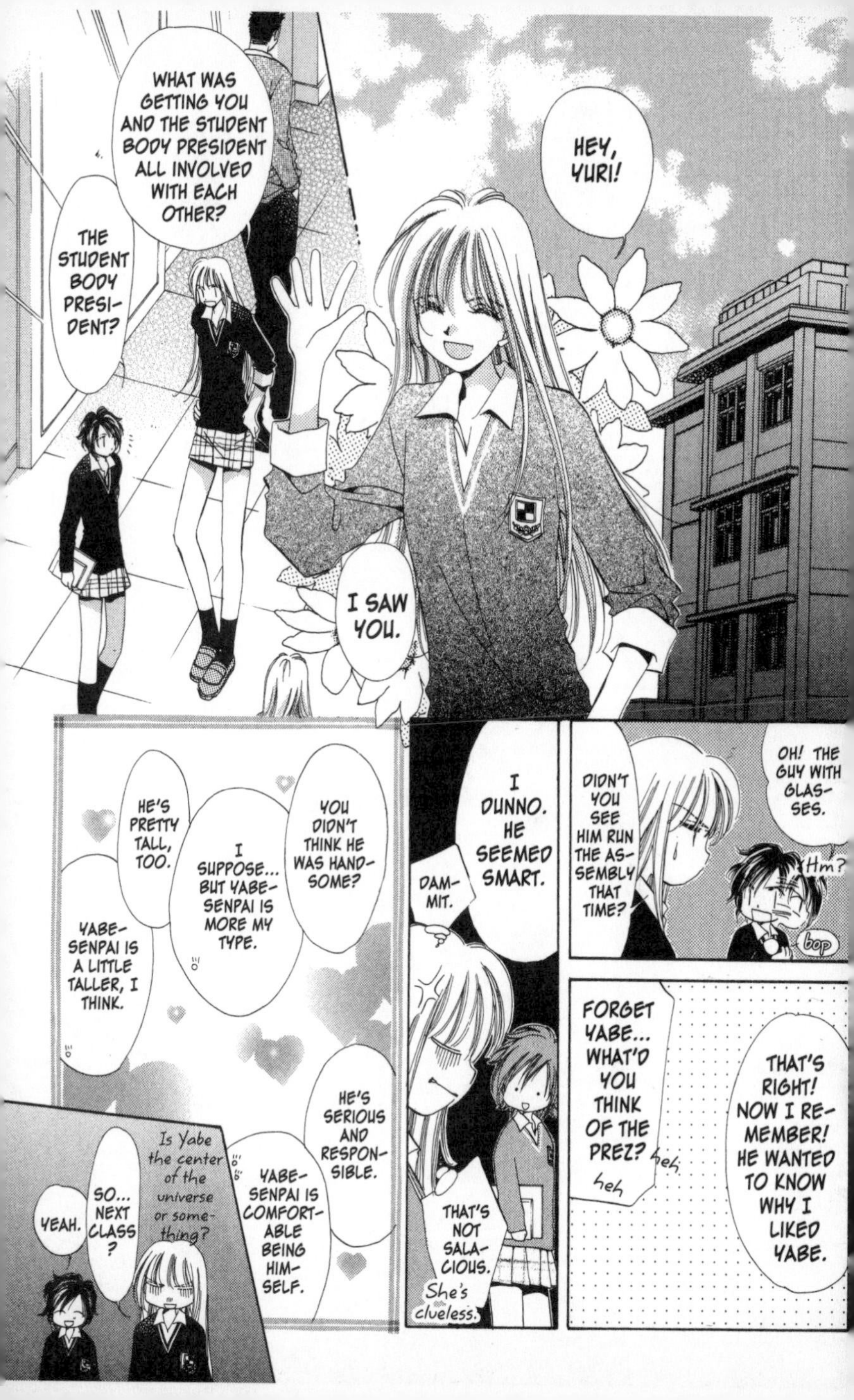

HEY, YURI!
I SAW YOU.
WHAT WAS GETTING YOU AND THE STUDENT BODY PRESIDENT ALL INVOLVED WITH EACH OTHER?
THE STUDENT BODY PRESIDENT?
OH! THE GUY WITH GLASSES.
Hm?
bop
DIDN'T YOU SEE HIM RUN THE ASSEMBLY THAT TIME?
THAT'S RIGHT! NOW I REMEMBER! HE WANTED TO KNOW WHY I LIKED YABE.
FORGET YABE... WHAT'D YOU THINK OF THE PREZ?
heh heh
I DUNNO. HE SEEMED SMART.
DAMMIT.
THAT'S NOT SALACIOUS.
She's clueless.
YOU DIDN'T THINK HE WAS HANDSOME?
I SUPPOSE... BUT YABE-SENPAI IS MORE MY TYPE.
HE'S PRETTY TALL, TOO.
YABE-SENPAI IS A LITTLE TALLER, I THINK.
HE'S SERIOUS AND RESPONSIBLE.
YABE-SENPAI IS COMFORTABLE BEING HIMSELF.
Is Yabe the center of the universe or something?
SO... NEXT CLASS?
YEAH.

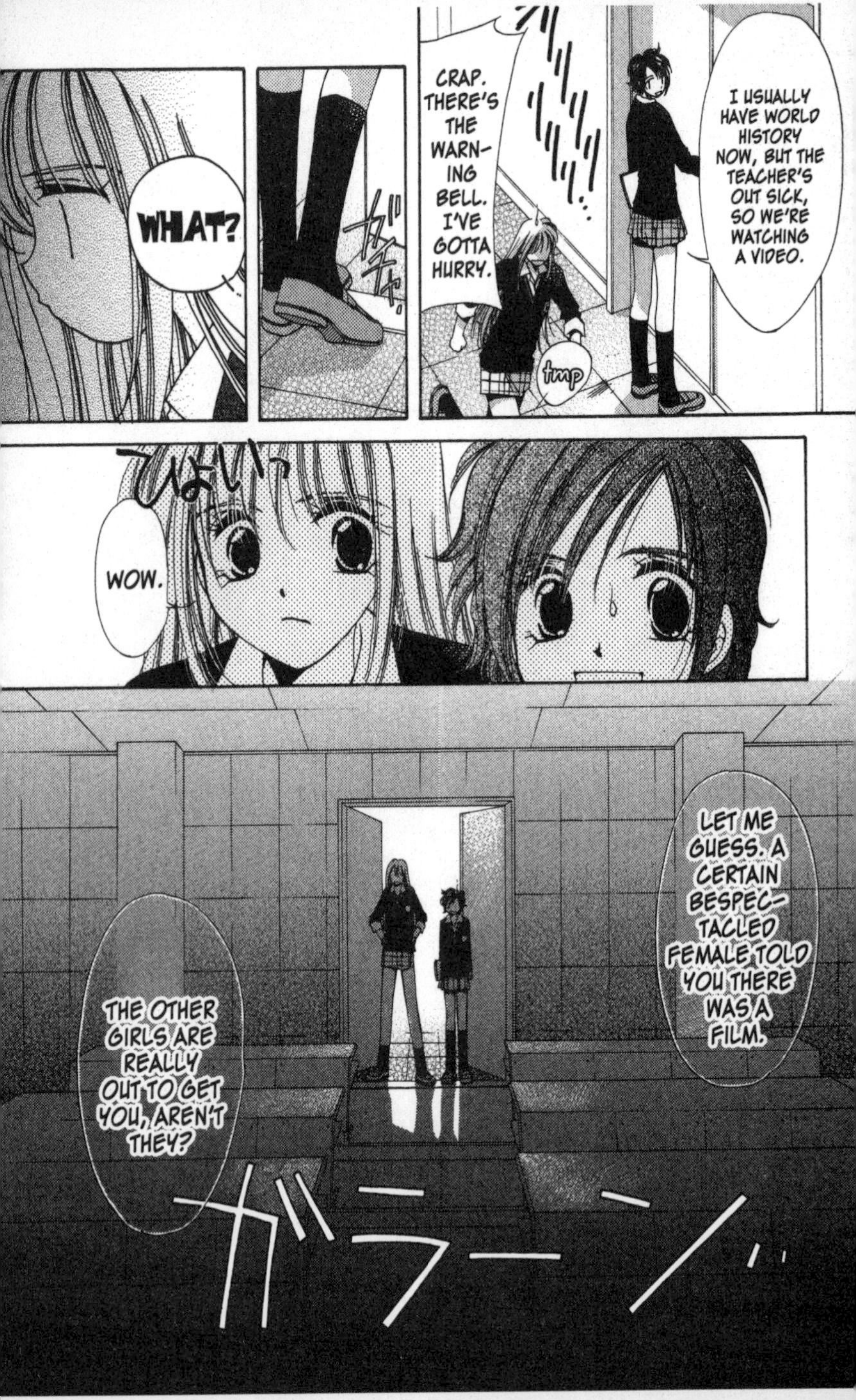
I USUALLY HAVE WORLD HISTORY NOW, BUT THE TEACHER'S OUT SICK, SO WE'RE WATCHING A VIDEO.
CRAP. THERE'S THE WARNING BELL. I'VE GOTTA HURRY.
tmp
WHAT?
WOW.
LET ME GUESS. A CERTAIN BESPECTACLED FEMALE TOLD YOU THERE WAS A FILM.
THE OTHER GIRLS ARE REALLY OUT TO GET YOU, AREN'T THEY?

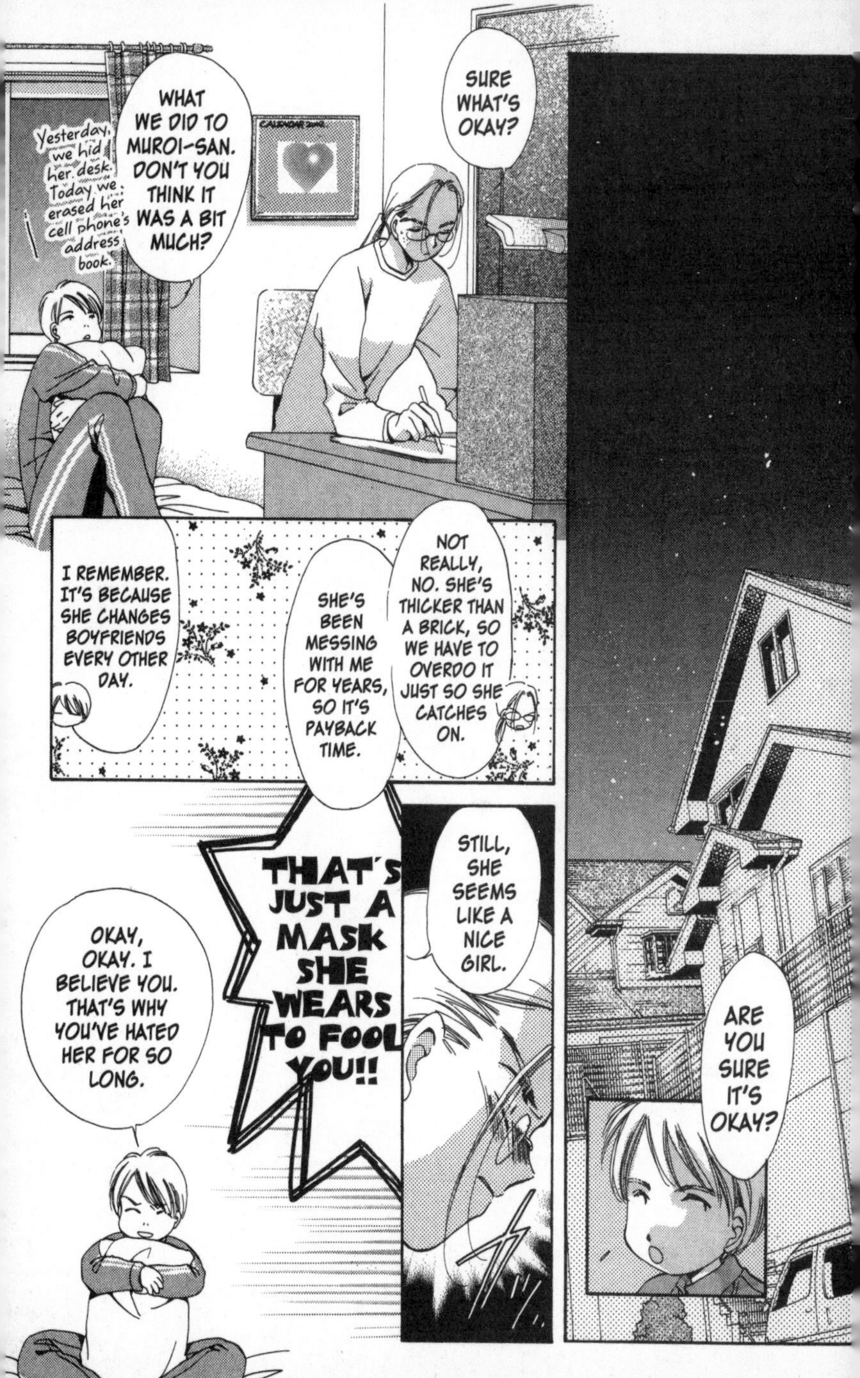
ARE YOU SURE IT'S OKAY?
SURE WHAT'S OKAY?
WHAT WE DID TO MUROI-SAN. DON'T YOU THINK IT WAS A BIT MUCH?
Yesterday, we hid her desk. Today we erased her cell phone's address book.
NOT REALLY, NO. SHE'S THICKER THAN A BRICK, SO WE HAVE TO OVERDO IT JUST SO SHE CATCHES ON.
SHE'S BEEN MESSING WITH ME FOR YEARS, SO IT'S PAYBACK TIME.
I REMEMBER. IT'S BECAUSE SHE CHANGES BOYFRIENDS EVERY OTHER DAY.
STILL, SHE SEEMS LIKE A NICE GIRL.
THAT'S JUST A MASK SHE WEARS TO FOOL YOU!!
OKAY, OKAY. I BELIEVE YOU. THAT'S WHY YOU'VE HATED HER FOR SO LONG.

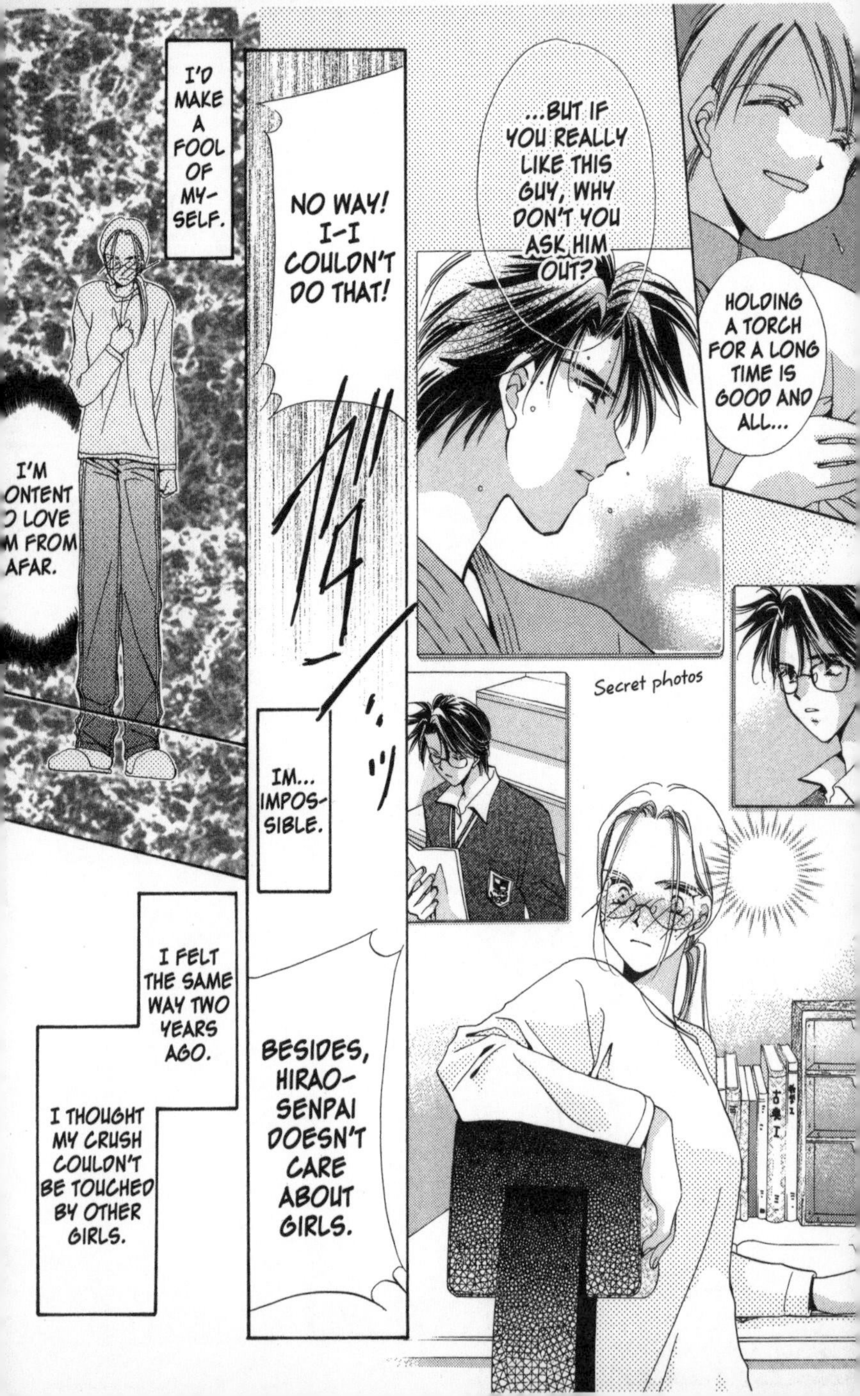
HOLDING A TORCH FOR A LONG TIME IS GOOD AND ALL...
...BUT IF YOU REALLY LIKE THIS GUY, WHY DON'T YOU ASK HIM OUT?
Secret photos
NO WAY! I-I COULDN'T DO THAT!
IM... IMPOSSIBLE.
I'D MAKE A FOOL OF MY-SELF.
I'M ONTENT LOVE M FROM AFAR.
BESIDES, HIRAO-SENPAI DOESN'T CARE ABOUT GIRLS.
I FELT THE SAME WAY TWO YEARS AGO.
I THOUGHT MY CRUSH COULDN'T BE TOUCHED BY OTHER GIRLS.

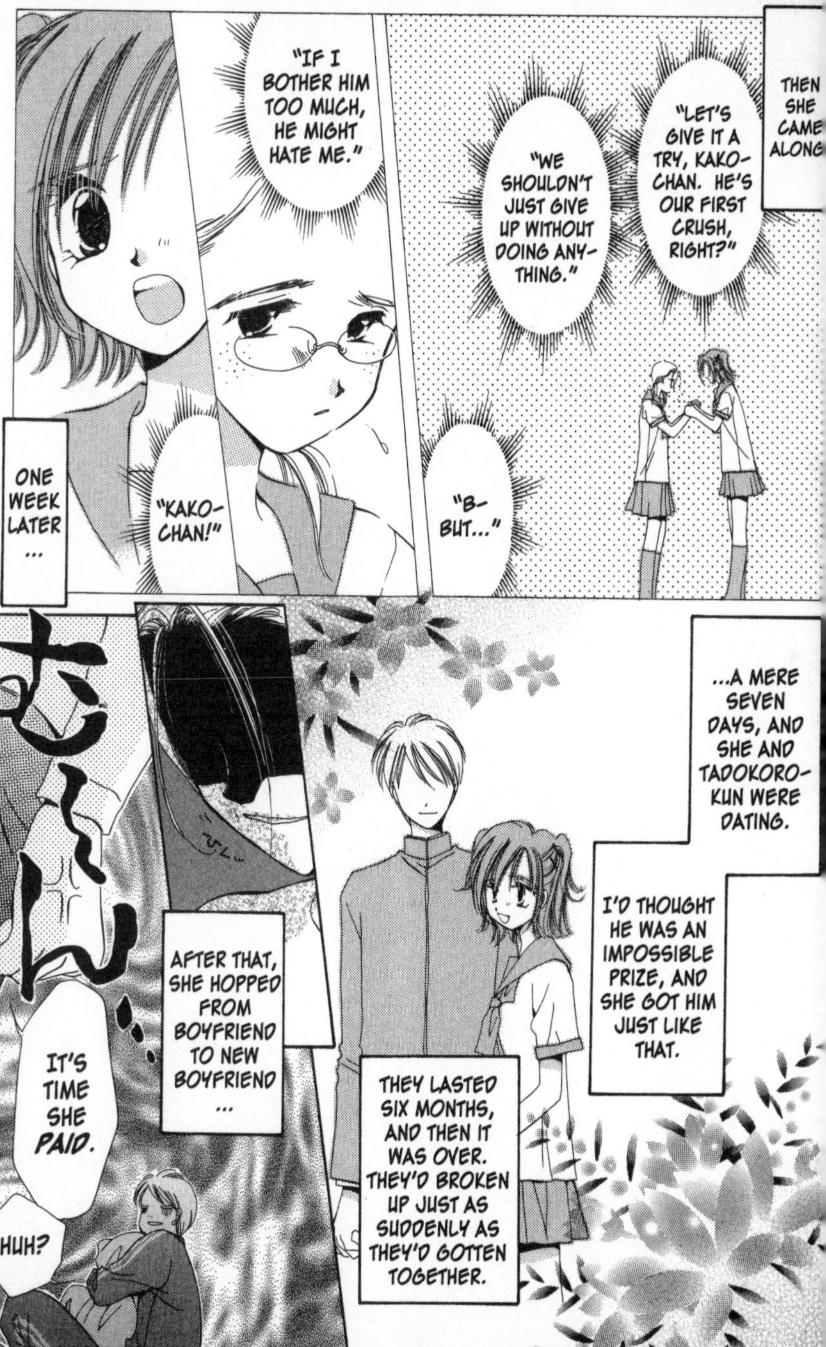
THEN SHE CAME ALONG
"LET'S GIVE IT A TRY, KAKO-CHAN. HE'S OUR FIRST CRUSH, RIGHT?"
"WE SHOULDN'T JUST GIVE UP WITHOUT DOING ANY-THING."
"B-BUT..."
"IF I BOTHER HIM TOO MUCH, HE MIGHT HATE ME."
"KAKO-CHAN!"
ONE WEEK LATER ...
...A MERE SEVEN DAYS, AND SHE AND TADOKORO-KUN WERE DATING.
I'D THOUGHT HE WAS AN IMPOSSIBLE PRIZE, AND SHE GOT HIM JUST LIKE THAT.
THEY LASTED SIX MONTHS, AND THEN IT WAS OVER. THEY'D BROKEN UP JUST AS SUDDENLY AS THEY'D GOTTEN TOGETHER.
AFTER THAT, SHE HOPPED FROM BOYFRIEND TO NEW BOYFRIEND ...
む〜ん...
IT'S TIME SHE *PAID*.
HUH?

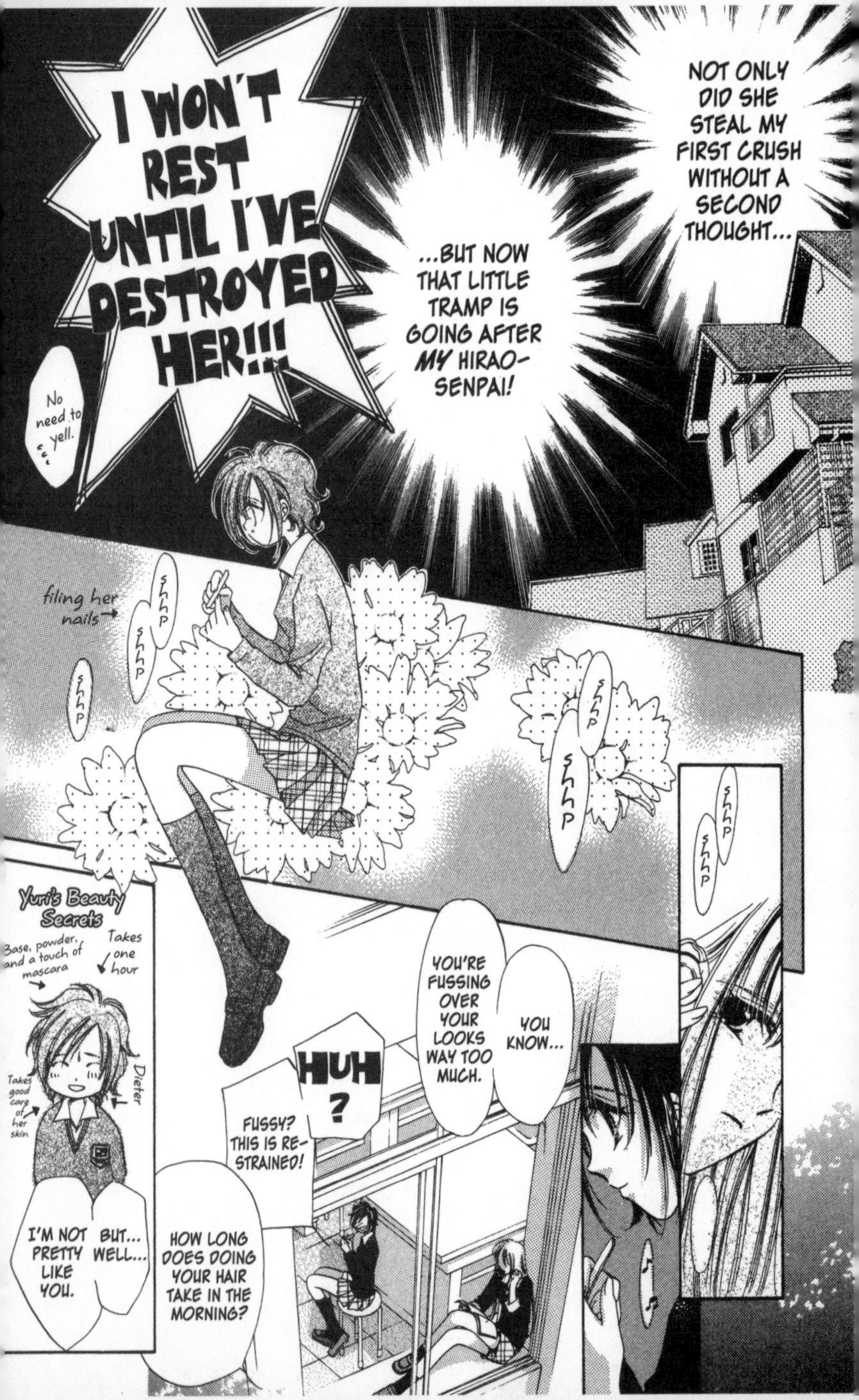
NOT ONLY DID SHE STEAL MY FIRST CRUSH WITHOUT A SECOND THOUGHT...
...BUT NOW THAT LITTLE TRAMP IS GOING AFTER *MY* HIRAO-SENPAI!
I WON'T REST UNTIL I'VE DESTROYED HER!!!
No need to yell.
shhp
shhp
shhp
shhp
shhp
filing her nails
shhp
shhp
YOU KNOW...
YOU'RE FUSSING OVER YOUR LOOKS WAY TOO MUCH.
HUH?
FUSSY? THIS IS RE-STRAINED!
HOW LONG DOES DOING YOUR HAIR TAKE IN THE MORNING?
BUT... WELL...
I'M NOT PRETTY LIKE YOU.
Yuri's Beauty Secrets
Base, powder, and a touch of mascara
Takes one hour
Dieter
Takes good care of her skin

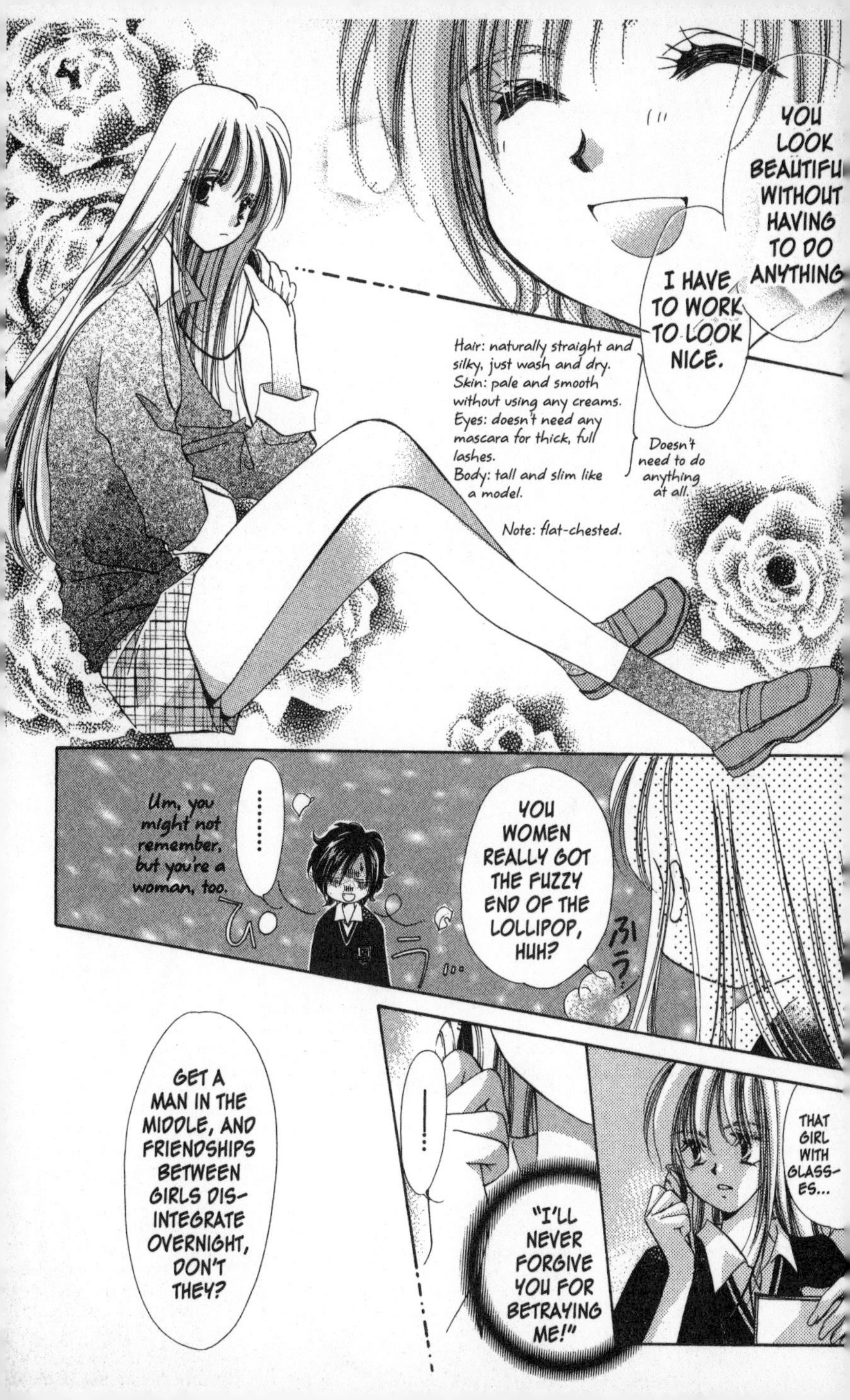
YOU LOOK BEAUTIFU WITHOUT HAVING TO DO ANYTHING
I HAVE TO WORK TO LOOK NICE.
Hair: naturally straight and silky, just wash and dry.
Skin: pale and smooth without using any creams.
Eyes: doesn't need any mascara for thick, full lashes.
Body: tall and slim like a model.
Doesn't need to do anything at all.
Note: flat-chested.
ふラ
YOU WOMEN REALLY GOT THE FUZZY END OF THE LOLLIPOP, HUH?
ひ
ラ
....
Um, you might not remember, but you're a woman, too.
THAT GIRL WITH GLASSES...
"I'LL NEVER FORGIVE YOU FOR BETRAYING ME!"
......!
GET A MAN IN THE MIDDLE, AND FRIENDSHIPS BETWEEN GIRLS DIS-INTEGRATE OVERNIGHT, DON'T THEY?

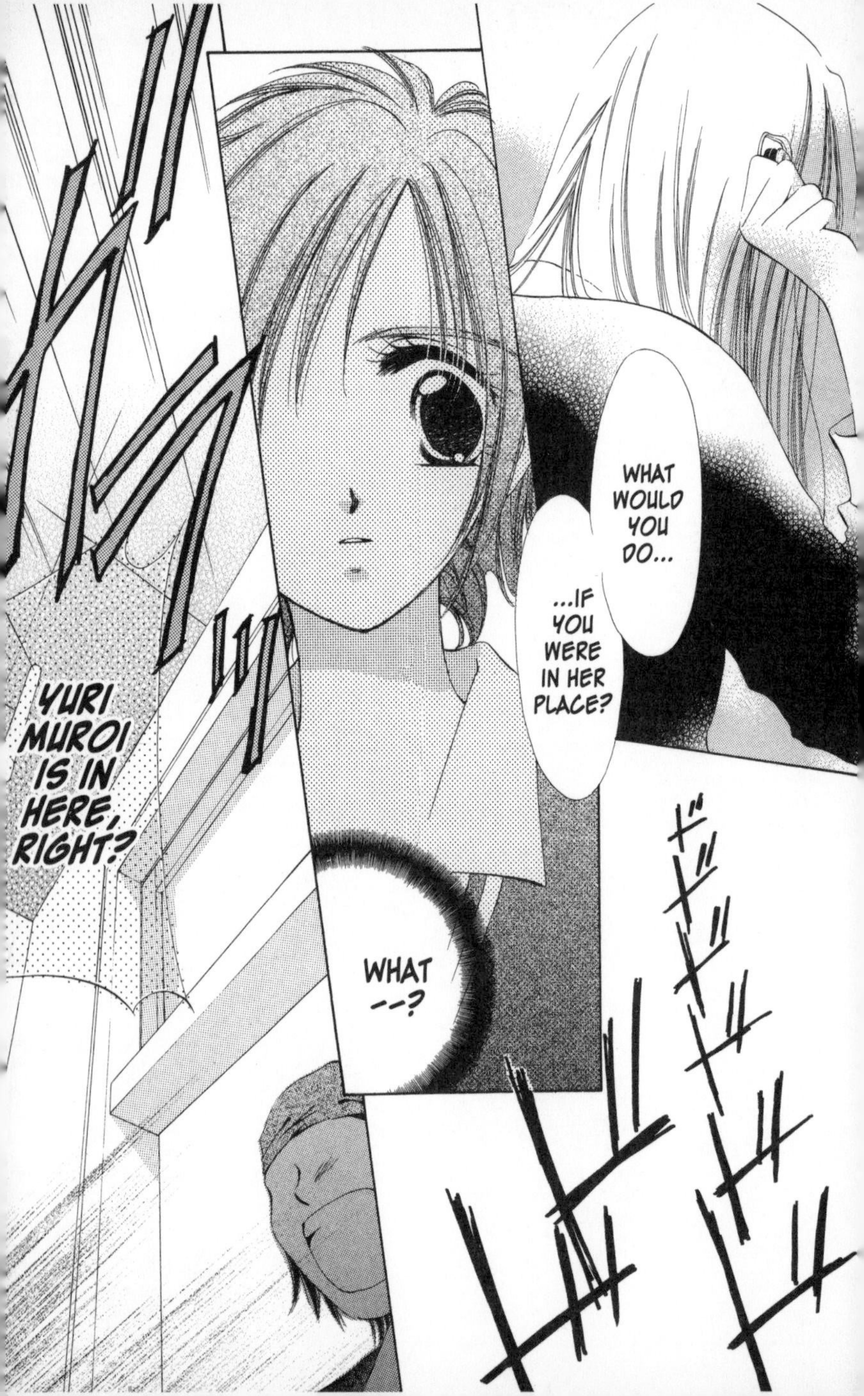
WHAT WOULD YOU DO...
...IF YOU WERE IN HER PLACE?
WHAT --?
YURI MUROI IS IN HERE, RIGHT?

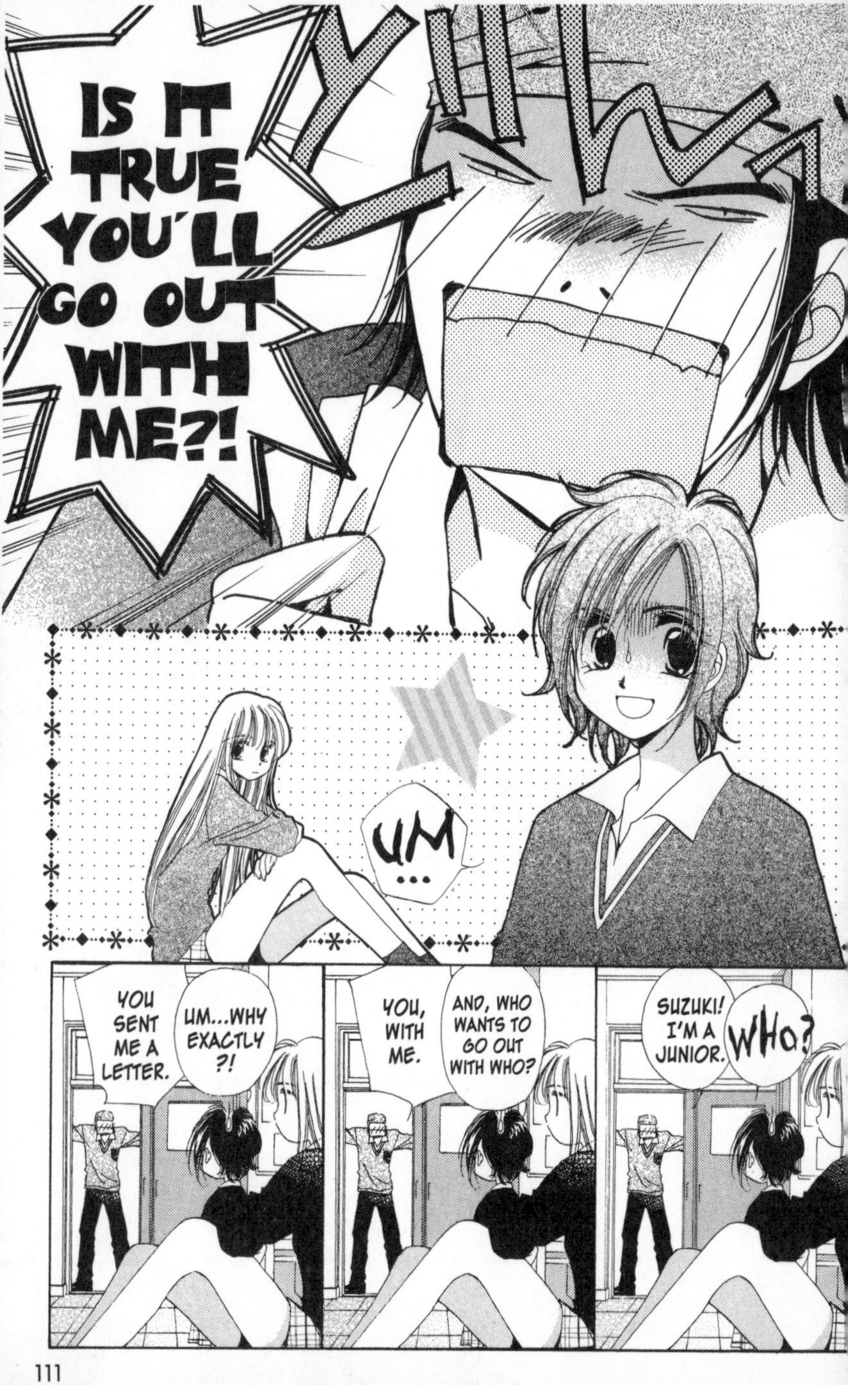
IS IT TRUE YOU'LL GO OUT WITH ME?!
UM...
WHO?
SUZUKI! I'M A JUNIOR.
AND, WHO WANTS TO GO OUT WITH WHO?
YOU, WITH ME.
UM...WHY EXACTLY ?!
YOU SENT ME A LETTER.

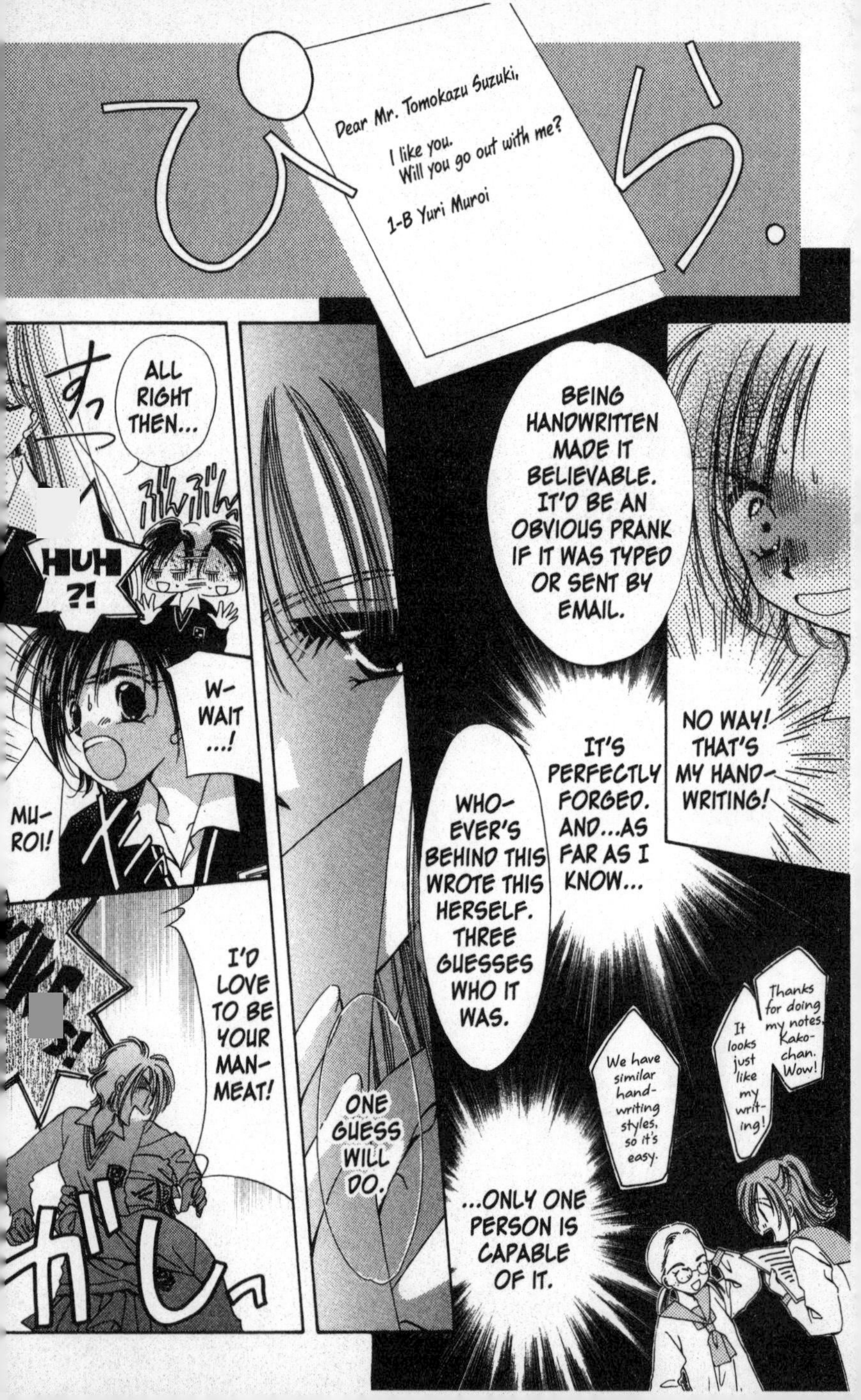
ぴら。
Dear Mr. Tomokazu Suzuki,
I like you.
Will you go out with me?
1-B Yuri Muroi
NO WAY! THAT'S MY HAND-WRITING!
BEING HANDWRITTEN MADE IT BELIEVABLE. IT'D BE AN OBVIOUS PRANK IF IT WAS TYPED OR SENT BY EMAIL.
IT'S PERFECTLY FORGED. AND...AS FAR AS I KNOW...
WHO-EVER'S BEHIND THIS WROTE THIS HERSELF. THREE GUESSES WHO IT WAS.
Thanks for doing my notes, Kako-chan. Wow!
It looks just like my writing!
We have similar hand-writing styles, so it's easy.
...ONLY ONE PERSON IS CAPABLE OF IT.
ONE GUESS WILL DO.
ALL RIGHT THEN...
すっ
ぶんぶん
HUH ?!
W-WAIT ...!
MU-ROI!
I'D LOVE TO BE YOUR MAN-MEAT!
がしっ

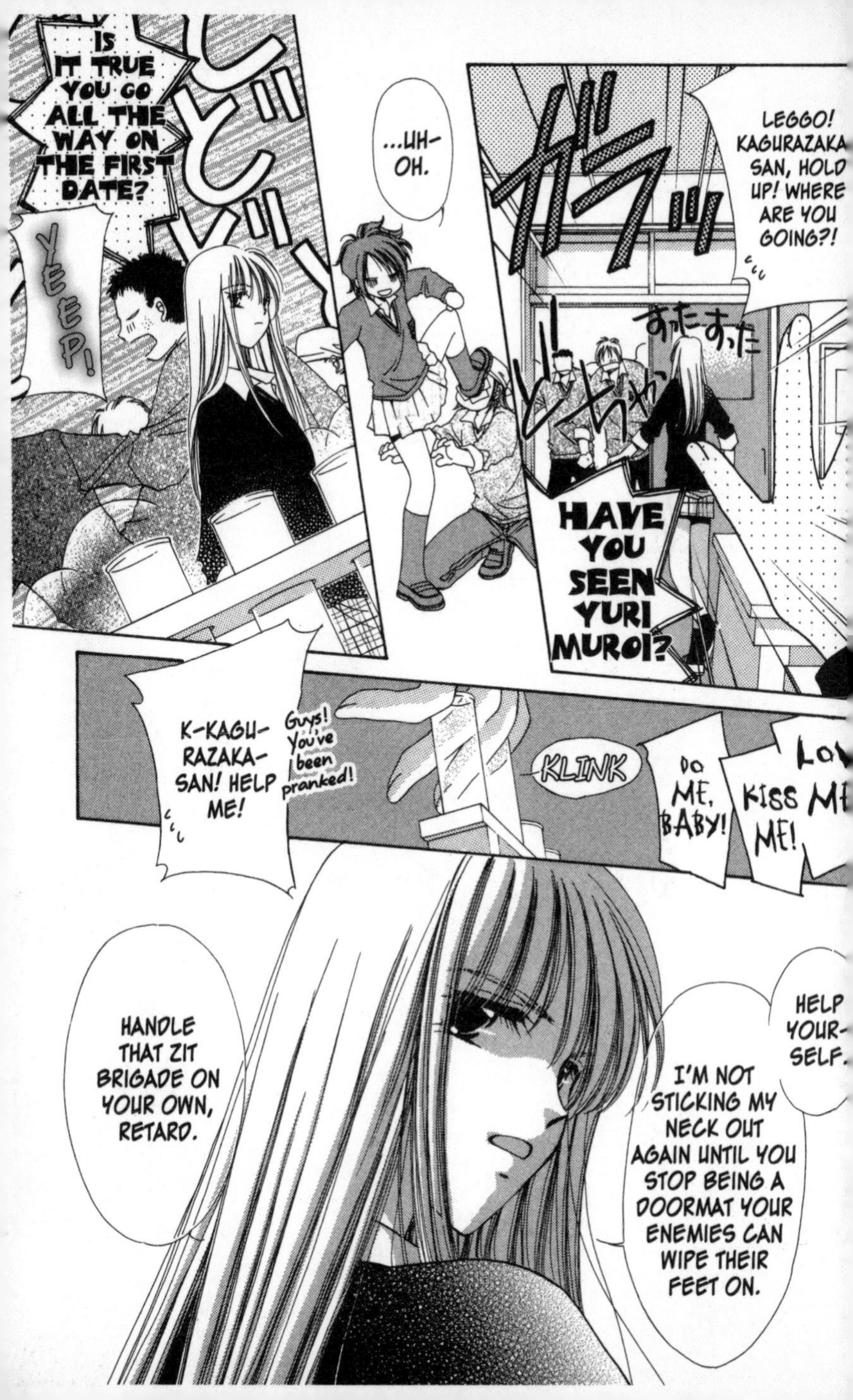
LEGGO! KAGURAZAKA SAN, HOLD UP! WHERE ARE YOU GOING?!
すたすた
HAVE YOU SEEN YURI MUROI?
...UH-OH.
IS IT TRUE YOU GO ALL THE WAY ON THE FIRST DATE?
YEEP!
KISS ME!
DO ME, BABY!
KLINK
Guys! You've been pranked!
K-KAGURAZAKA-SAN! HELP ME!
HELP YOURSELF.
I'M NOT STICKING MY NECK OUT AGAIN UNTIL YOU STOP BEING A DOORMAT YOUR ENEMIES CAN WIPE THEIR FEET ON.
HANDLE THAT ZIT BRIGADE ON YOUR OWN, RETARD.

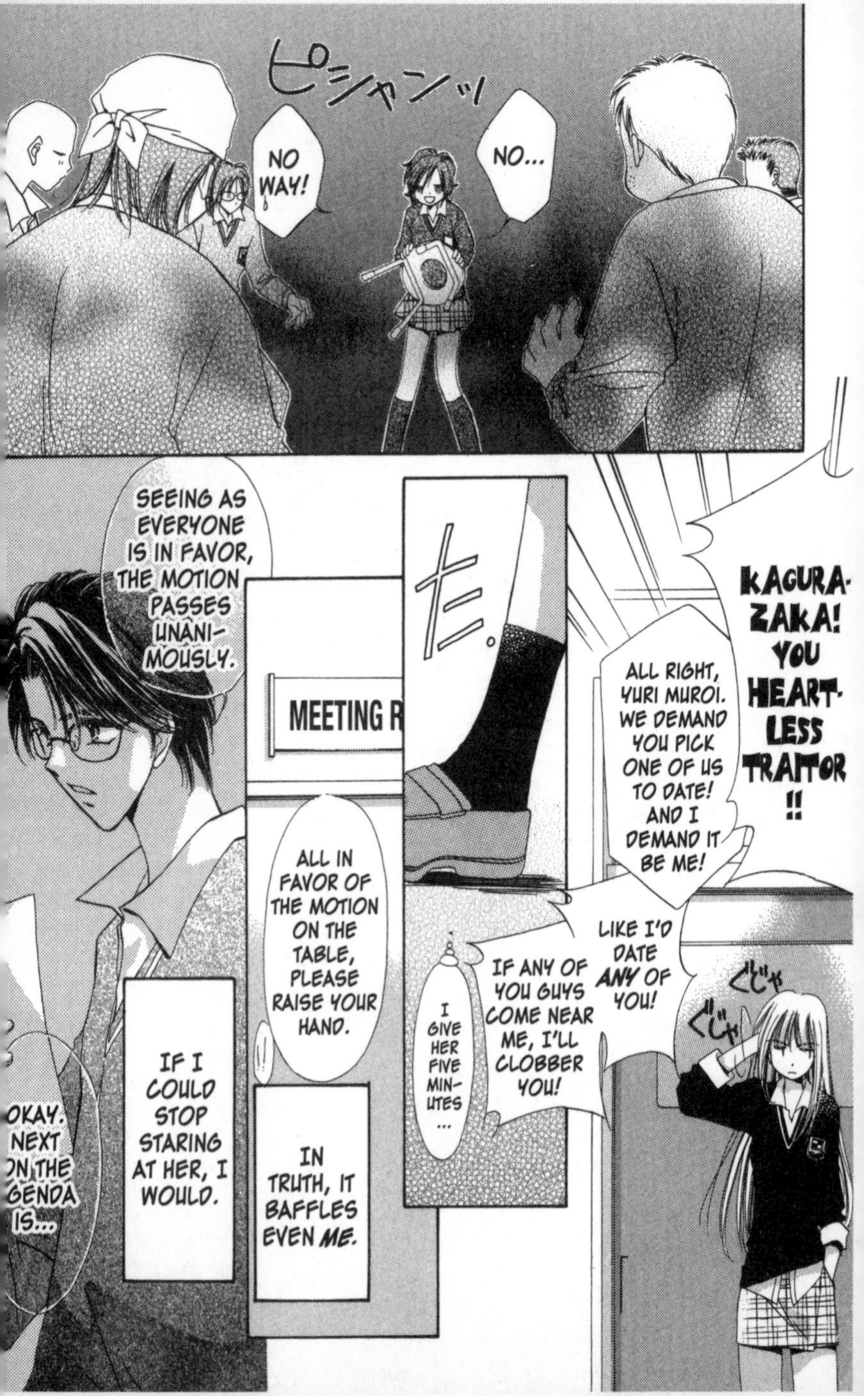
ピシャンッ
NO...
NO WAY!
KAGURAZAKA! YOU HEARTLESS TRAITOR!!
ALL RIGHT, YURI MUROI. WE DEMAND YOU PICK ONE OF US TO DATE! AND I DEMAND IT BE ME!
LIKE I'D DATE *ANY* OF YOU!
IF ANY OF YOU GUYS COME NEAR ME, I'LL CLOBBER YOU!
ぐじゃぐじゃ
I GIVE HER FIVE MINUTES...
た。
MEETING R
ALL IN FAVOR OF THE MOTION ON THE TABLE, PLEASE RAISE YOUR HAND.
!!
IN TRUTH, IT BAFFLES EVEN *ME*.
SEEING AS EVERYONE IS IN FAVOR, THE MOTION PASSES UNANIMOUSLY.
IF I COULD STOP STARING AT HER, I WOULD.
OKAY. NEXT ON THE GENDA IS...

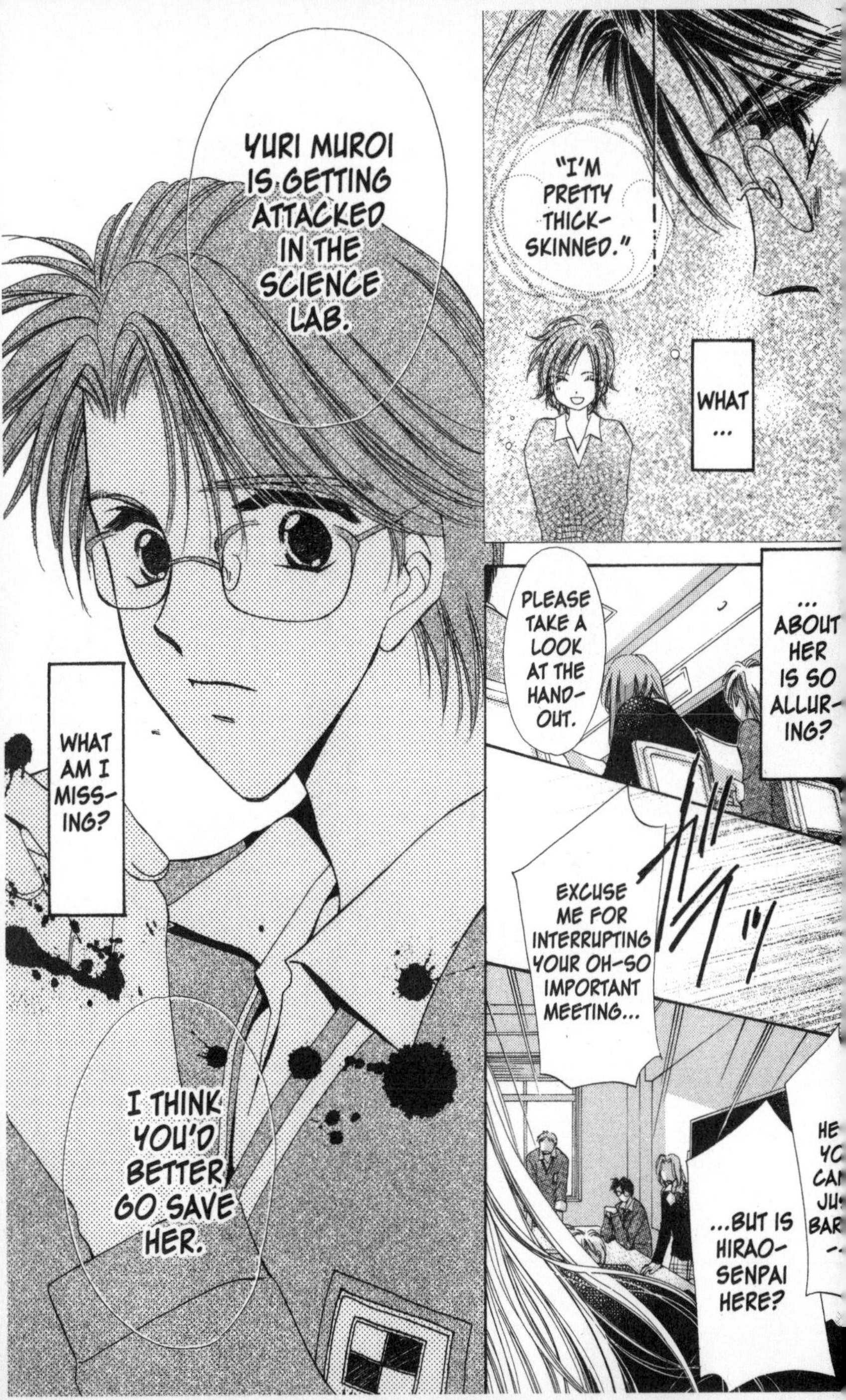
"I'M PRETTY THICK-SKINNED."
WHAT ...
... ABOUT HER IS SO ALLUR-ING?
PLEASE TAKE A LOOK AT THE HAND-OUT.
EXCUSE ME FOR INTERRUPTING YOUR OH-SO IMPORTANT MEETING...
...BUT IS HIRAO-SENPAI HERE?
YURI MUROI IS GETTING ATTACKED IN THE SCIENCE LAB.
WHAT AM I MISS-ING?
I THINK YOU'D BETTER GO SAVE HER.

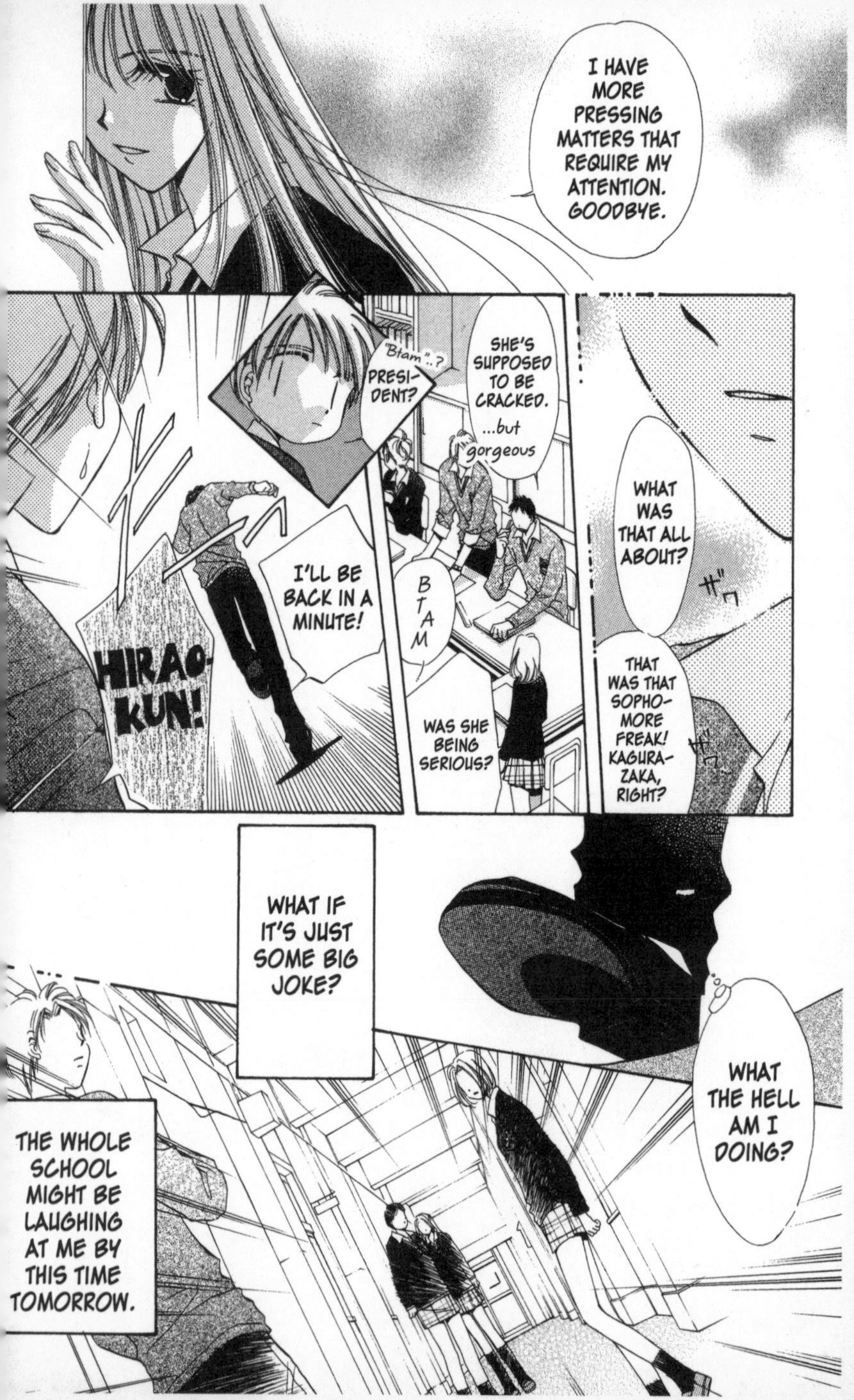
I HAVE MORE PRESSING MATTERS THAT REQUIRE MY ATTENTION. GOODBYE.
WHAT WAS THAT ALL ABOUT?
ザワ
THAT WAS THAT SOPHOMORE FREAK! KAGURAZAKA, RIGHT?
SHE'S SUPPOSED TO BE CRACKED.
...but gorgeous
BTAM
WAS SHE BEING SERIOUS?
"Btam"..? PRESIDENT?
I'LL BE BACK IN A MINUTE!
HIRAO-KUN!
WHAT THE HELL AM I DOING?
WHAT IF IT'S JUST SOME BIG JOKE?
THE WHOLE SCHOOL MIGHT BE LAUGHING AT ME BY THIS TIME TOMORROW.

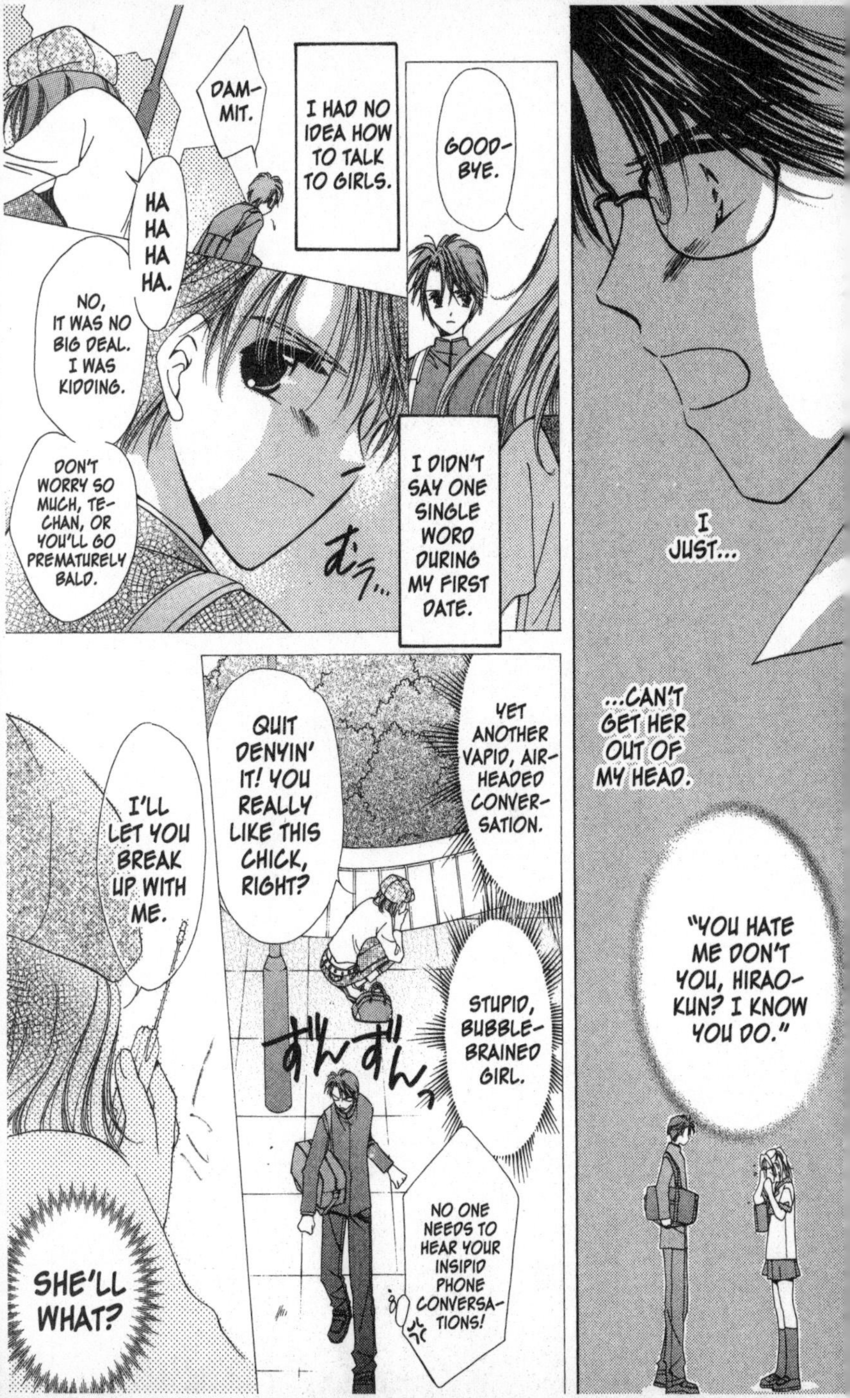
I JUST...
...CAN'T GET HER OUT OF MY HEAD.
"YOU HATE ME DON'T YOU, HIRAO-KUN? I KNOW YOU DO."
GOOD-BYE.
I HAD NO IDEA HOW TO TALK TO GIRLS.
I DIDN'T SAY ONE SINGLE WORD DURING MY FIRST DATE.
DAM-MIT.
HA HA HA HA.
NO, IT WAS NO BIG DEAL. I WAS KIDDING.
DON'T WORRY SO MUCH, TE-CHAN, OR YOU'LL GO PREMATURELY BALD.
むっ...
YET ANOTHER VAPID, AIR-HEADED CONVER-SATION.
QUIT DENYIN' IT! YOU REALLY LIKE THIS CHICK, RIGHT?
STUPID, BUBBLE-BRAINED GIRL.
ずんずんっ
NO ONE NEEDS TO HEAR YOUR INSIPID PHONE CONVERSA-TIONS!
I'LL LET YOU BREAK UP WITH ME.
SHE'LL WHAT?

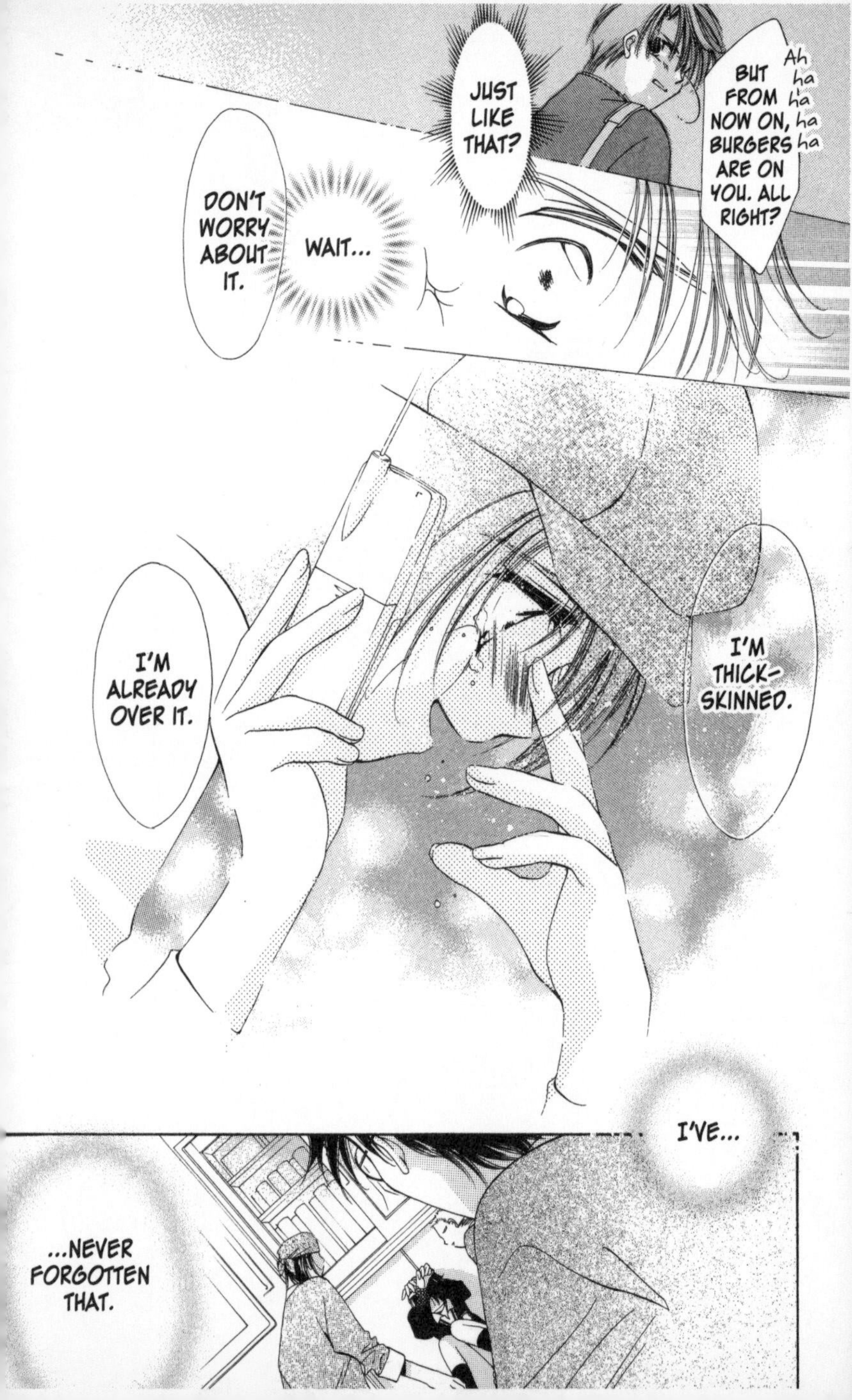
Ah ha ha ha ha
BUT FROM NOW ON, BURGERS ARE ON YOU. ALL RIGHT?
JUST LIKE THAT?
WAIT...
DON'T WORRY ABOUT IT.
I'M THICK-SKINNED.
I'M ALREADY OVER IT.
I'VE...
...NEVER FORGOTTEN THAT.

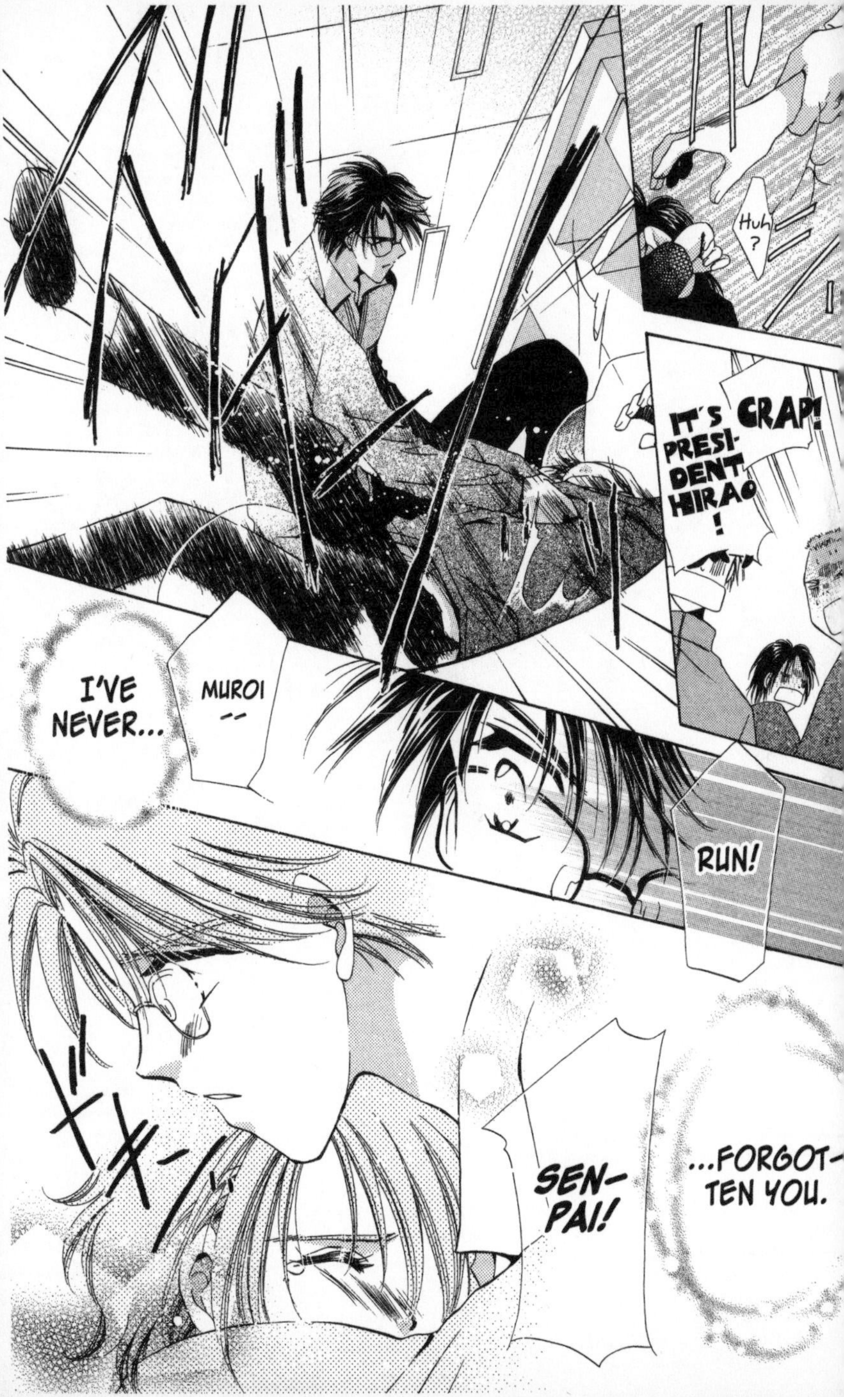

Huh?
CRAP!
IT'S PRESIDENT HIRAO!
RUN!
MUROI--
I'VE NEVER...
...FORGOTTEN YOU.
SENPAI!

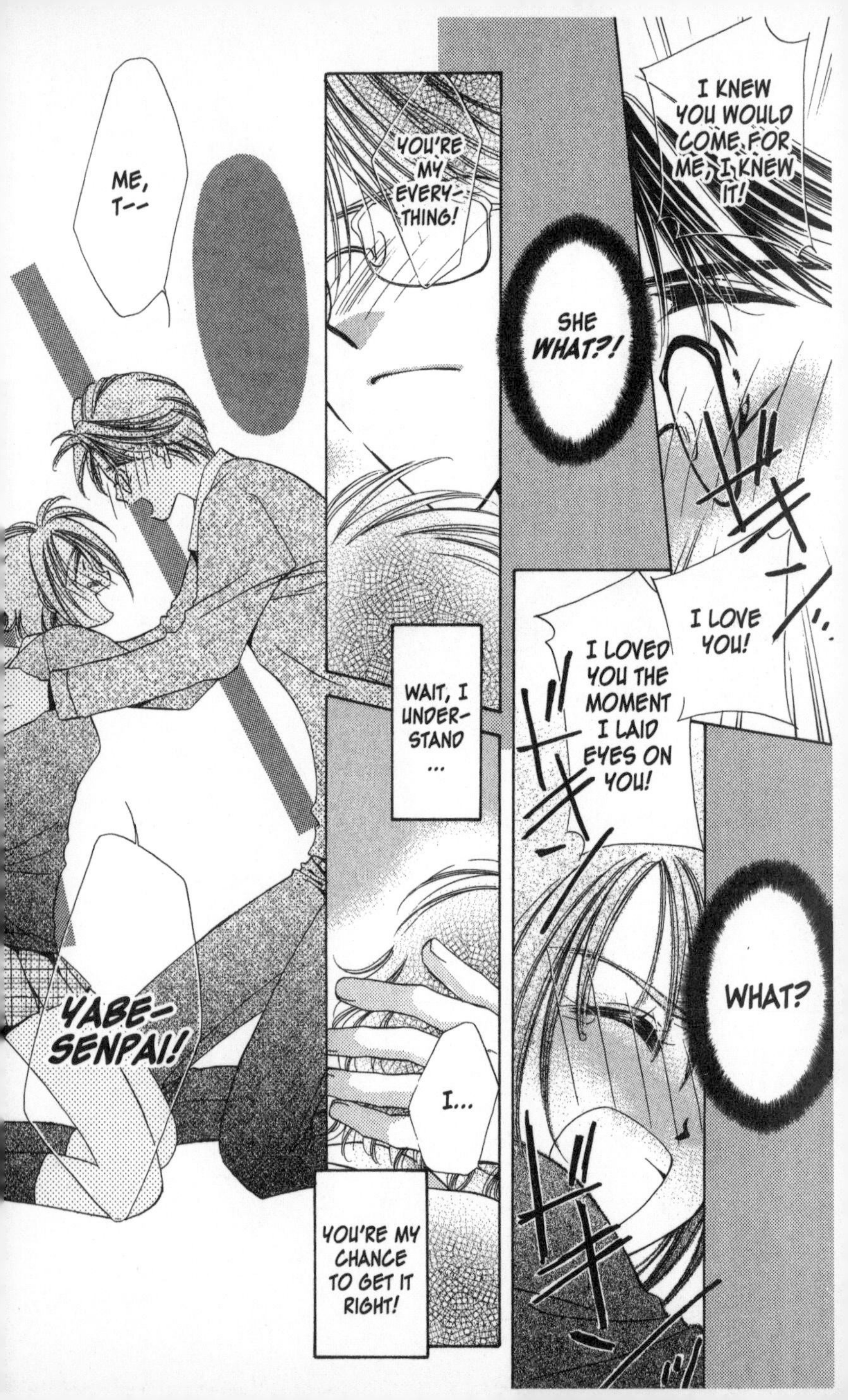
I KNEW YOU WOULD COME FOR ME, I KNEW IT!
SHE WHAT?!
I LOVE YOU!
I LOVED YOU THE MOMENT I LAID EYES ON YOU!
WHAT?
YOU'RE MY EVERYTHING!
WAIT, I UNDERSTAND...
I...
YOU'RE MY CHANCE TO GET IT RIGHT!
ME, T--
YABE-SENPAI!

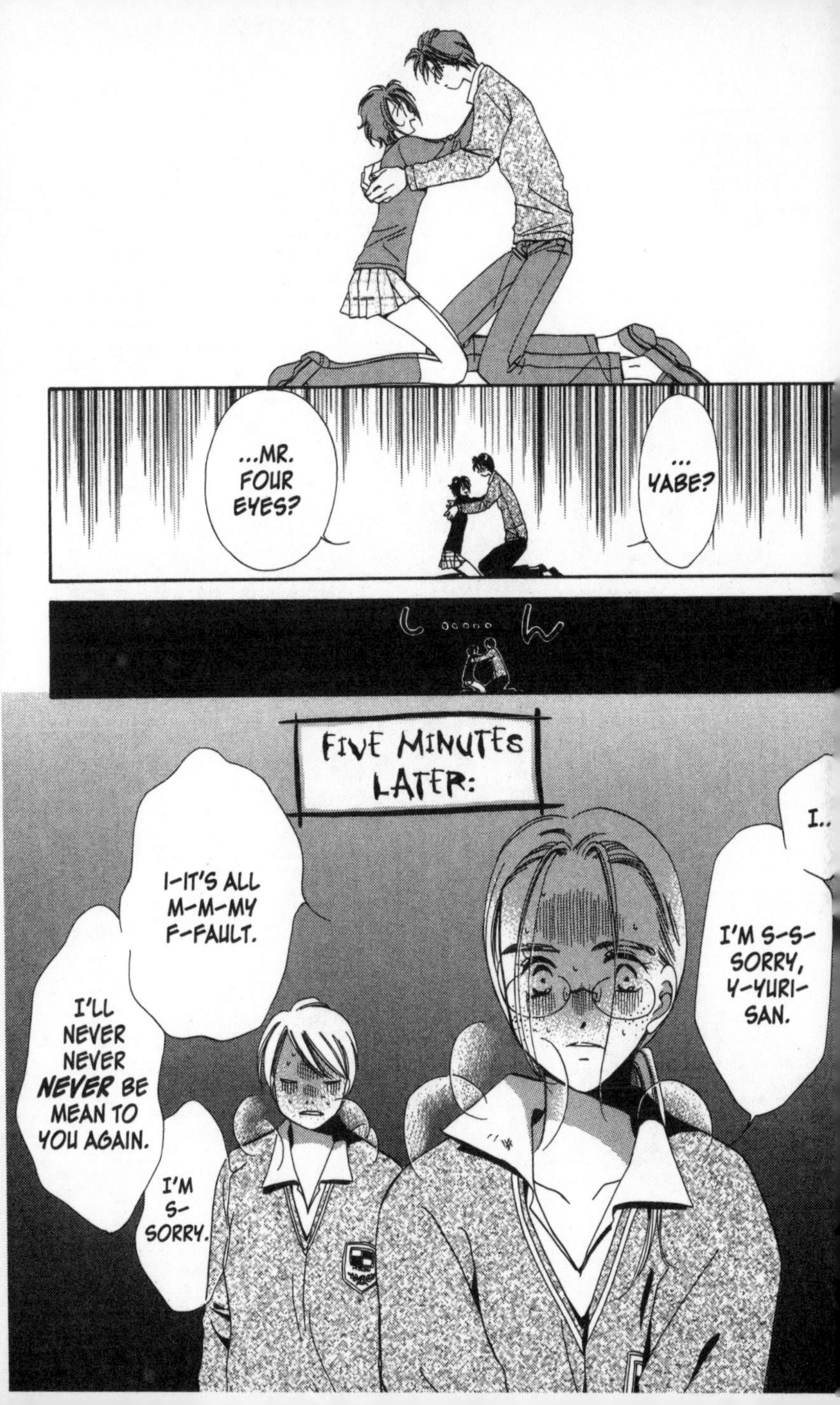
...YABE?
...MR. FOUR EYES?
し.....ん
FIVE MINUTES LATER:
I...
I'M S-S-SORRY, Y-YURI-SAN.
I-IT'S ALL M-M-MY F-FAULT.
I'LL NEVER NEVER NEVER BE MEAN TO YOU AGAIN.
I'M S-SORRY.

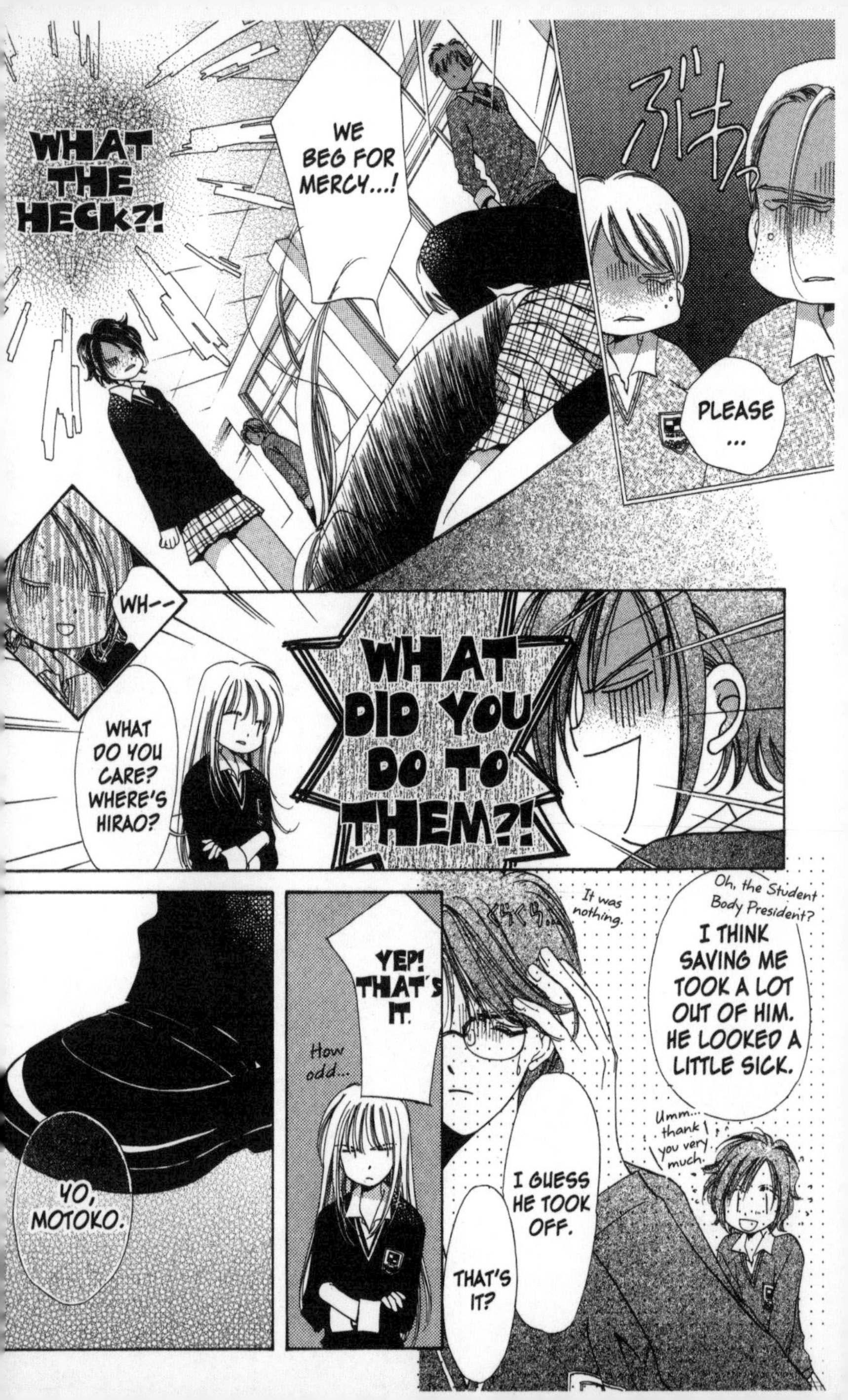

ぶわっ
PLEASE ...
WE BEG FOR MERCY...!
WHAT THE HECK?!
WHAT DID YOU DO TO THEM?!
WHAT DO YOU CARE? WHERE'S HIRAO?
WH--
Oh, the Student Body President?
I THINK SAVING ME TOOK A LOT OUT OF HIM. HE LOOKED A LITTLE SICK.
It was nothing.
くらくら...
Umm... thank you very much.
I GUESS HE TOOK OFF.
THAT'S IT?
YEP! THAT'S IT.
How odd...
YO, MOTOKO.

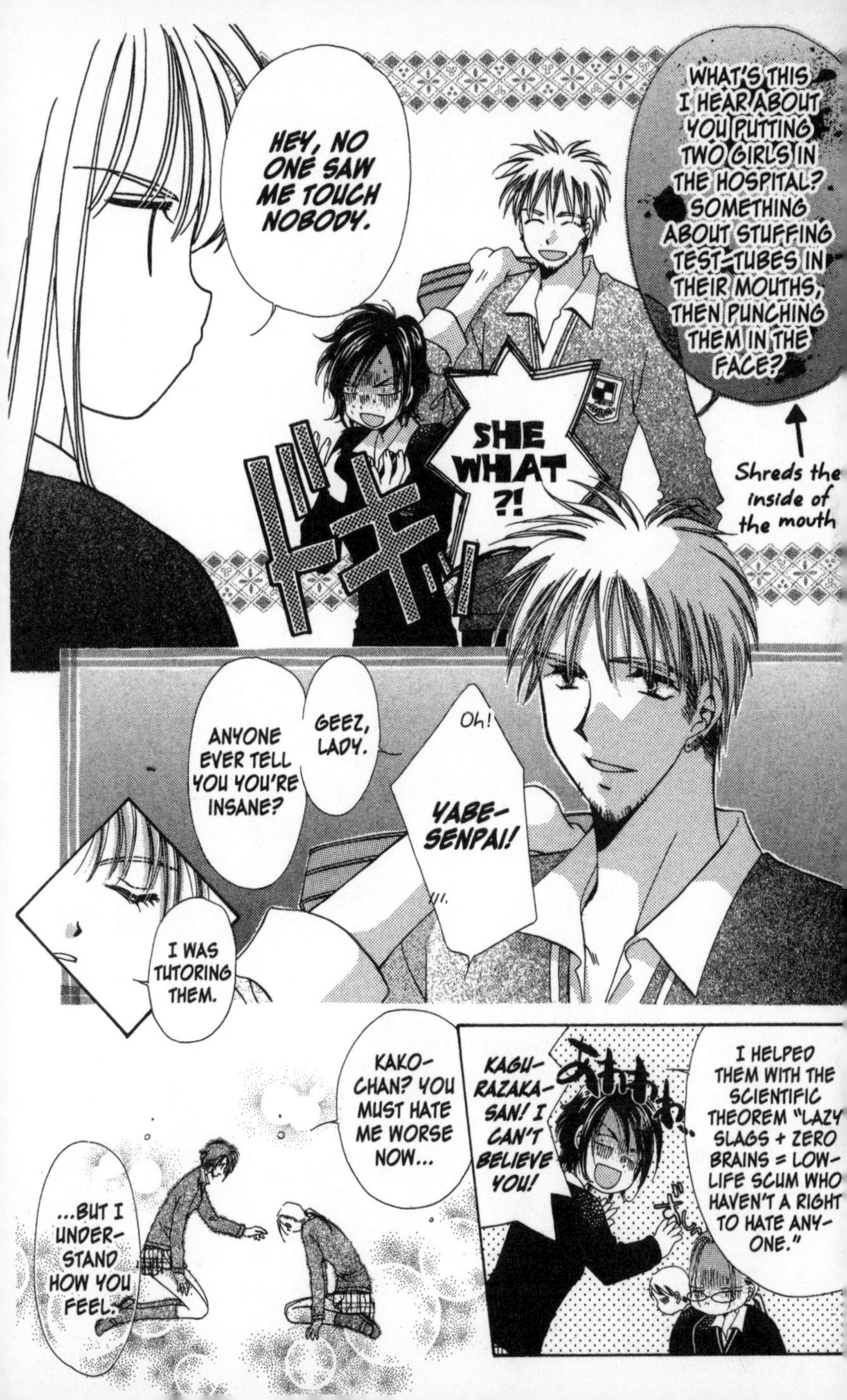
WHAT'S THIS I HEAR ABOUT YOU PUTTING TWO GIRLS IN THE HOSPITAL? SOMETHING ABOUT STUFFING TEST-TUBES IN THEIR MOUTHS, THEN PUNCHING THEM IN THE FACE?
Shreds the inside of the mouth
SHE WHAT ?!
HEY, NO ONE SAW ME TOUCH NOBODY.
Oh!
YABE-SENPAI!
GEEZ, LADY.
ANYONE EVER TELL YOU YOU'RE INSANE?
I WAS TUTORING THEM.
I HELPED THEM WITH THE SCIENTIFIC THEOREM "LAZY SLAGS + ZERO BRAINS = LOW-LIFE SCUM WHO HAVEN'T A RIGHT TO HATE ANY-ONE."
KAGU-RAZAKA-SAN! I CAN'T BELIEVE YOU!
KAKO-CHAN? YOU MUST HATE ME WORSE NOW...
...BUT I UNDER-STAND HOW YOU FEEL.

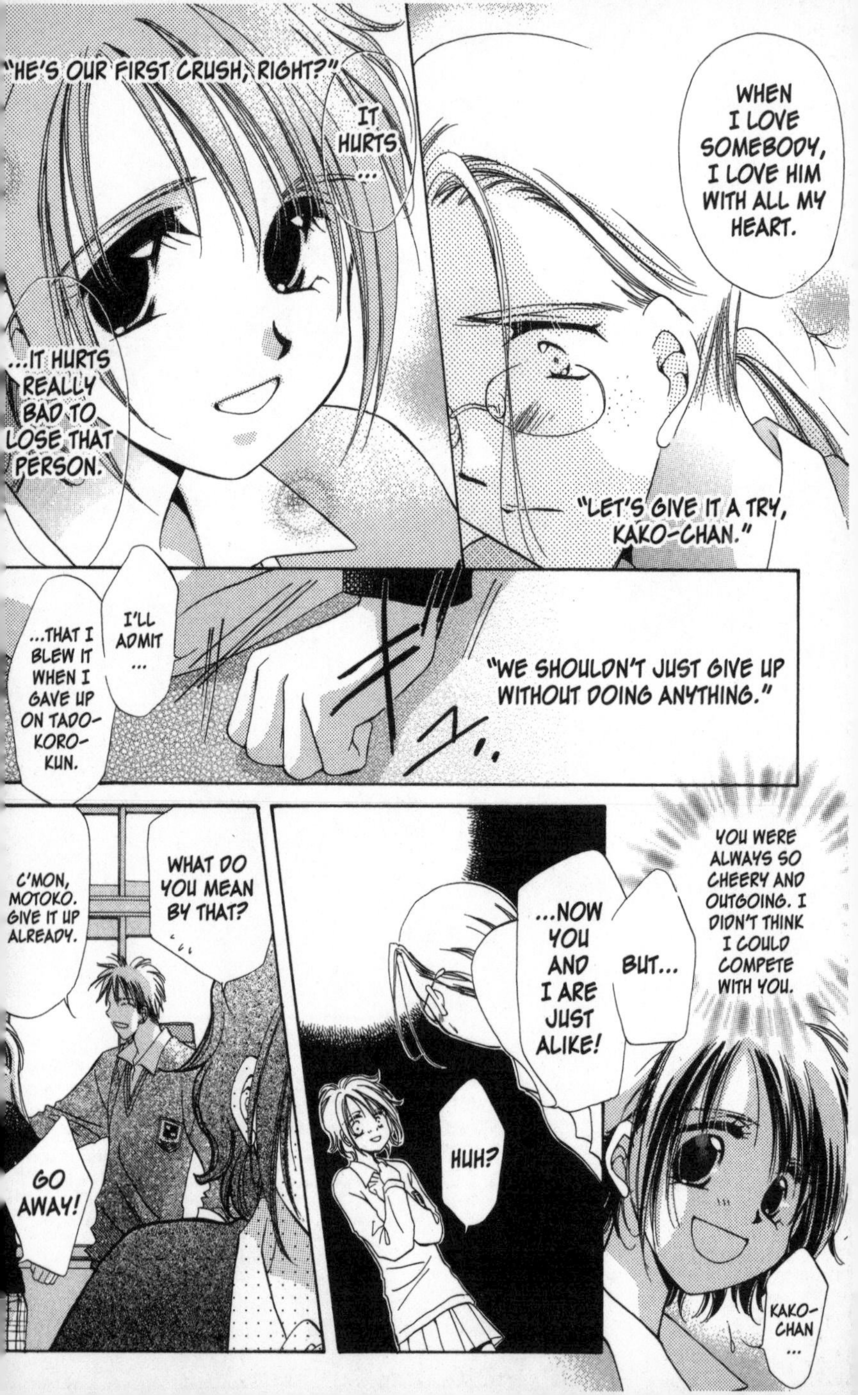
WHEN I LOVE SOMEBODY, I LOVE HIM WITH ALL MY HEART.
"LET'S GIVE IT A TRY, KAKO-CHAN."
"HE'S OUR FIRST CRUSH, RIGHT?"
IT HURTS...
...IT HURTS REALLY BAD TO LOSE THAT PERSON.
"WE SHOULDN'T JUST GIVE UP WITHOUT DOING ANYTHING."
I'LL ADMIT...
...THAT I BLEW IT WHEN I GAVE UP ON TADO-KORO-KUN.
YOU WERE ALWAYS SO CHEERY AND OUTGOING. I DIDN'T THINK I COULD COMPETE WITH YOU.
BUT...
...NOW YOU AND I ARE JUST ALIKE!
KAKO-CHAN...
HUH?
WHAT DO YOU MEAN BY THAT?
C'MON, MOTOKO. GIVE IT UP ALREADY.
GO AWAY!

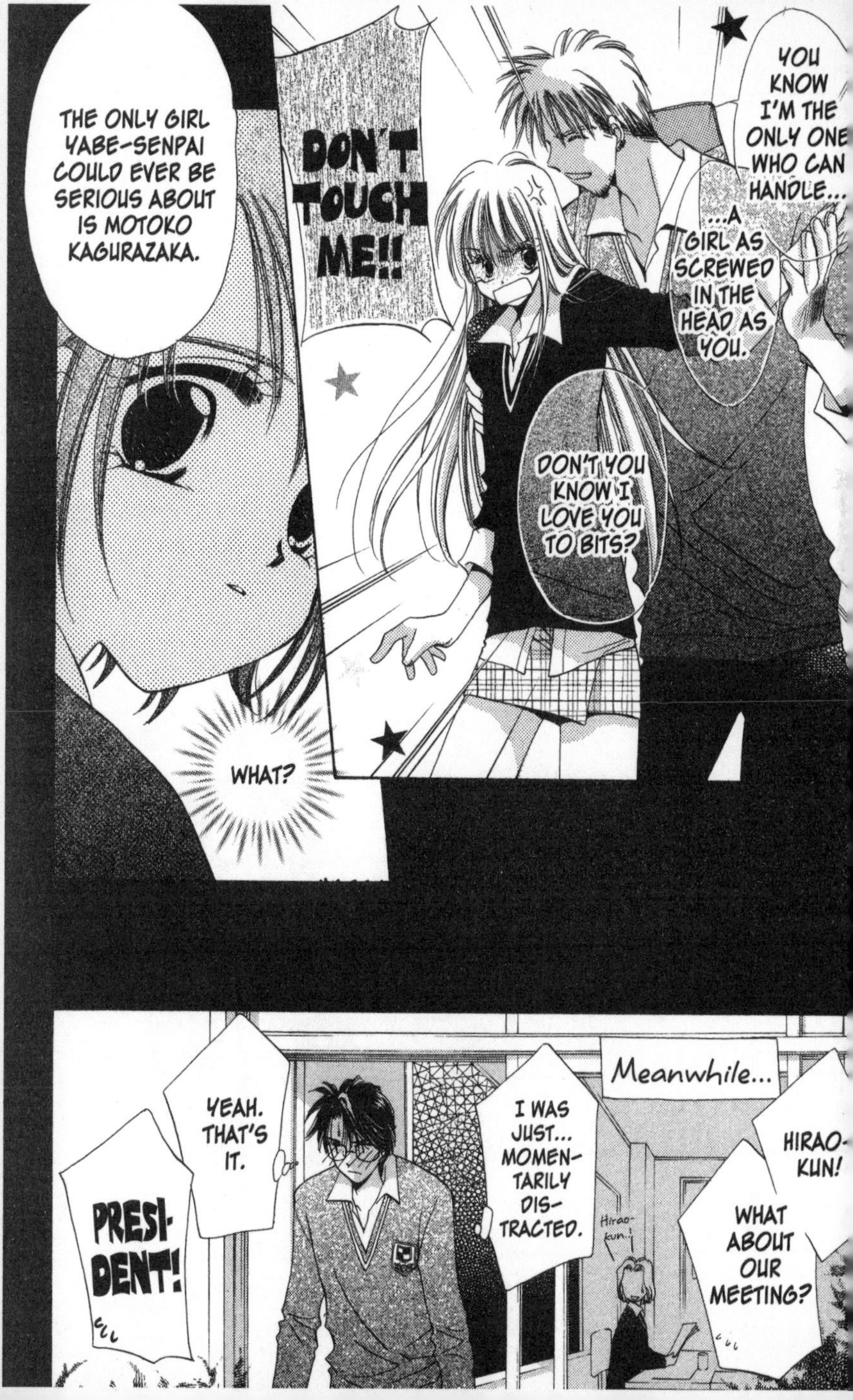
YOU KNOW I'M THE ONLY ONE WHO CAN HANDLE...
...A GIRL AS SCREWED IN THE HEAD AS YOU.
DON'T YOU KNOW I LOVE YOU TO BITS?
DON'T TOUCH ME!!
THE ONLY GIRL YABE-SENPAI COULD EVER BE SERIOUS ABOUT IS MOTOKO KAGURAZAKA.
WHAT?
Meanwhile...
HIRAO-KUN!
WHAT ABOUT OUR MEETING?
Hirao-kun
I WAS JUST... MOMEN-TARILY DIS-TRACTED.
YEAH. THAT'S IT.
PRESI-DENT!

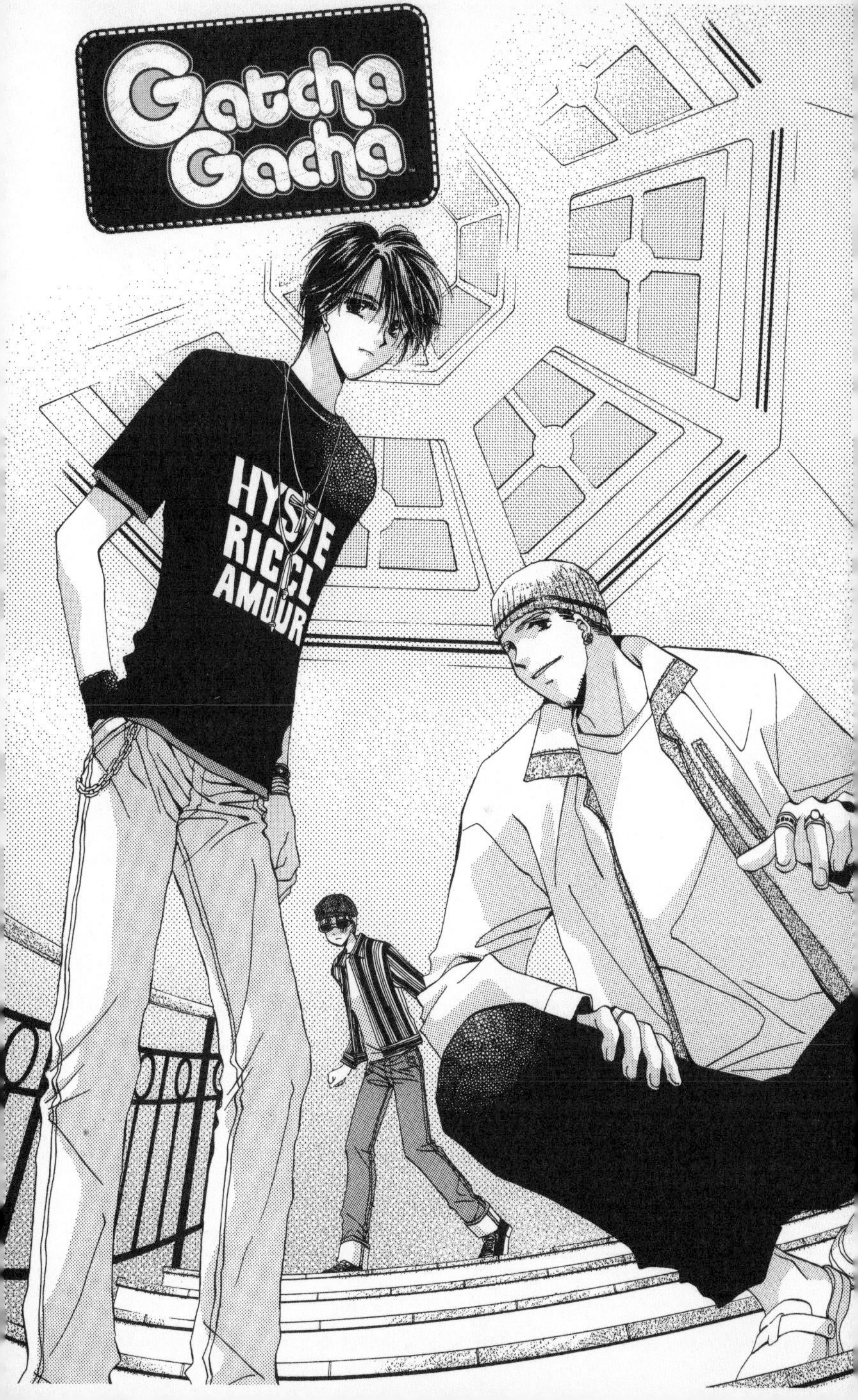
Gatcha Gacha™
HYSTE RIC CL AMOUR

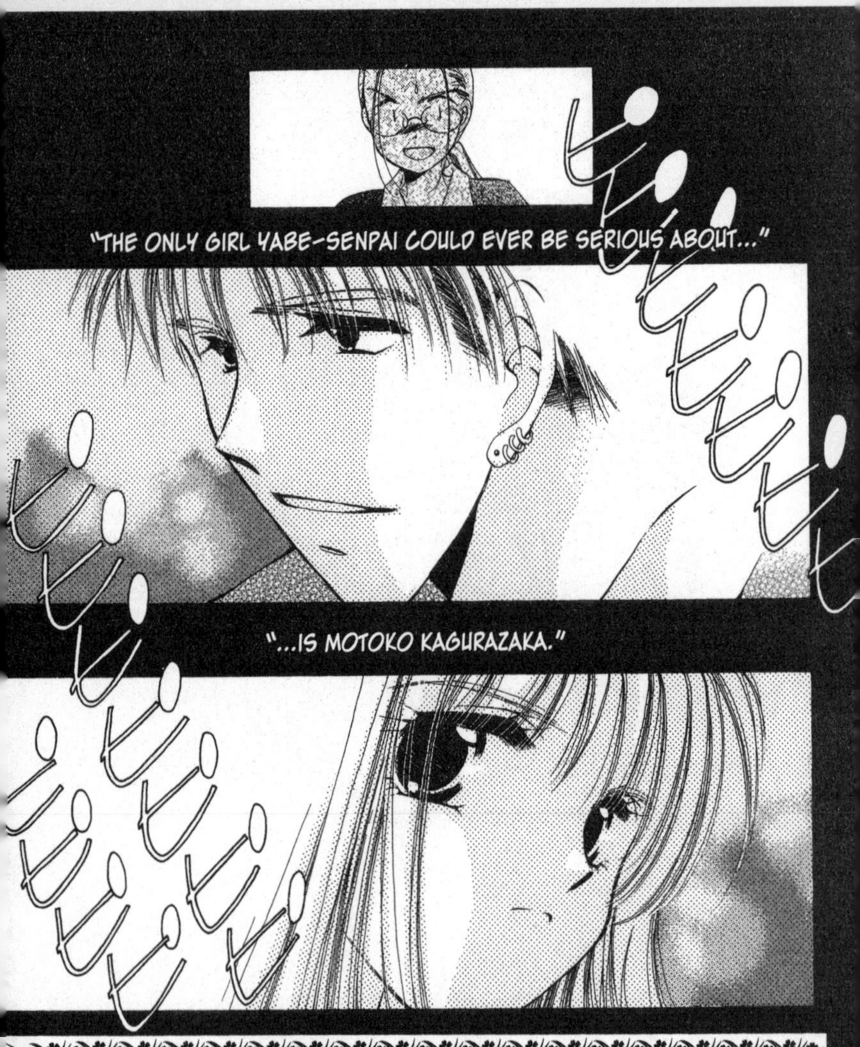
"THE ONLY GIRL YABE-SENPAI COULD EVER BE SERIOUS ABOUT..."
"...IS MOTOKO KAGURAZAKA."

Tachibana's Movie Recommendations

Little Dancer (English production)

Watch it with the knowledge that they're trying to trick you. It'll be good for your soul.

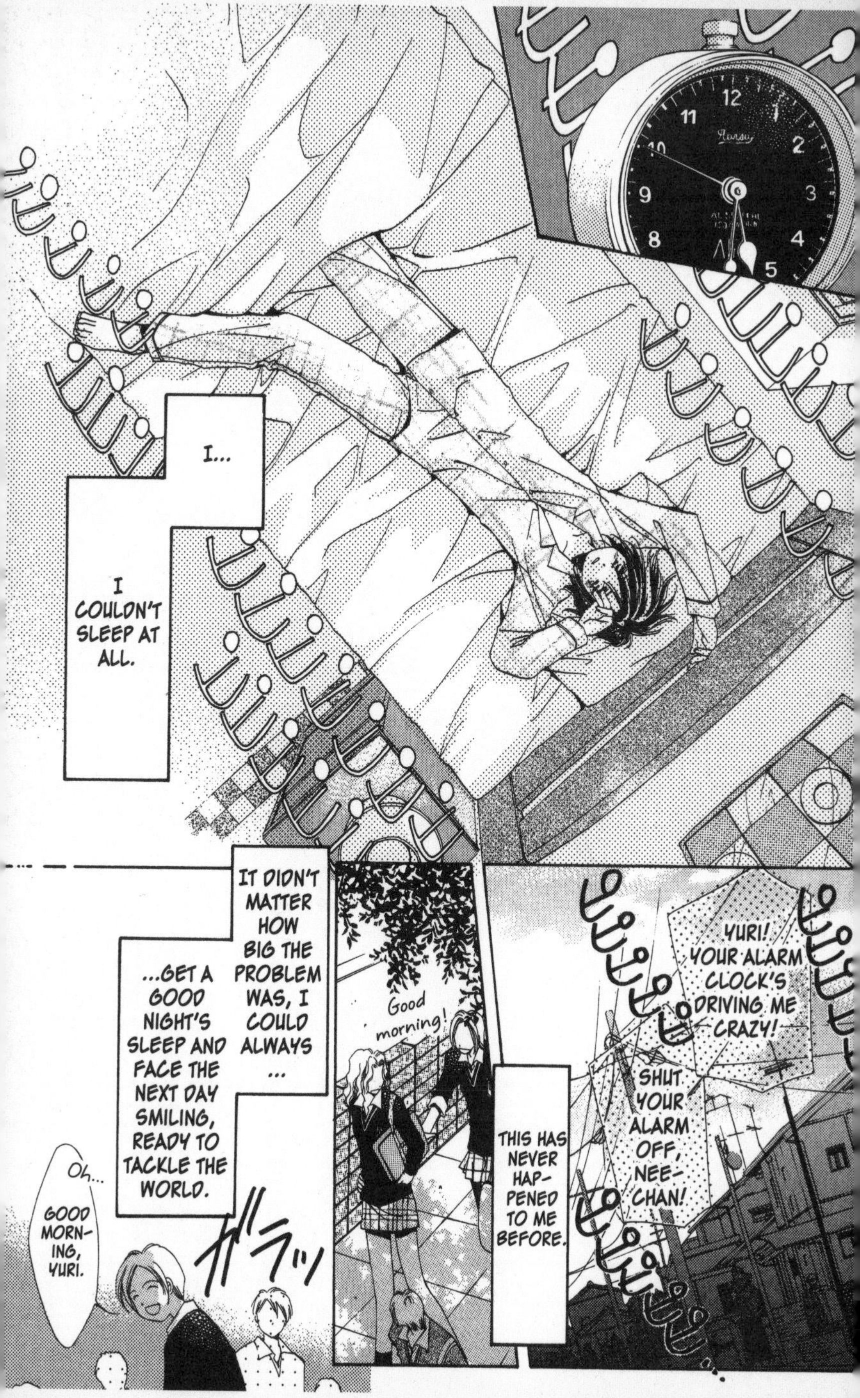
I...
I COULDN'T SLEEP AT ALL.
YURI! YOUR ALARM CLOCK'S DRIVING ME CRAZY!
SHUT YOUR ALARM OFF, NEE-CHAN!
THIS HAS NEVER HAPPENED TO ME BEFORE.
Good morning!
IT DIDN'T MATTER HOW BIG THE PROBLEM WAS, I COULD ALWAYS ...
...GET A GOOD NIGHT'S SLEEP AND FACE THE NEXT DAY SMILING, READY TO TACKLE THE WORLD.
ガラッ
Oh... GOOD MORNING, YURI.

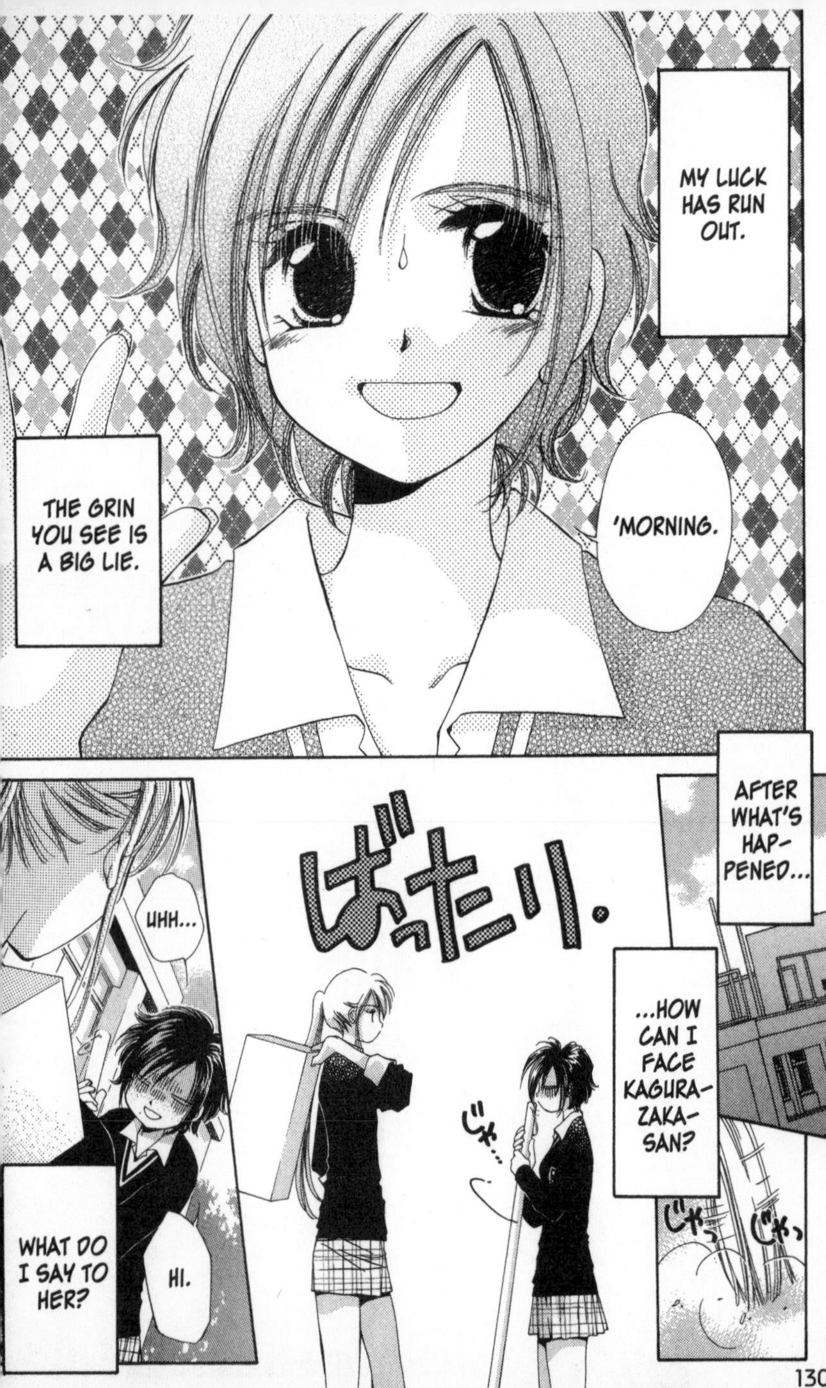
MY LUCK HAS RUN OUT.
'MORNING.
THE GRIN YOU SEE IS A BIG LIE.
AFTER WHAT'S HAP-PENED...
...HOW CAN I FACE KAGURA-ZAKA-SAN?
じゃっ
じゃっ
ばったり。
じゃ…
UHH...
HI.
WHAT DO I SAY TO HER?

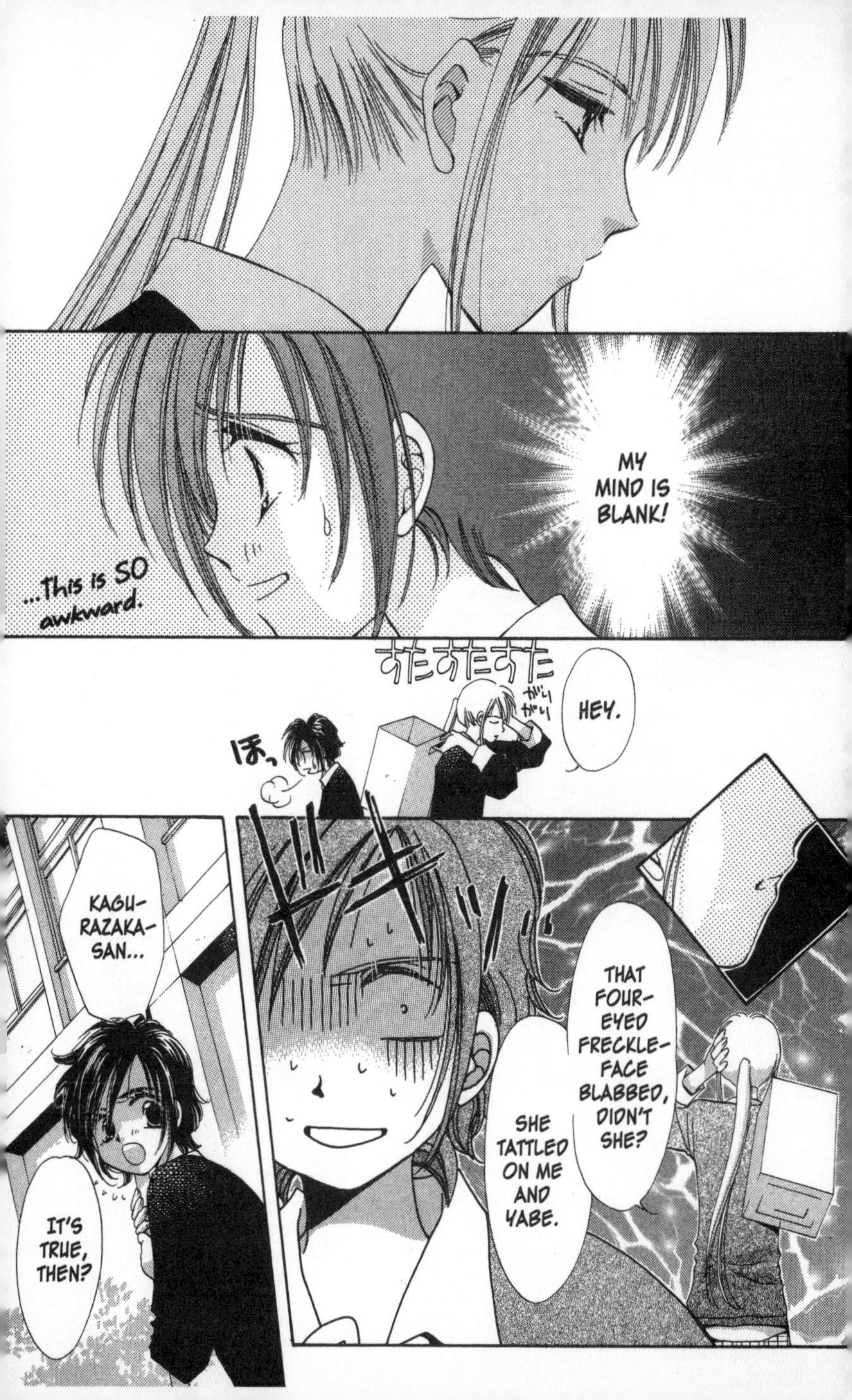

MY MIND IS BLANK!
...This is SO awkward.
HEY.
がりがり
すたすたすた
ほっ
THAT FOUR-EYED FRECKLE-FACE BLABBED, DIDN'T SHE?
SHE TATTLED ON ME AND YABE.
KAGURAZAKA-SAN...
IT'S TRUE, THEN?

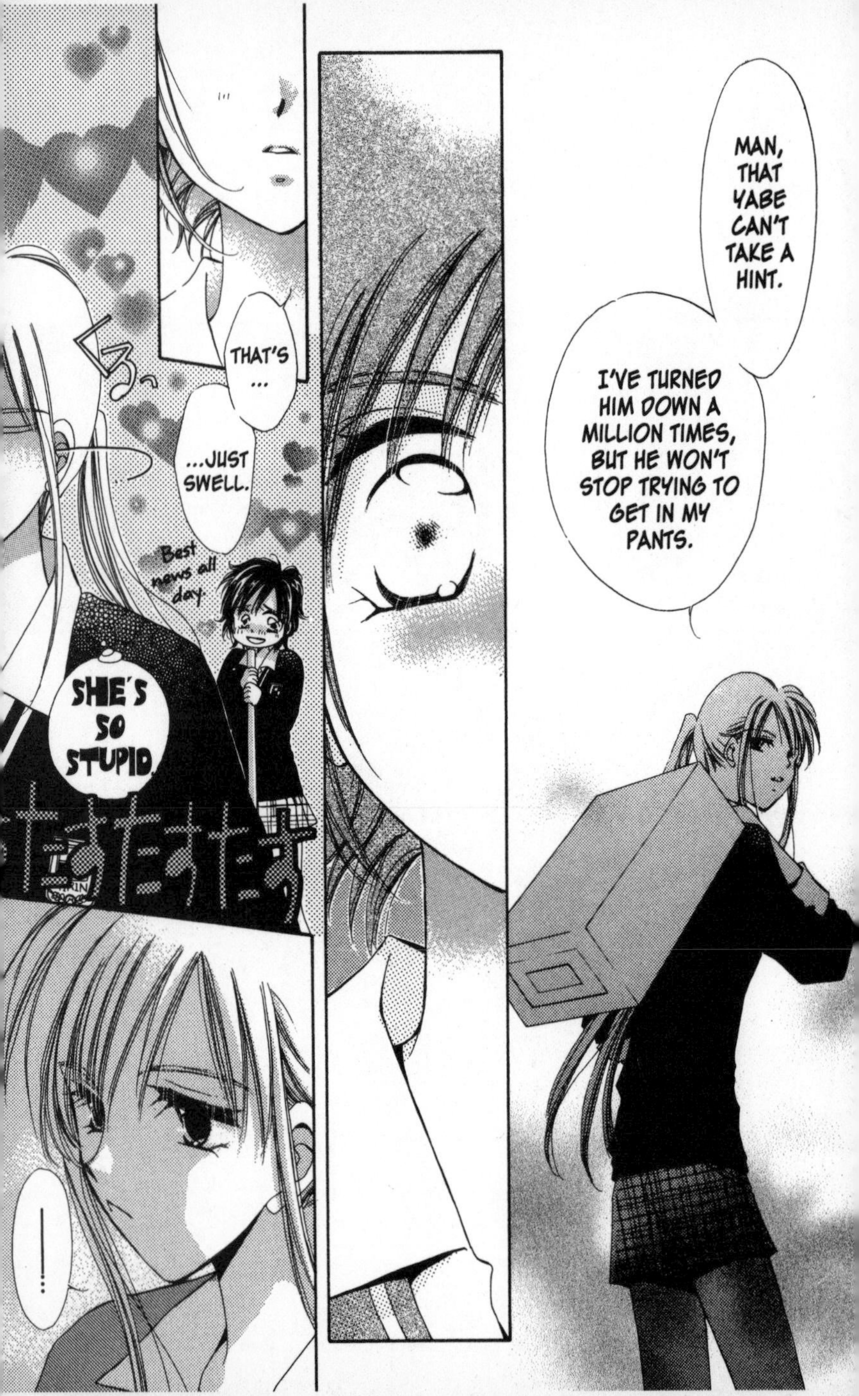
MAN, THAT YABE CAN'T TAKE A HINT.
I'VE TURNED HIM DOWN A MILLION TIMES, BUT HE WON'T STOP TRYING TO GET IN MY PANTS.
THAT'S ...
...JUST SWELL.
Best news all day.
SHE'S SO STUPID.

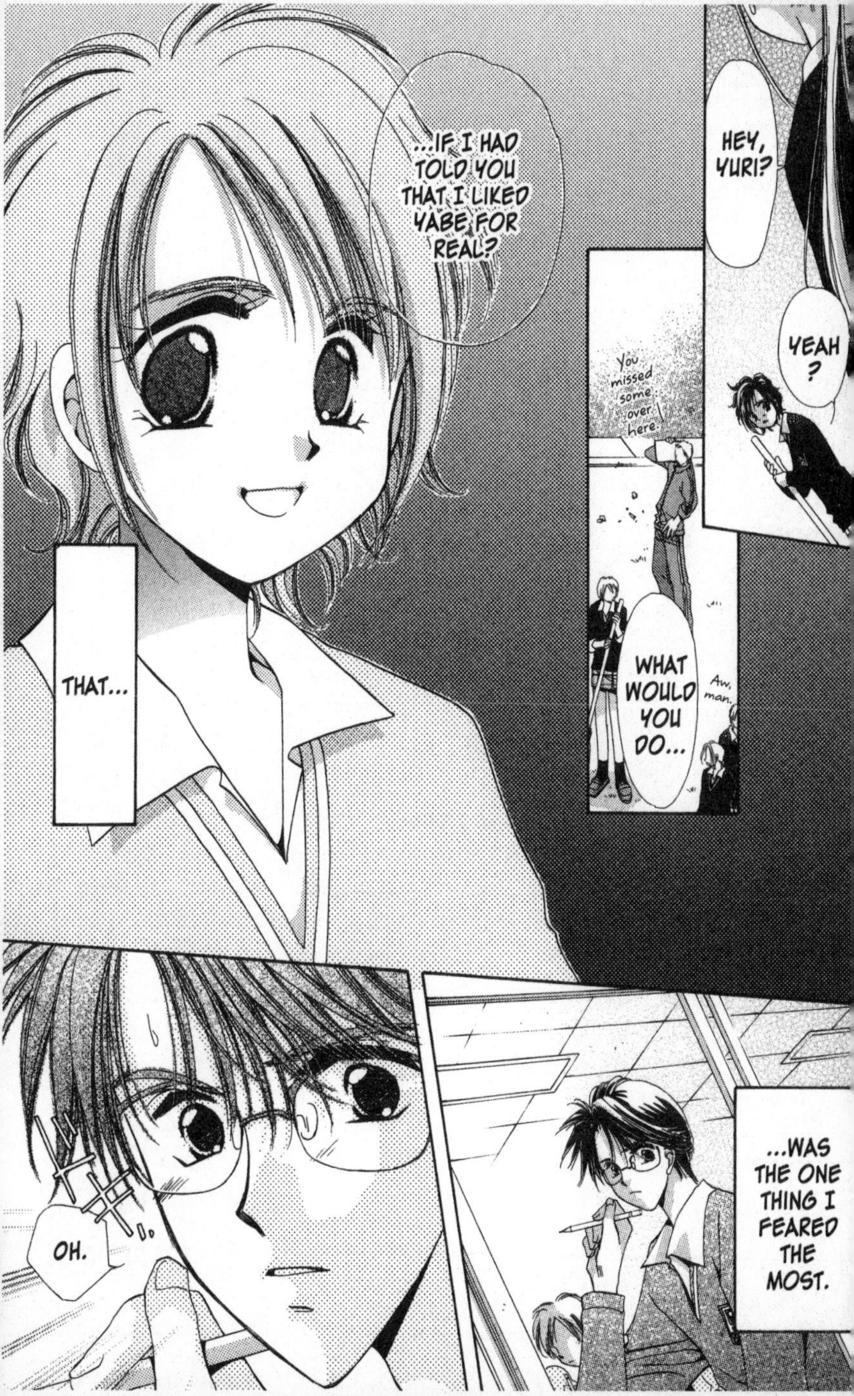
HEY, YURI?
YEAH?
You missed some over here
WHAT WOULD YOU DO...
Aw, man.
...IF I HAD TOLD YOU THAT I LIKED YABE FOR REAL?
THAT...
...WAS THE ONE THING I FEARED THE MOST.
OH.

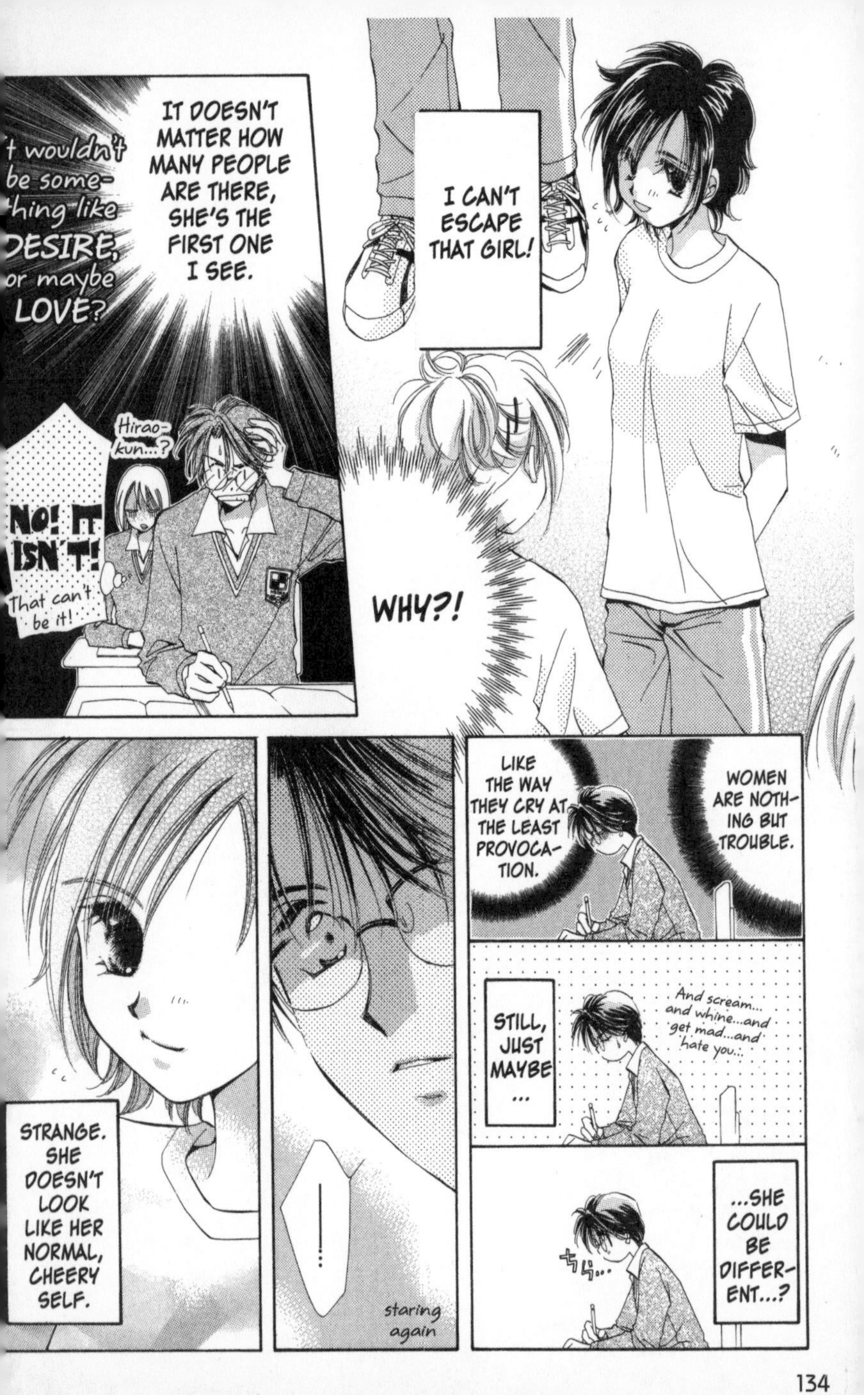

I CAN'T ESCAPE THAT GIRL!
WHY?!
IT DOESN'T MATTER HOW MANY PEOPLE ARE THERE, SHE'S THE FIRST ONE I SEE.
t wouldn't be some-thing like DESIRE, or maybe LOVE?
Hirao-kun...?
NO! IT ISN'T!
That can't be it!
WOMEN ARE NOTH-ING BUT TROUBLE.
LIKE THE WAY THEY CRY AT THE LEAST PROVOCA-TION.
And scream... and whine...and get mad...and hate you...
STILL, JUST MAYBE ...
...SHE COULD BE DIFFER-ENT...?
ちら...
......
staring again
STRANGE. SHE DOESN'T LOOK LIKE HER NORMAL, CHEERY SELF.

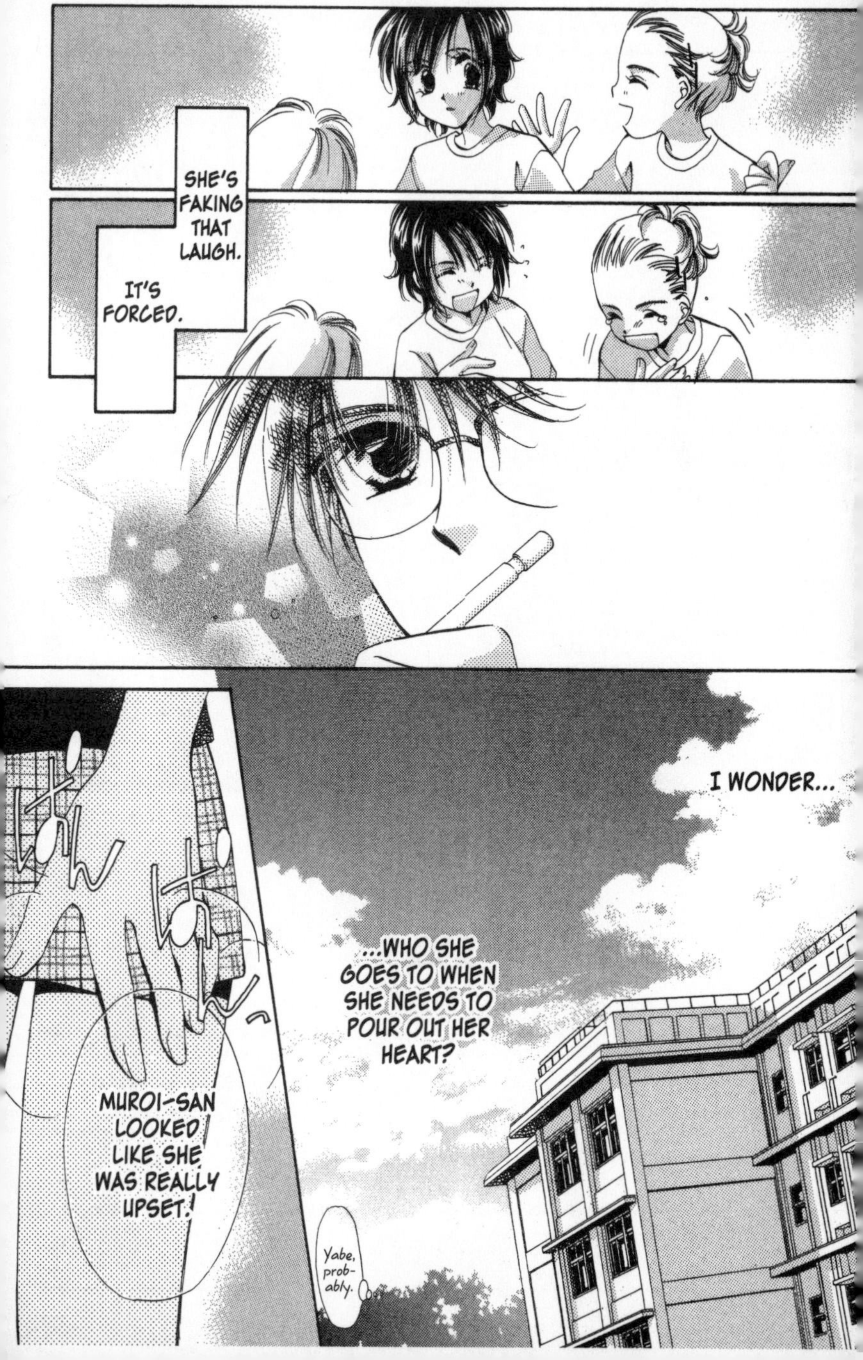
SHE'S FAKING THAT LAUGH.
IT'S FORCED.
I WONDER...
...WHO SHE GOES TO WHEN SHE NEEDS TO POUR OUT HER HEART?
MUROI-SAN LOOKED LIKE SHE WAS REALLY UPSET!
Yabe, probably.

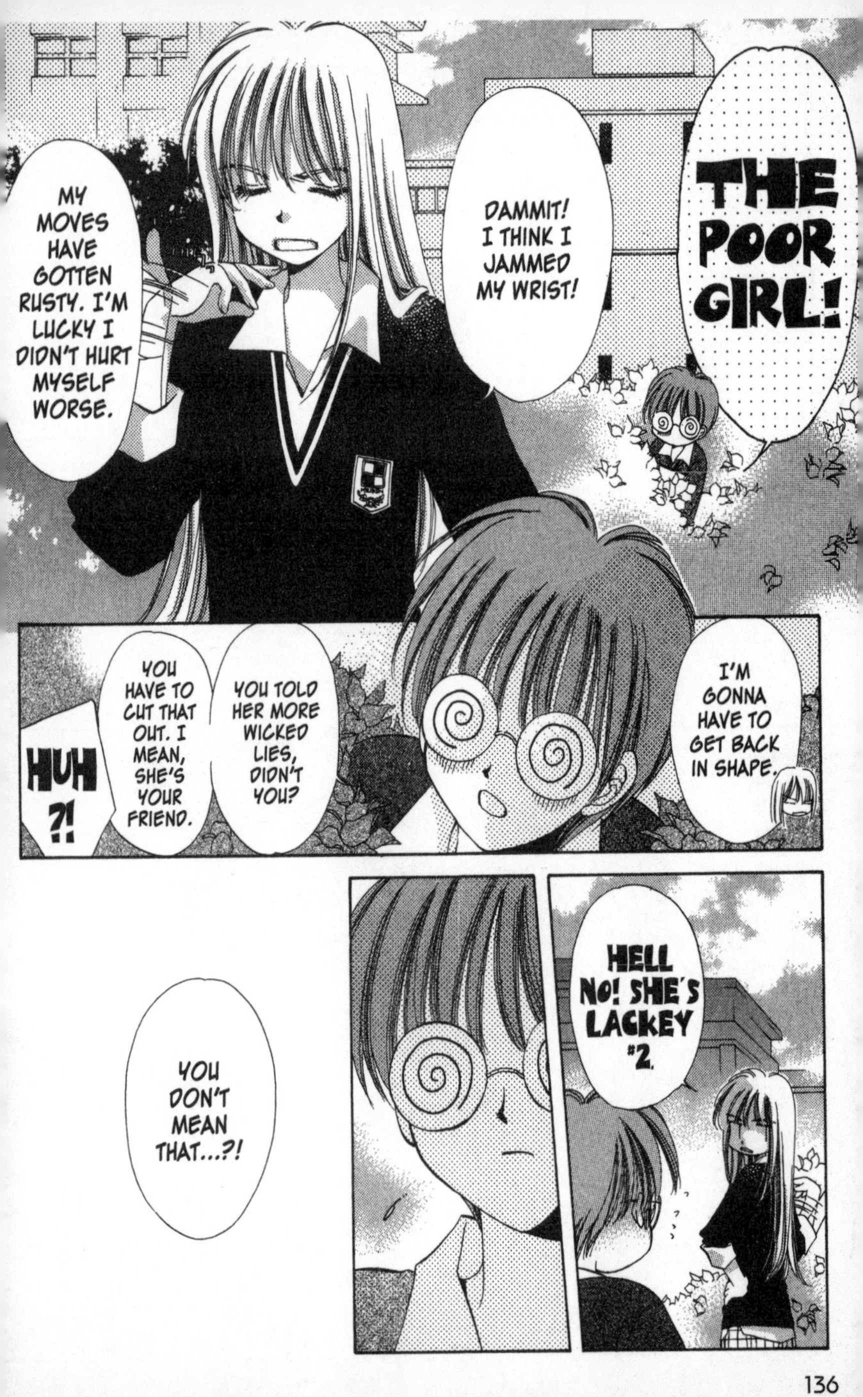
THE POOR GIRL!
DAMMIT! I THINK I JAMMED MY WRIST!
MY MOVES HAVE GOTTEN RUSTY. I'M LUCKY I DIDN'T HURT MYSELF WORSE.
I'M GONNA HAVE TO GET BACK IN SHAPE.
YOU TOLD HER MORE WICKED LIES, DIDN'T YOU?
YOU HAVE TO CUT THAT OUT. I MEAN, SHE'S YOUR FRIEND.
HUH ?!
HELL NO! SHE'S LACKEY #2.
YOU DON'T MEAN THAT...?!

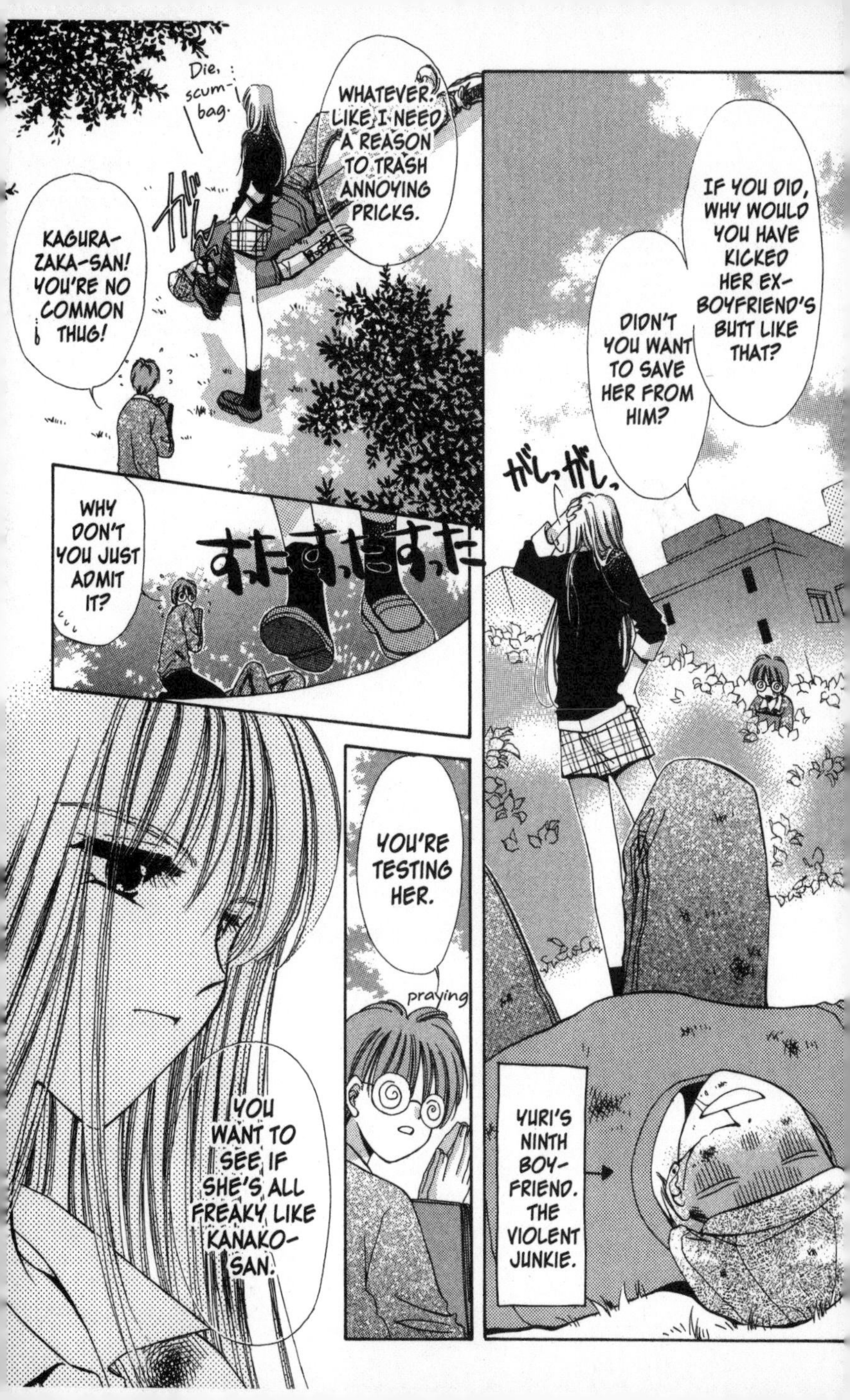
IF YOU DID, WHY WOULD YOU HAVE KICKED HER EX-BOYFRIEND'S BUTT LIKE THAT?
DIDN'T YOU WANT TO SAVE HER FROM HIM?
がしっ がしっ
WHATEVER. LIKE I NEED A REASON TO TRASH ANNOYING PRICKS.
Die, scum-bag.
KAGURA-ZAKA-SAN! YOU'RE NO COMMON THUG!
WHY DON'T YOU JUST ADMIT IT?
すたすたすた
YURI'S NINTH BOY-FRIEND. THE VIOLENT JUNKIE.
YOU'RE TESTING HER.
praying
YOU WANT TO SEE IF SHE'S ALL FREAKY LIKE KANAKO-SAN.

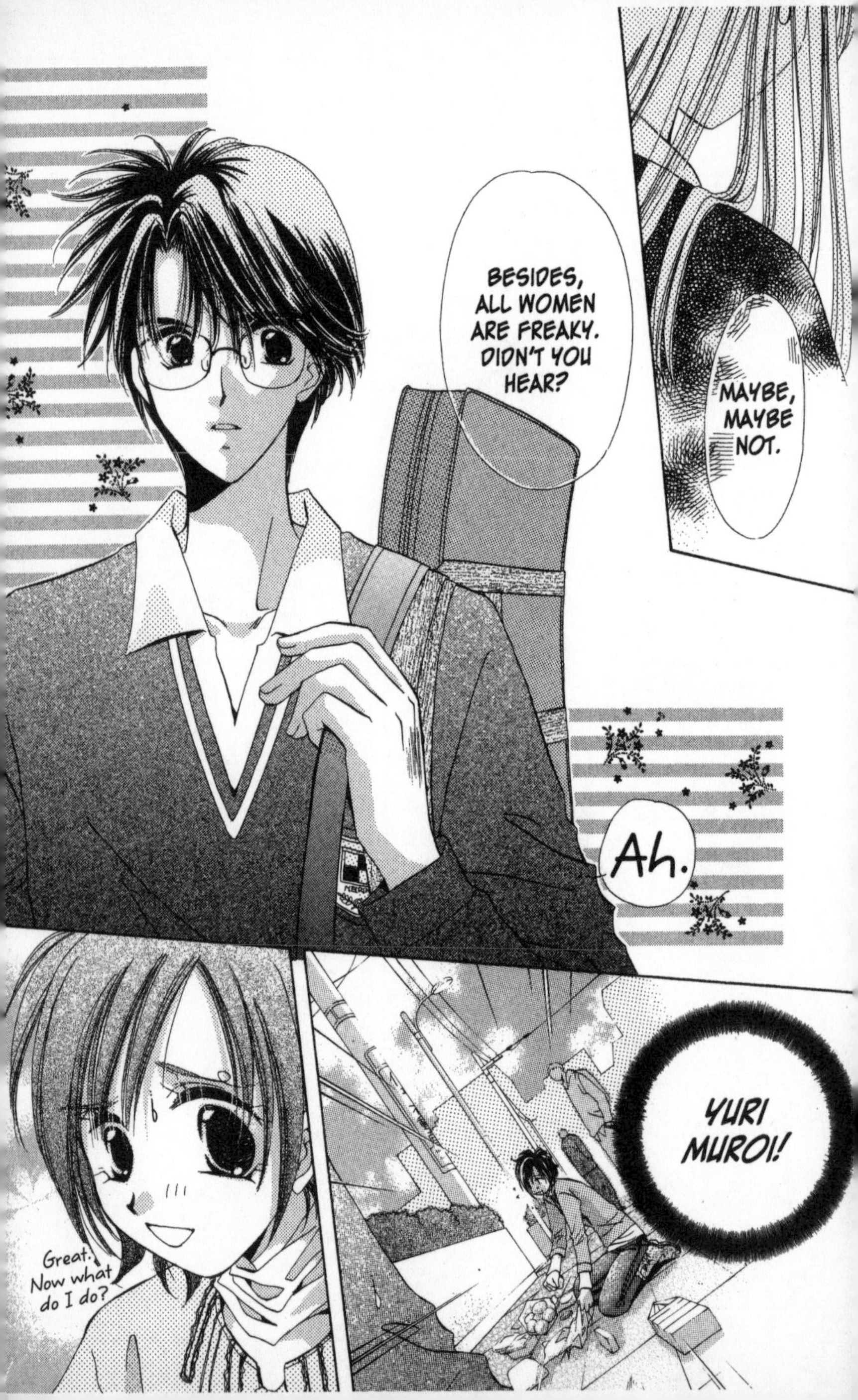
MAYBE, MAYBE NOT.
BESIDES, ALL WOMEN ARE FREAKY. DIDN'T YOU HEAR?
Ah.
YURI MUROI!
Great. Now what do I do?

Takahiro Yabe

On one hand, he's a smooth-talking, lazy punk who's good in a fight. On the other, he's always the sweetest gentleman when it comes to the ladies.

Truth be told, with his big body, droopy eyes, and scraggly goatee, he's precisely my type of guy. A thousand apologies since, for the first time, I have ignored the needs of all you young girls out there to draw what I personally think is the hottest type of fella.

He really is useless as a human being, but he's so much fun to draw. Trying to do teenage guys has always been a source of headaches for me (what a thing for a shojo manga artist to say!), but Yabe is different.

But if you should ever meet someone like him in real life, never date him. He'll just take advantage of you.

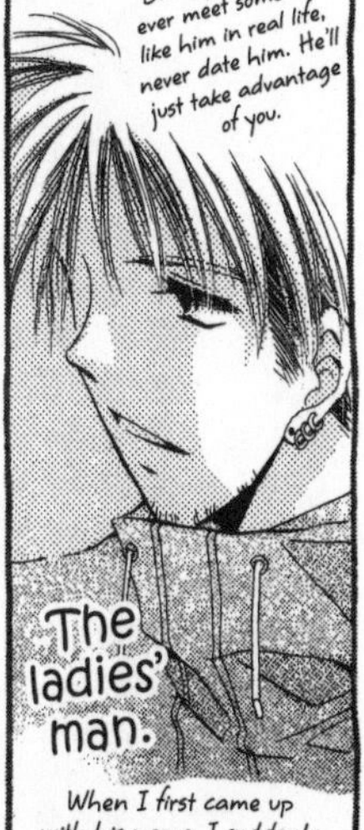
The ladies' man.

When I first came up with his name, I suddenly remembered 99 no Yabecchi, and got a little worried that some people might think I was copying him or something.

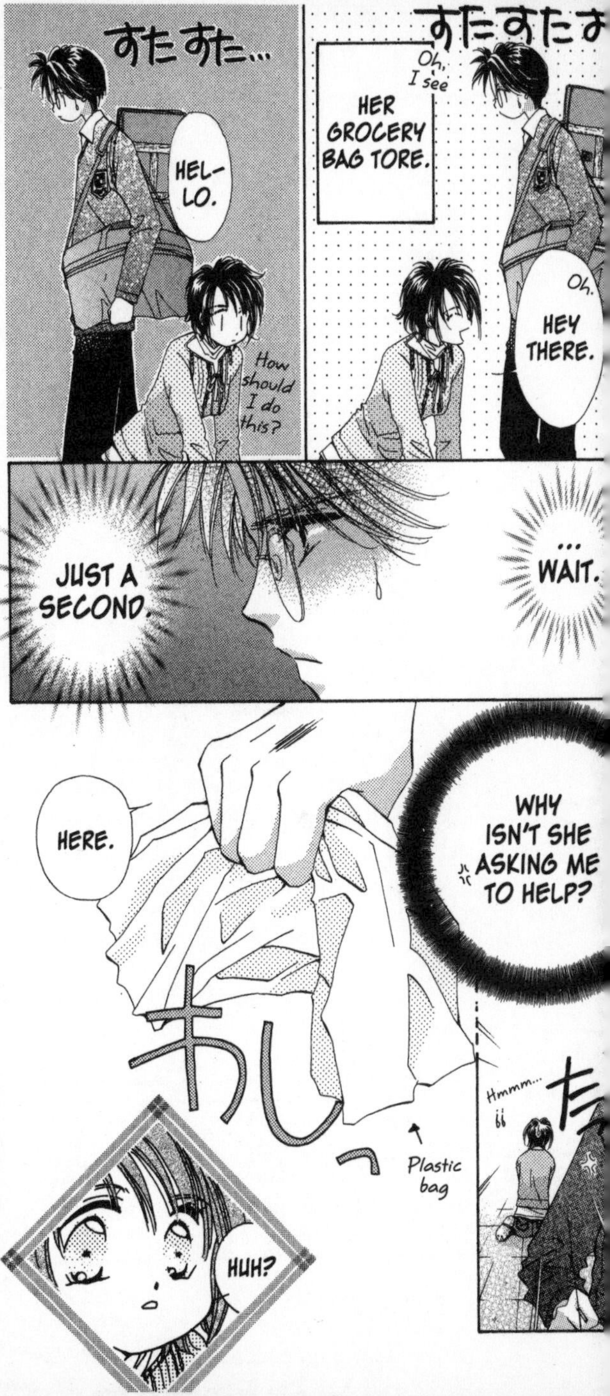
すたすた
Oh, I see
HER GROCERY BAG TORE.
Oh.
HEY THERE.
すたすた...
HEL-LO.
How should I do this?
... WAIT.
JUST A SECOND.
WHY ISN'T SHE ASKING ME TO HELP?
Hmmm...
HERE.
わしっ
Plastic bag
HUH?

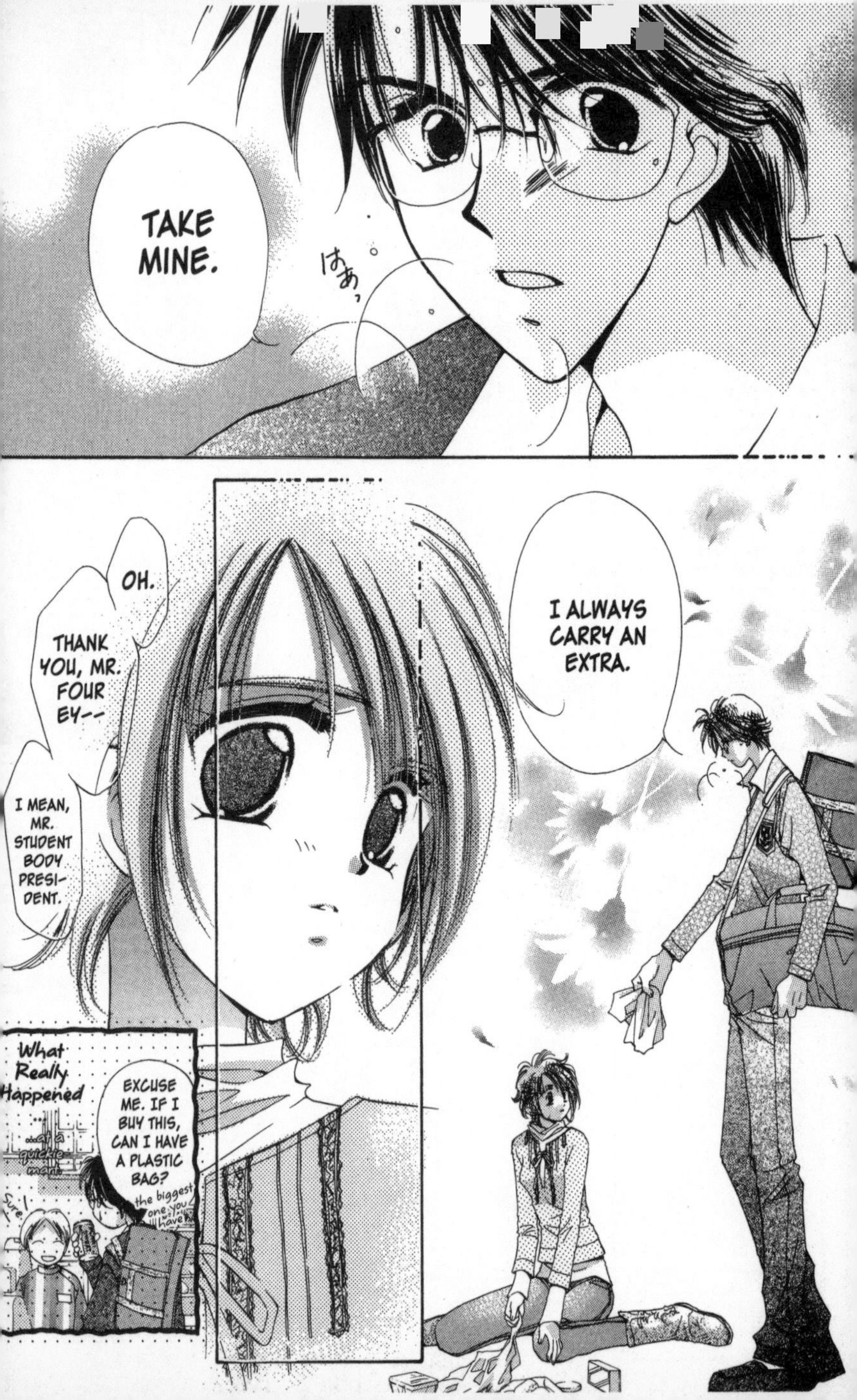

TAKE MINE.
はあ、
I ALWAYS CARRY AN EXTRA.
OH.
THANK YOU, MR. FOUR EY--
I MEAN, MR. STUDENT BODY PRESI-DENT.
What Really Happened
...at a quickie-mart
EXCUSE ME. IF I BUY THIS, CAN I HAVE A PLASTIC BAG?
the biggest one you have
Sure!

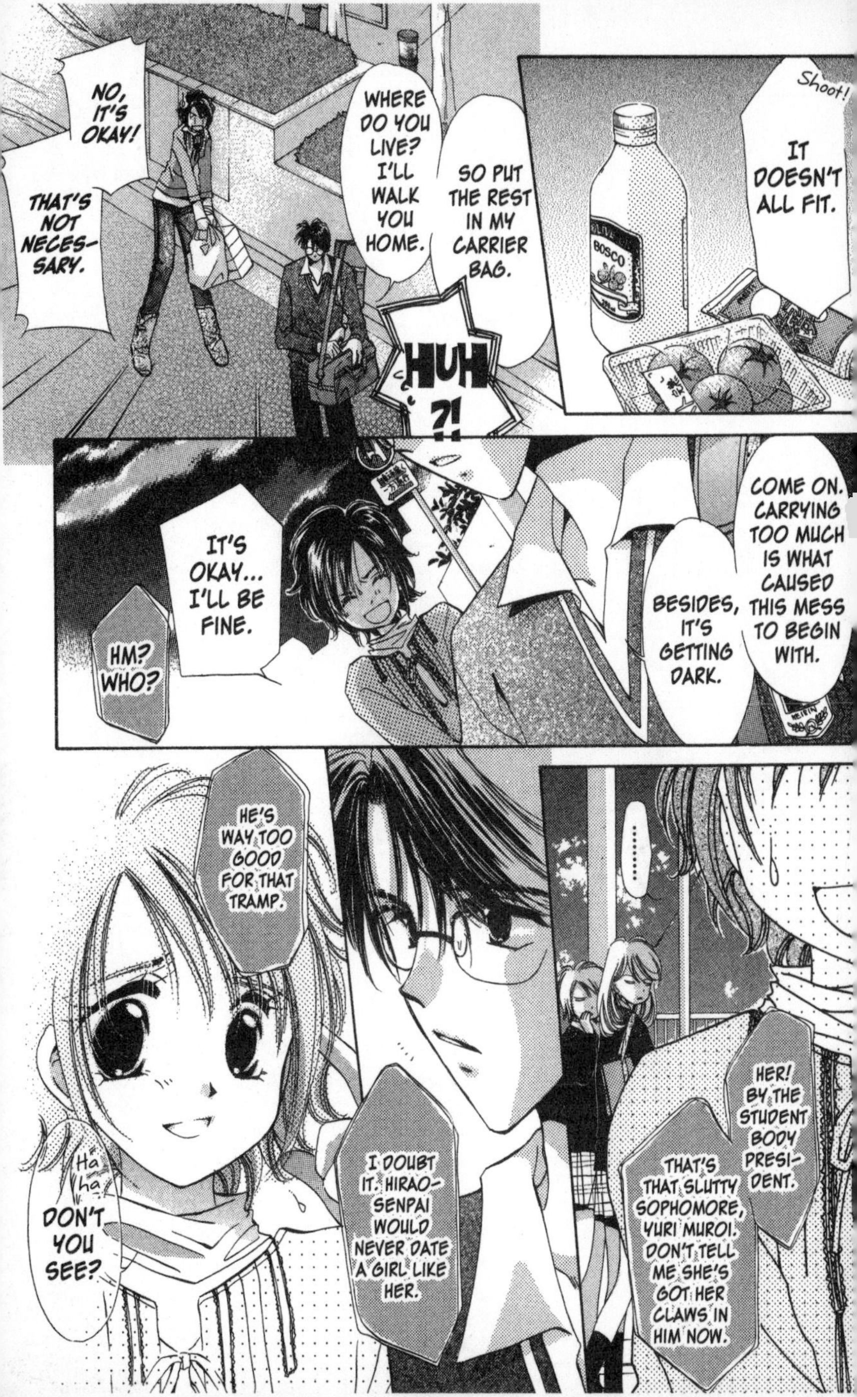
Shoot!
IT DOESN'T ALL FIT.
SO PUT THE REST IN MY CARRIER BAG.
WHERE DO YOU LIVE? I'LL WALK YOU HOME.
HUH ?!
NO, IT'S OKAY!
THAT'S NOT NECES-SARY.
COME ON. CARRYING TOO MUCH IS WHAT CAUSED THIS MESS TO BEGIN WITH.
BESIDES, IT'S GETTING DARK.
IT'S OKAY... I'LL BE FINE.
HM? WHO?
......
HER! BY THE STUDENT BODY PRESI-DENT.
THAT'S THAT SLUTTY SOPHOMORE, YURI MUROI. DON'T TELL ME SHE'S GOT HER CLAWS IN HIM NOW.
I DOUBT IT. HIRAO-SENPAI WOULD NEVER DATE A GIRL LIKE HER.
HE'S WAY TOO GOOD FOR THAT TRAMP.
Ha ha
DON'T YOU SEE?

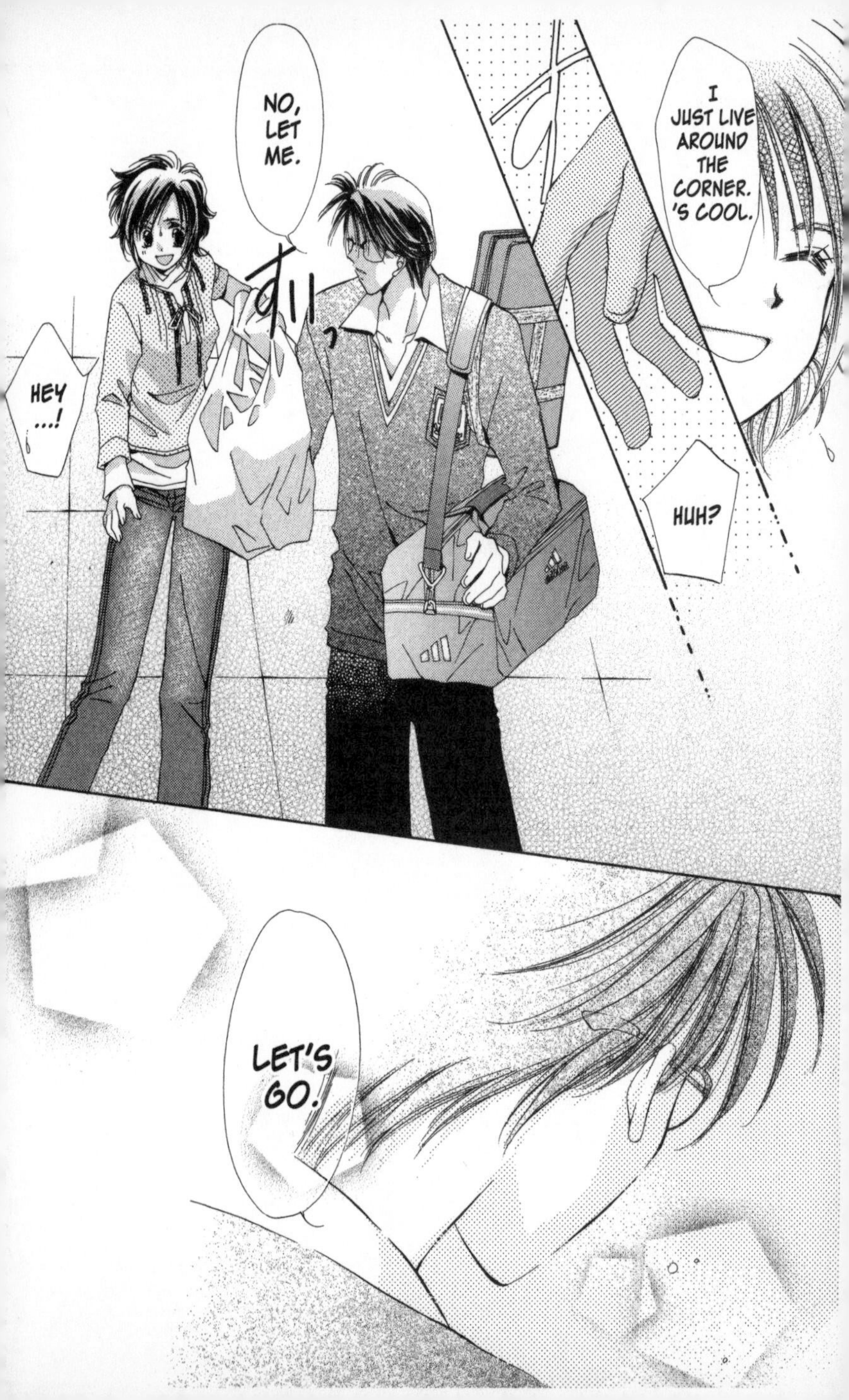
I JUST LIVE AROUND THE CORNER. 'S COOL.
HUH?
NO, LET ME.
すいっ
HEY ...!
LET'S GO.

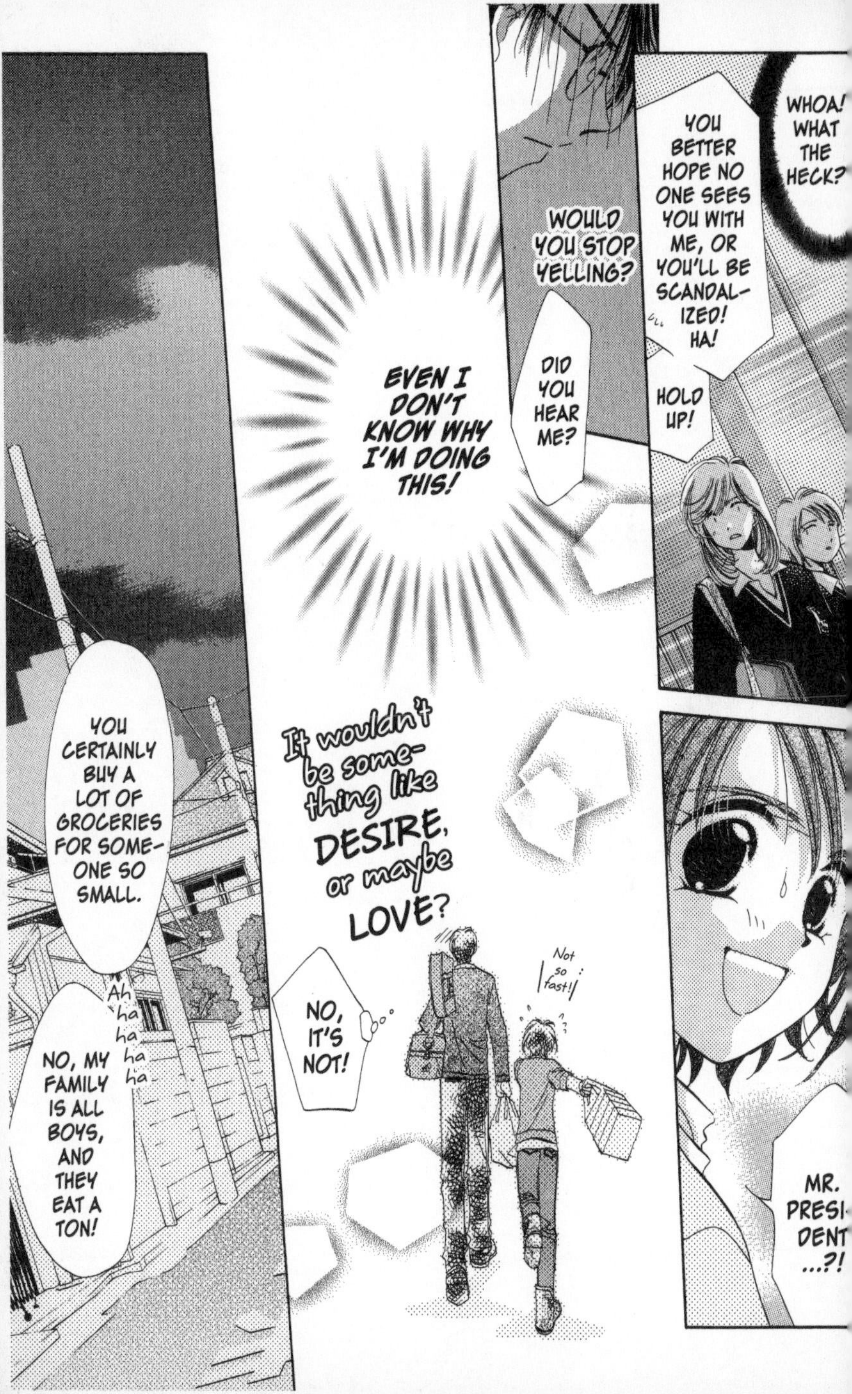
WHOA! WHAT THE HECK?
YOU BETTER HOPE NO ONE SEES YOU WITH ME, OR YOU'LL BE SCANDAL-IZED! HA!
HOLD UP!
MR. PRESI-DENT ...?!
WOULD YOU STOP YELLING?
DID YOU HEAR ME?
EVEN I DON'T KNOW WHY I'M DOING THIS!
It wouldn't be some-thing like DESIRE, or maybe LOVE?
NO, IT'S NOT!
Not so fast!
YOU CERTAINLY BUY A LOT OF GROCERIES FOR SOME-ONE SO SMALL.
Ah ha ha ha ha
NO, MY FAMILY IS ALL BOYS, AND THEY EAT A TON!

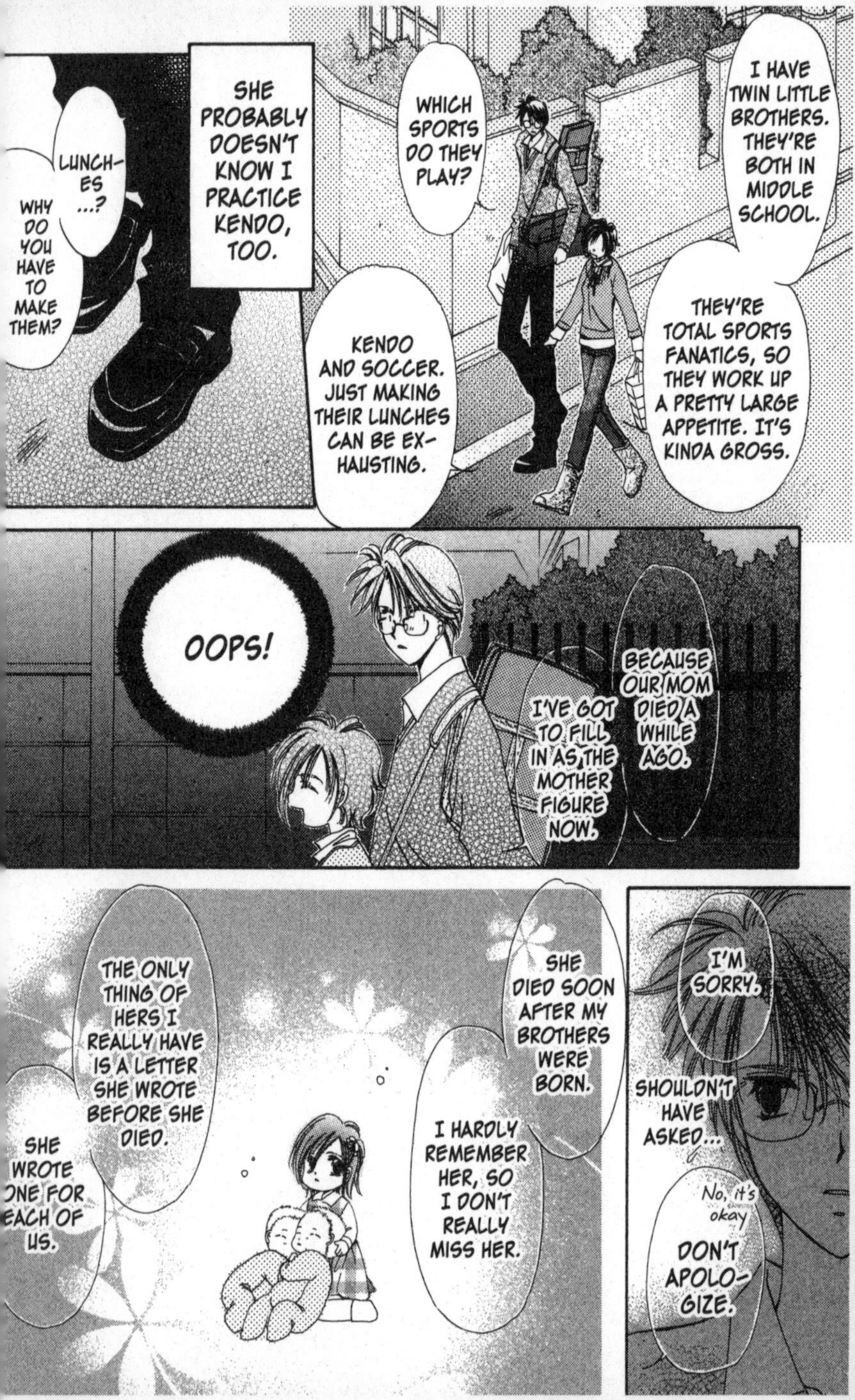
I HAVE TWIN LITTLE BROTHERS. THEY'RE BOTH IN MIDDLE SCHOOL.
THEY'RE TOTAL SPORTS FANATICS, SO THEY WORK UP A PRETTY LARGE APPETITE. IT'S KINDA GROSS.
WHICH SPORTS DO THEY PLAY?
KENDO AND SOCCER. JUST MAKING THEIR LUNCHES CAN BE EX-HAUSTING.
SHE PROBABLY DOESN'T KNOW I PRACTICE KENDO, TOO.
LUNCH-ES ...?
WHY DO YOU HAVE TO MAKE THEM?
BECAUSE OUR MOM DIED A WHILE AGO.
I'VE GOT TO FILL IN AS THE MOTHER FIGURE NOW.
OOPS!
I'M SORRY.
SHOULDN'T HAVE ASKED...
No, it's okay
DON'T APOLO-GIZE.
SHE DIED SOON AFTER MY BROTHERS WERE BORN.
I HARDLY REMEMBER HER, SO I DON'T REALLY MISS HER.
THE ONLY THING OF HERS I REALLY HAVE IS A LETTER SHE WROTE BEFORE SHE DIED.
SHE WROTE ONE FOR EACH OF US.

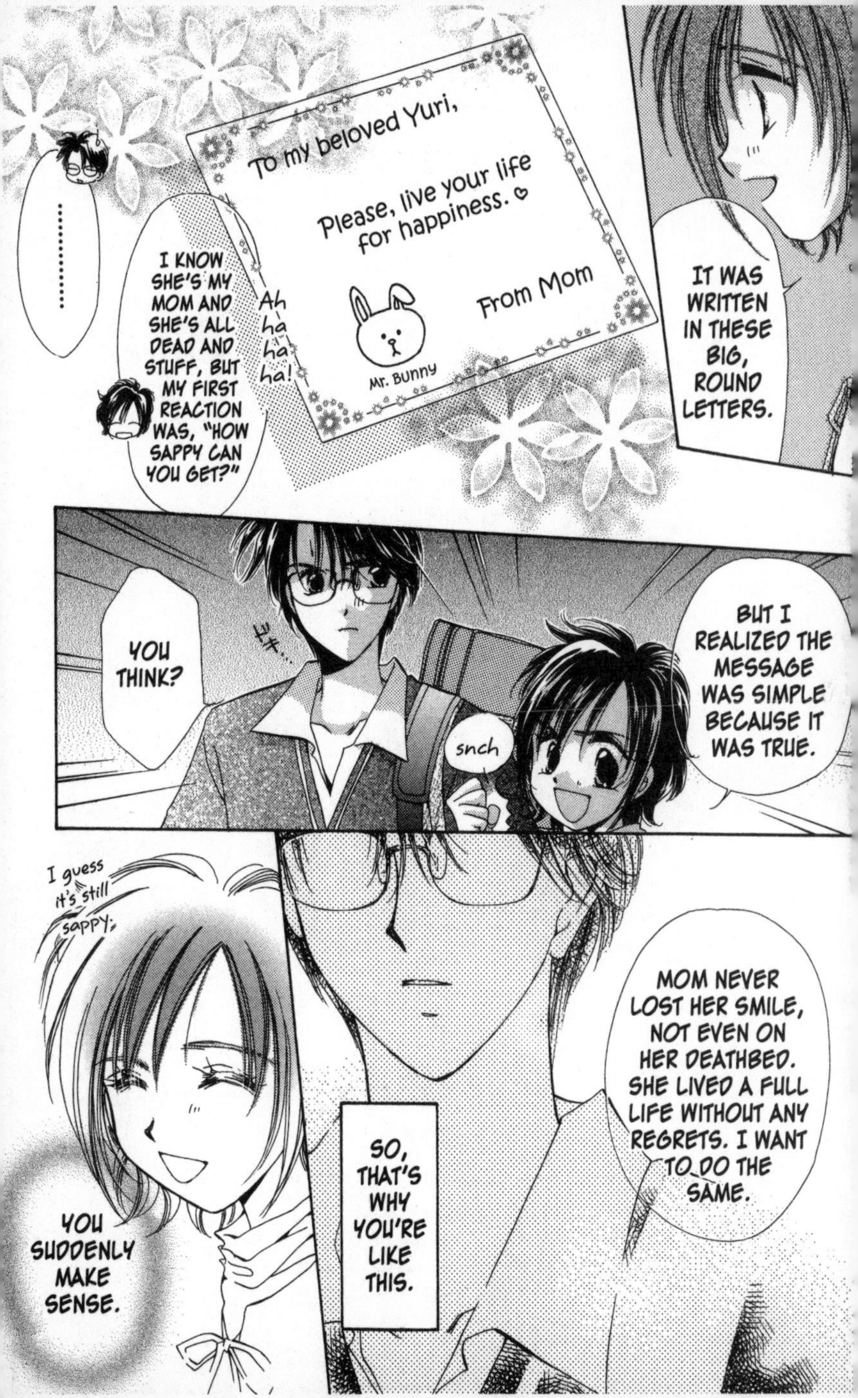
IT WAS WRITTEN IN THESE BIG, ROUND LETTERS.
To my beloved Yuri,
Please, live your life for happiness.
From Mom
Mr. Bunny
I KNOW SHE'S MY MOM AND SHE'S ALL DEAD AND STUFF, BUT MY FIRST REACTION WAS, "HOW SAPPY CAN YOU GET?"
Ah ha ha ha!
....
BUT I REALIZED THE MESSAGE WAS SIMPLE BECAUSE IT WAS TRUE.
snch
YOU THINK?
MOM NEVER LOST HER SMILE, NOT EVEN ON HER DEATHBED. SHE LIVED A FULL LIFE WITHOUT ANY REGRETS. I WANT TO DO THE SAME.
SO, THAT'S WHY YOU'RE LIKE THIS.
I guess it's still sappy.
YOU SUDDENLY MAKE SENSE.

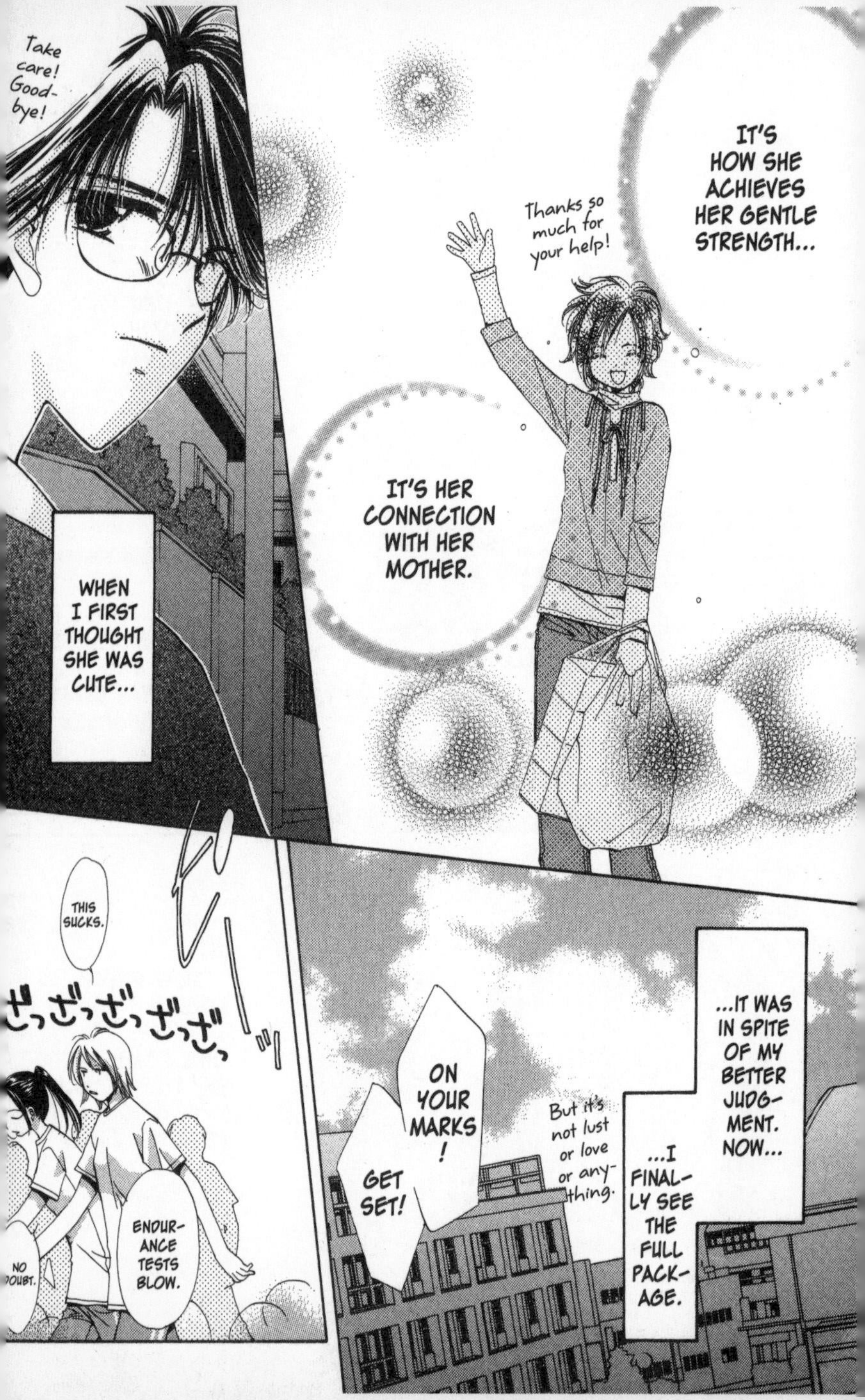
IT'S HOW SHE ACHIEVES HER GENTLE STRENGTH...
Thanks so much for your help!
IT'S HER CONNECTION WITH HER MOTHER.
Take care! Good-bye!
WHEN I FIRST THOUGHT SHE WAS CUTE...
...IT WAS IN SPITE OF MY BETTER JUDGMENT. NOW...
...I FINALLY SEE THE FULL PACKAGE.
But it's not lust or love or anything.
ON YOUR MARKS!
GET SET!
THIS SUCKS.
ざっざっざっざっ
ENDURANCE TESTS BLOW.
NO DOUBT.

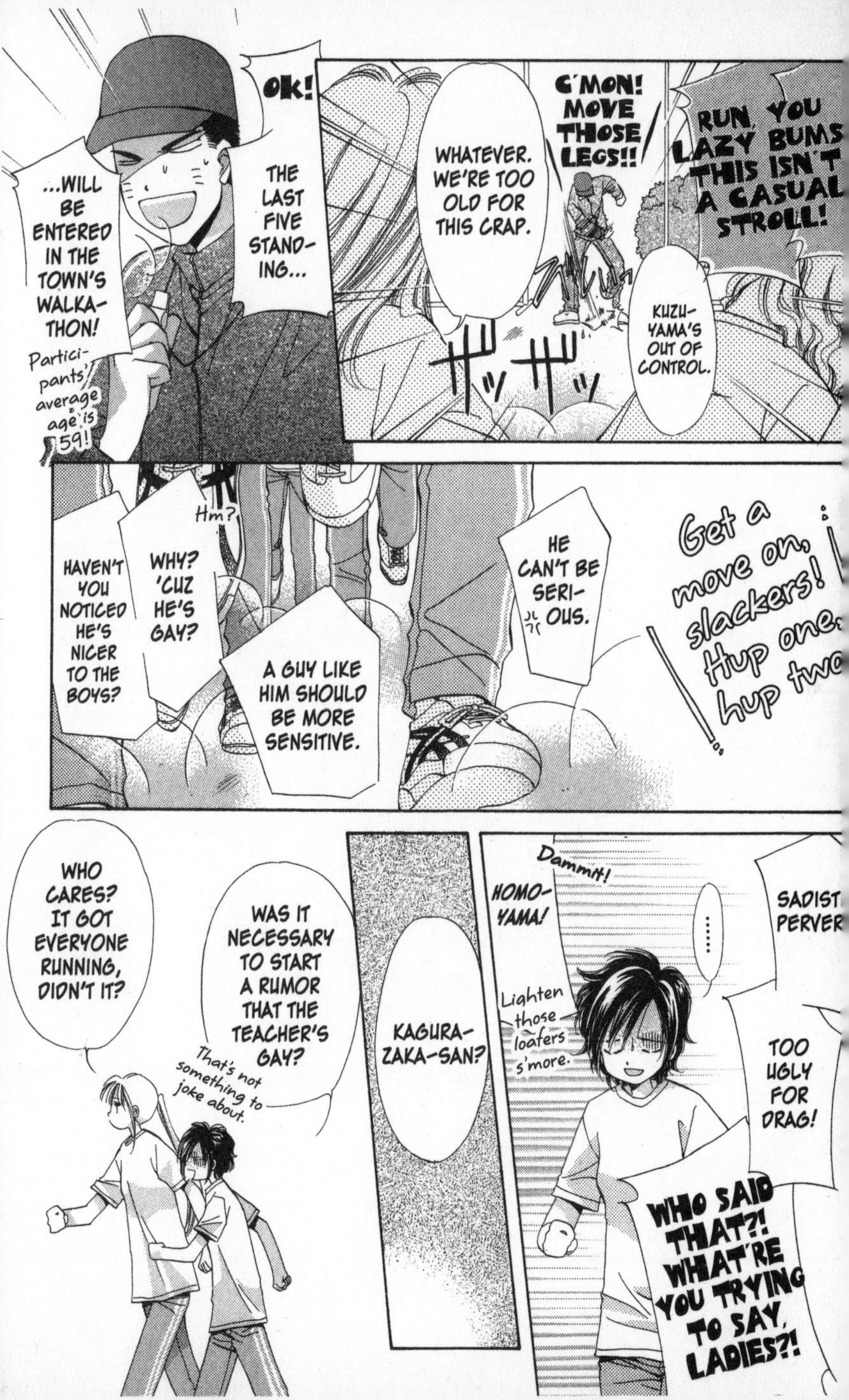
RUN YOU LAZY BUMS THIS ISN'T A CASUAL STROLL!
C'MON! MOVE THOSE LEGS!!
KUZUYAMA'S OUT OF CONTROL.
WHATEVER. WE'RE TOO OLD FOR THIS CRAP.
OK!
THE LAST FIVE STANDING...
...WILL BE ENTERED IN THE TOWN'S WALKATHON!
Participants' average age is 59!
Get a move on, slackers! Hup one, hup two
HE CAN'T BE SERIOUS.
A GUY LIKE HIM SHOULD BE MORE SENSITIVE.
Hm?
WHY? 'CUZ HE'S GAY?
HAVEN'T YOU NOTICED HE'S NICER TO THE BOYS?
SADIST PERVER
TOO UGLY FOR DRAG!
WHO SAID THAT?! WHAT'RE YOU TRYING TO SAY, LADIES?!
......
Dammit!
HOMOYAMA!
Lighten those loafers s'more.
KAGURAZAKA-SAN?
WAS IT NECESSARY TO START A RUMOR THAT THE TEACHER'S GAY?
WHO CARES? IT GOT EVERYONE RUNNING, DIDN'T IT?
That's not something to joke about.

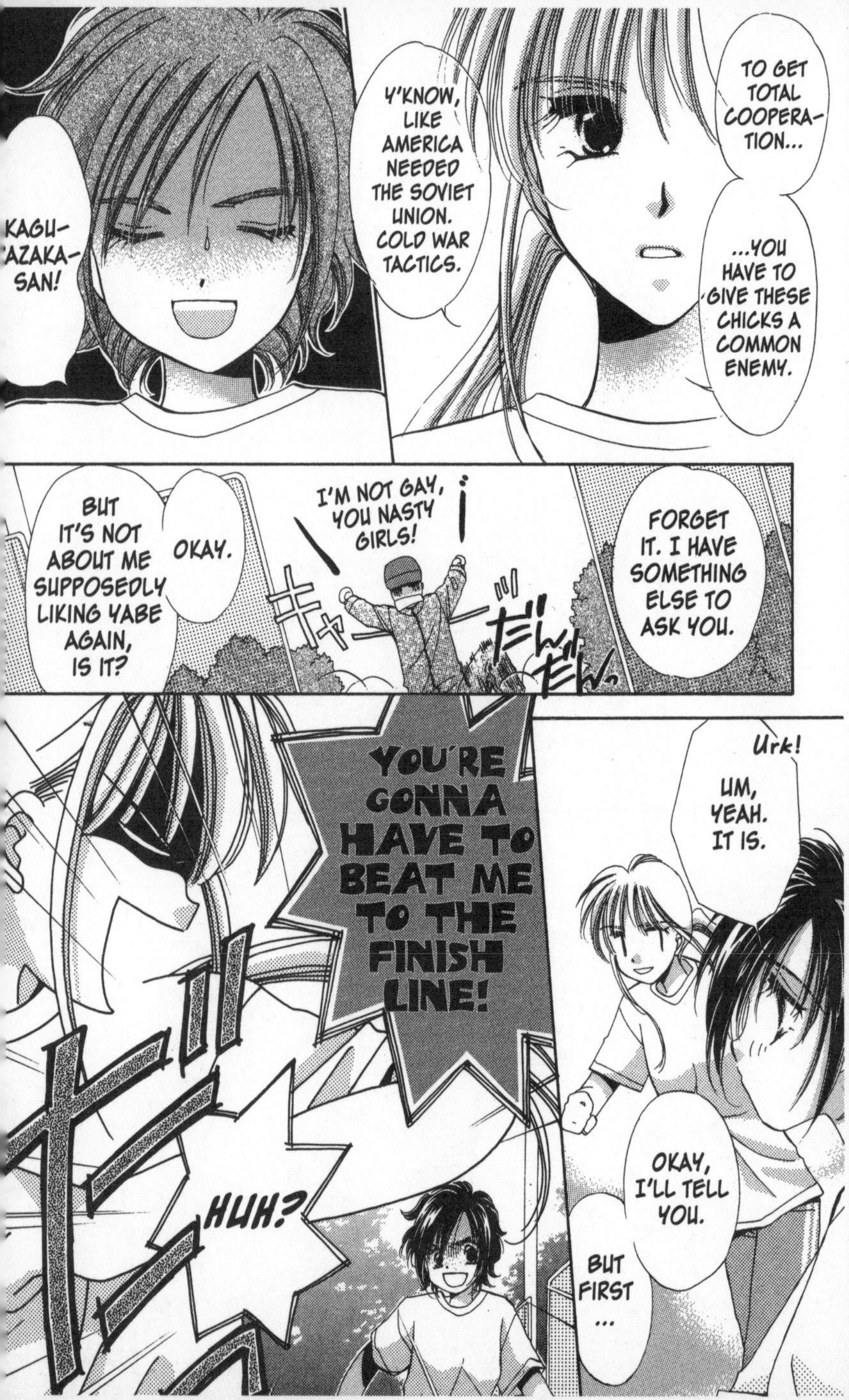
TO GET TOTAL COOPERA-TION...
...YOU HAVE TO GIVE THESE CHICKS A COMMON ENEMY.
Y'KNOW, LIKE AMERICA NEEDED THE SOVIET UNION. COLD WAR TACTICS.
KAGU- AZAKA- SAN!
FORGET IT. I HAVE SOMETHING ELSE TO ASK YOU.
だん だん
I'M NOT GAY, YOU NASTY GIRLS!
キャー
OKAY.
BUT IT'S NOT ABOUT ME SUPPOSEDLY LIKING YABE AGAIN, IS IT?
Urk!
UM, YEAH. IT IS.
OKAY, I'LL TELL YOU.
BUT FIRST ...
YOU'RE GONNA HAVE TO BEAT ME TO THE FINISH LINE!
HUH?

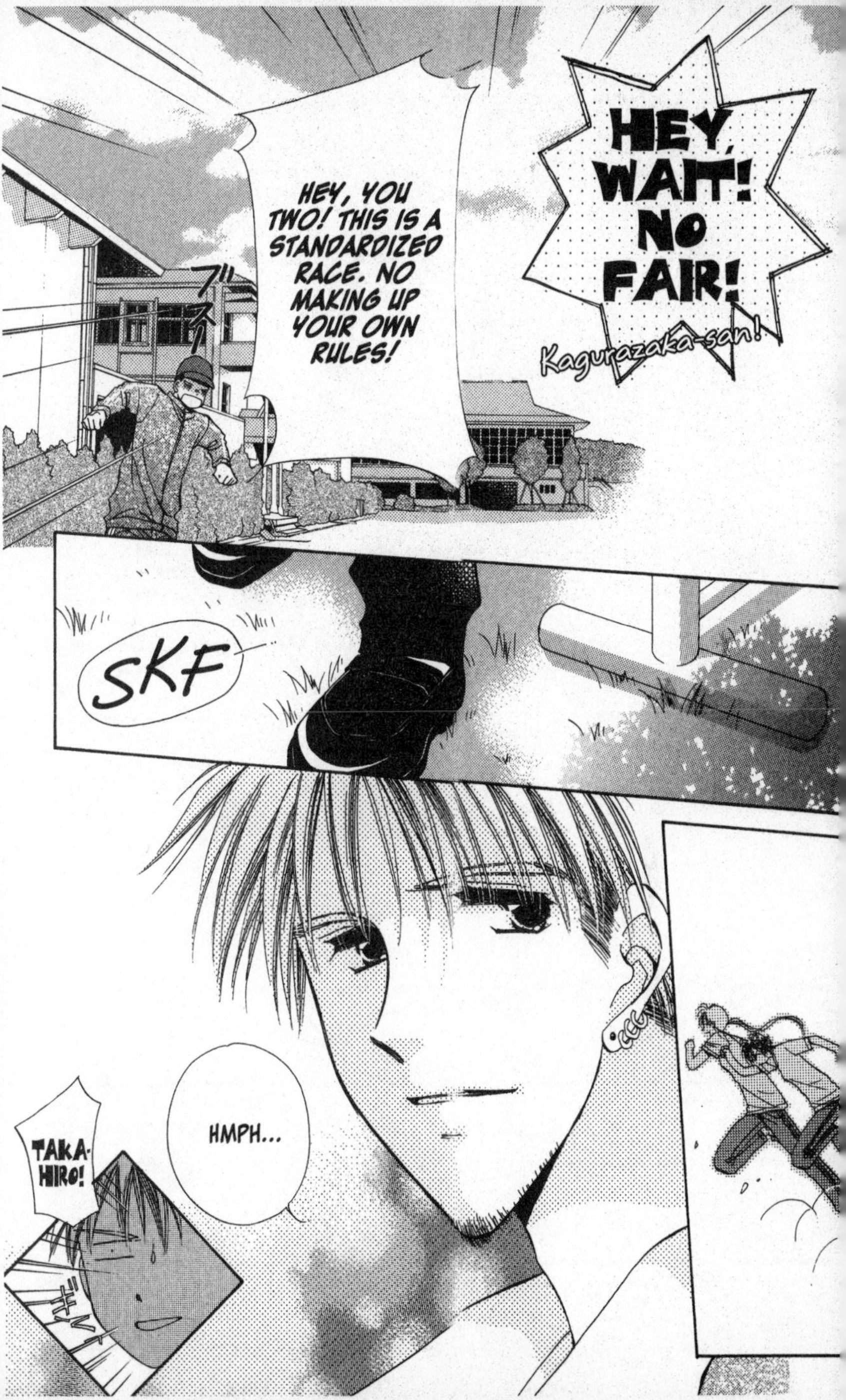
HEY, WAIT! NO FAIR!
Kagurazaka-san!
HEY, YOU TWO! THIS IS A STANDARDIZED RACE. NO MAKING UP YOUR OWN RULES!
SKF
HMPH...
TAKA-HIRO!

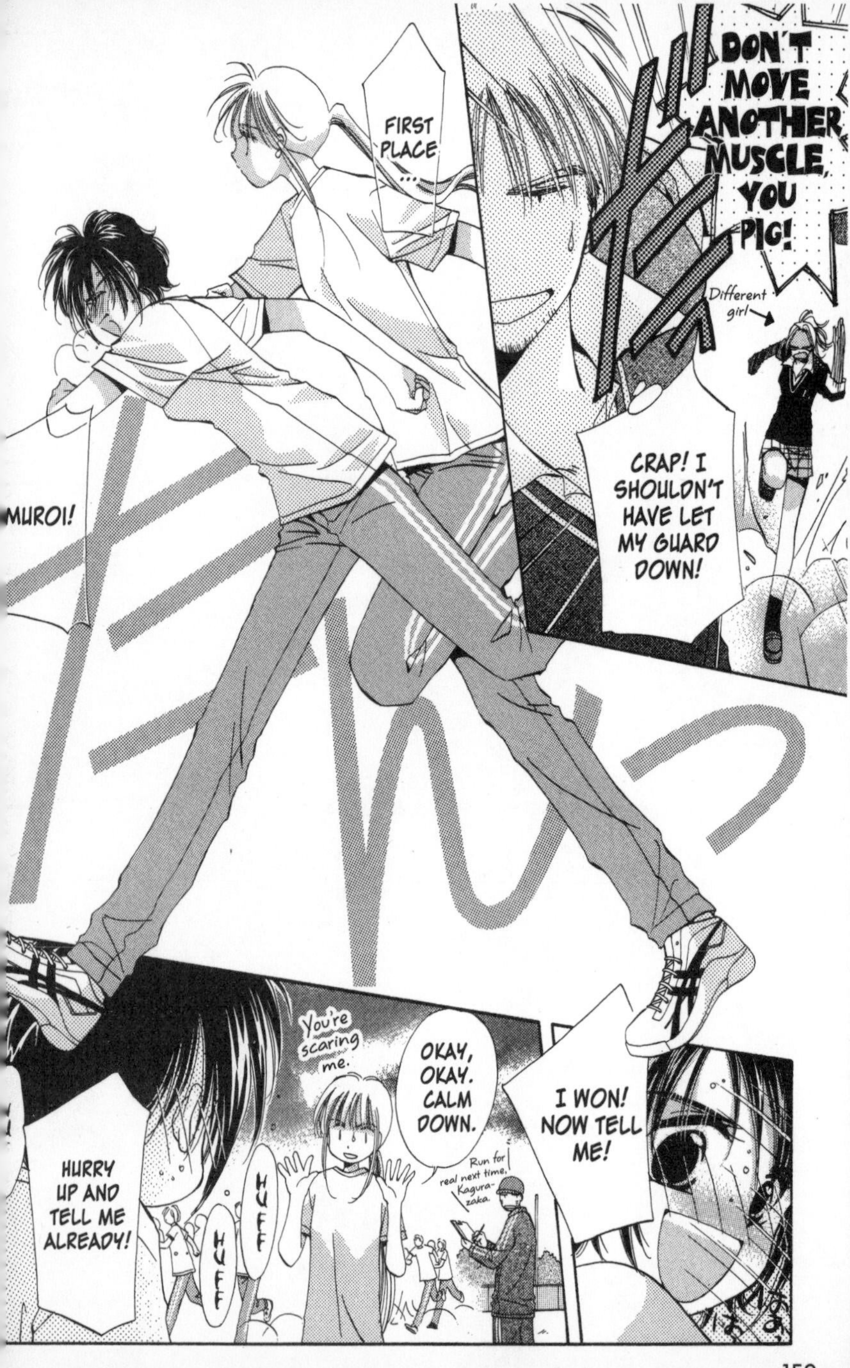
DON'T MOVE ANOTHER MUSCLE, YOU PIG!
Different girl
CRAP! I SHOULDN'T HAVE LET MY GUARD DOWN!
FIRST PLACE...
MUROI!
I WON! NOW TELL ME!
OKAY, OKAY. CALM DOWN.
You're scaring me.
Run for real next time, Kagura-zaka.
HUFF
HUFF
HURRY UP AND TELL ME ALREADY!

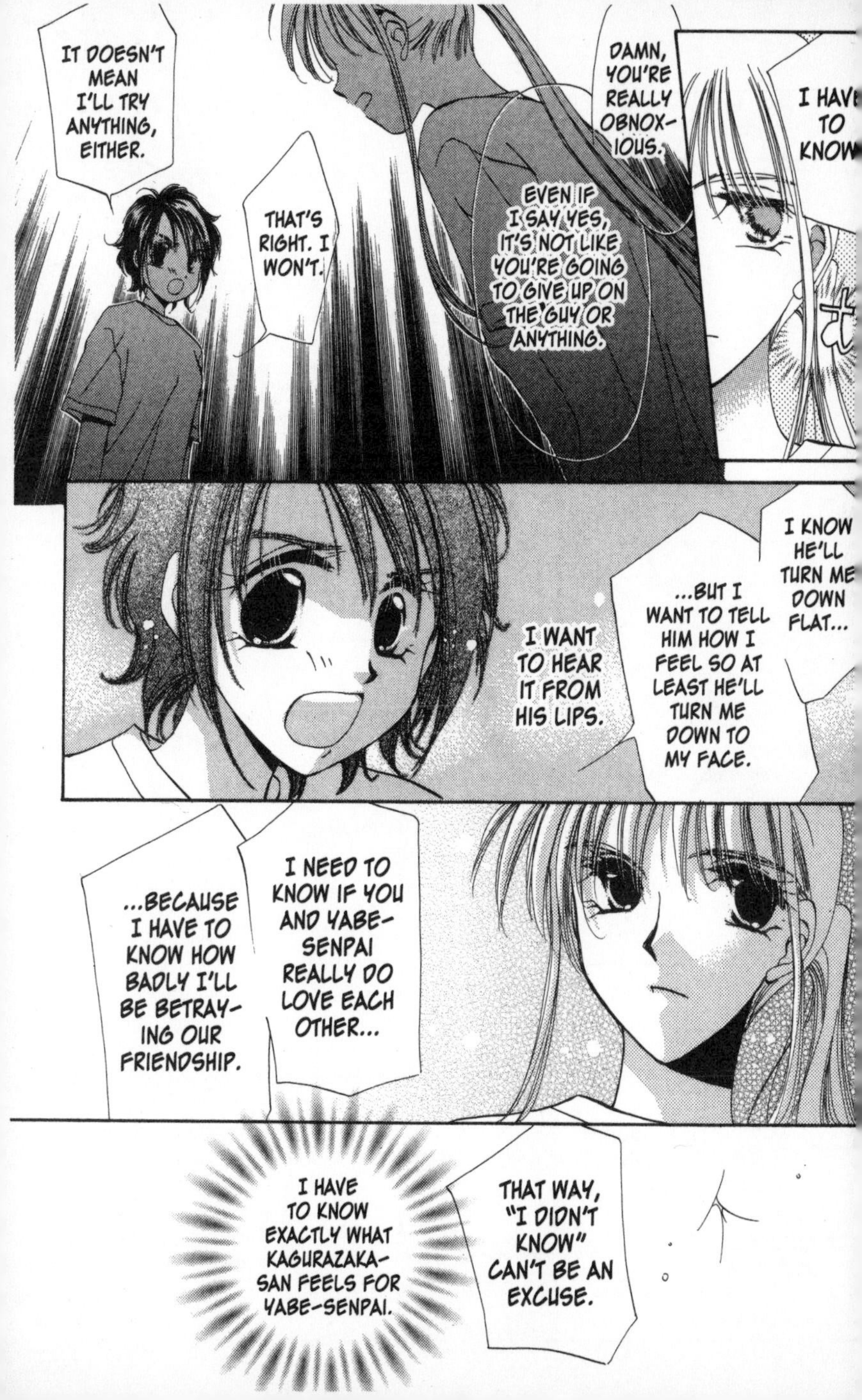
I HAVE TO KNOW
DAMN, YOU'RE REALLY OBNOXIOUS.
EVEN IF I SAY YES, IT'S NOT LIKE YOU'RE GOING TO GIVE UP ON THE GUY OR ANYTHING.
IT DOESN'T MEAN I'LL TRY ANYTHING, EITHER.
THAT'S RIGHT. I WON'T.
I KNOW HE'LL TURN ME DOWN FLAT...
...BUT I WANT TO TELL HIM HOW I FEEL SO AT LEAST HE'LL TURN ME DOWN TO MY FACE.
I WANT TO HEAR IT FROM HIS LIPS.
I NEED TO KNOW IF YOU AND YABE-SENPAI REALLY DO LOVE EACH OTHER...
...BECAUSE I HAVE TO KNOW HOW BADLY I'LL BE BETRAYING OUR FRIENDSHIP.
THAT WAY, "I DIDN'T KNOW" CAN'T BE AN EXCUSE.
I HAVE TO KNOW EXACTLY WHAT KAGURAZAKA-SAN FEELS FOR YABE-SENPAI.

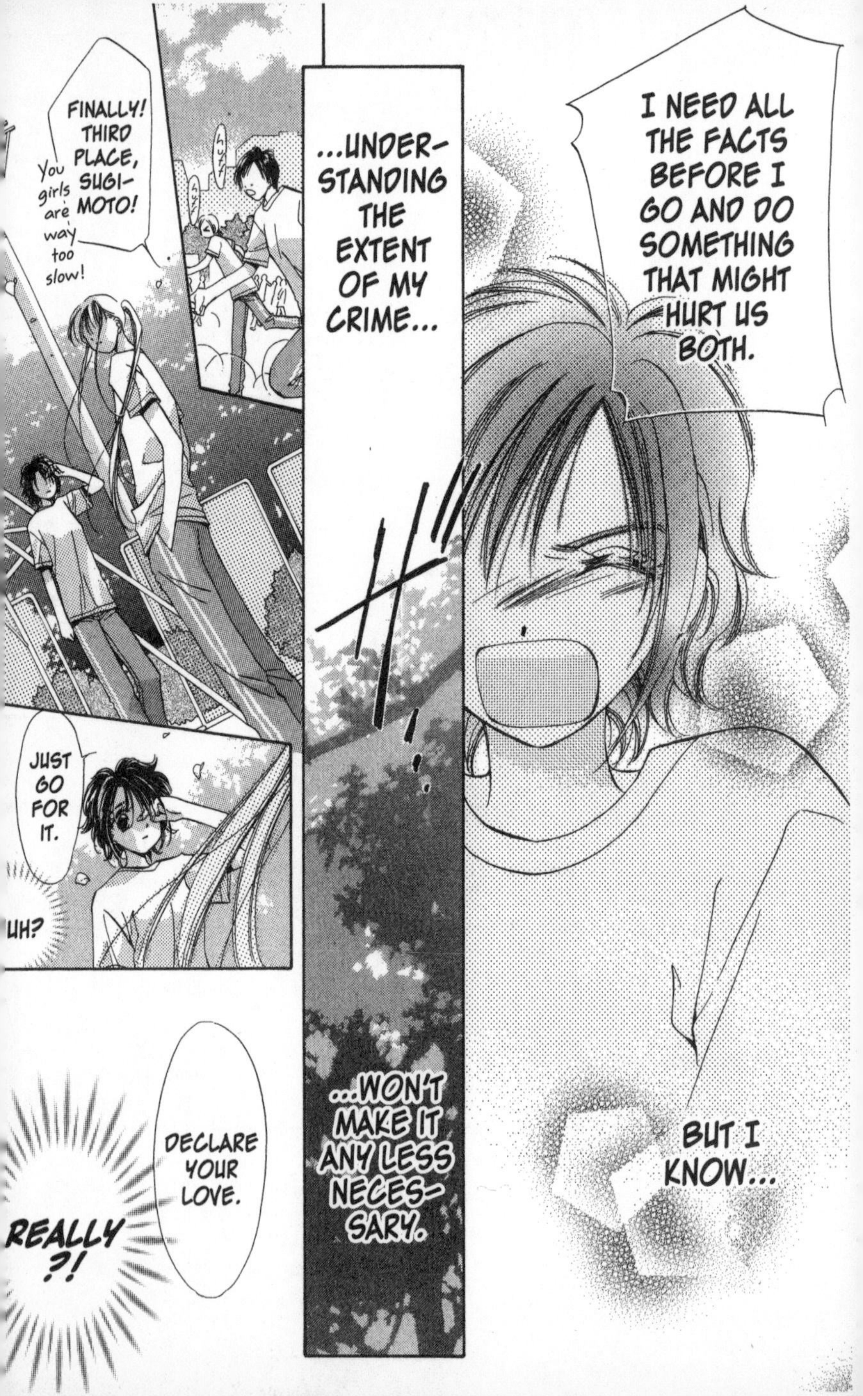

I NEED ALL THE FACTS BEFORE I GO AND DO SOMETHING THAT MIGHT HURT US BOTH.
BUT I KNOW...
...UNDER-STANDING THE EXTENT OF MY CRIME...
...WON'T MAKE IT ANY LESS NECES-SARY.
FINALLY! THIRD PLACE, SUGI-MOTO!
You girls are way too slow!
JUST GO FOR IT.
UH?
DECLARE YOUR LOVE.
REALLY ?!

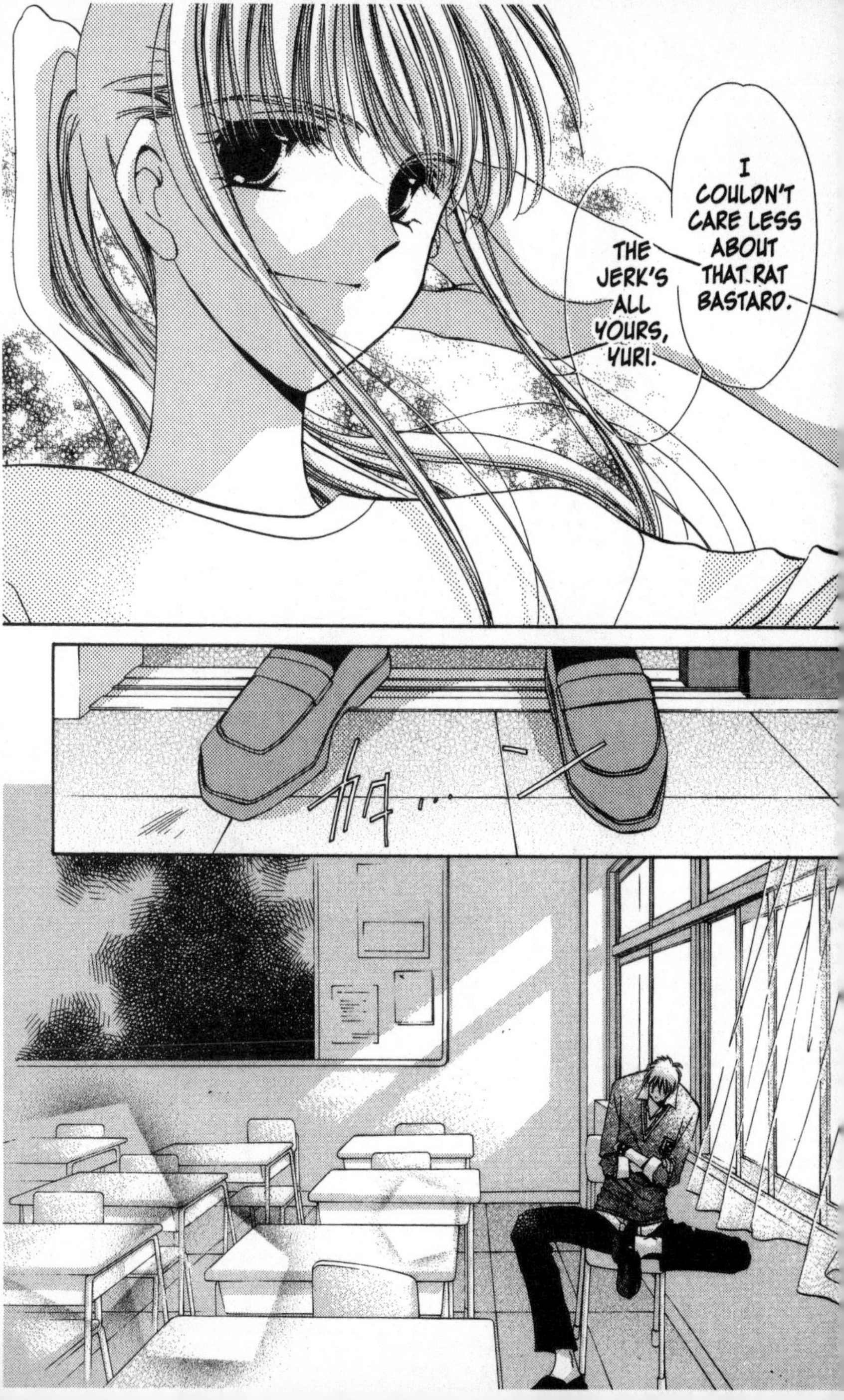
I COULDN'T CARE LESS ABOUT THAT RAT BASTARD.
THE JERK'S ALL YOURS, YURI.
カタ...

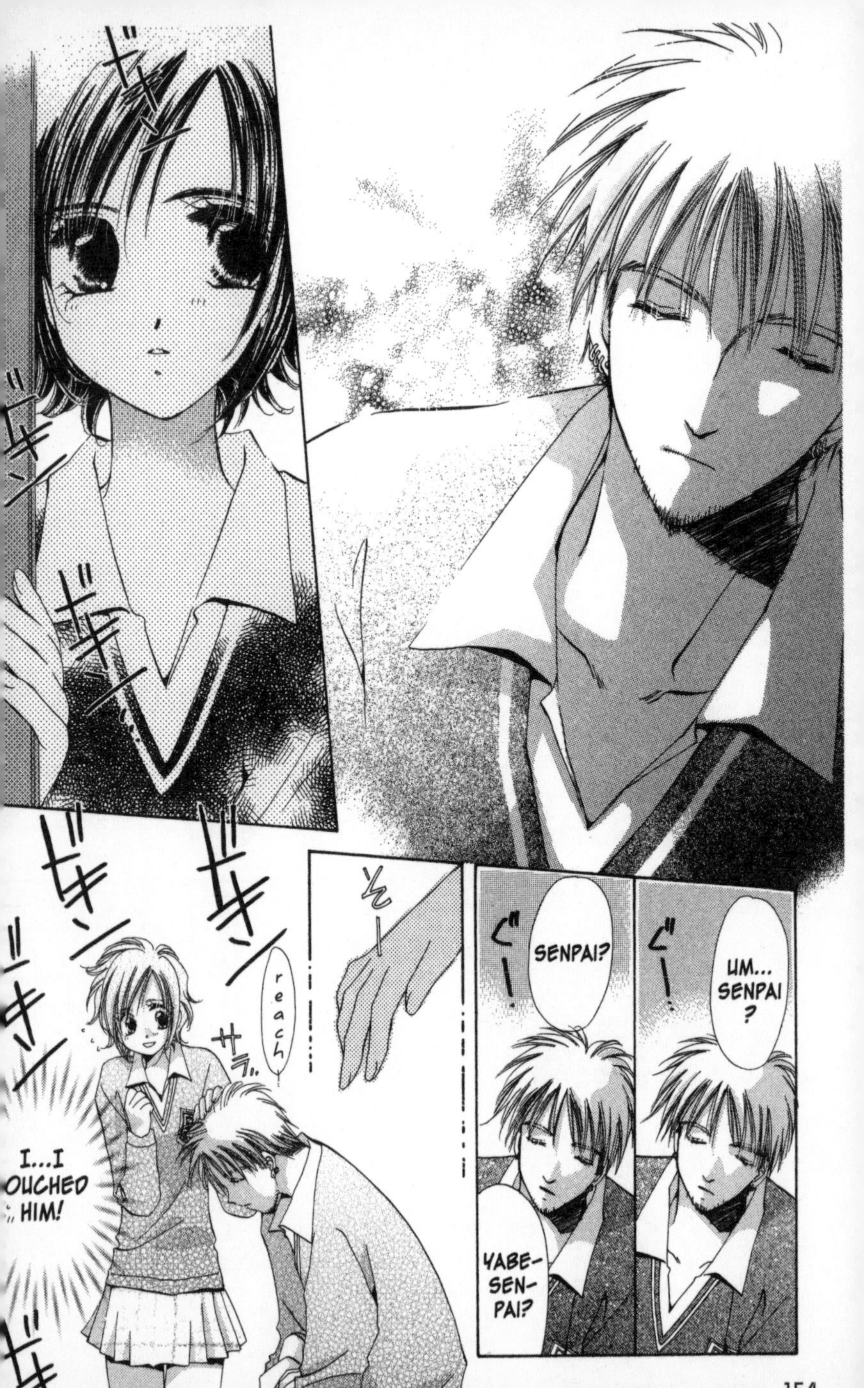
UM... SENPAI?
SENPAI?
YABE-SENPAI?
reach
I...I OUCHED HIM!

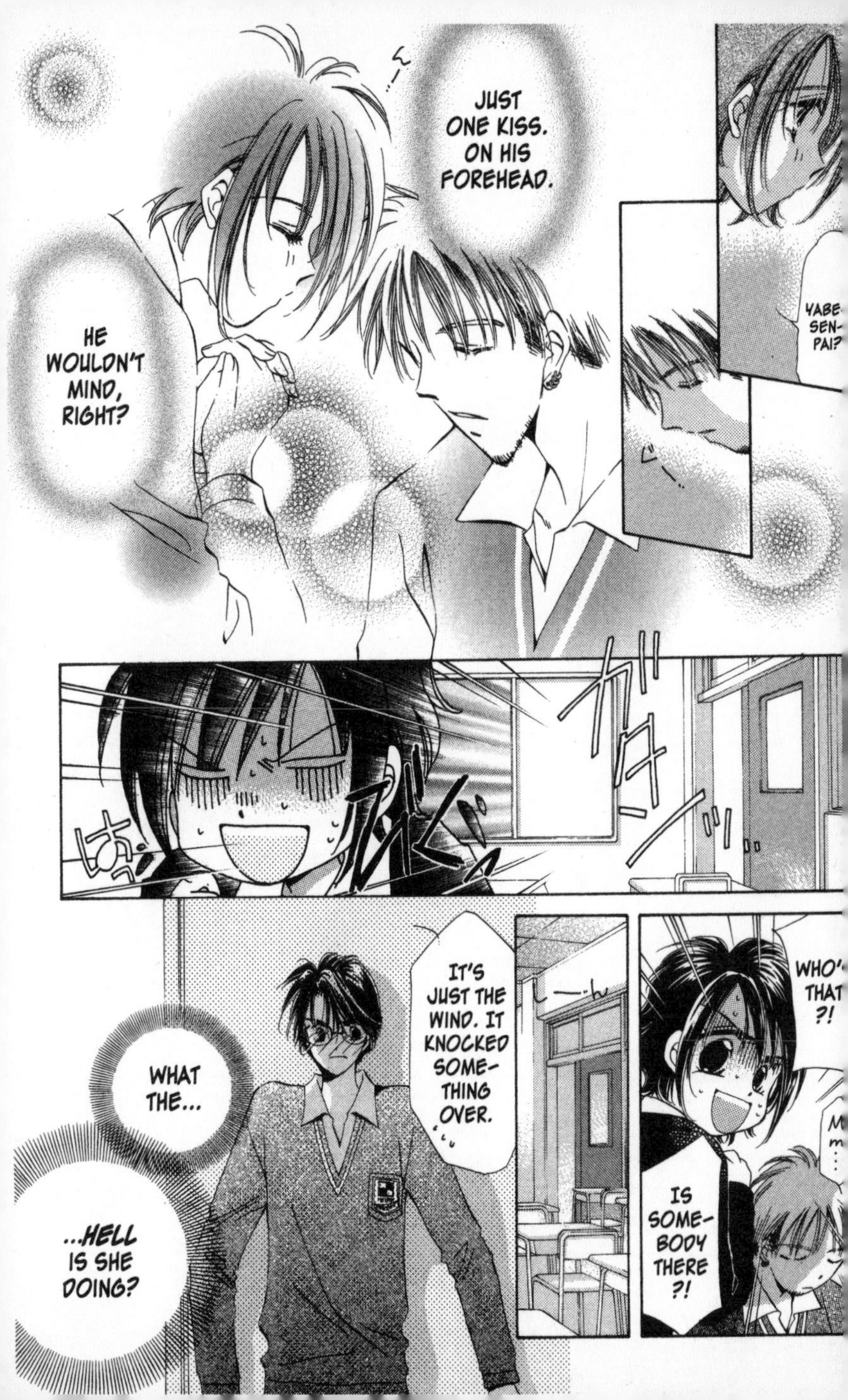
YABE-SENPAI?
JUST ONE KISS. ON HIS FOREHEAD.
HE WOULDN'T MIND, RIGHT?
WHO' THAT?!
IS SOMEBODY THERE?!
IT'S JUST THE WIND. IT KNOCKED SOMETHING OVER.
WHAT THE...
...HELL IS SHE DOING?

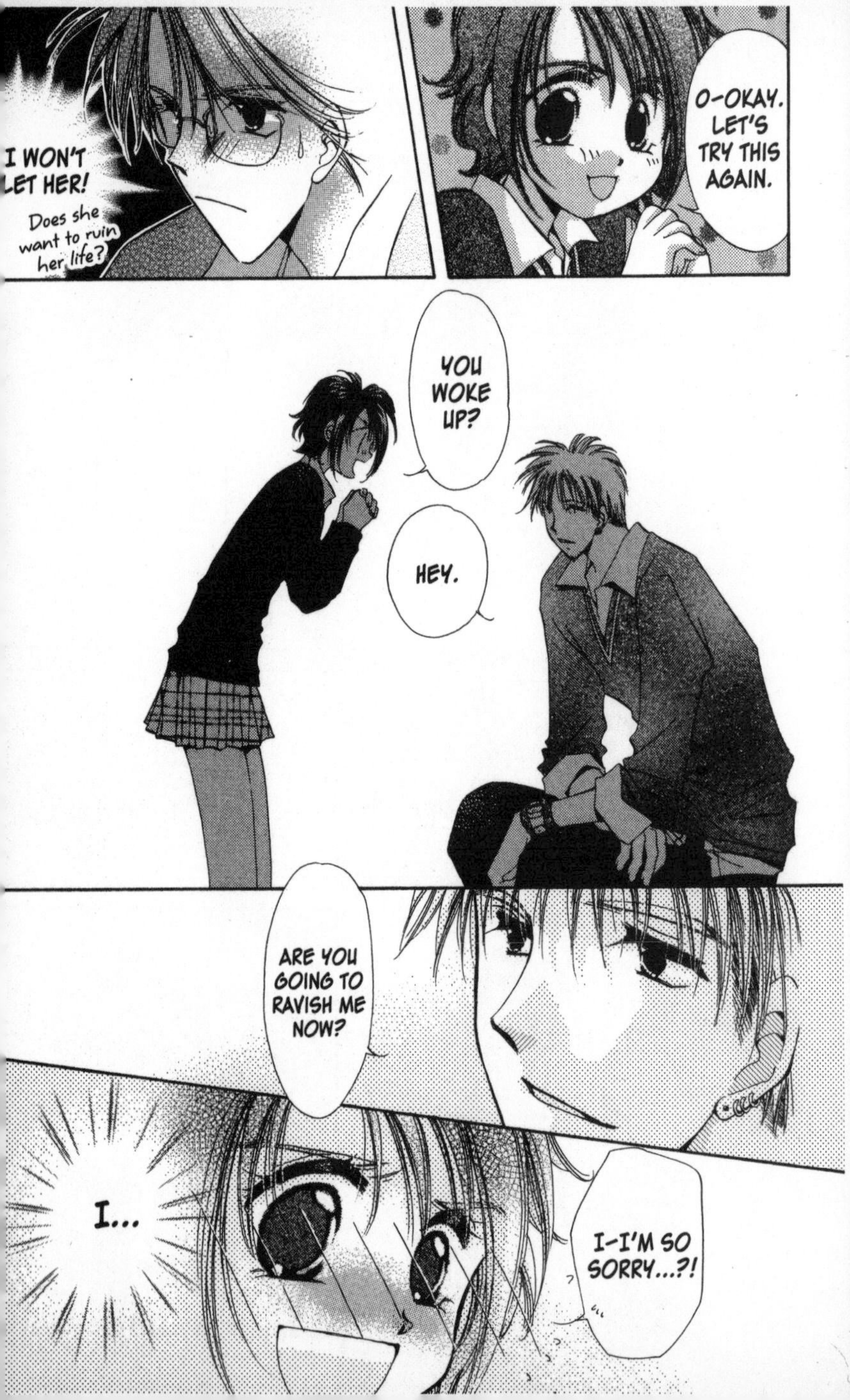
O-OKAY. LET'S TRY THIS AGAIN.
I WON'T LET HER!
Does she want to ruin her life?
YOU WOKE UP?
HEY.
ARE YOU GOING TO RAVISH ME NOW?
I-I'M SO SORRY...?!
I...

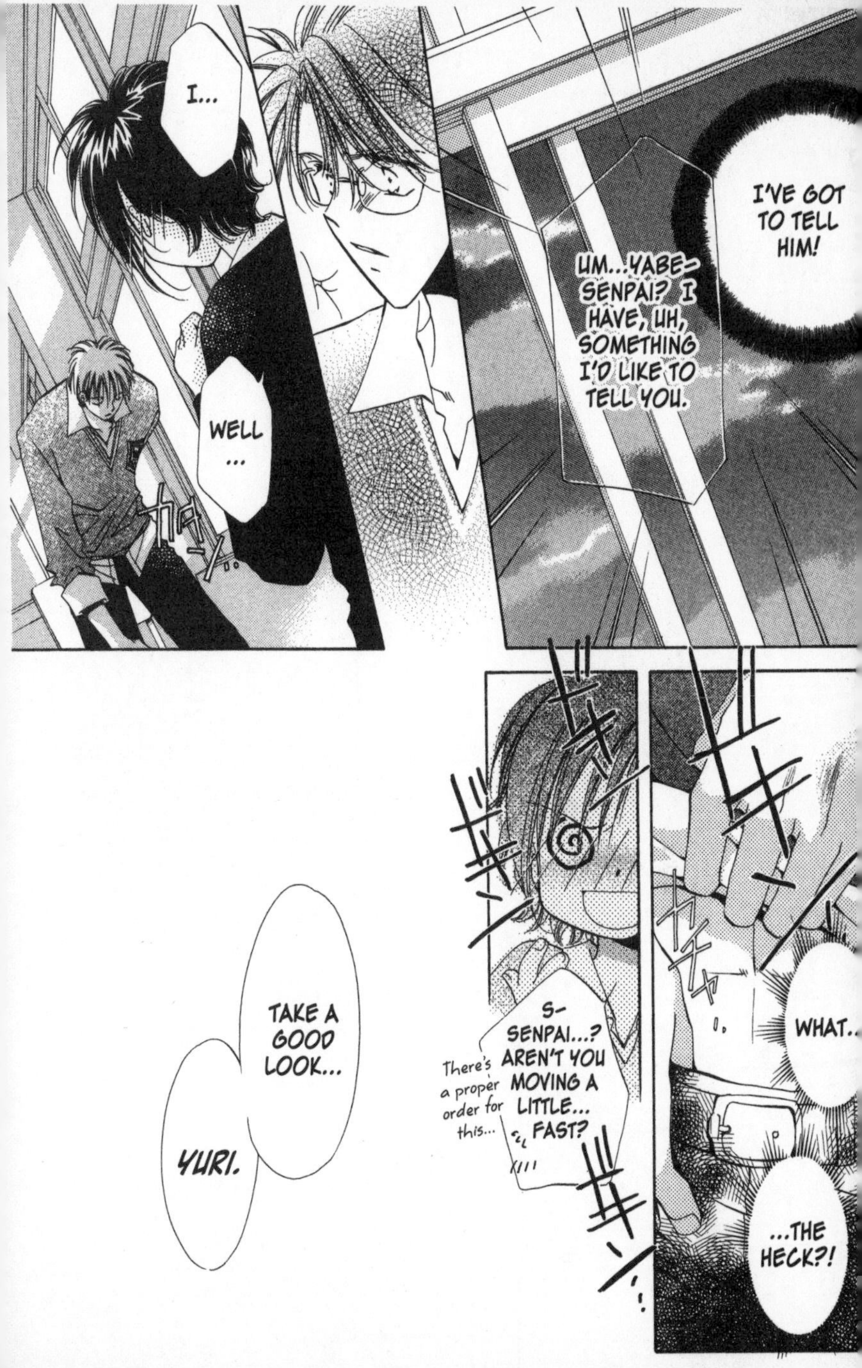
I'VE GOT TO TELL HIM!
UM...YABE-SENPAI? I HAVE, UH, SOMETHING I'D LIKE TO TELL YOU.
I...
WELL ...
WHAT...
...THE HECK?!
S-SENPAI...? AREN'T YOU MOVING A LITTLE... FAST?
There's a proper order for this...
TAKE A GOOD LOOK...
YURI.

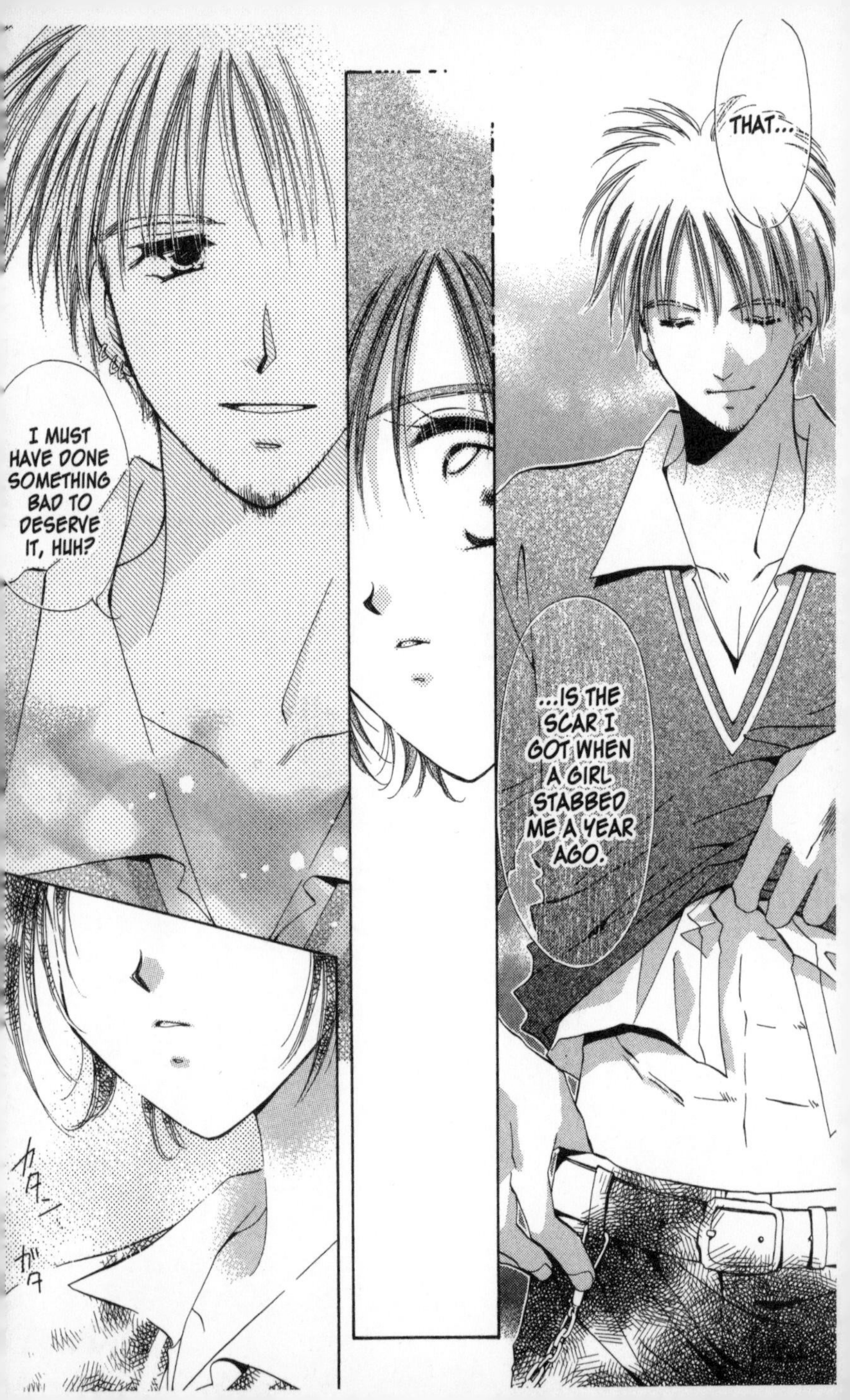
THAT...
...IS THE SCAR I GOT WHEN A GIRL STABBED ME A YEAR AGO.
I MUST HAVE DONE SOMETHING BAD TO DESERVE IT, HUH?

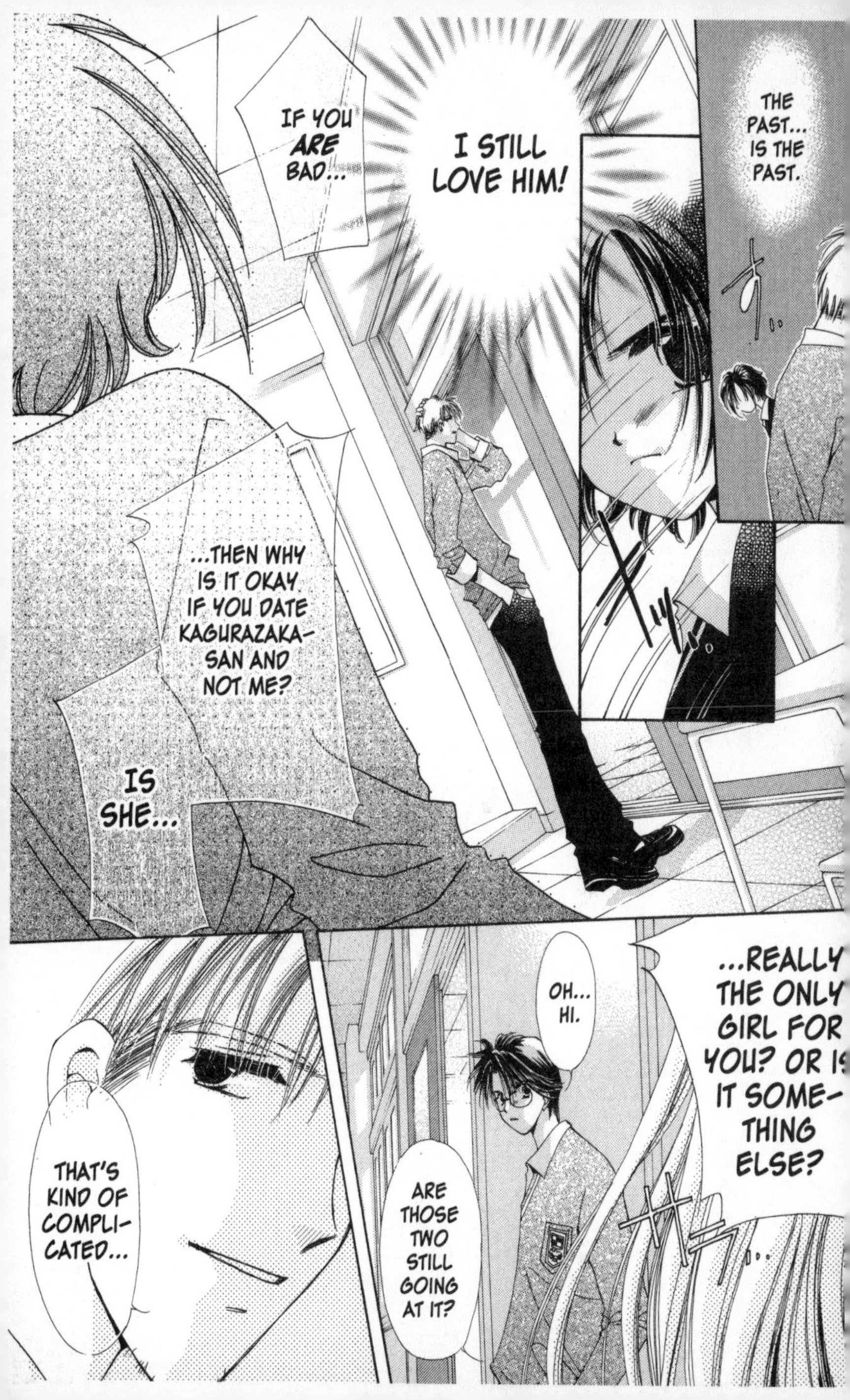
THE PAST... IS THE PAST.
I STILL LOVE HIM!
IF YOU ARE BAD...
...THEN WHY IS IT OKAY IF YOU DATE KAGURAZAKA-SAN AND NOT ME?
IS SHE...
...REALLY THE ONLY GIRL FOR YOU? OR IS IT SOME-THING ELSE?
OH... HI.
ARE THOSE TWO STILL GOING AT IT?
THAT'S KIND OF COMPLI-CATED...

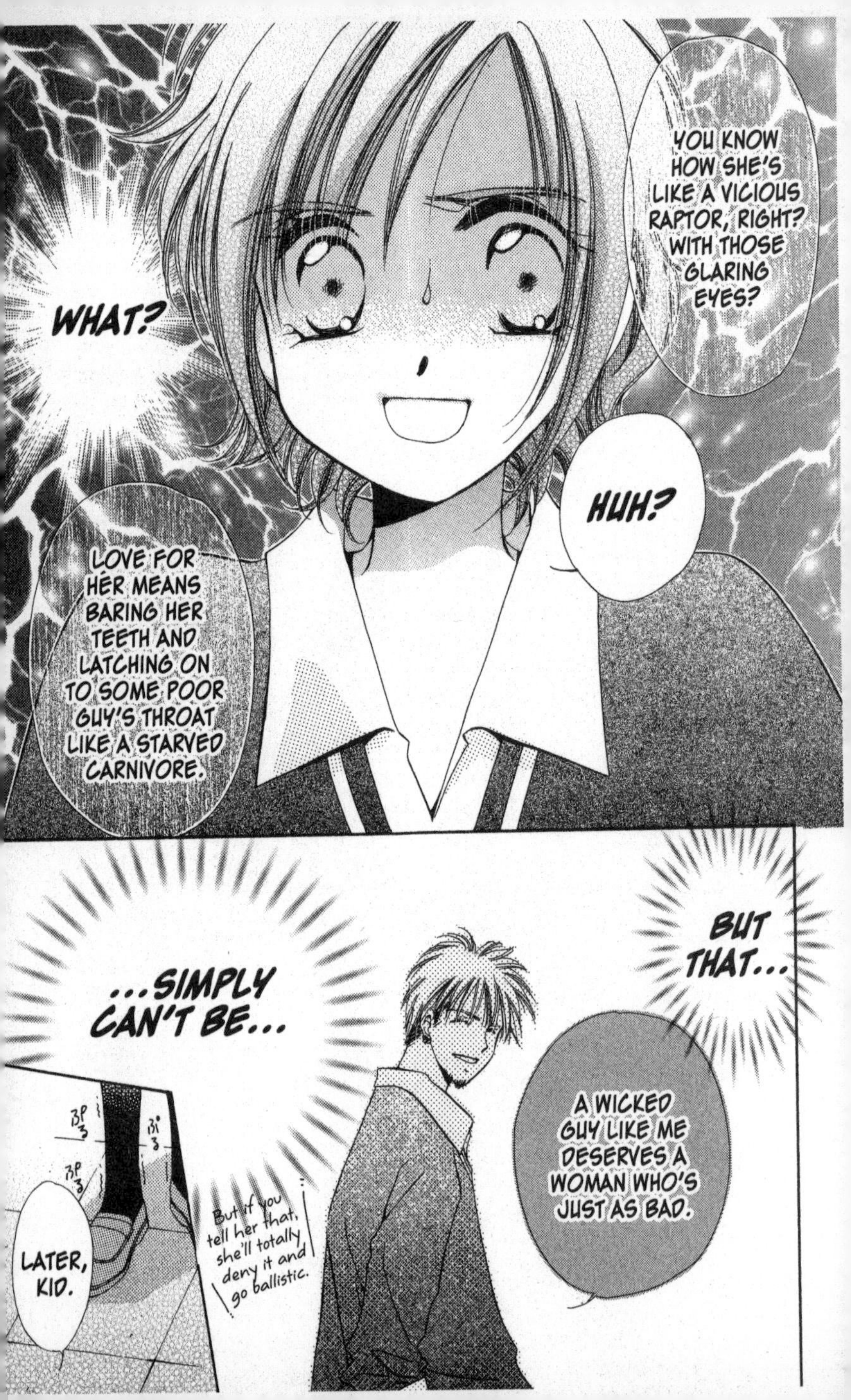
YOU KNOW HOW SHE'S LIKE A VICIOUS RAPTOR, RIGHT? WITH THOSE GLARING EYES?
WHAT?
HUH?
LOVE FOR HER MEANS BARING HER TEETH AND LATCHING ON TO SOME POOR GUY'S THROAT LIKE A STARVED CARNIVORE.
BUT THAT...
...SIMPLY CAN'T BE...
A WICKED GUY LIKE ME DESERVES A WOMAN WHO'S JUST AS BAD.
But if you tell her that, she'll totally deny it and go ballistic.
LATER, KID.

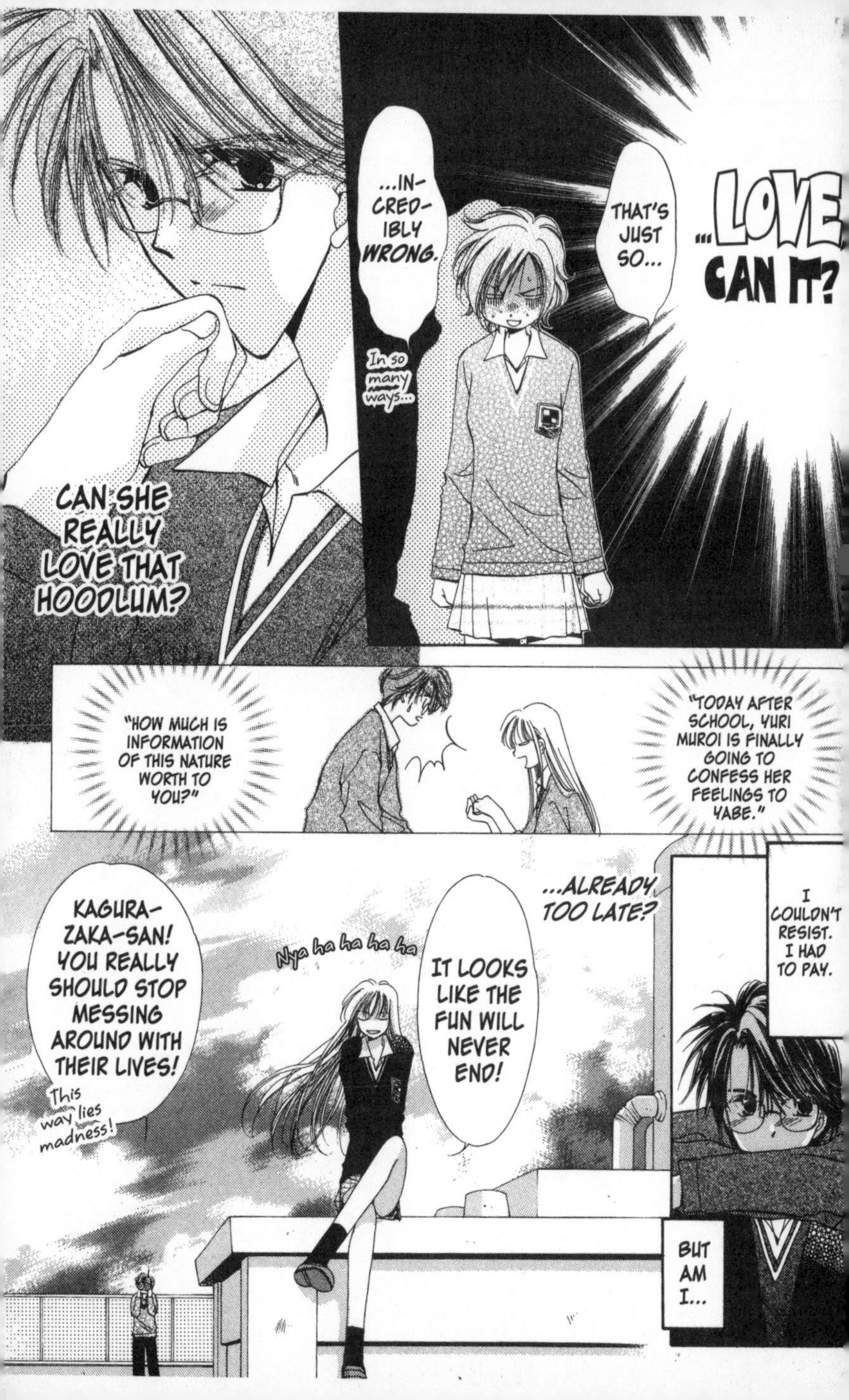
...LOVE CAN IT?
THAT'S JUST SO...
...IN-CREDIBLY WRONG.
In so many ways...
CAN SHE REALLY LOVE THAT HOODLUM?
"TODAY AFTER SCHOOL, YURI MUROI IS FINALLY GOING TO CONFESS HER FEELINGS TO YABE."
"HOW MUCH IS INFORMATION OF THIS NATURE WORTH TO YOU?"
I COULDN'T RESIST. I HAD TO PAY.
BUT AM I...
...ALREADY TOO LATE?
IT LOOKS LIKE THE FUN WILL NEVER END!
Nya ha ha ha ha
KAGURA-ZAKA-SAN! YOU REALLY SHOULD STOP MESSING AROUND WITH THEIR LIVES!
This way lies madness!

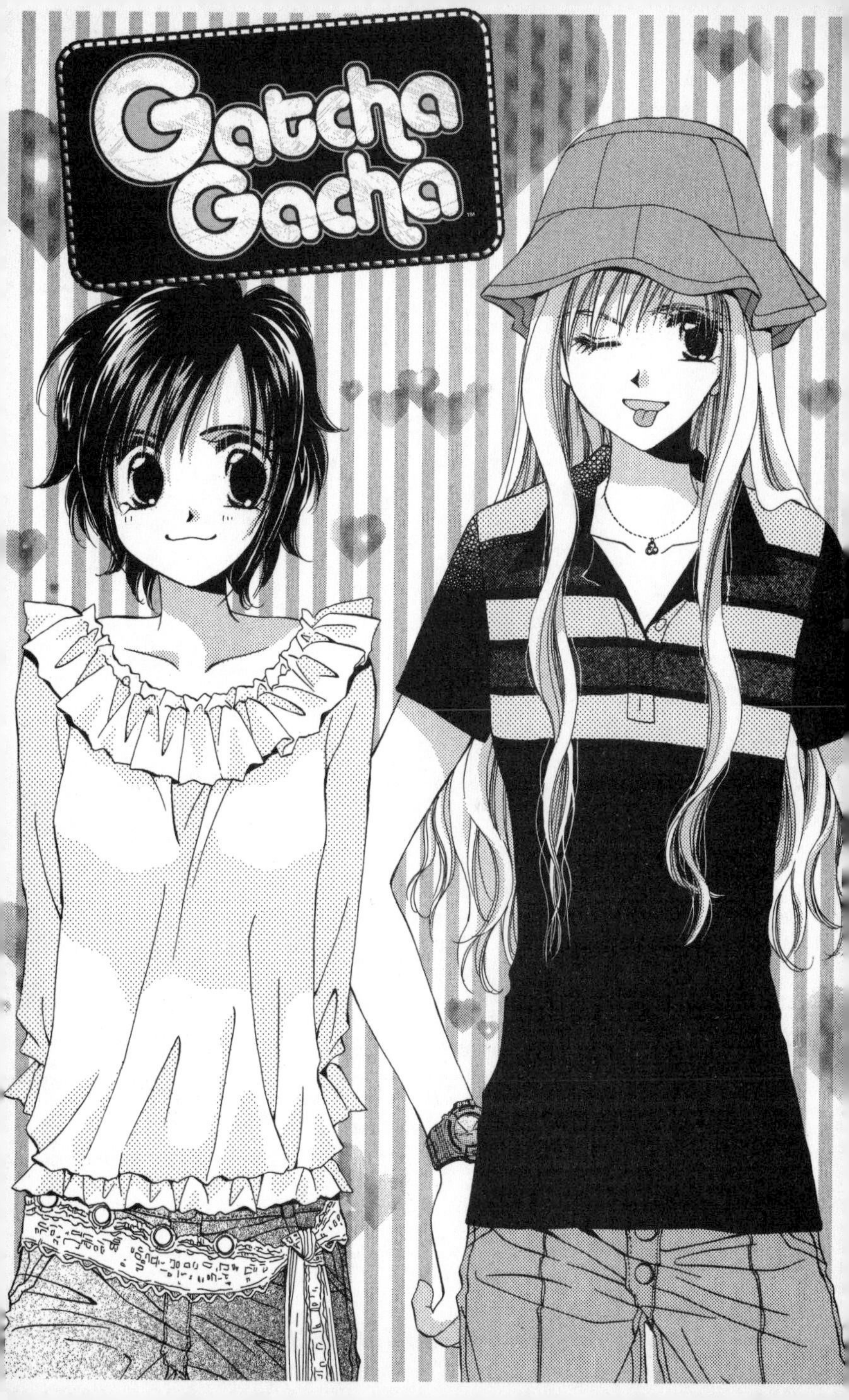
Gatcha Gacha™

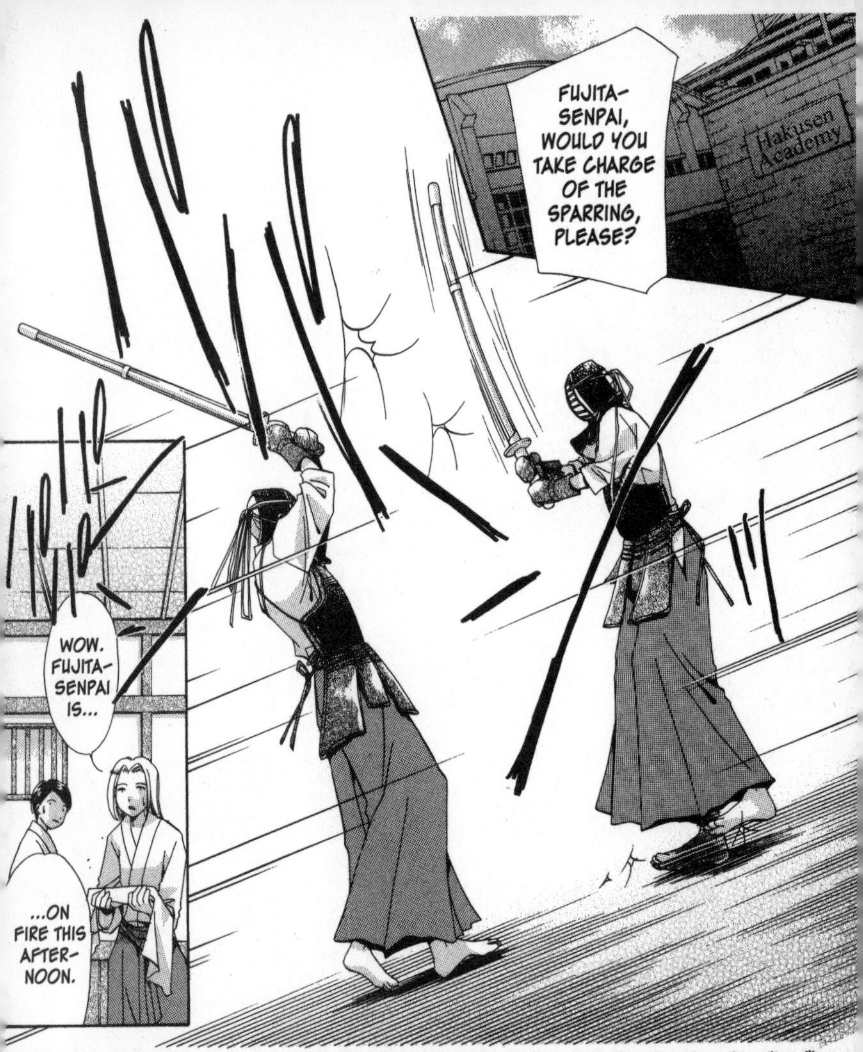
Hakusen Academy
FUJITA-SENPAI, WOULD YOU TAKE CHARGE OF THE SPARRING, PLEASE?
WOW. FUJITA-SENPAI IS...
...ON FIRE THIS AFTERNOON.

PLEASE DIRECT FAN LETTERS OF LOVE AND ADORATION FOR TACHIBANA-SENSEI TO:

Yutaka Tachibana
TokyoPop
5900 Wilshire Blvd. Suite 2000
Los Angeles, CA 90036
USA

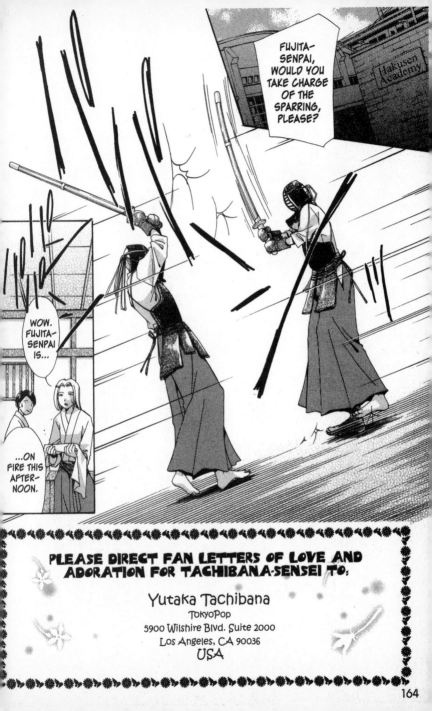

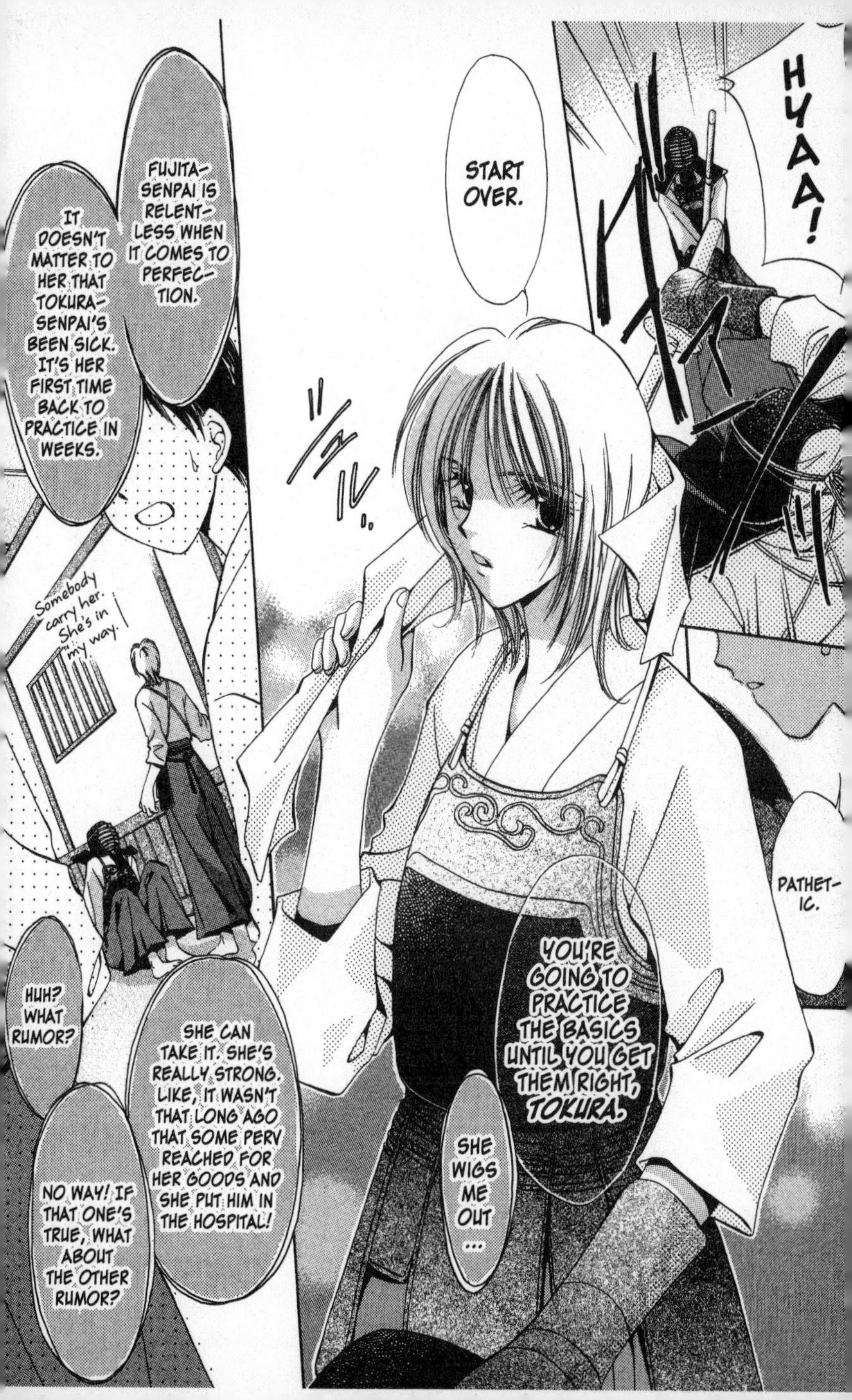
HYAA!
START OVER.
PATHETIC.
YOU'RE GOING TO PRACTICE THE BASICS UNTIL YOU GET THEM RIGHT, TOKURA.
SHE WIGS ME OUT...
FUJITA-SENPAI IS RELENTLESS WHEN IT COMES TO PERFECTION.
IT DOESN'T MATTER TO HER THAT TOKURA-SENPAI'S BEEN SICK. IT'S HER FIRST TIME BACK TO PRACTICE IN WEEKS.
Somebody carry her. She's in my way.
HUH? WHAT RUMOR?
SHE CAN TAKE IT. SHE'S REALLY STRONG. LIKE, IT WASN'T THAT LONG AGO THAT SOME PERV REACHED FOR HER GOODS AND SHE PUT HIM IN THE HOSPITAL!
NO WAY! IF THAT ONE'S TRUE, WHAT ABOUT THE OTHER RUMOR?

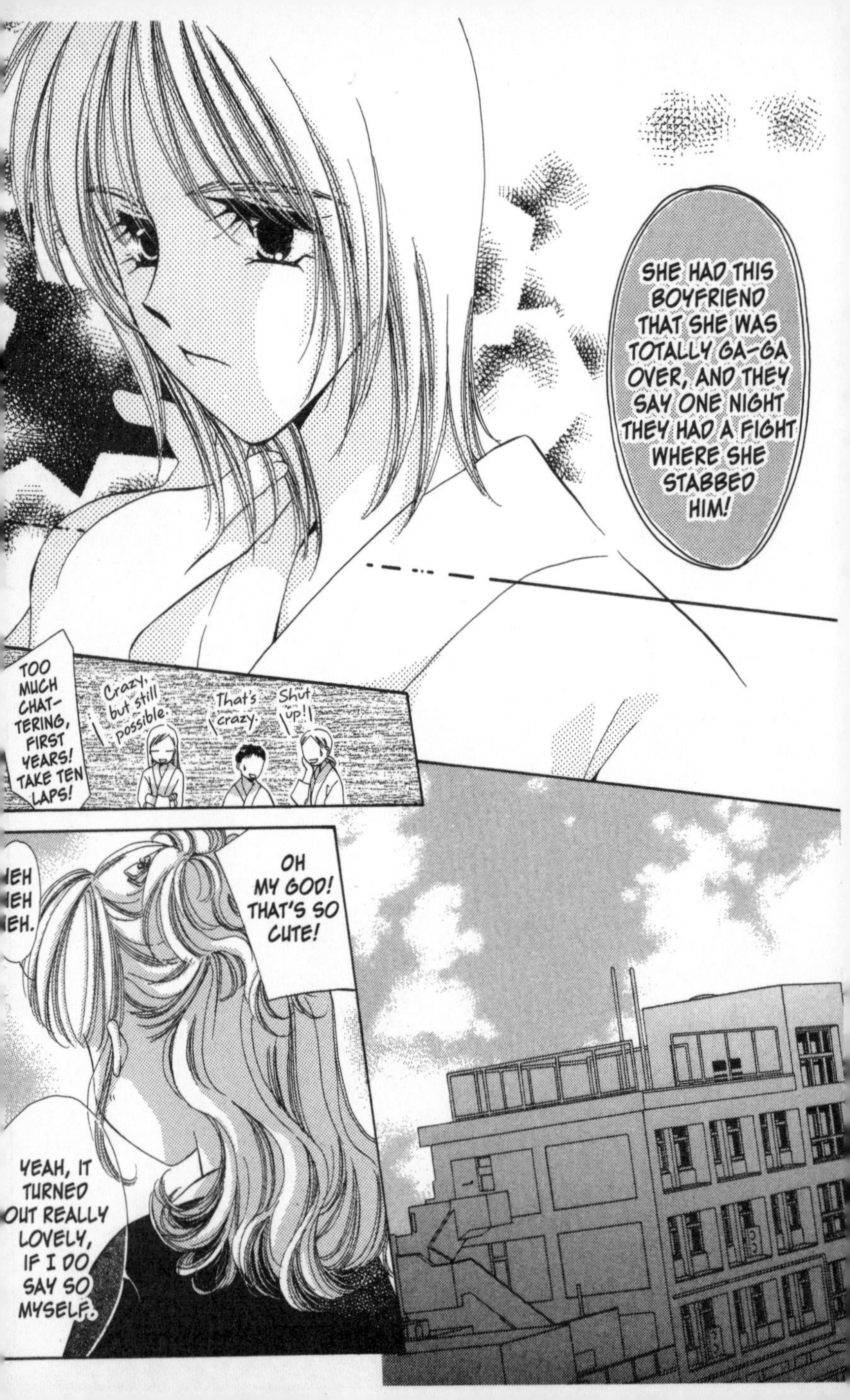
SHE HAD THIS BOYFRIEND THAT SHE WAS TOTALLY GA-GA OVER, AND THEY SAY ONE NIGHT THEY HAD A FIGHT WHERE SHE STABBED HIM!
Shut up!
That's crazy.
Crazy, but still possible.
TOO MUCH CHAT-TERING, FIRST YEARS! TAKE TEN LAPS!
OH MY GOD! THAT'S SO CUTE!
EH EH EH.
YEAH, IT TURNED OUT REALLY LOVELY, IF I DO SAY SO MYSELF.

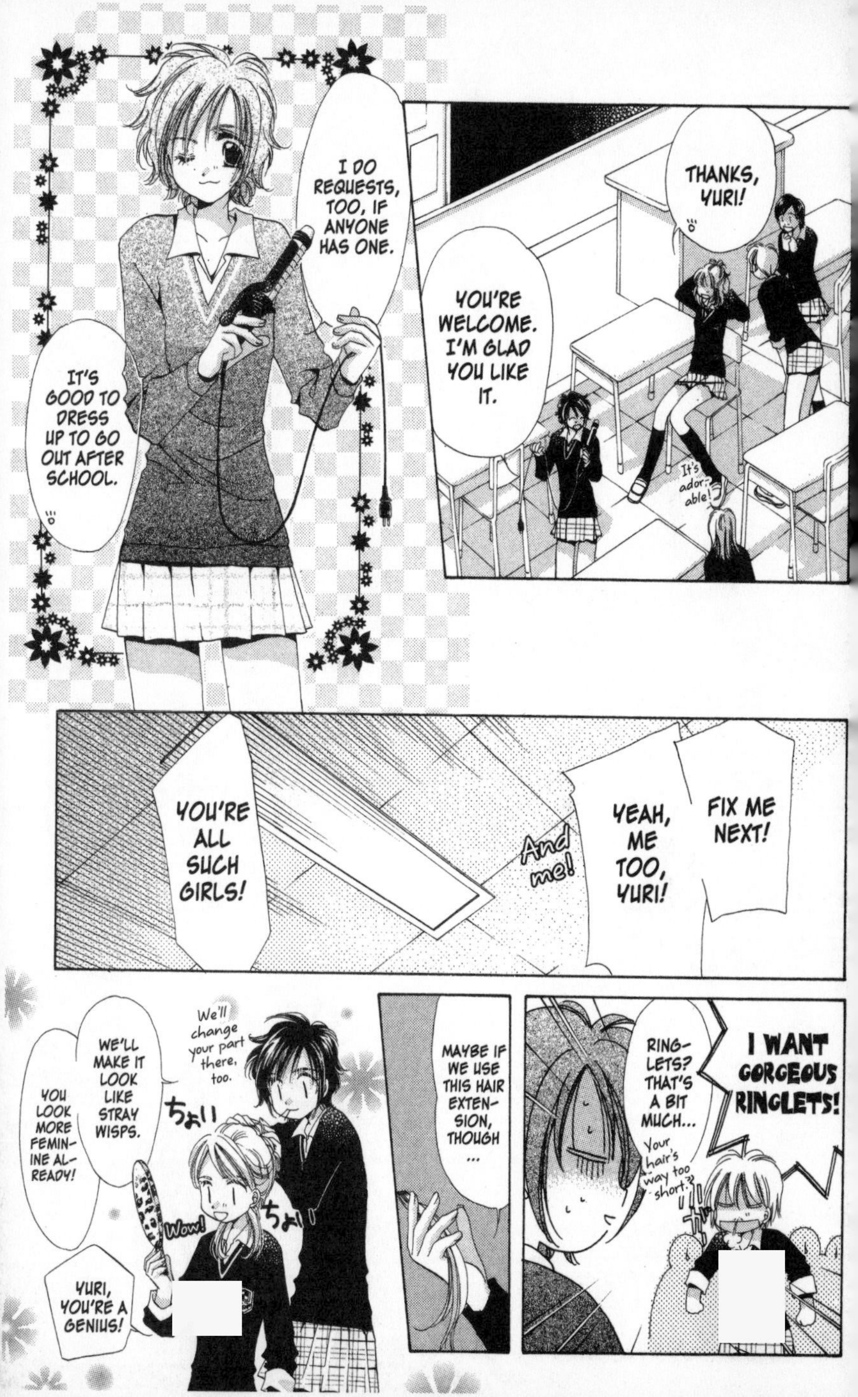
THANKS, YURI!
YOU'RE WELCOME. I'M GLAD YOU LIKE IT.
It's adorable!
I DO REQUESTS, TOO, IF ANYONE HAS ONE.
IT'S GOOD TO DRESS UP TO GO OUT AFTER SCHOOL.
FIX ME NEXT!
YEAH, ME TOO, YURI!
And me!
YOU'RE ALL SUCH GIRLS!
I WANT GORGEOUS RINGLETS!
RINGLETS? THAT'S A BIT MUCH...
Your hair's way too short.
MAYBE IF WE USE THIS HAIR EXTENSION, THOUGH ...
We'll change your part there, too.
WE'LL MAKE IT LOOK LIKE STRAY WISPS.
ちょい
YOU LOOK MORE FEMININE ALREADY!
Wow!
YURI, YOU'RE A GENIUS!

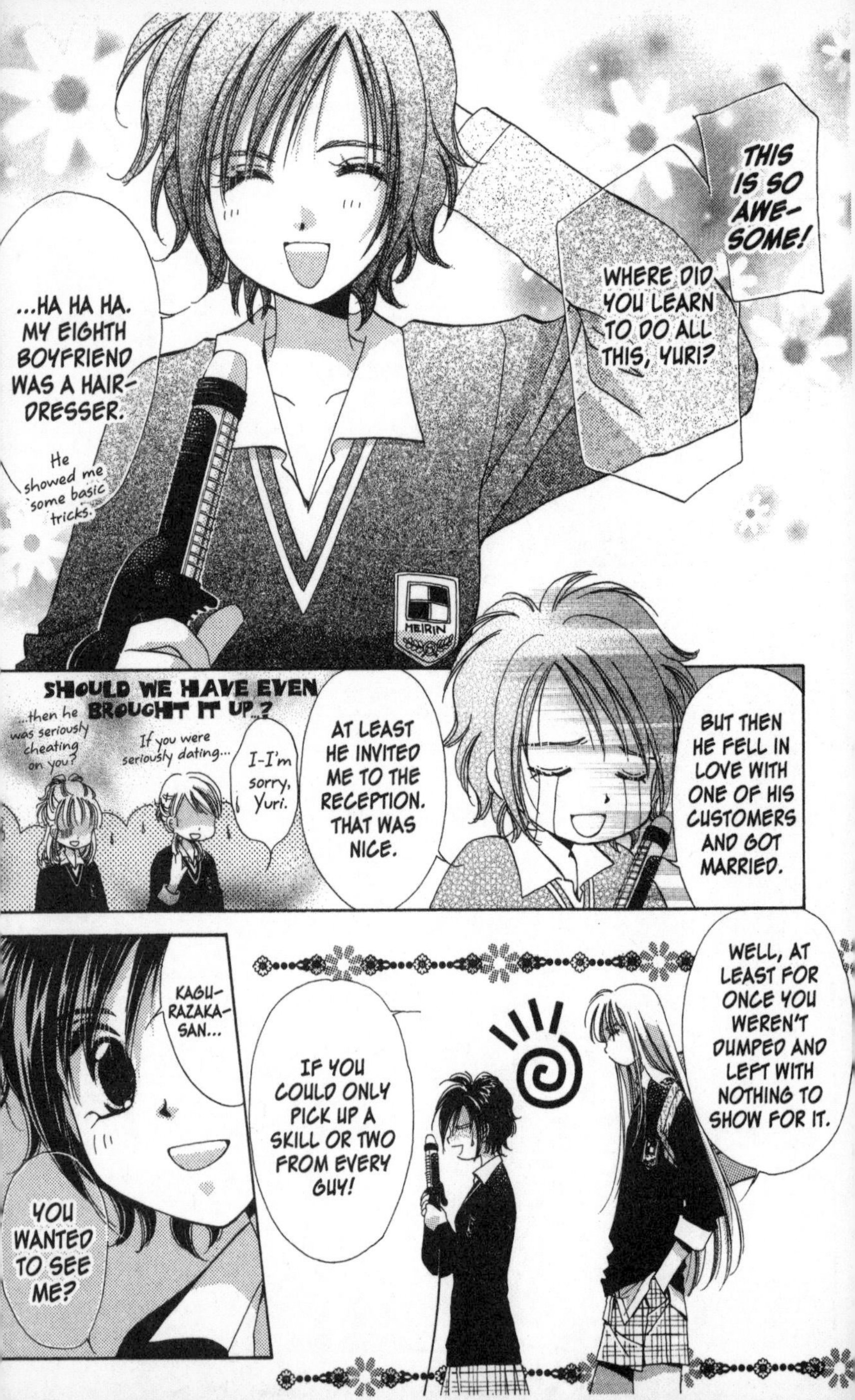
THIS IS SO AWE-SOME!
WHERE DID YOU LEARN TO DO ALL THIS, YURI?
...HA HA HA. MY EIGHTH BOYFRIEND WAS A HAIR-DRESSER.
He showed me some basic tricks.
BUT THEN HE FELL IN LOVE WITH ONE OF HIS CUSTOMERS AND GOT MARRIED.
AT LEAST HE INVITED ME TO THE RECEPTION. THAT WAS NICE.
I-I'm sorry, Yuri.
SHOULD WE HAVE EVEN BROUGHT IT UP..?
If you were seriously dating...
...then he was seriously cheating on you?
WELL, AT LEAST FOR ONCE YOU WEREN'T DUMPED AND LEFT WITH NOTHING TO SHOW FOR IT.
IF YOU COULD ONLY PICK UP A SKILL OR TWO FROM EVERY GUY!
KAGU-RAZAKA-SAN...
YOU WANTED TO SEE ME?

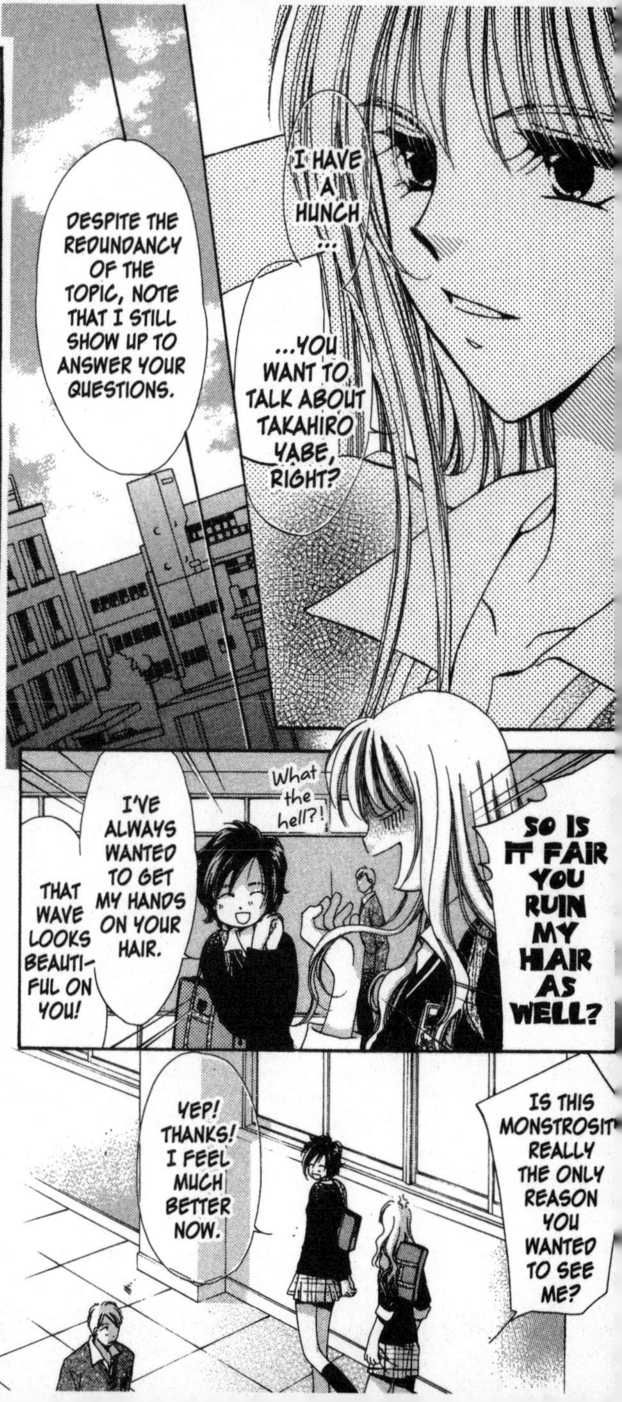
I HAVE A HUNCH...
...YOU WANT TO TALK ABOUT TAKAHIRO YABE, RIGHT?
DESPITE THE REDUNDANCY OF THE TOPIC, NOTE THAT I STILL SHOW UP TO ANSWER YOUR QUESTIONS.
SO IS IT FAIR YOU RUIN MY HAIR AS WELL?
What the hell?!
I'VE ALWAYS WANTED TO GET MY HANDS ON YOUR HAIR.
THAT WAVE LOOKS BEAUTI-FUL ON YOU!
IS THIS MONSTROSIT REALLY THE ONLY REASON YOU WANTED TO SEE ME?
YEP! THANKS! I FEEL MUCH BETTER NOW.

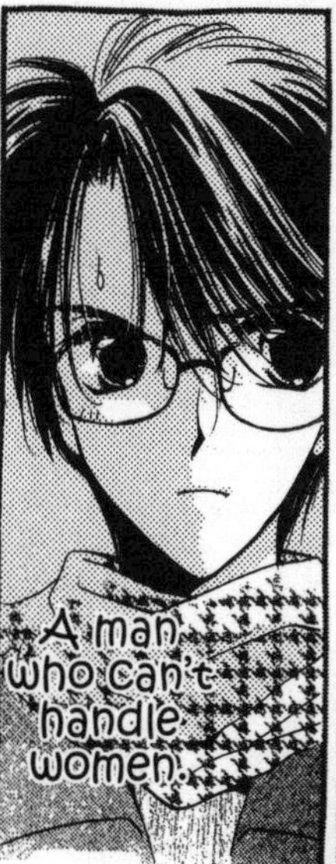
A man who can't handle women.

Sho Hirao

He's the only serious, responsible, normal human being in the whole bunch. At least, that's what you think when you first meet him. Scratch the surface and it turns out he has just as many issues as the rest of them. (This manga is held together by the quirks of messed-up characters and the good will of our wonderful readers.)

I don't know if it's because of his looks or what, but he is far and away the most popular character among our lady readers. Hmmm. I'd kinda figured this would happen, but I still can't really decide how I feel about it. Don't get me wrong, I'm not saying this is a bad thing. But still...

Secretly, I call him the Pathetic Prez. Let's all call him that.

(I don't mean to imply that I dislike all neat, smart-looking men. But just because I like Ed Harris and Sean Connery doesn't mean I like every distinguished bald man, either.)

But you do have to wonder if poor Hirao will ever find happiness...

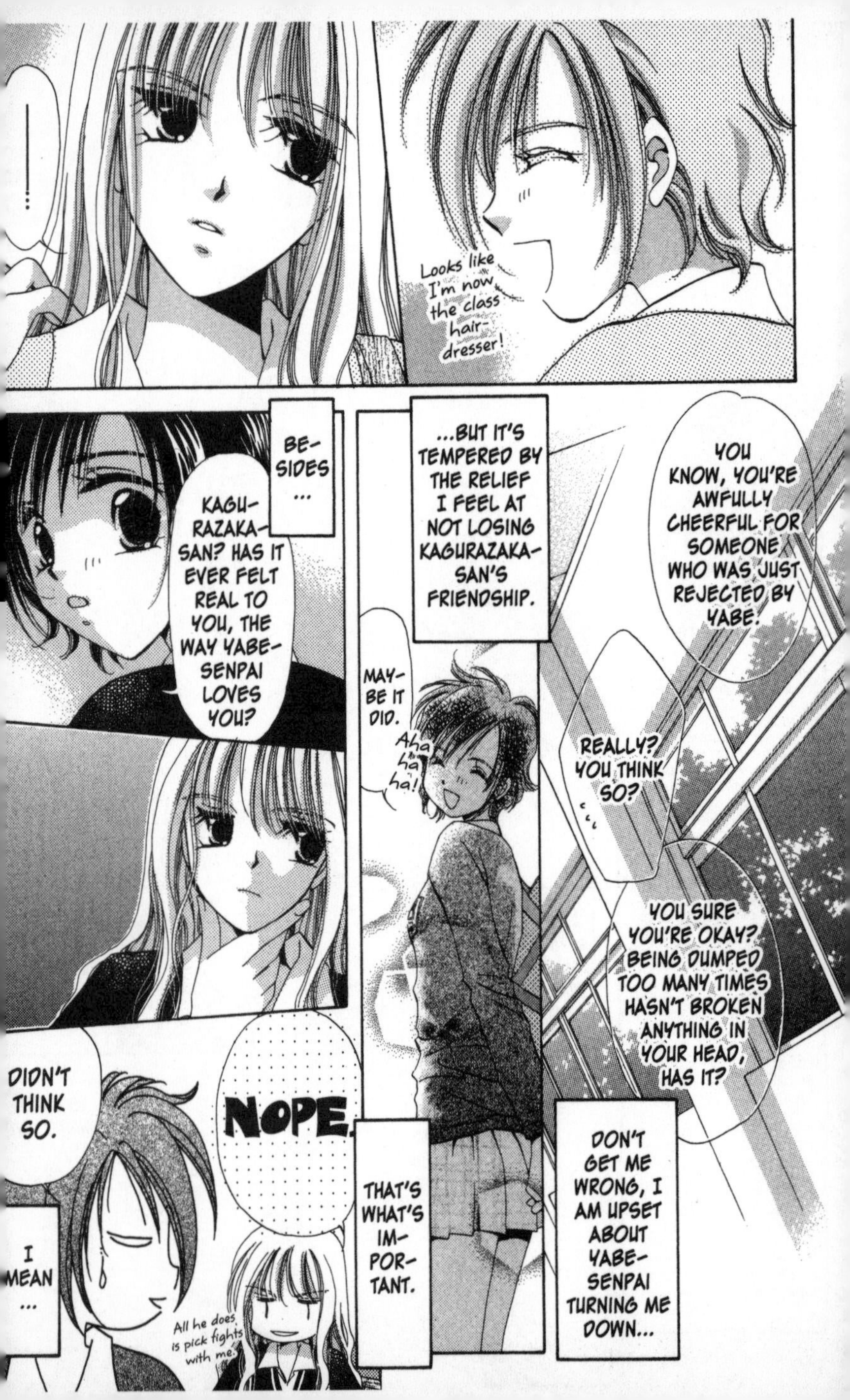
Looks like I'm now the class hairdresser!
......
YOU KNOW, YOU'RE AWFULLY CHEERFUL FOR SOMEONE WHO WAS JUST REJECTED BY YABE.
REALLY? YOU THINK SO?
YOU SURE YOU'RE OKAY? BEING DUMPED TOO MANY TIMES HASN'T BROKEN ANYTHING IN YOUR HEAD, HAS IT?
DON'T GET ME WRONG, I AM UPSET ABOUT YABE-SENPAI TURNING ME DOWN...
...BUT IT'S TEMPERED BY THE RELIEF I FEEL AT NOT LOSING KAGURAZAKA-SAN'S FRIENDSHIP.
MAY-BE IT DID.
Aha ha ha!
THAT'S WHAT'S IM-POR-TANT.
BE-SIDES...
KAGU-RAZAKA-SAN? HAS IT EVER FELT REAL TO YOU, THE WAY YABE-SENPAI LOVES YOU?
NOPE.
DIDN'T THINK SO.
I MEAN...
All he does is pick fights with me.

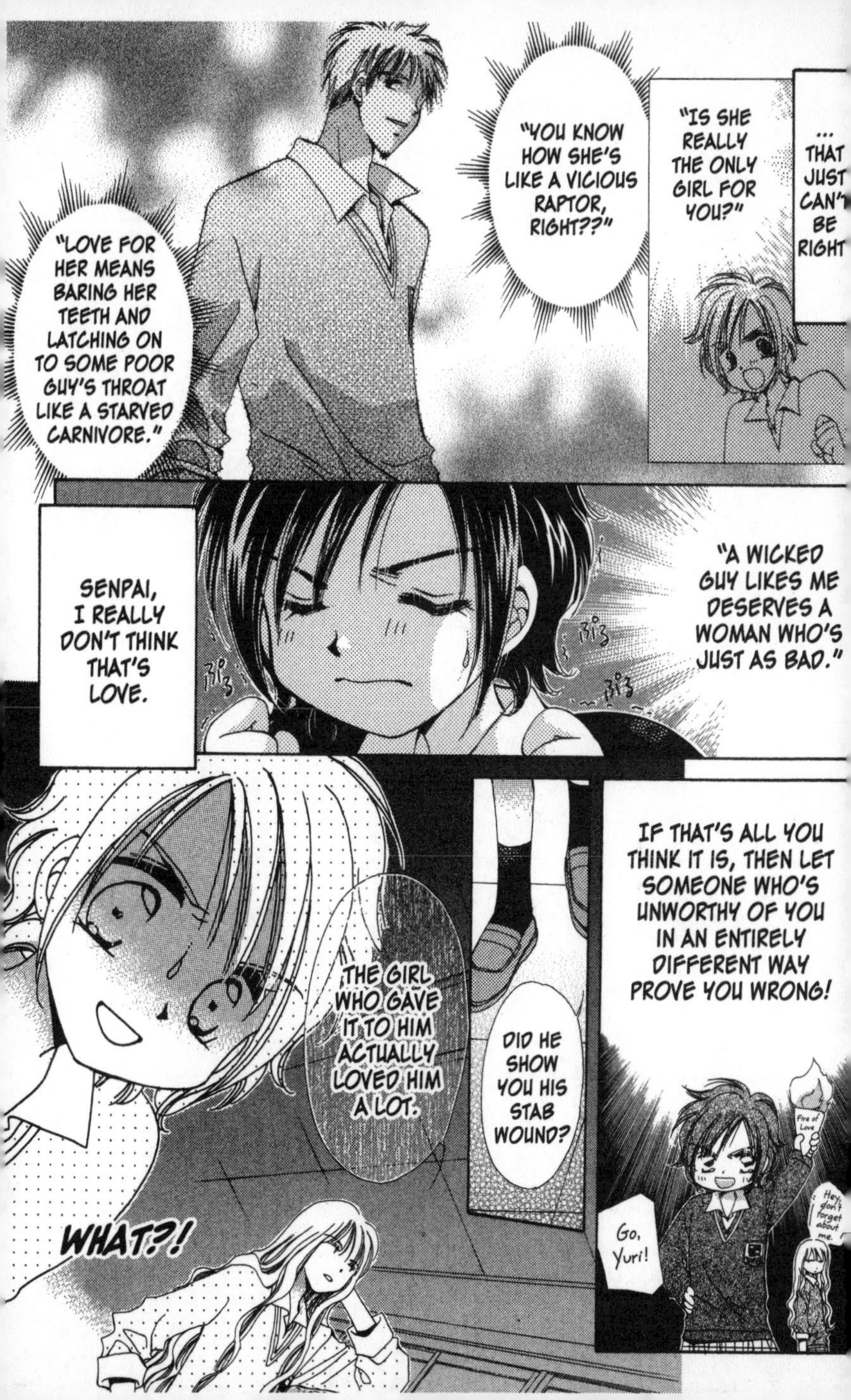
... THAT JUST CAN'T BE RIGHT
"IS SHE REALLY THE ONLY GIRL FOR YOU?"
"YOU KNOW HOW SHE'S LIKE A VICIOUS RAPTOR, RIGHT??"
"LOVE FOR HER MEANS BARING HER TEETH AND LATCHING ON TO SOME POOR GUY'S THROAT LIKE A STARVED CARNIVORE."
"A WICKED GUY LIKES ME DESERVES A WOMAN WHO'S JUST AS BAD."
SENPAI, I REALLY DON'T THINK THAT'S LOVE.
IF THAT'S ALL YOU THINK IT IS, THEN LET SOMEONE WHO'S UNWORTHY OF YOU IN AN ENTIRELY DIFFERENT WAY PROVE YOU WRONG!
Fire of Love
Hey, don't forget about me.
Go, Yuri!
DID HE SHOW YOU HIS STAB WOUND?
THE GIRL WHO GAVE IT TO HIM ACTUALLY LOVED HIM A LOT.
WHAT?!

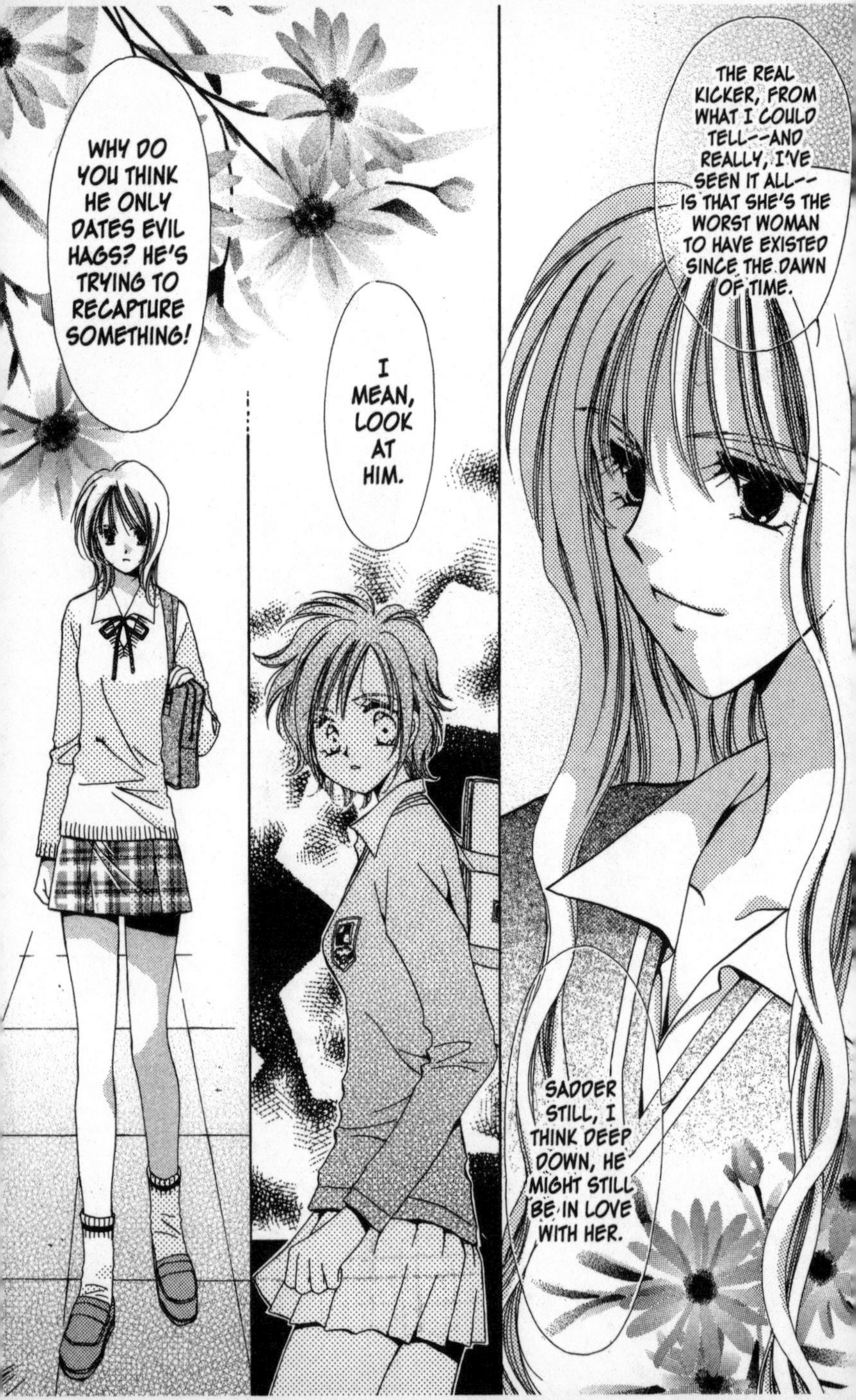
THE REAL KICKER, FROM WHAT I COULD TELL--AND REALLY, I'VE SEEN IT ALL--IS THAT SHE'S THE WORST WOMAN TO HAVE EXISTED SINCE THE DAWN OF TIME.
SADDER STILL, I THINK DEEP DOWN, HE MIGHT STILL BE IN LOVE WITH HER.
I MEAN, LOOK AT HIM.
WHY DO YOU THINK HE ONLY DATES EVIL HAGS? HE'S TRYING TO RECAPTURE SOMETHING!

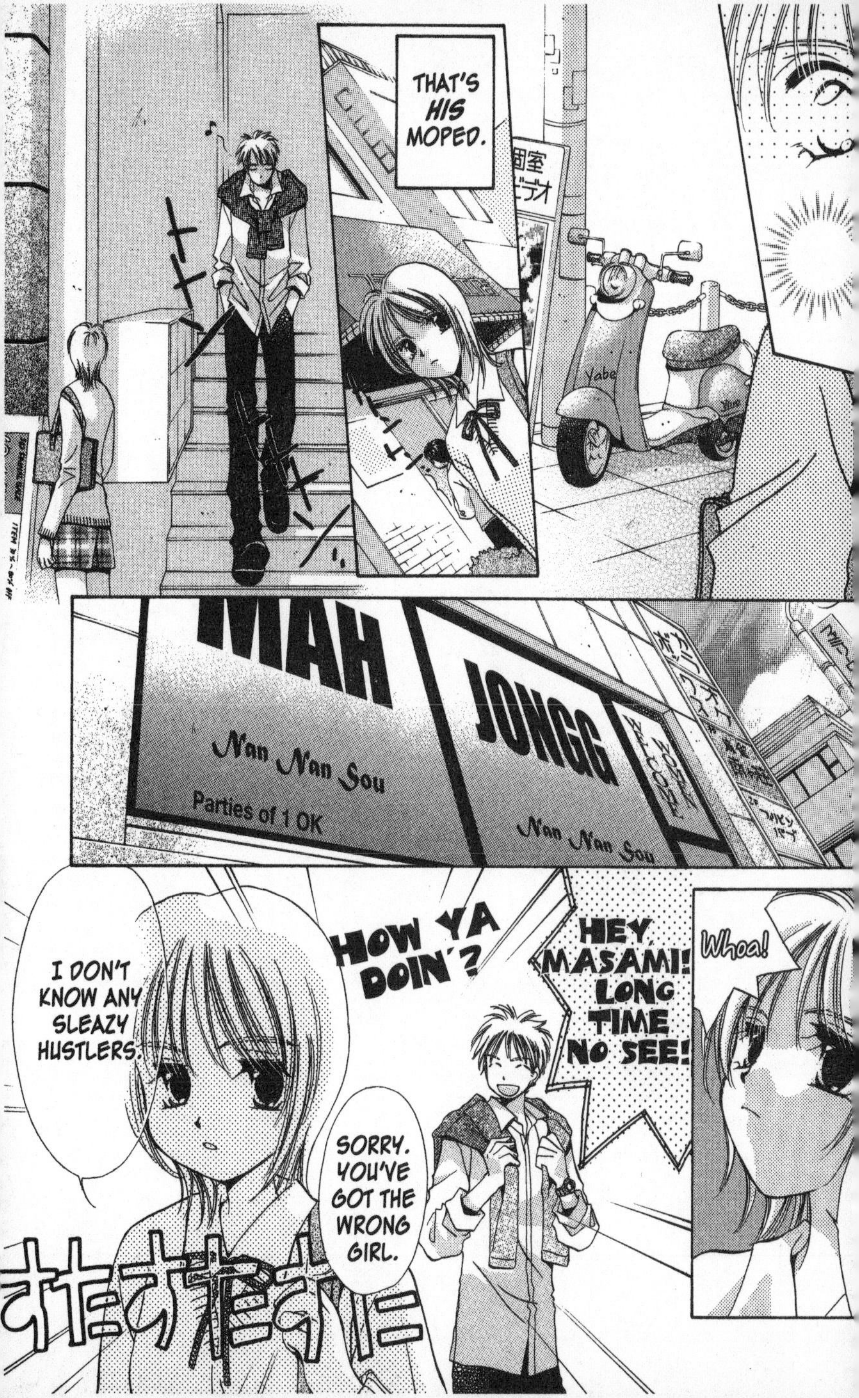

THAT'S HIS MOPED.
Yabe
MAH JONGG
Nan Nan Sou
Parties of 1 OK
WOMEN WELCOME
Nan Nan Sou
Whoa!
HEY MASAMI! LONG TIME NO SEE!
HOW YA DOIN'?
SORRY. YOU'VE GOT THE WRONG GIRL.
I DON'T KNOW ANY SLEAZY HUSTLERS.

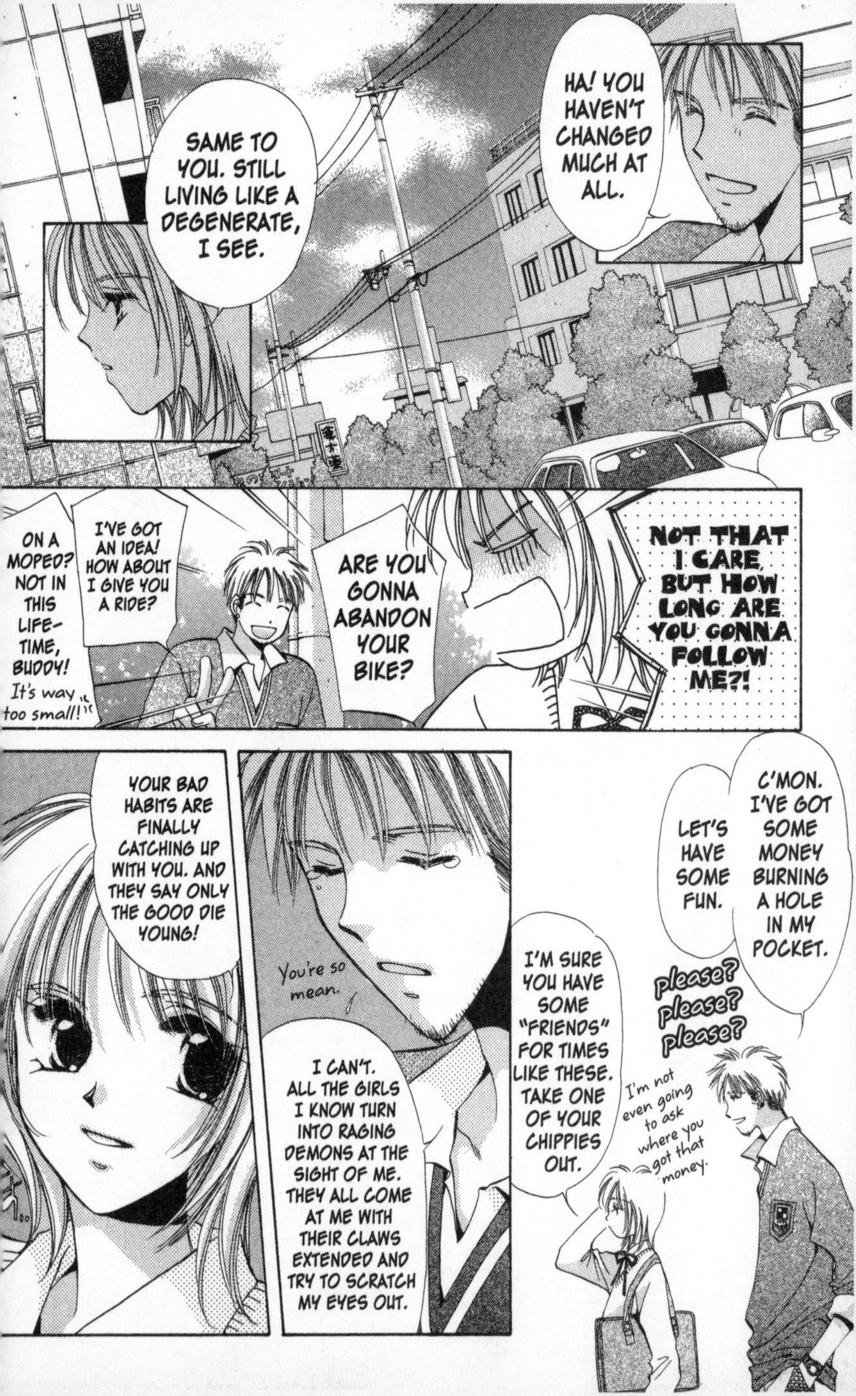
HA! YOU HAVEN'T CHANGED MUCH AT ALL.
SAME TO YOU. STILL LIVING LIKE A DEGENERATE, I SEE.
NOT THAT I CARE, BUT HOW LONG ARE YOU GONNA FOLLOW ME?!
ARE YOU GONNA ABANDON YOUR BIKE?
I'VE GOT AN IDEA! HOW ABOUT I GIVE YOU A RIDE?
ON A MOPED? NOT IN THIS LIFE-TIME, BUDDY!
It's way too small!!
C'MON. I'VE GOT SOME MONEY BURNING A HOLE IN MY POCKET.
LET'S HAVE SOME FUN.
please? please? please?
I'm not even going to ask where you got that money.
I'M SURE YOU HAVE SOME "FRIENDS" FOR TIMES LIKE THESE. TAKE ONE OF YOUR CHIPPIES OUT.
I CAN'T. ALL THE GIRLS I KNOW TURN INTO RAGING DEMONS AT THE SIGHT OF ME. THEY ALL COME AT ME WITH THEIR CLAWS EXTENDED AND TRY TO SCRATCH MY EYES OUT.
You're so mean.
YOUR BAD HABITS ARE FINALLY CATCHING UP WITH YOU. AND THEY SAY ONLY THE GOOD DIE YOUNG!

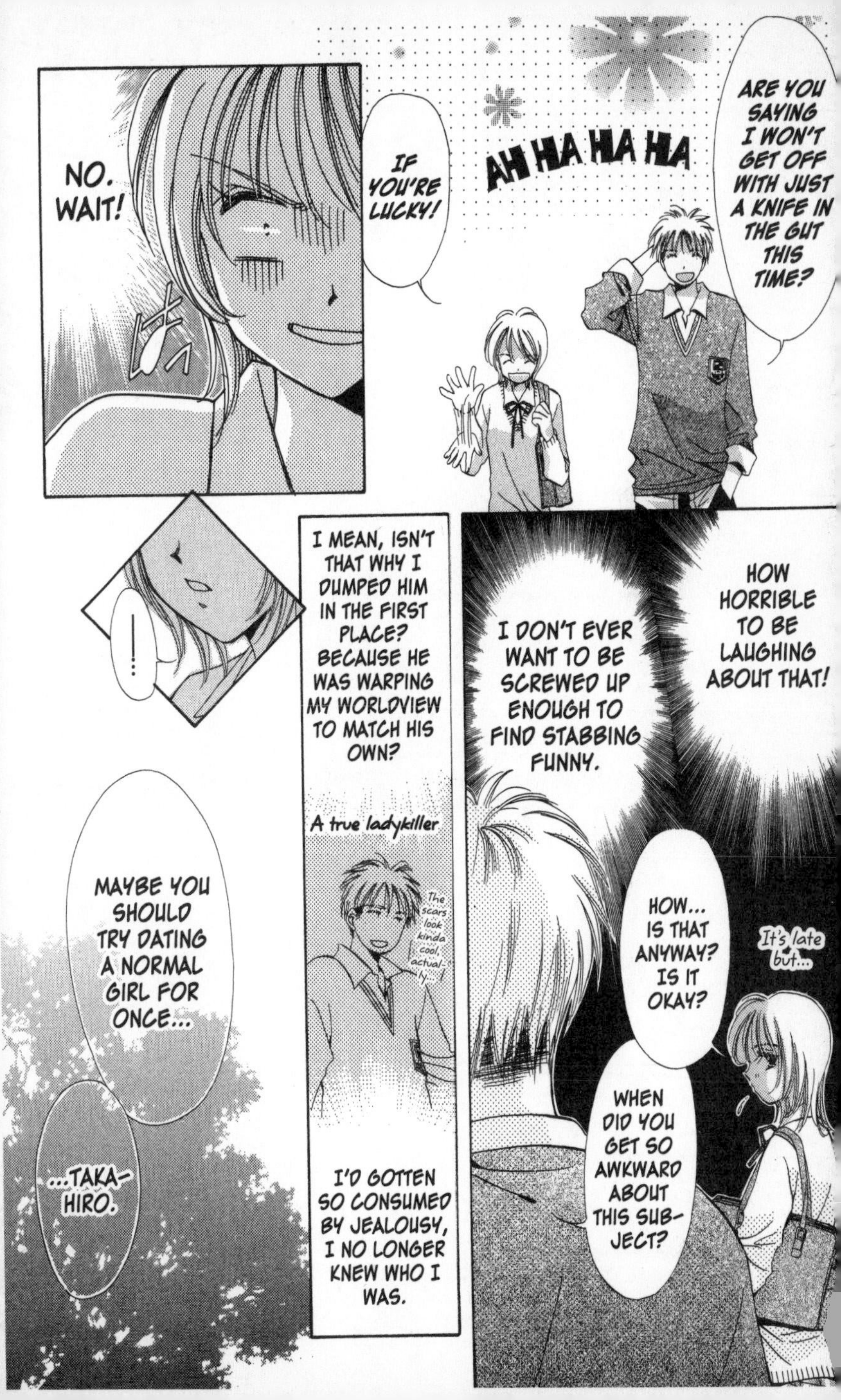

ARE YOU SAYING I WON'T GET OFF WITH JUST A KNIFE IN THE GUT THIS TIME?
AH HA HA HA
IF YOU'RE LUCKY!
NO. WAIT!
HOW HORRIBLE TO BE LAUGHING ABOUT THAT!
I DON'T EVER WANT TO BE SCREWED UP ENOUGH TO FIND STABBING FUNNY.
It's late but...
HOW... IS THAT ANYWAY? IS IT OKAY?
WHEN DID YOU GET SO AWKWARD ABOUT THIS SUBJECT?
I MEAN, ISN'T THAT WHY I DUMPED HIM IN THE FIRST PLACE? BECAUSE HE WAS WARPING MY WORLDVIEW TO MATCH HIS OWN?
A true ladykiller
The scars look kinda cool, actually...
I'D GOTTEN SO CONSUMED BY JEALOUSY, I NO LONGER KNEW WHO I WAS.
!...
MAYBE YOU SHOULD TRY DATING A NORMAL GIRL FOR ONCE...
...TAKA-HIRO.

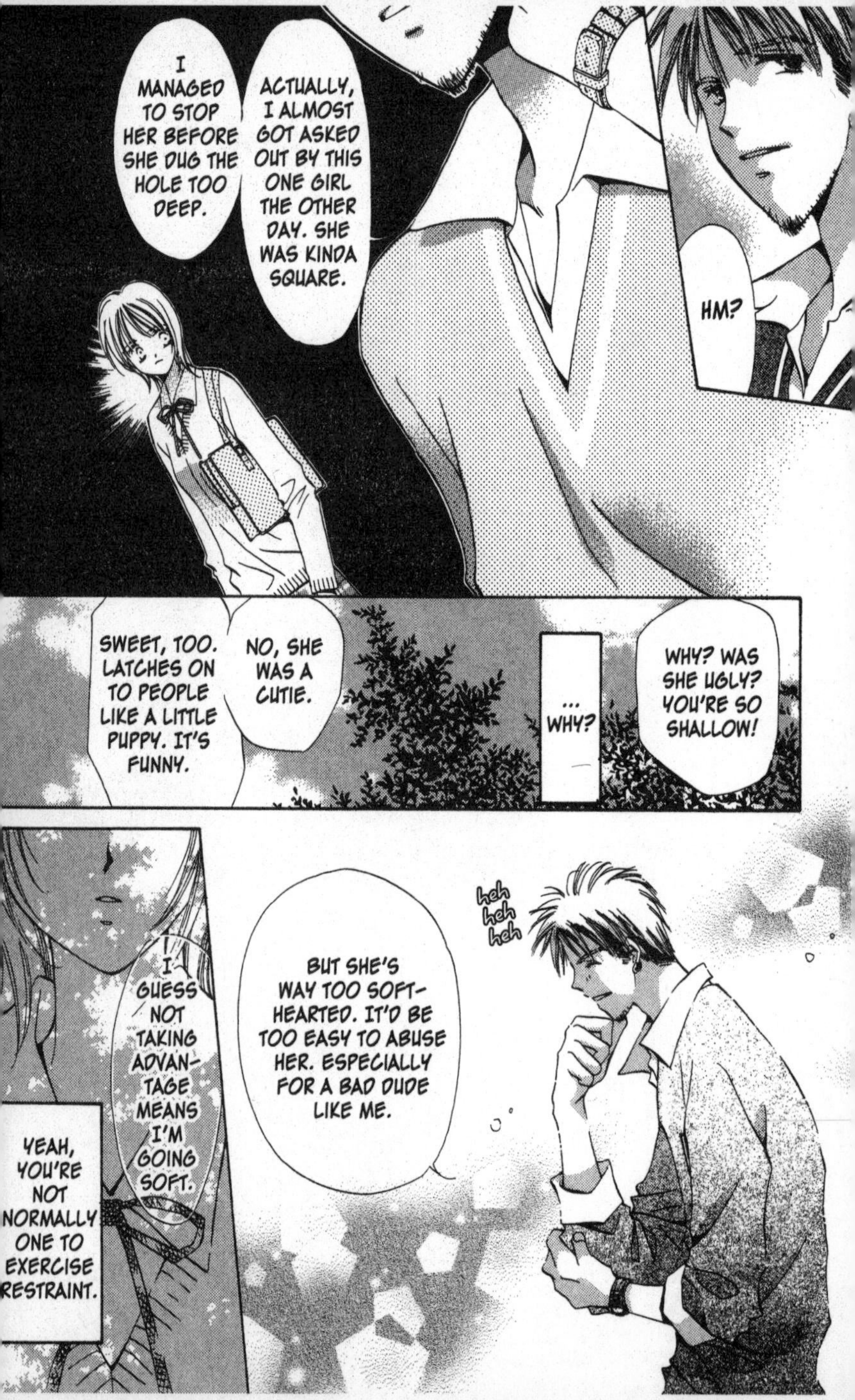
HM?
ACTUALLY, I ALMOST GOT ASKED OUT BY THIS ONE GIRL THE OTHER DAY. SHE WAS KINDA SQUARE.
I MANAGED TO STOP HER BEFORE SHE DUG THE HOLE TOO DEEP.
WHY? WAS SHE UGLY? YOU'RE SO SHALLOW!
... WHY?
NO, SHE WAS A CUTIE.
SWEET, TOO. LATCHES ON TO PEOPLE LIKE A LITTLE PUPPY. IT'S FUNNY.
heh heh heh
BUT SHE'S WAY TOO SOFT-HEARTED. IT'D BE TOO EASY TO ABUSE HER. ESPECIALLY FOR A BAD DUDE LIKE ME.
I GUESS NOT TAKING ADVAN-TAGE MEANS I'M GOING SOFT.
YEAH, YOU'RE NOT NORMALLY ONE TO EXERCISE RESTRAINT.

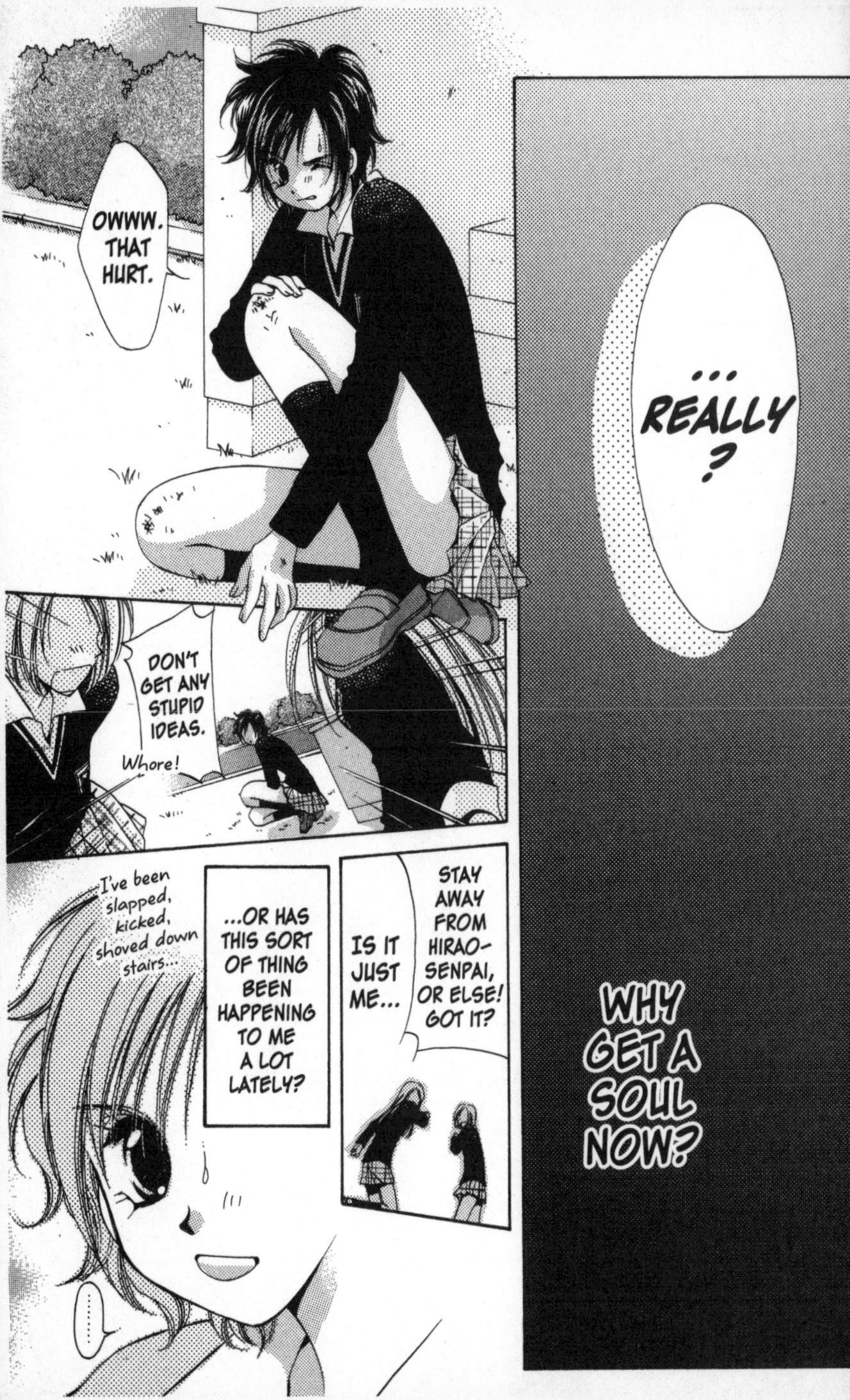
...REALLY?
WHY GET A SOUL NOW?
OWWW. THAT HURT.
DON'T GET ANY STUPID IDEAS.
Whore!
STAY AWAY FROM HIRAO-SENPAI, OR ELSE! GOT IT?
IS IT JUST ME...
...OR HAS THIS SORT OF THING BEEN HAPPENING TO ME A LOT LATELY?
I've been slapped, kicked, shoved down stairs...
......

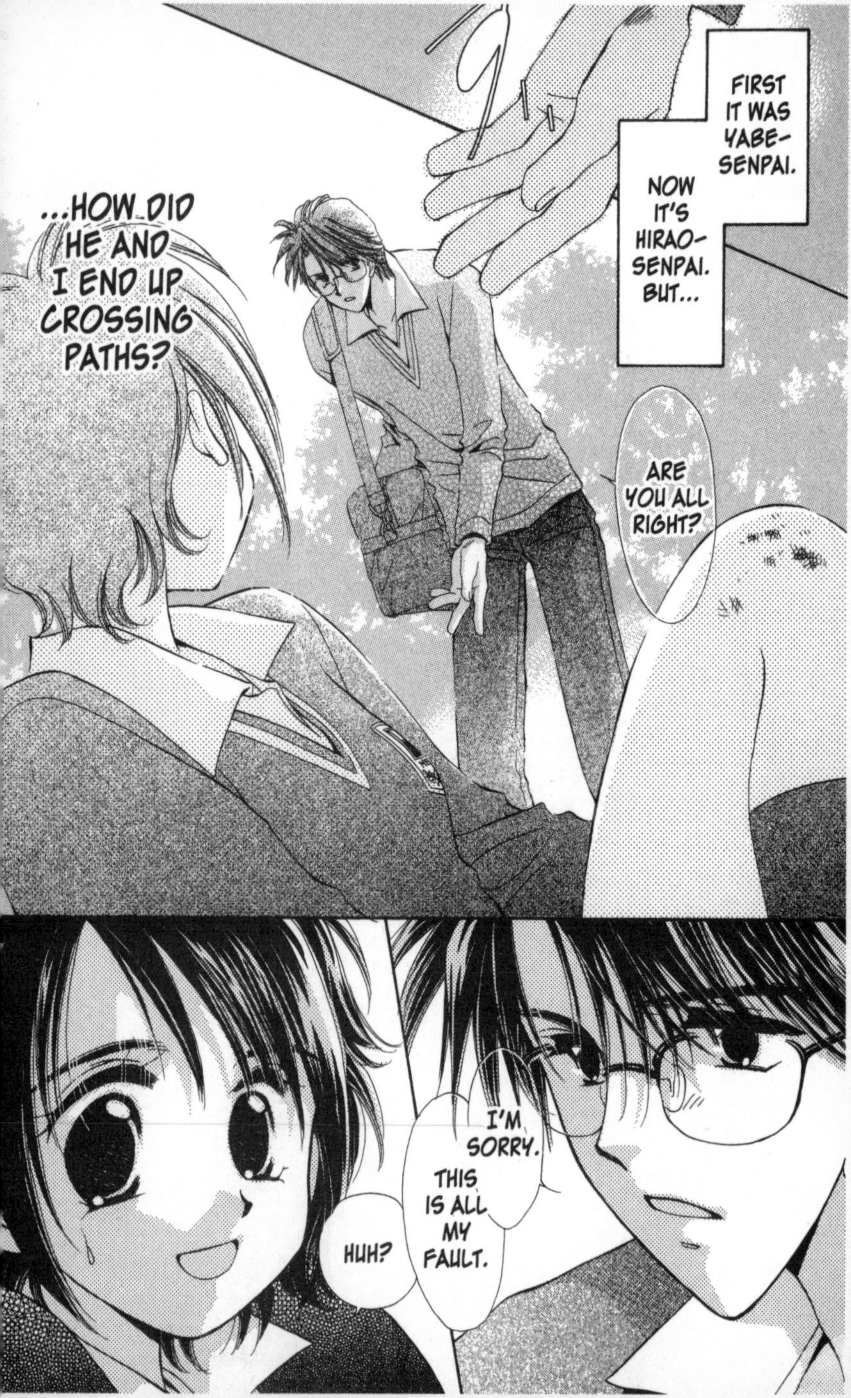
FIRST IT WAS YABE-SENPAI.
NOW IT'S HIRAO-SENPAI. BUT...
ARE YOU ALL RIGHT?
...HOW DID HE AND I END UP CROSSING PATHS?
I'M SORRY.
THIS IS ALL MY FAULT.
HUH?

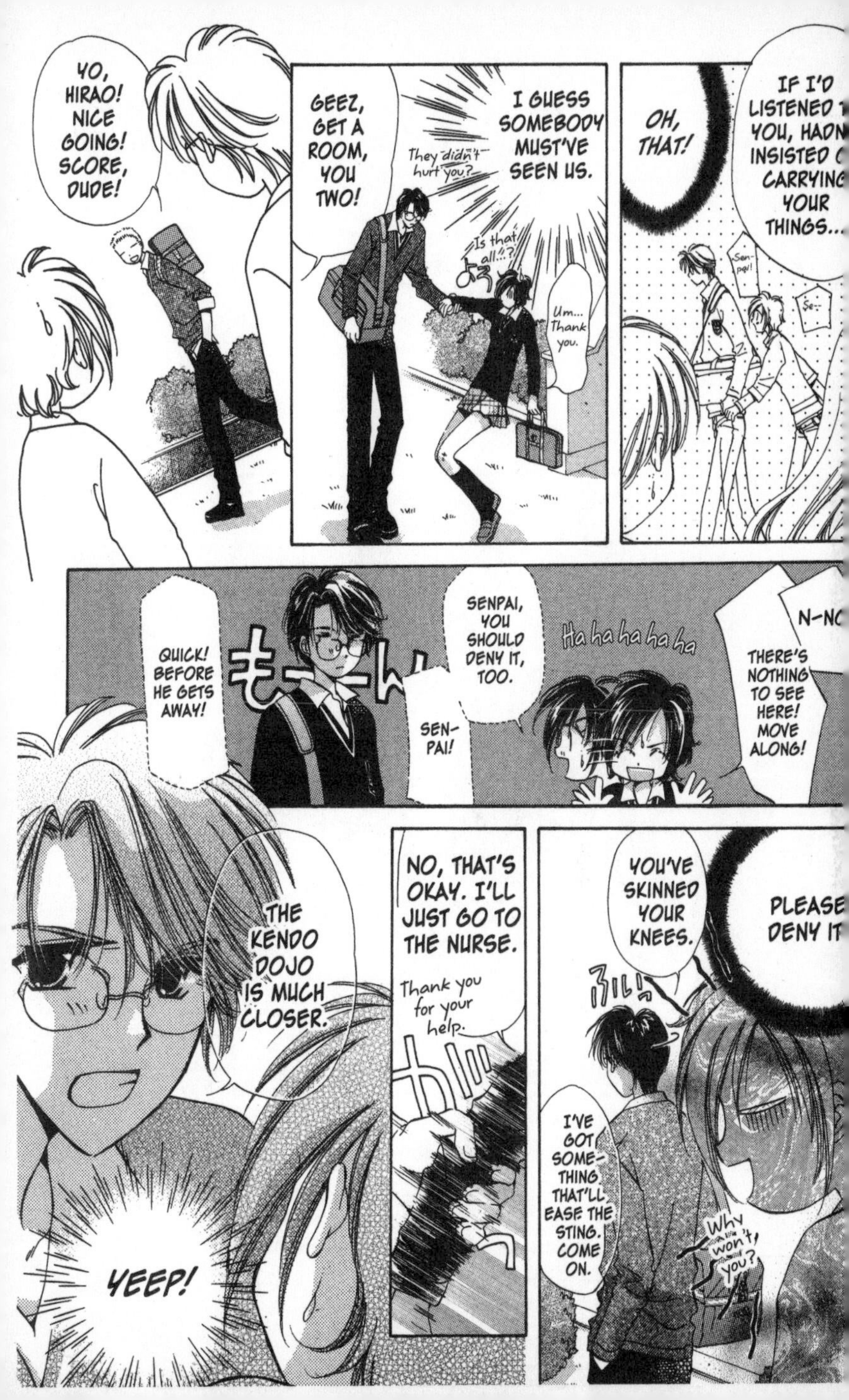
IF I'D LISTENED T YOU, HADN INSISTED C CARRYING YOUR THINGS...
Sen-pai!
Se--
OH, THAT!
I GUESS SOMEBODY MUST'VE SEEN US.
They didn't hurt you?
Is that all!!?
Um... Thank you.
GEEZ, GET A ROOM, YOU TWO!
YO, HIRAO! NICE GOING! SCORE, DUDE!
N-NC
THERE'S NOTHING TO SEE HERE! MOVE ALONG!
Ha ha ha ha ha ha
SENPAI, YOU SHOULD DENY IT, TOO.
SEN-PAI!
QUICK! BEFORE HE GETS AWAY!
PLEASE DENY IT
Why won't you?
YOU'VE SKINNED YOUR KNEES.
I'VE GOT SOME-THING THAT'LL EASE THE STING. COME ON.
NO, THAT'S OKAY. I'LL JUST GO TO THE NURSE.
Thank you for your help.
THE KENDO DOJO IS MUCH CLOSER.
YEEP!

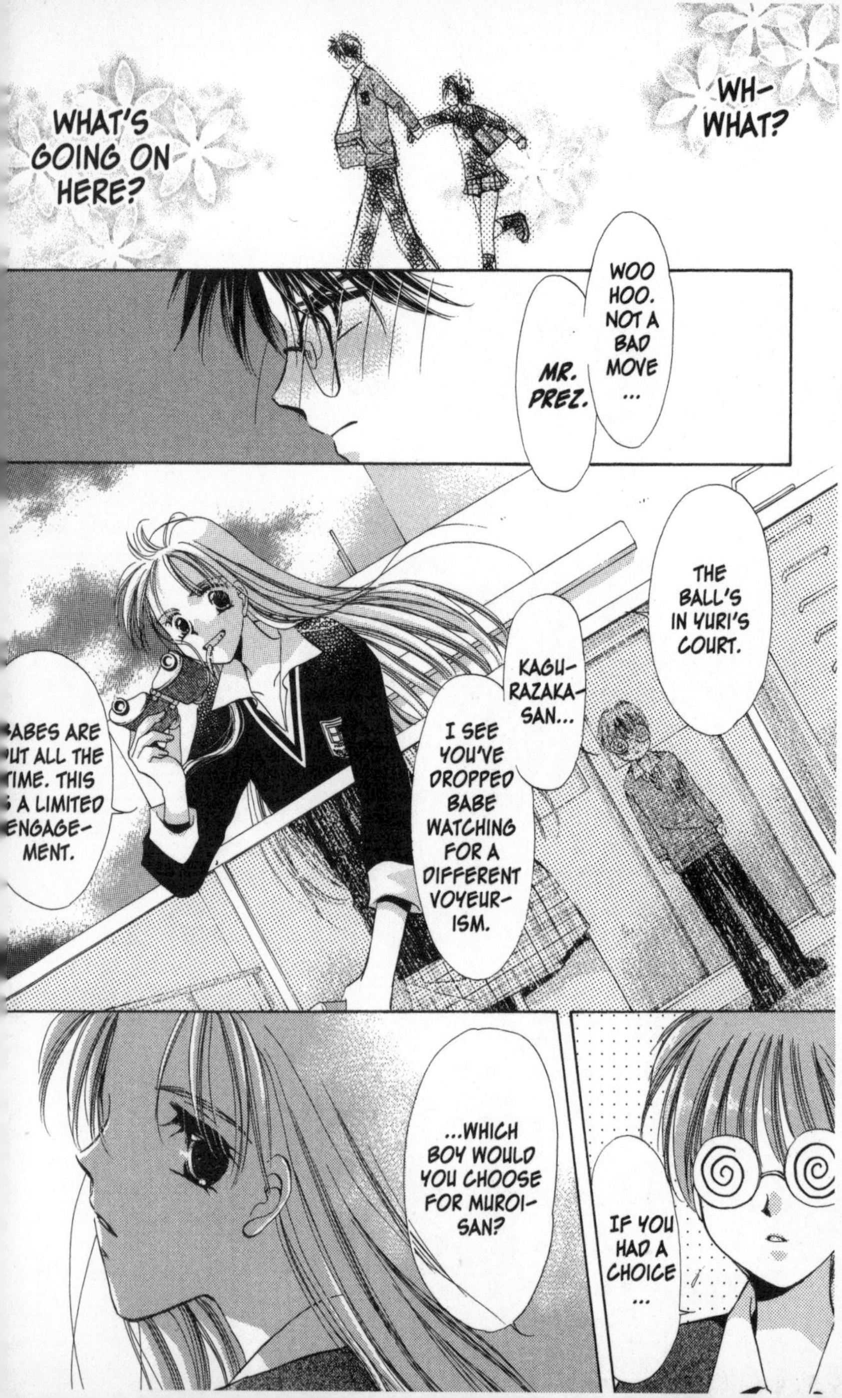
WH- WHAT?
WHAT'S GOING ON HERE?
WOO HOO. NOT A BAD MOVE ...
MR. PREZ.
THE BALL'S IN YURI'S COURT.
KAGURAZAKA-SAN...
I SEE YOU'VE DROPPED BABE WATCHING FOR A DIFFERENT VOYEURISM.
ABES ARE UT ALL THE TIME. THIS A LIMITED ENGAGEMENT.
IF YOU HAD A CHOICE ...
...WHICH BOY WOULD YOU CHOOSE FOR MUROI-SAN?

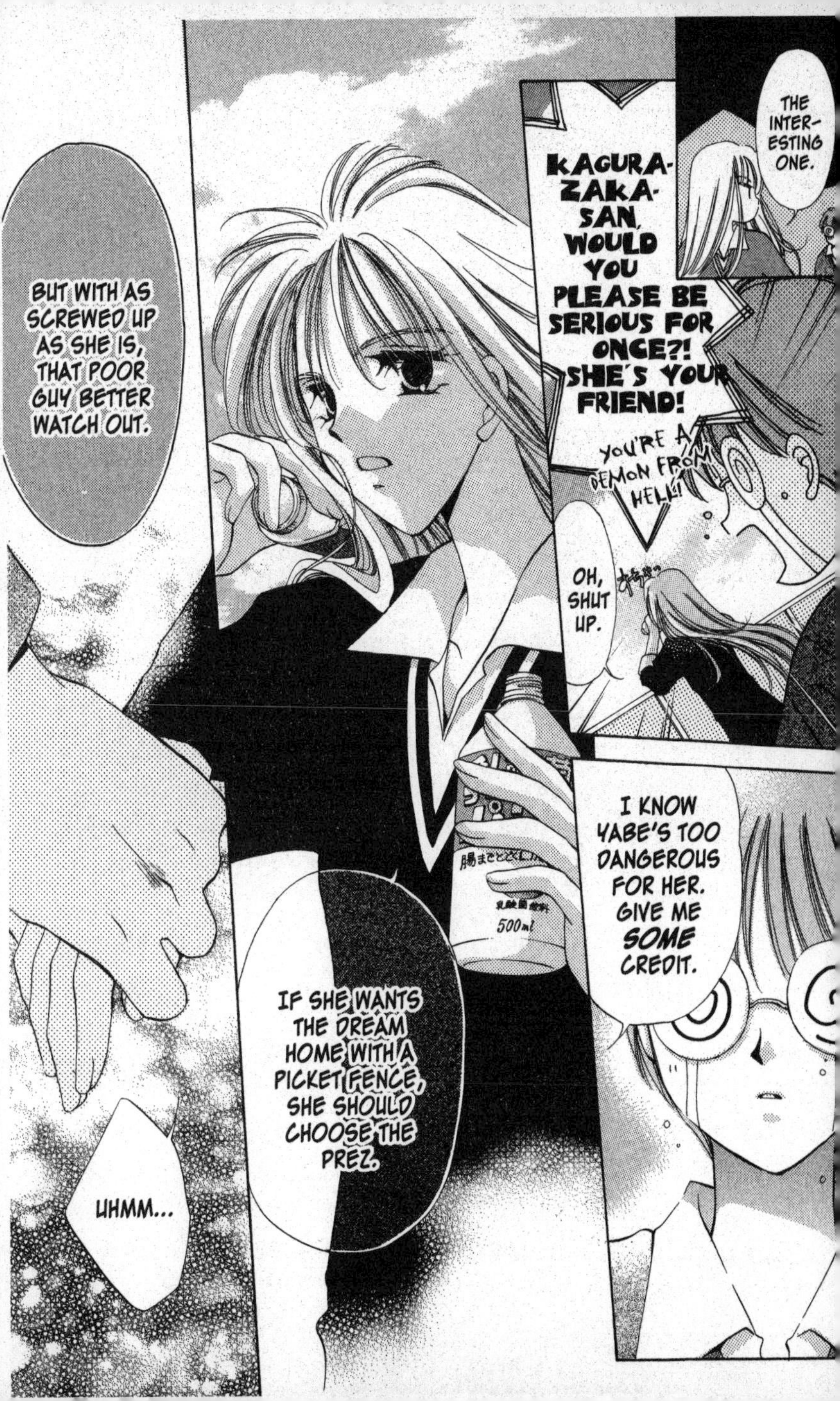
THE INTER-ESTING ONE.
KAGURA-ZAKA-SAN, WOULD YOU PLEASE BE SERIOUS FOR ONCE?! SHE'S YOUR FRIEND!
YOU'RE A DEMON FROM HELL!
OH, SHUT UP.
I KNOW YABE'S TOO DANGEROUS FOR HER. GIVE ME *SOME* CREDIT.
IF SHE WANTS THE DREAM HOME WITH A PICKET FENCE, SHE SHOULD CHOOSE THE PREZ.
BUT WITH AS SCREWED UP AS SHE IS, THAT POOR GUY BETTER WATCH OUT.
UHMM...

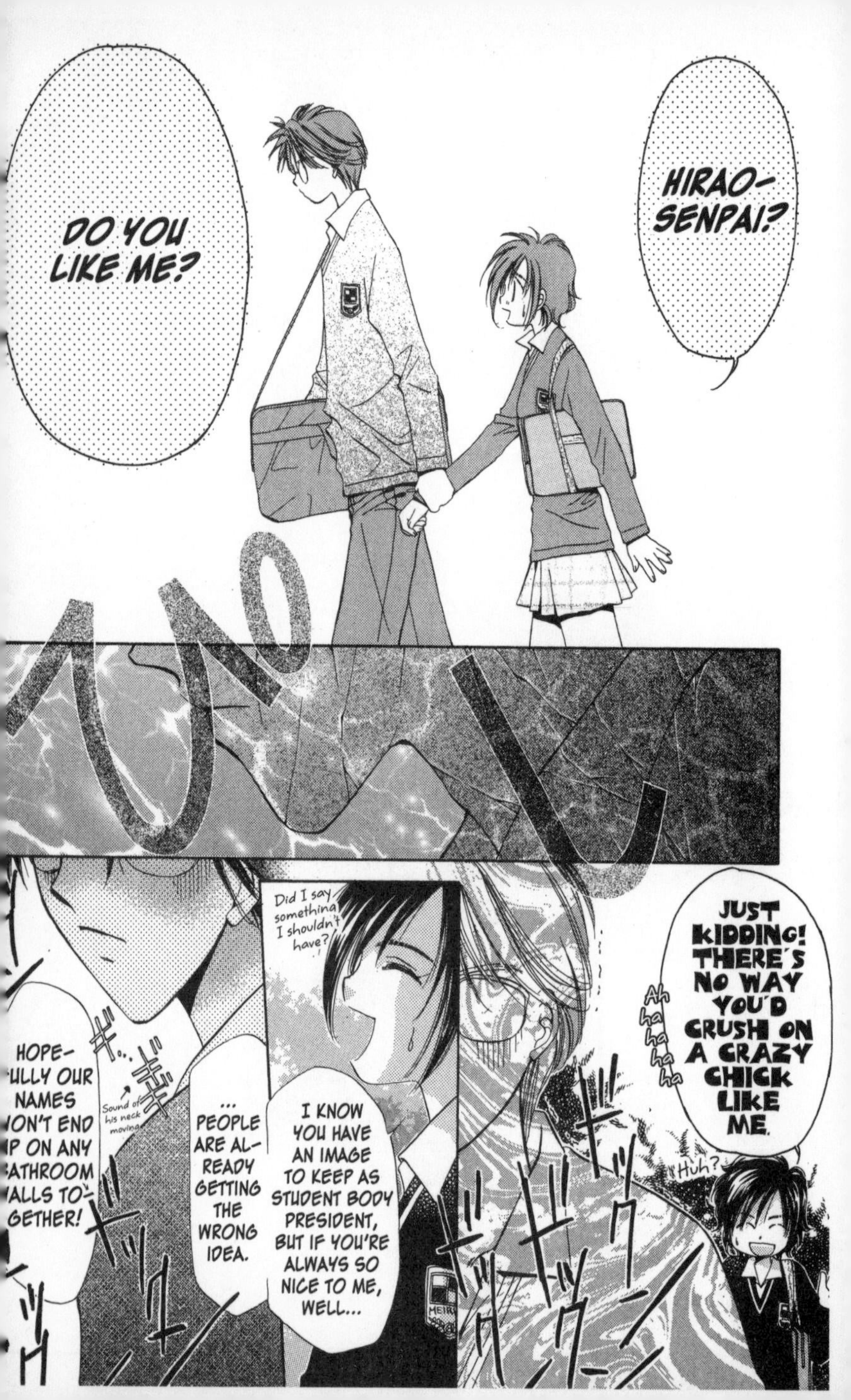
HIRAO-SENPAI?
DO YOU LIKE ME?
JUST KIDDING! THERE'S NO WAY YOU'D CRUSH ON A CRAZY CHICK LIKE ME.
Ah ha ha ha ha
Huh?
Did I say something I shouldn't have?
I KNOW YOU HAVE AN IMAGE TO KEEP AS STUDENT BODY PRESIDENT, BUT IF YOU'RE ALWAYS SO NICE TO ME, WELL...
... PEOPLE ARE AL-READY GETTING THE WRONG IDEA.
Sound of his neck moving
HOPE-ULLY OUR NAMES ON'T END P ON ANY ATHROOM ALLS TO-GETHER!

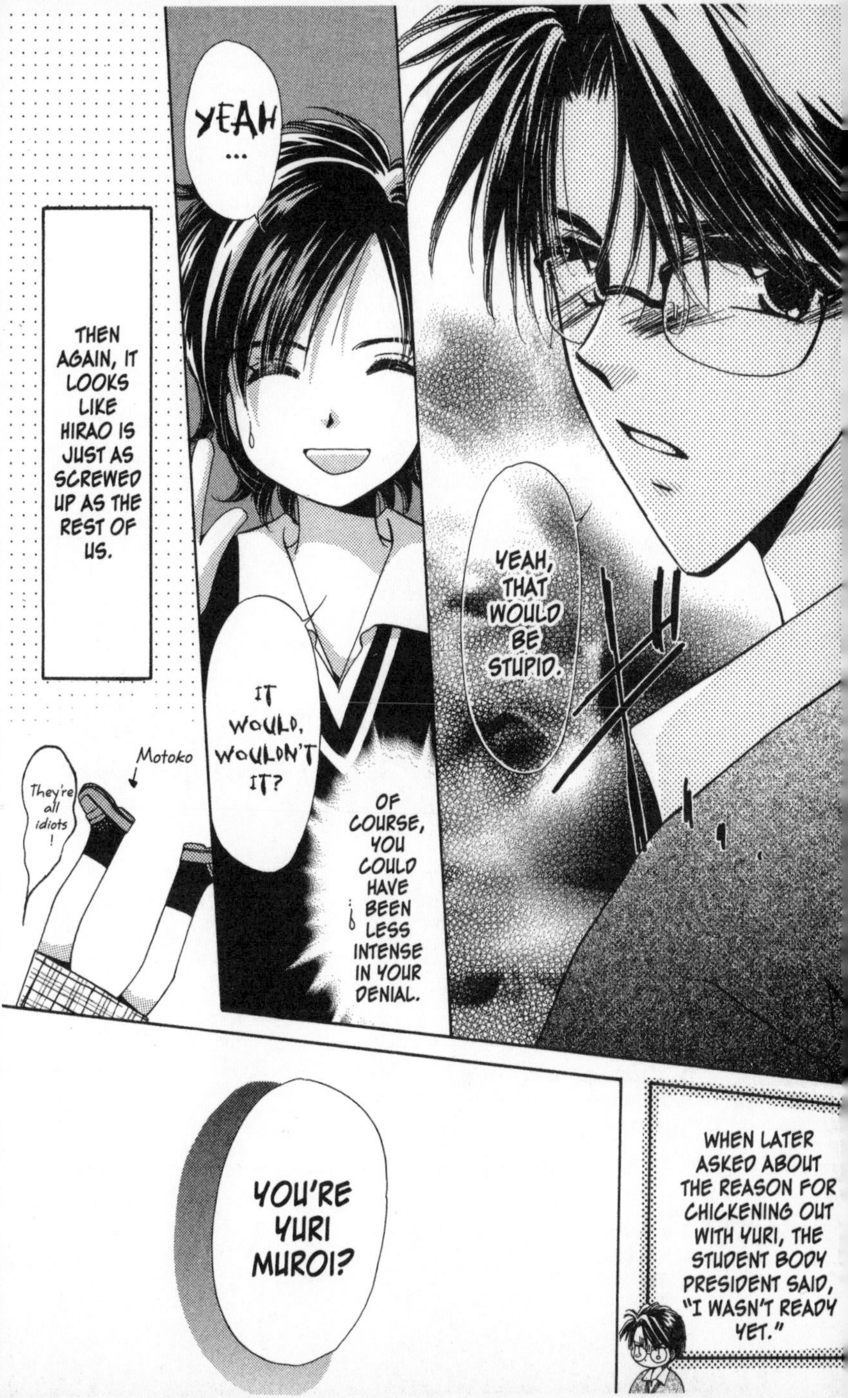
YEAH, THAT WOULD BE STUPID.
YEAH ...
IT WOULD, WOULDN'T IT?
OF COURSE, YOU COULD HAVE BEEN LESS INTENSE IN YOUR DENIAL.
THEN AGAIN, IT LOOKS LIKE HIRAO IS JUST AS SCREWED UP AS THE REST OF US.
Motoko
They're all idiots!
WHEN LATER ASKED ABOUT THE REASON FOR CHICKENING OUT WITH YURI, THE STUDENT BODY PRESIDENT SAID, "I WASN'T READY YET."
YOU'RE YURI MUROI?

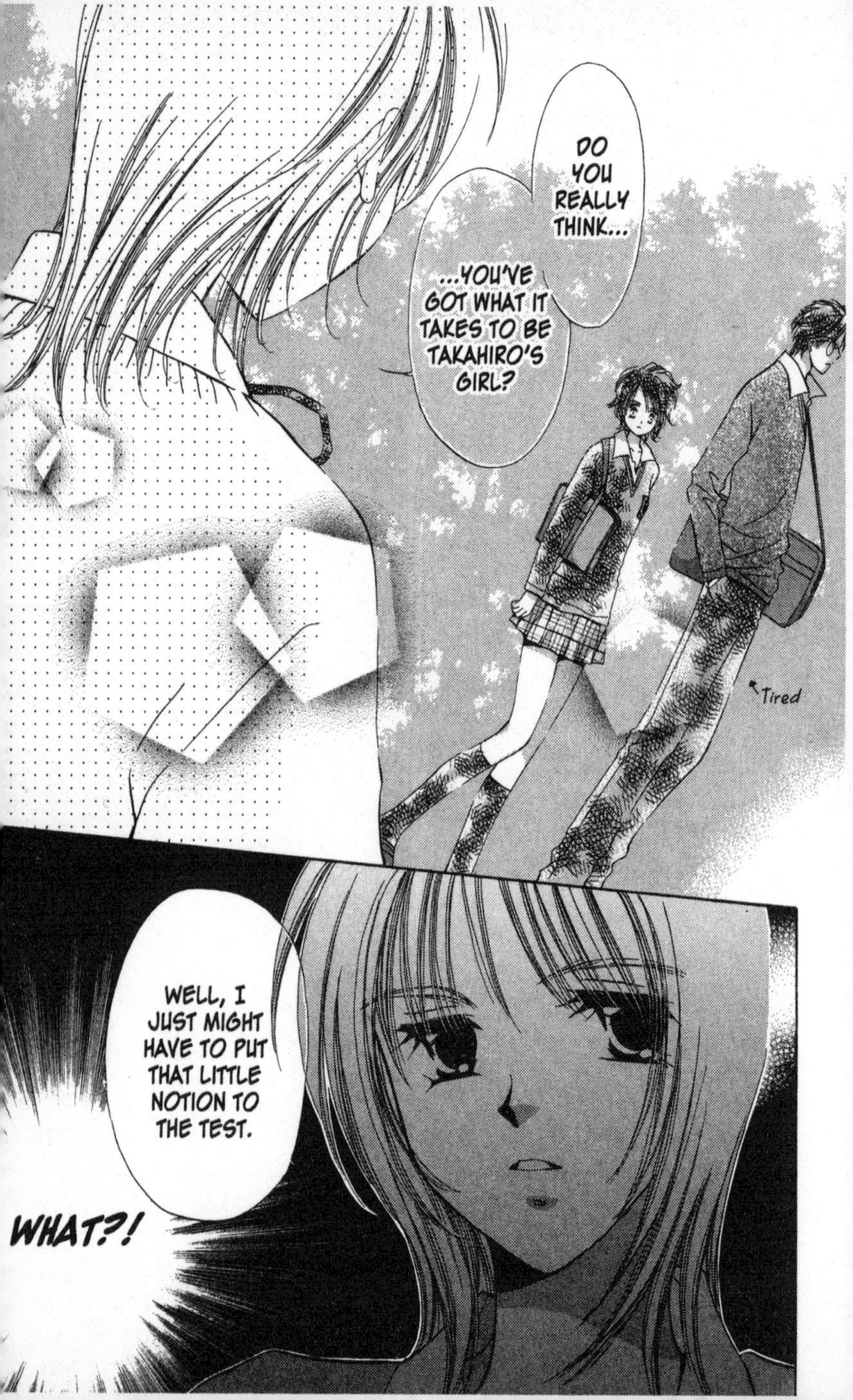
DO YOU REALLY THINK...
...YOU'VE GOT WHAT IT TAKES TO BE TAKAHIRO'S GIRL?
Tired
WELL, I JUST MIGHT HAVE TO PUT THAT LITTLE NOTION TO THE TEST.
WHAT?!

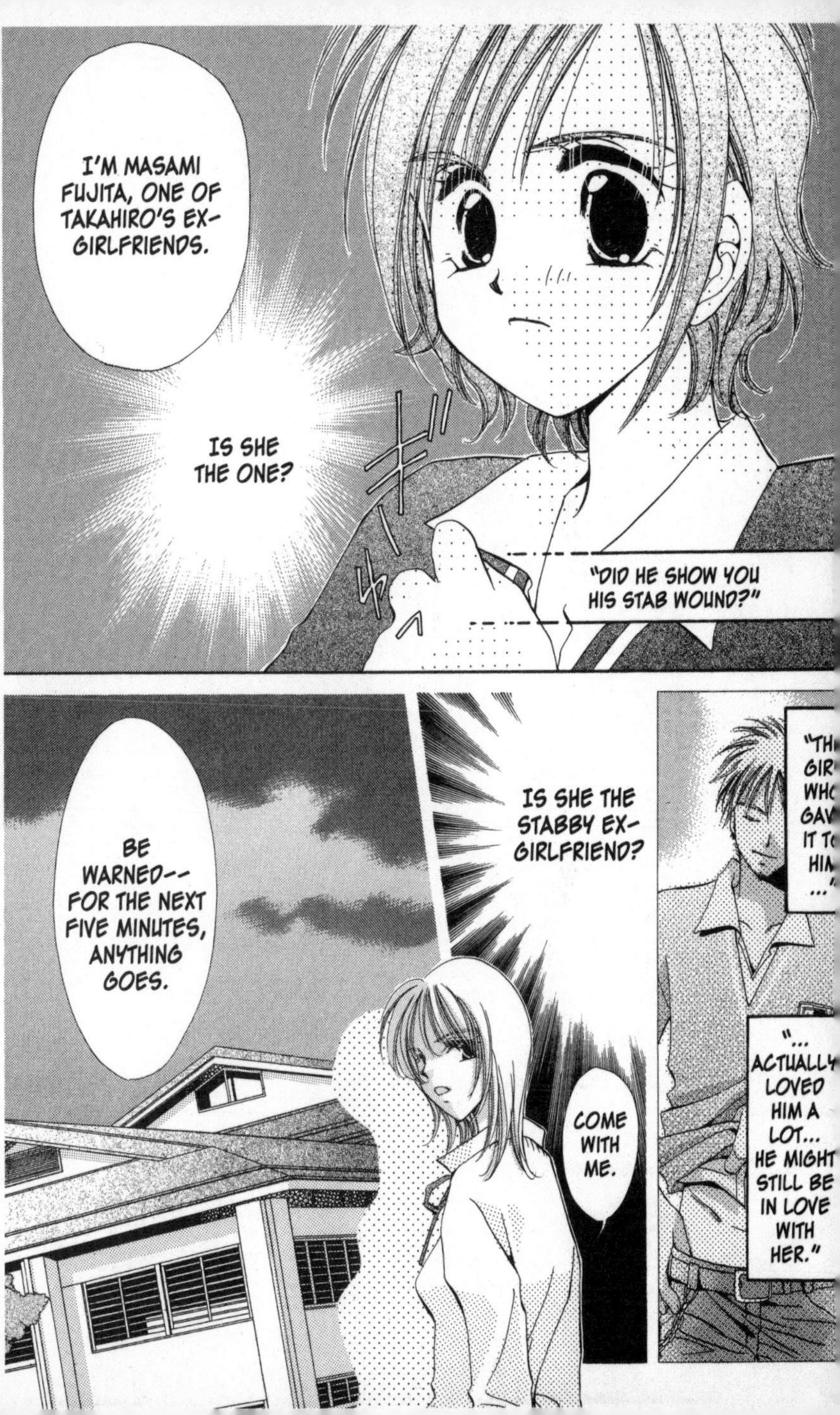
I'M MASAMI FUJITA, ONE OF TAKAHIRO'S EX-GIRLFRIENDS.
IS SHE THE ONE?
"DID HE SHOW YOU HIS STAB WOUND?"
"TH GIR WH GAV IT T HIM ..."
"... ACTUALLY LOVED HIM A LOT... HE MIGHT STILL BE IN LOVE WITH HER."
IS SHE THE STABBY EX-GIRLFRIEND?
COME WITH ME.
BE WARNED-- FOR THE NEXT FIVE MINUTES, ANYTHING GOES.

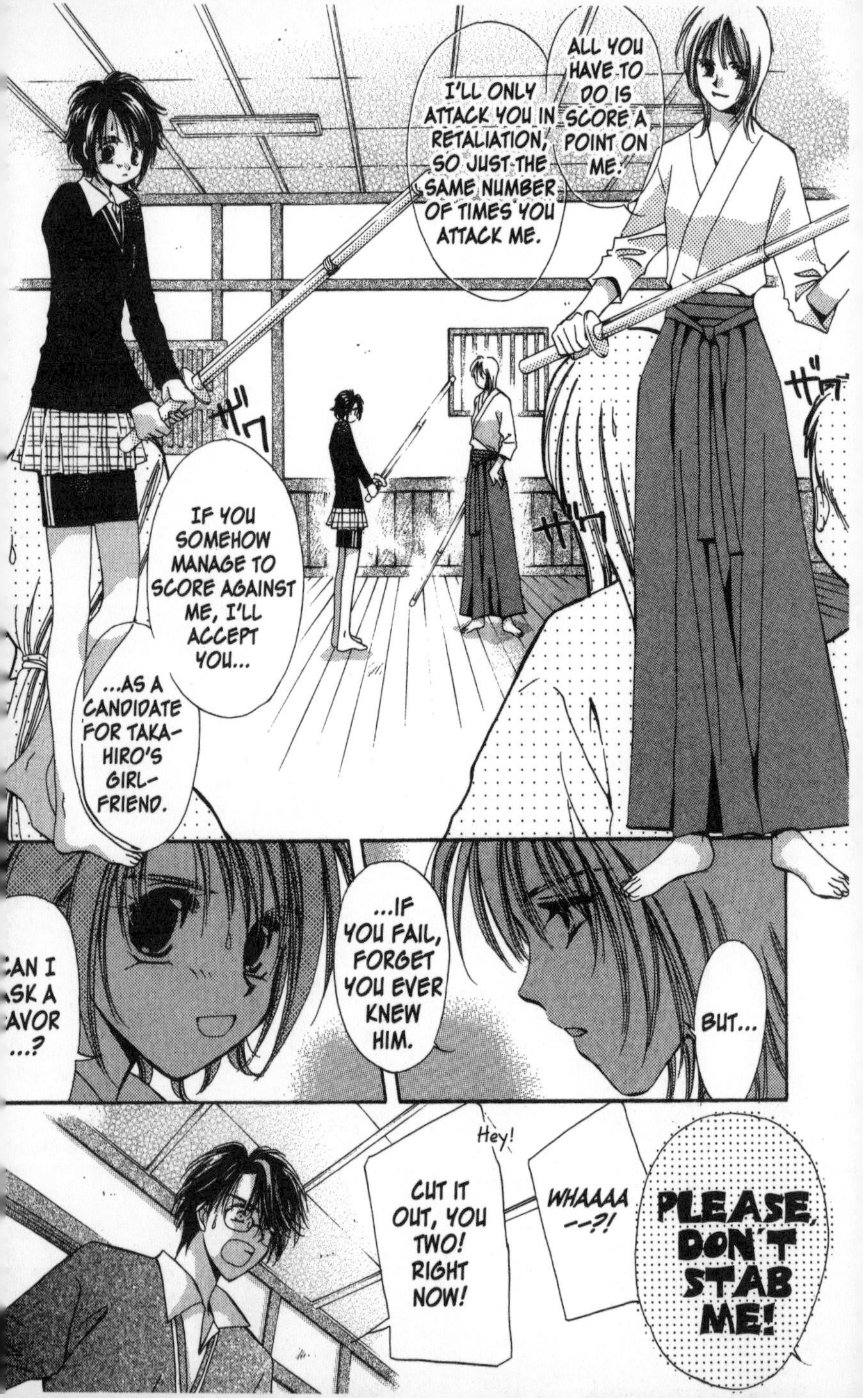

ALL YOU HAVE TO DO IS SCORE A POINT ON ME.
I'LL ONLY ATTACK YOU IN RETALIATION, SO JUST THE SAME NUMBER OF TIMES YOU ATTACK ME.
IF YOU SOMEHOW MANAGE TO SCORE AGAINST ME, I'LL ACCEPT YOU...
...AS A CANDIDATE FOR TAKA-HIRO'S GIRL-FRIEND.
BUT...
...IF YOU FAIL, FORGET YOU EVER KNEW HIM.
CAN I ASK A FAVOR ...?
PLEASE, DON'T STAB ME!
WHAAAA--?!
Hey!
CUT IT OUT, YOU TWO! RIGHT NOW!

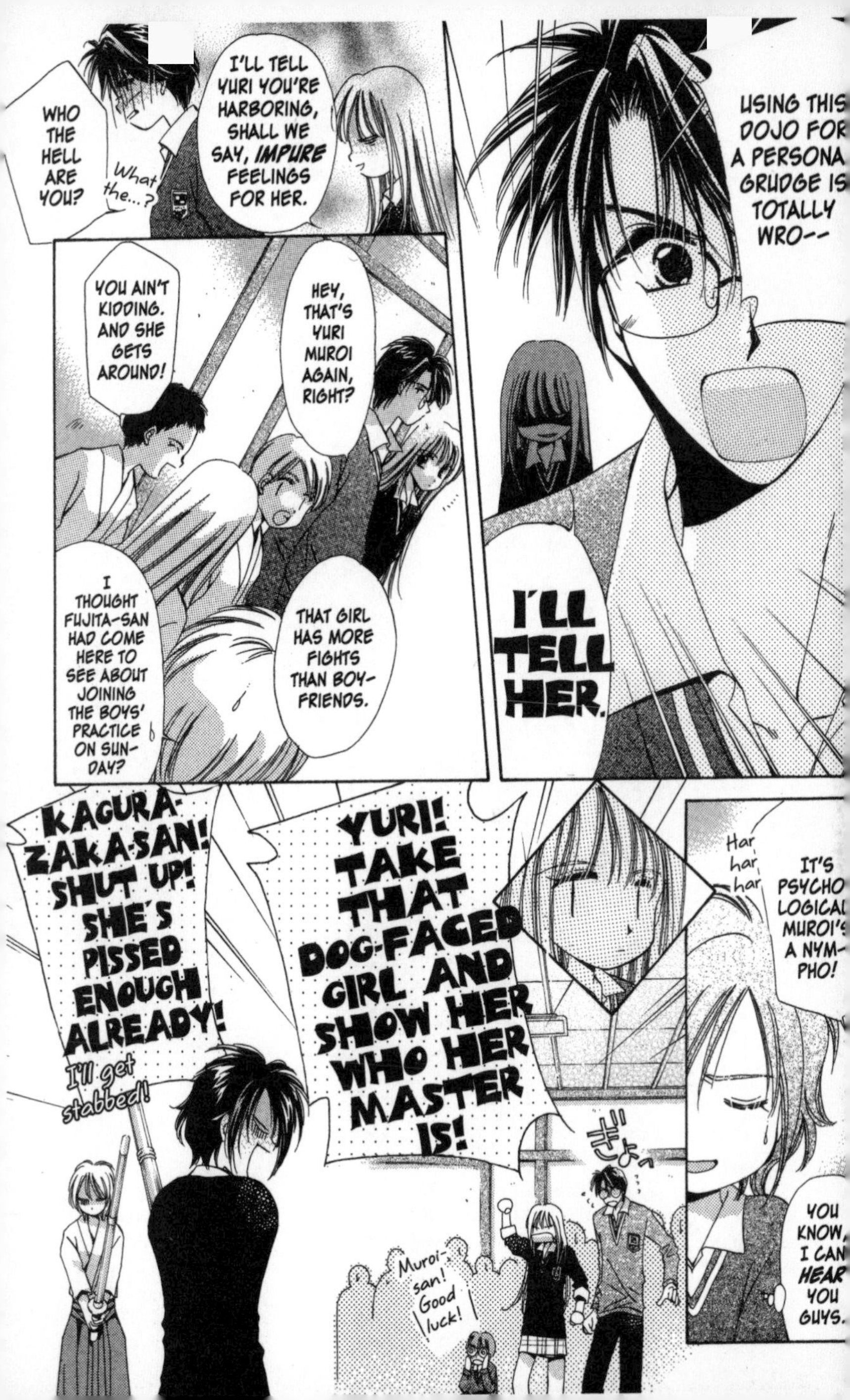
USING THIS DOJO FOR A PERSONA GRUDGE IS TOTALLY WRO--
I'LL TELL HER.
I'LL TELL YURI YOU'RE HARBORING, SHALL WE SAY, *IMPURE* FEELINGS FOR HER.
WHO THE HELL ARE YOU?
What the...?
HEY, THAT'S YURI MUROI AGAIN, RIGHT?
YOU AIN'T KIDDING. AND SHE GETS AROUND!
THAT GIRL HAS MORE FIGHTS THAN BOY-FRIENDS.
I THOUGHT FUJITA-SAN HAD COME HERE TO SEE ABOUT JOINING THE BOYS' PRACTICE ON SUN-DAY?
Har har har
IT'S PSYCHO LOGICAL MUROI'S A NYM-PHO!
YOU KNOW, I CAN *HEAR* YOU GUYS.
YURI! TAKE THAT DOG-FACED GIRL AND SHOW HER WHO HER MASTER IS!
ぎょ
KAGURA-ZAKA-SAN! SHUT UP! SHE'S PISSED ENOUGH ALREADY!
I'll get stabbed!
Muroi-san! Good luck!

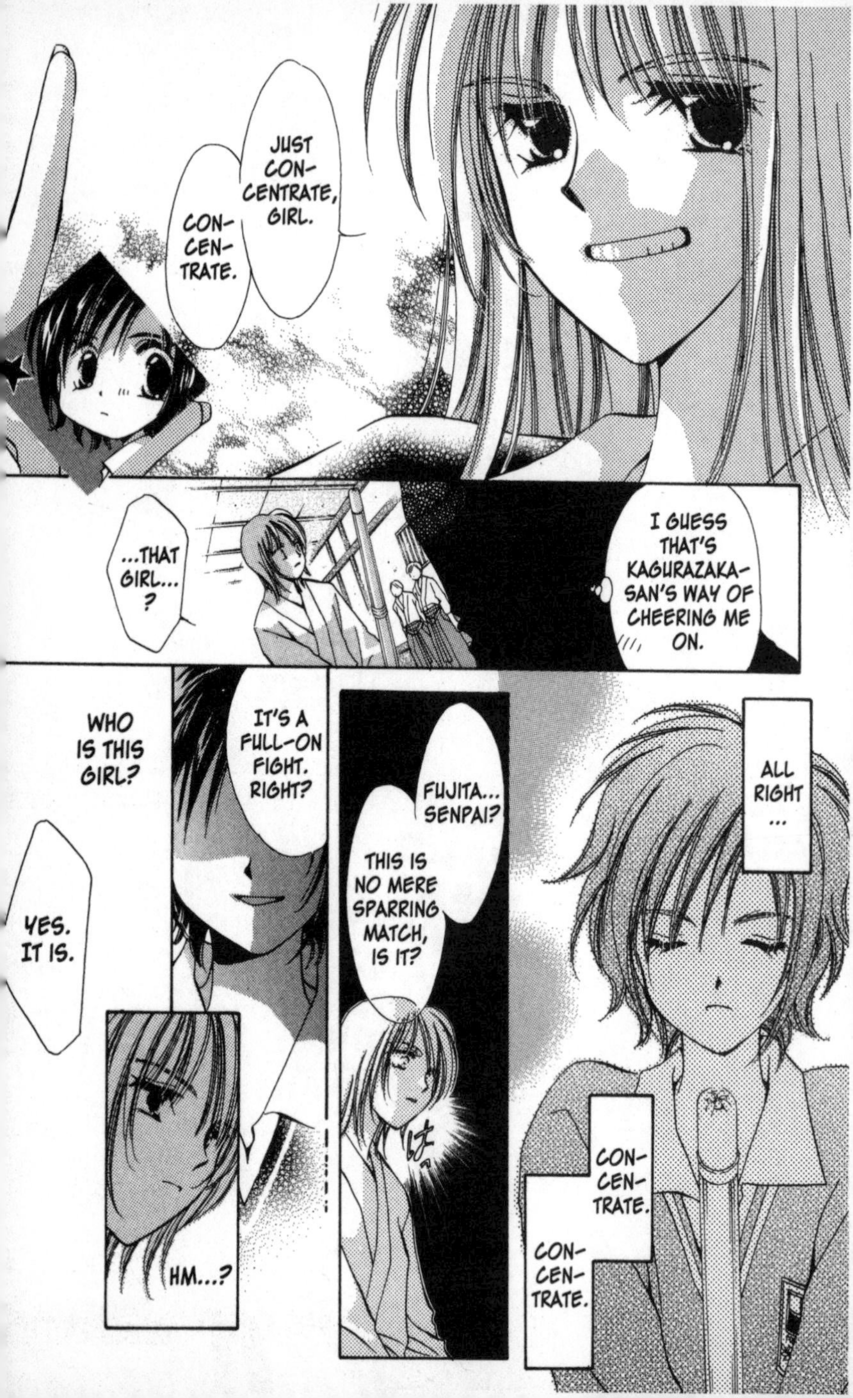
JUST CON-CENTRATE, GIRL.
CON-CEN-TRATE.
I GUESS THAT'S KAGURAZAKA-SAN'S WAY OF CHEERING ME ON.
...THAT GIRL...?
ALL RIGHT...
CON-CEN-TRATE.
CON-CEN-TRATE.
FUJITA... SENPAI?
THIS IS NO MERE SPARRING MATCH, IS IT?
IT'S A FULL-ON FIGHT. RIGHT?
WHO IS THIS GIRL?
YES. IT IS.
HM...?

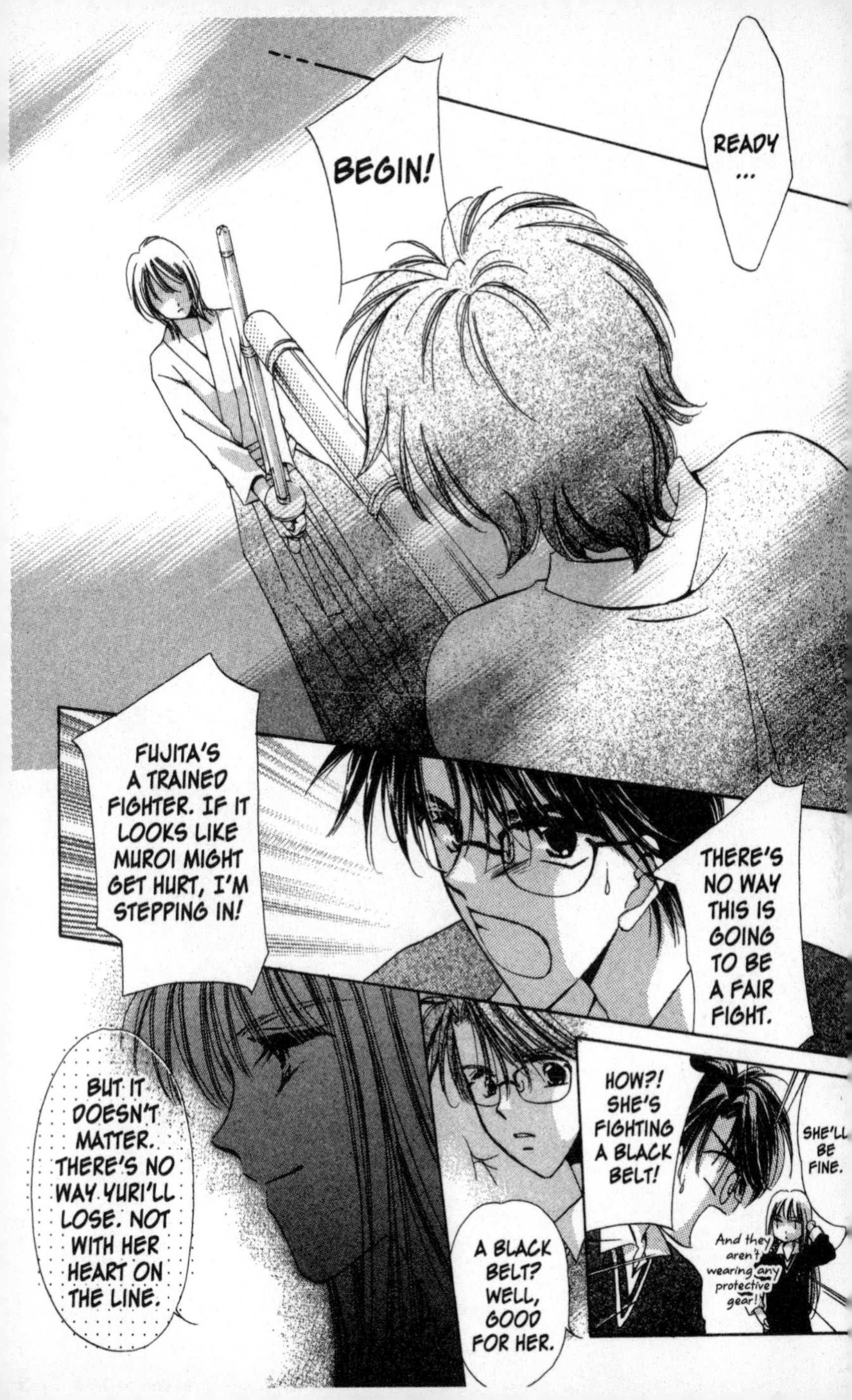
READY ...
BEGIN!
THERE'S NO WAY THIS IS GOING TO BE A FAIR FIGHT.
FUJITA'S A TRAINED FIGHTER. IF IT LOOKS LIKE MUROI MIGHT GET HURT, I'M STEPPING IN!
HOW?! SHE'S FIGHTING A BLACK BELT!
SHE'LL BE FINE.
And they aren't wearing any protective gear!
A BLACK BELT? WELL, GOOD FOR HER.
BUT IT DOESN'T MATTER. THERE'S NO WAY YURI'LL LOSE. NOT WITH HER HEART ON THE LINE.

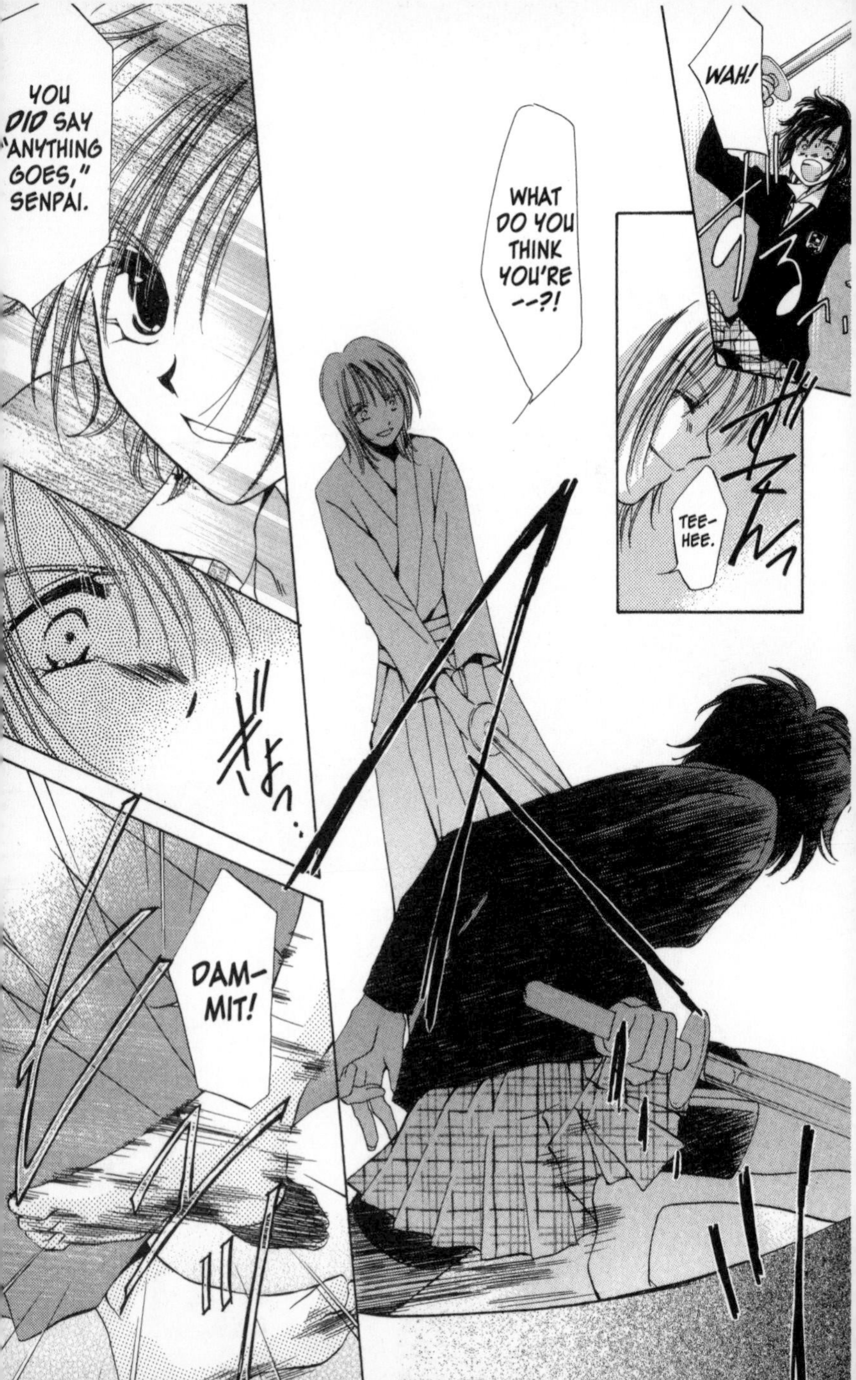
WAH!
TEE-HEE.
WHAT DO YOU THINK YOU'RE --?!
YOU DID SAY "ANYTHING GOES," SENPAI.
DAM-MIT!

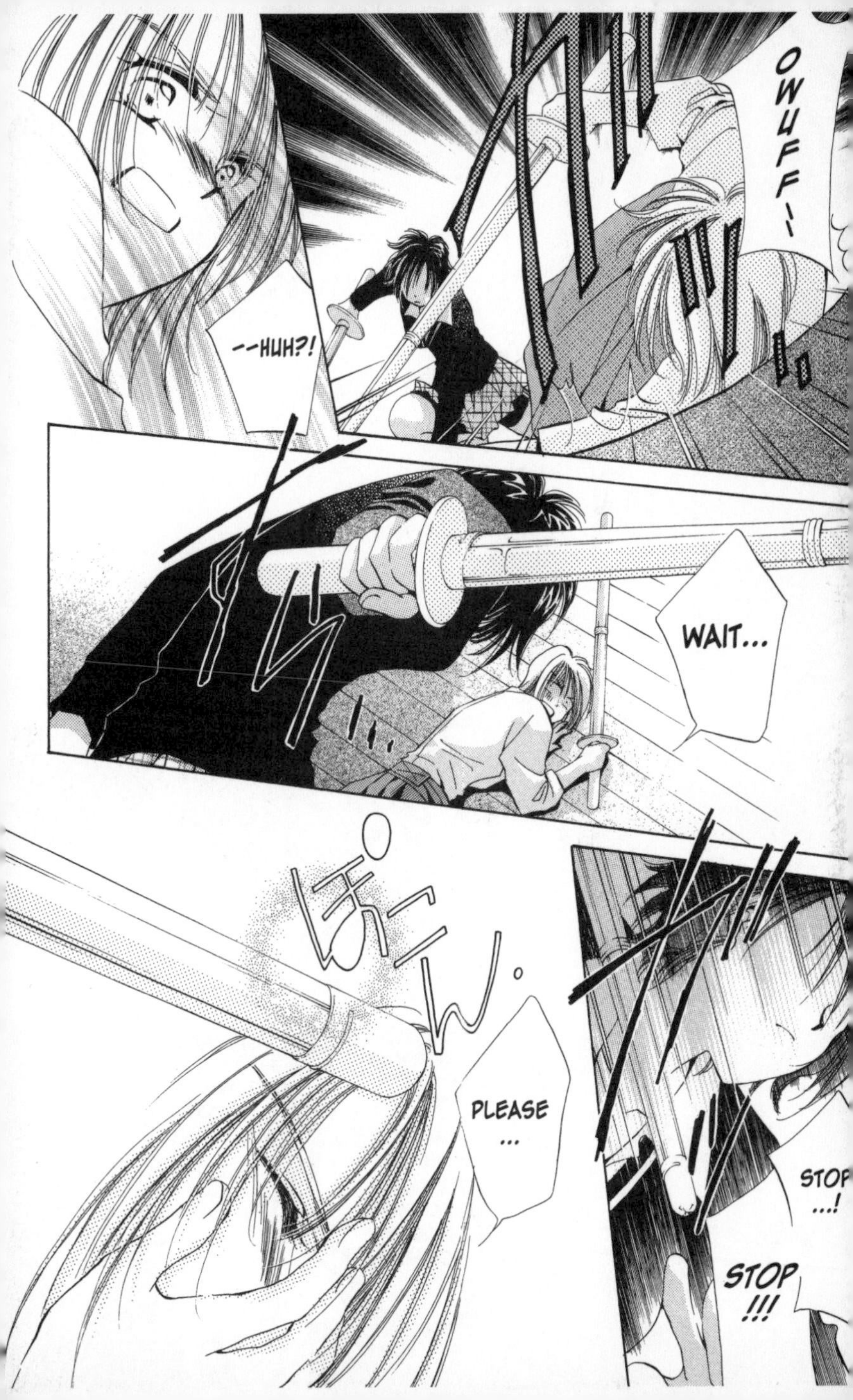
OWUFF..!
--HUH?!
WAIT...
STOP ...!
STOP !!!
ぽこん。
PLEASE ...

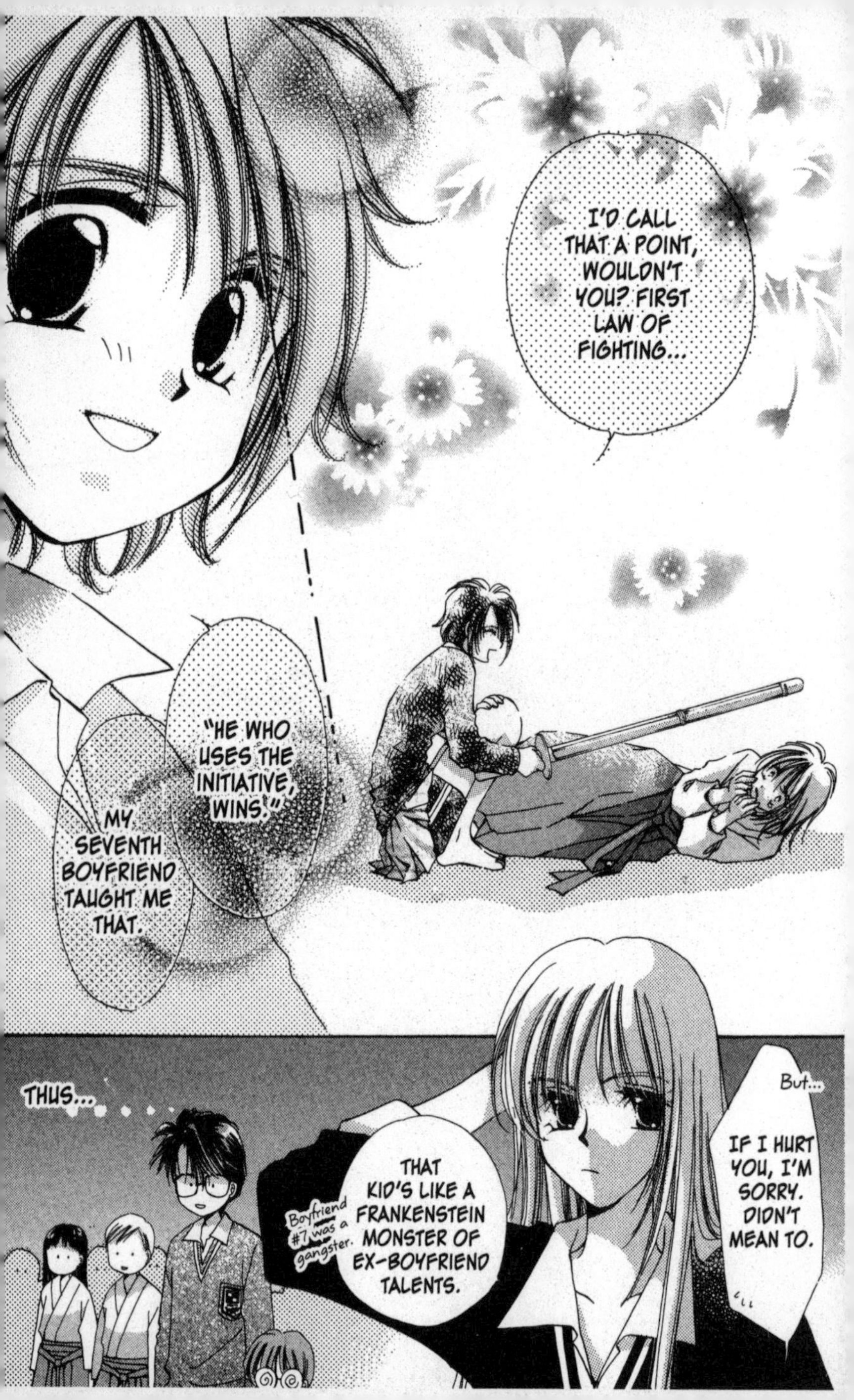
I'D CALL THAT A POINT, WOULDN'T YOU? FIRST LAW OF FIGHTING...
"HE WHO USES THE INITIATIVE, WINS."
MY SEVENTH BOYFRIEND TAUGHT ME THAT.
But...
IF I HURT YOU, I'M SORRY. DIDN'T MEAN TO.
THAT KID'S LIKE A FRANKENSTEIN MONSTER OF EX-BOYFRIEND TALENTS.
Boyfriend #7 was a gangster.
THUS......

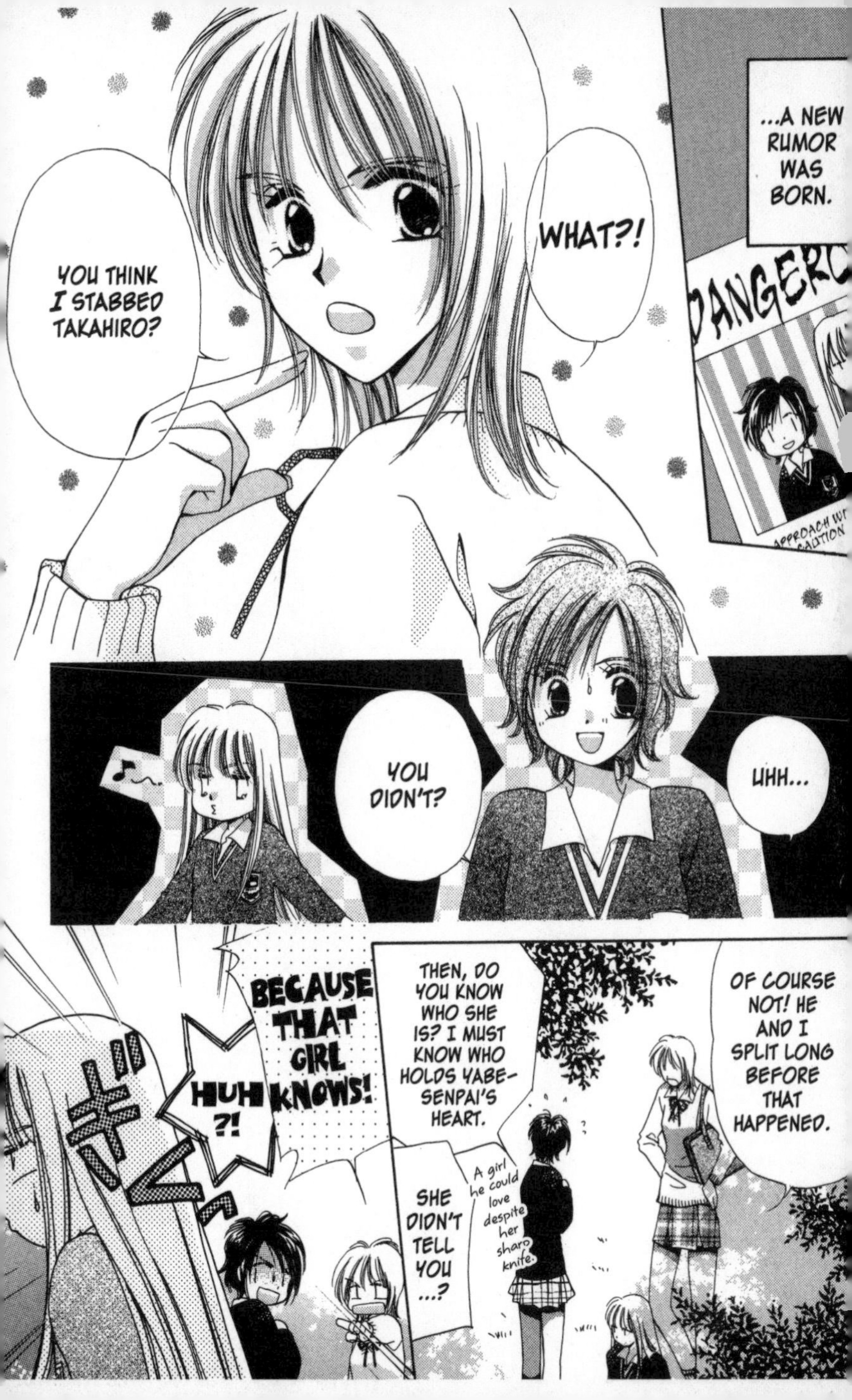
...A NEW RUMOR WAS BORN.
WHAT?!
YOU THINK I STABBED TAKAHIRO?
UHH...
YOU DIDN'T?
OF COURSE NOT! HE AND I SPLIT LONG BEFORE THAT HAPPENED.
THEN, DO YOU KNOW WHO SHE IS? I MUST KNOW WHO HOLDS YABE-SENPAI'S HEART.
A girl he could love despite her sharp knife.
SHE DIDN'T TELL YOU ...?
BECAUSE THAT GIRL KNOWS!
HUH ?!

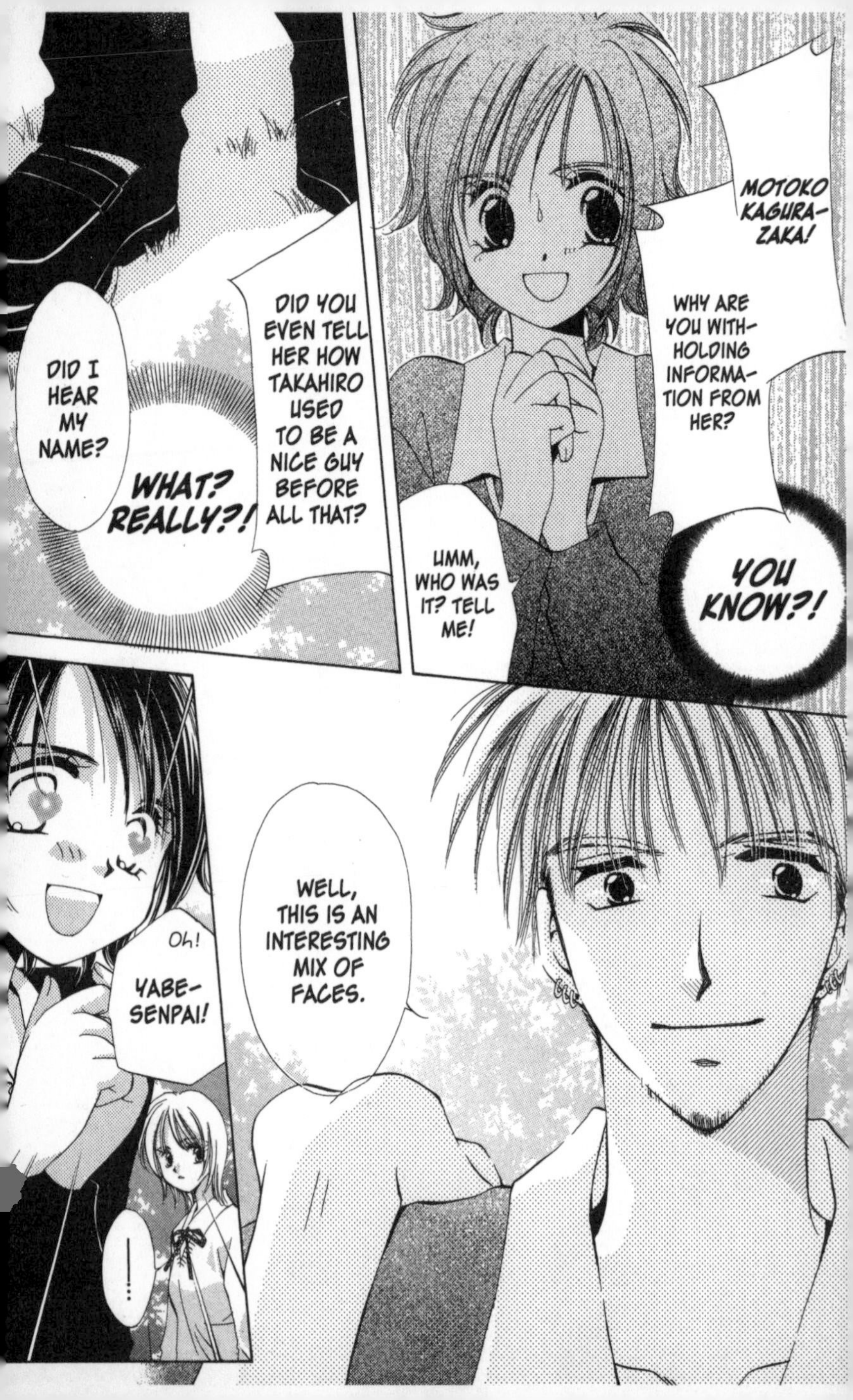
MOTOKO KAGURA-ZAKA!
WHY ARE YOU WITH-HOLDING INFORMATION FROM HER?
YOU KNOW?!
UMM, WHO WAS IT? TELL ME!
DID YOU EVEN TELL HER HOW TAKAHIRO USED TO BE A NICE GUY BEFORE ALL THAT?
WHAT? REALLY?!
DID I HEAR MY NAME?
WELL, THIS IS AN INTERESTING MIX OF FACES.
Oh!
YABE-SENPAI!
...!

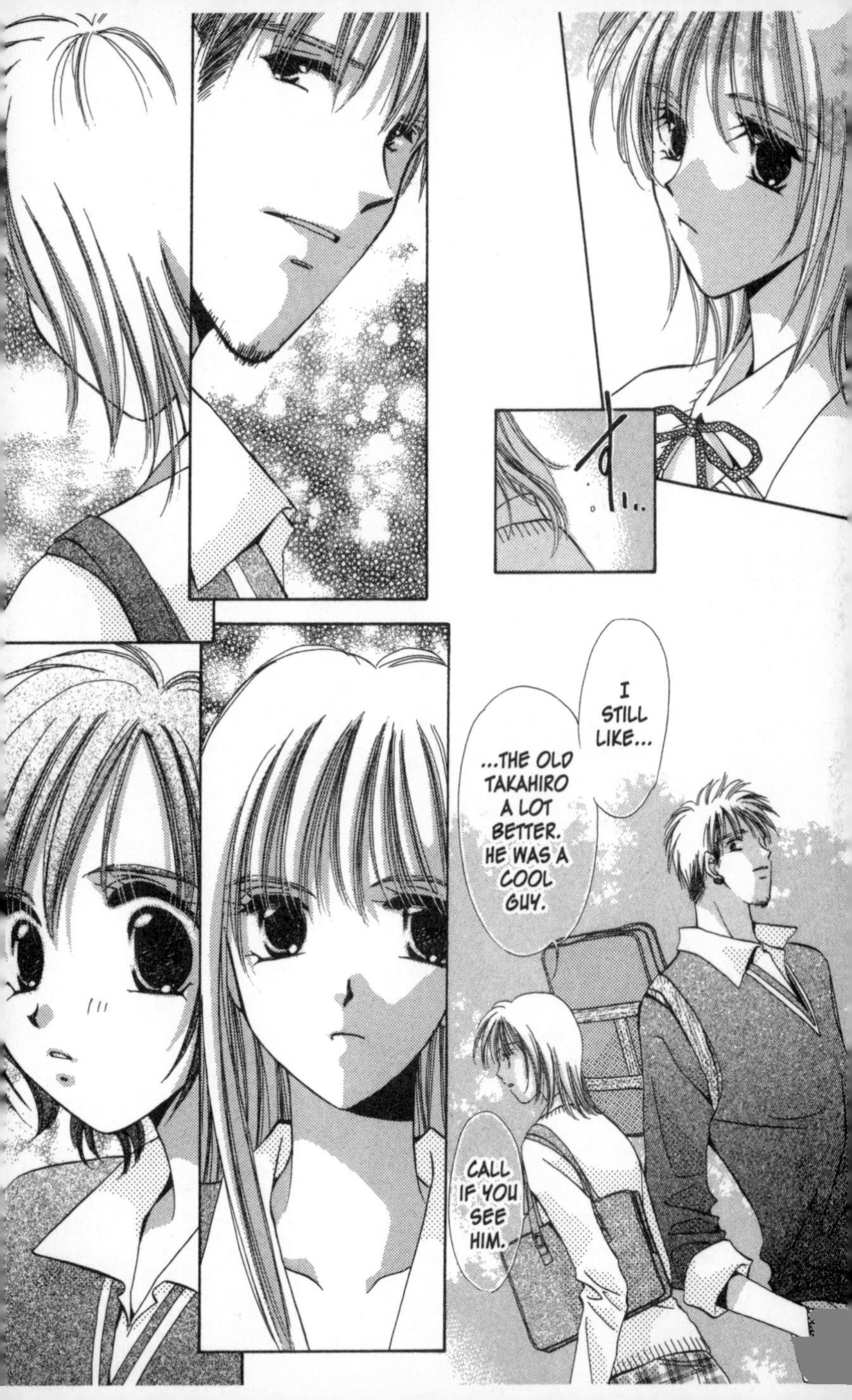
I STILL LIKE...
...THE OLD TAKAHIRO A LOT BETTER. HE WAS A COOL GUY.
CALL IF YOU SEE HIM.

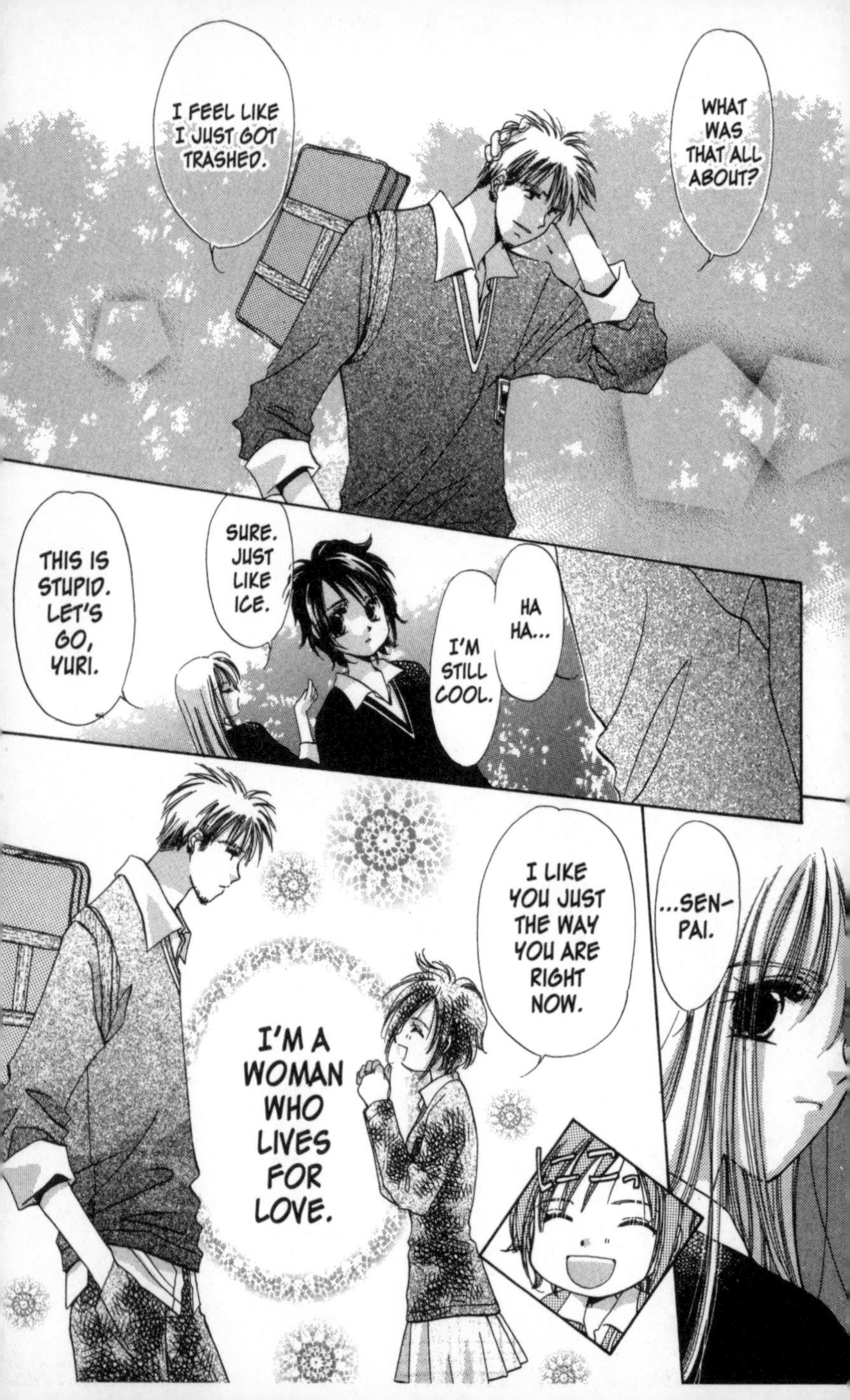
WHAT WAS THAT ALL ABOUT?
I FEEL LIKE I JUST GOT TRASHED.
HA HA...
I'M STILL COOL.
SURE. JUST LIKE ICE.
THIS IS STUPID. LET'S GO, YURI.
...SEN-PAI.
I LIKE YOU JUST THE WAY YOU ARE RIGHT NOW.
I'M A WOMAN WHO LIVES FOR LOVE.

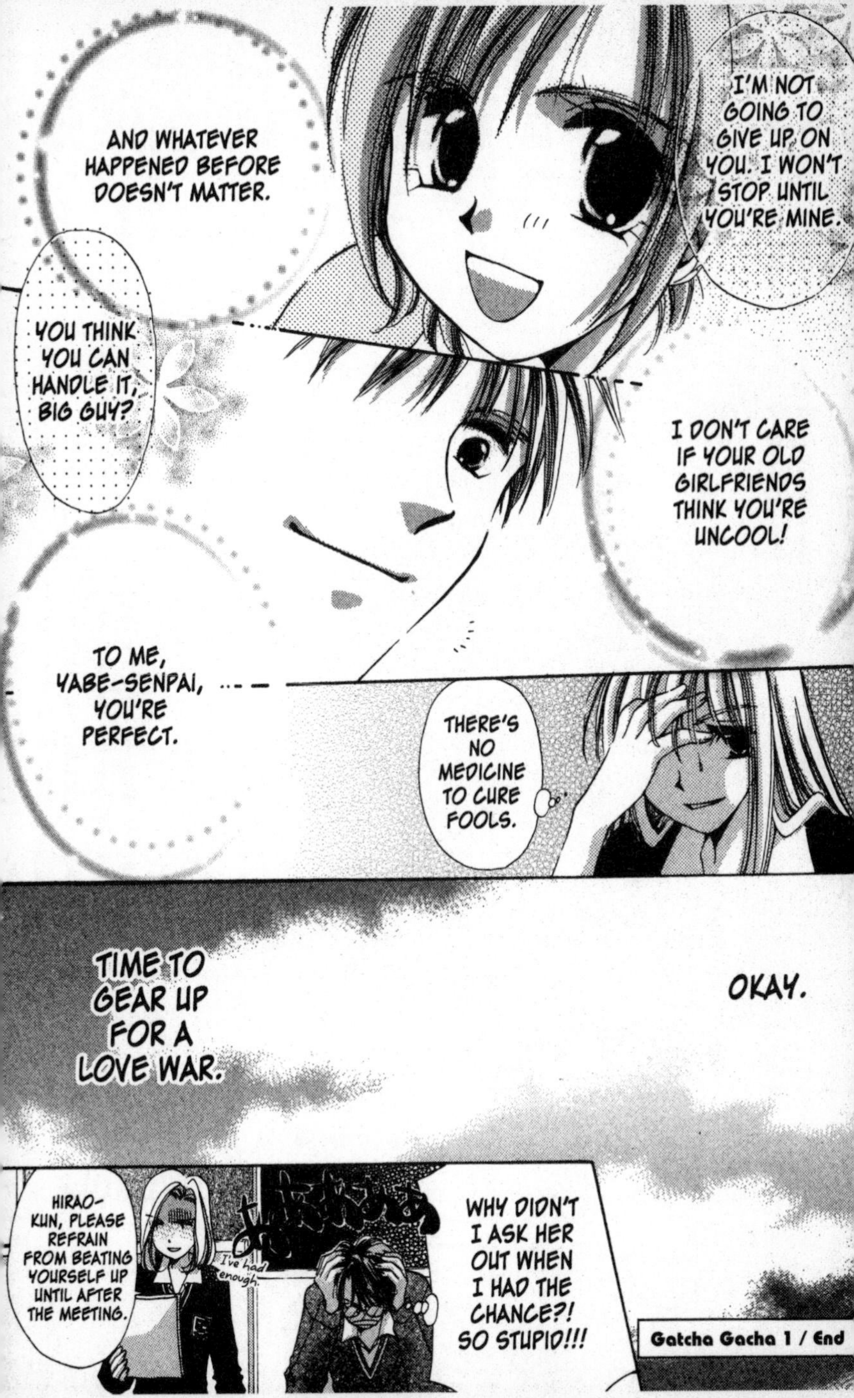
I'M NOT GOING TO GIVE UP ON YOU. I WON'T STOP UNTIL YOU'RE MINE.
AND WHATEVER HAPPENED BEFORE DOESN'T MATTER.
I DON'T CARE IF YOUR OLD GIRLFRIENDS THINK YOU'RE UNCOOL!
TO ME, YABE-SENPAI, YOU'RE PERFECT.
YOU THINK YOU CAN HANDLE IT, BIG GUY?
THERE'S NO MEDICINE TO CURE FOOLS.
OKAY.
TIME TO GEAR UP FOR A LOVE WAR.
WHY DIDN'T I ASK HER OUT WHEN I HAD THE CHANCE?! SO STUPID!!!
I've had enough.
HIRAO-KUN, PLEASE REFRAIN FROM BEATING YOURSELF UP UNTIL AFTER THE MEETING.
Gatcha Gacha 1 / End

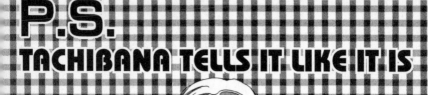

P.S.
TACHIBANA TELLS IT LIKE IT IS

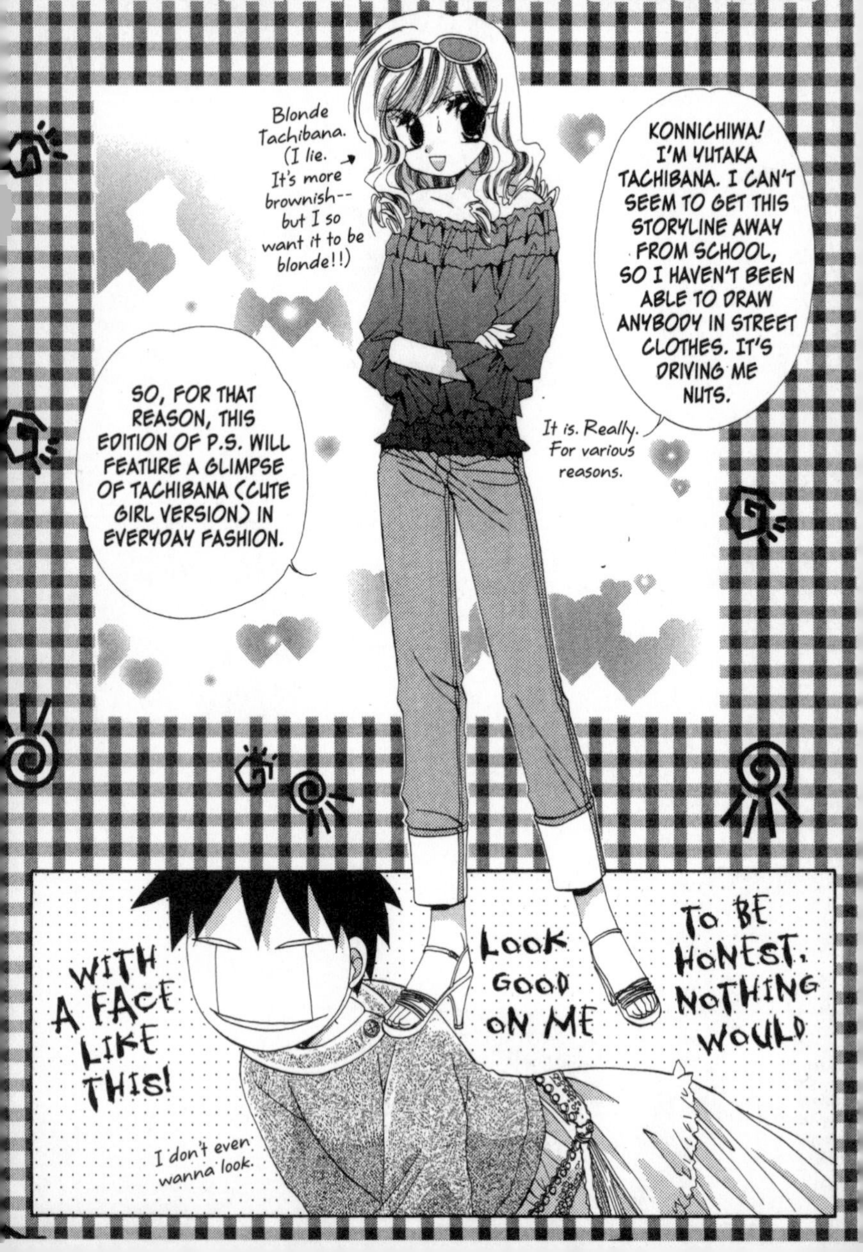
KONNICHIWA! I'M YUTAKA TACHIBANA. I CAN'T SEEM TO GET THIS STORYLINE AWAY FROM SCHOOL, SO I HAVEN'T BEEN ABLE TO DRAW ANYBODY IN STREET CLOTHES. IT'S DRIVING ME NUTS.
It is. Really. For various reasons.
Blonde Tachibana. (I lie. It's more brownish-- but I so want it to be blonde!!)
SO, FOR THAT REASON, THIS EDITION OF P.S. WILL FEATURE A GLIMPSE OF TACHIBANA (CUTE GIRL VERSION) IN EVERYDAY FASHION.
TO BE HONEST, NOTHING WOULD
LOOK GOOD ON ME
WITH A FACE LIKE THIS!
I don't even wanna look.

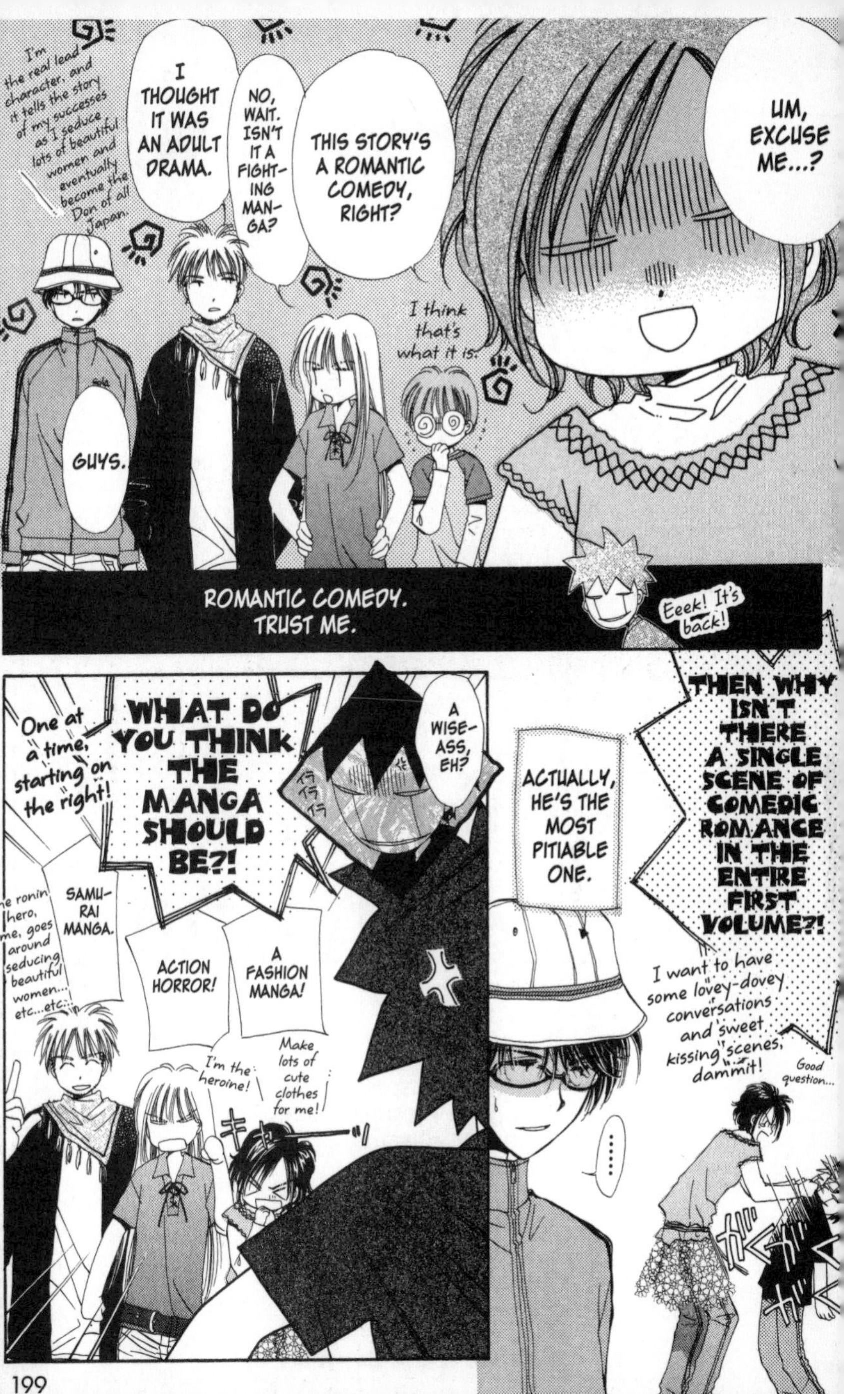
UM, EXCUSE ME...?
THIS STORY'S A ROMANTIC COMEDY, RIGHT?
NO, WAIT. ISN'T IT A FIGHTING MANGA?
I THOUGHT IT WAS AN ADULT DRAMA.
I'm the real lead character, and it tells the story of my successes as I seduce lots of beautiful women and eventually become the Don of all Japan.
I think that's what it is.
GUYS.
Eeek! It's back!
ROMANTIC COMEDY. TRUST ME.
THEN WHY ISN'T THERE A SINGLE SCENE OF COMEDIC ROMANCE IN THE ENTIRE FIRST VOLUME?!
I want to have some lovey-dovey conversations and sweet kissing scenes, dammit!
Good question...
ACTUALLY, HE'S THE MOST PITIABLE ONE.
......
A WISE-ASS, EH?
WHAT DO YOU THINK THE MANGA SHOULD BE?!
One at a time, starting on the right!
A FASHION MANGA!
Make lots of cute clothes for me!
ACTION HORROR!
I'm the heroine!
SAMURAI MANGA.
The ronin hero, me, goes around seducing beautiful women... etc...etc...

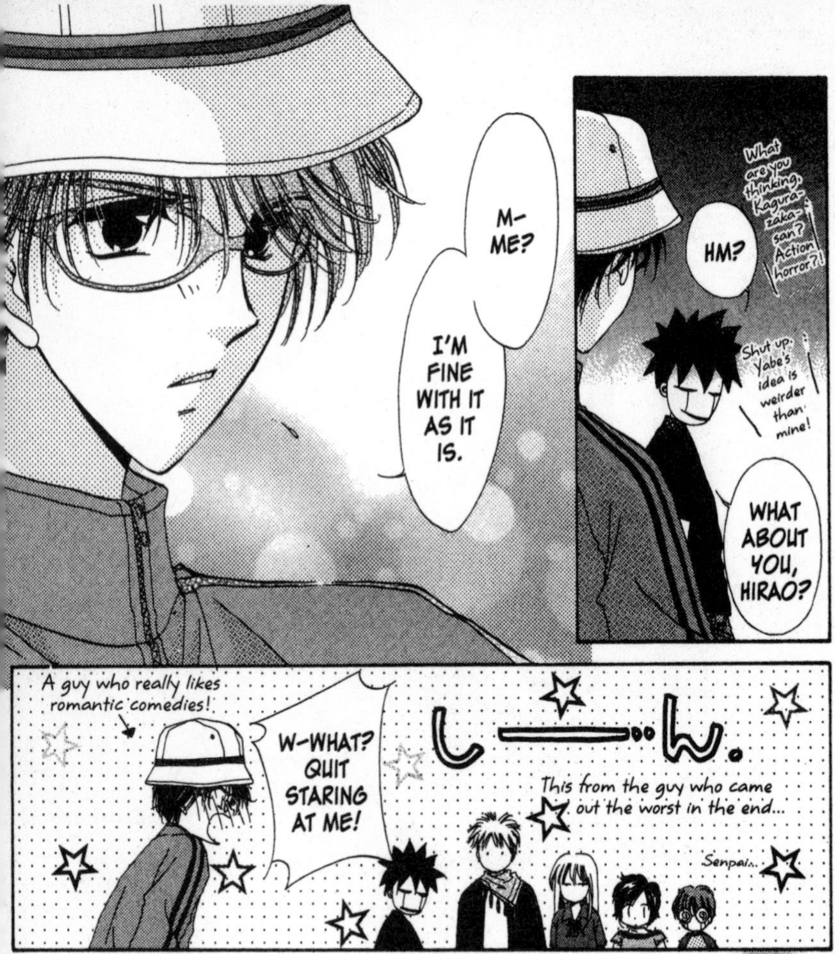
What are you thinking, Kagura-zaka-san? Action horror?!
HM?
Shut up. Yabe's idea is weirder than mine!
WHAT ABOUT YOU, HIRAO?
M-ME?
I'M FINE WITH IT AS IT IS.
しーん。
This from the guy who came out the worst in the end...
Senpai...
W-WHAT? QUIT STARING AT ME!
A guy who really likes romantic comedies!

So, paying respect to the
Student Body President's request,
on with the romantic comedy.

See y'all later!

P.S - Tachibana Tells It Like It Is / End

Gatcha Gacha
Volume 2

It's summer, and Yuri and Motoko have decided to go to the annual summer fireworks festival. Along the way, both Yabe and Hirao join them. Casual conversation ends up bringing up touchy subjects; Motoko's heritage, Yabe's past, Hirao's growing feelings for Yuri and how Hirao and Yabe first met (and what caused them to change so drastically from that time a year ago).

And just what mischief does Motoko have planned when she finds out Hirao has budding feelings for Yuri?

Though many questions are asked, the relationships between Yuri, Motoko, Yabe and Hirao only get more tangled in this second volume of *Gatcha Gacha*.

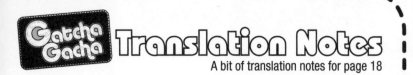

Gatcha Gacha

Translation Notes

A bit of translation notes for page 18

Usually we do our best to work these kinds of notes directly into the manga pages by either retouching the Japanese text into English or by adding the notes directly onto the pages. However, with this particular page neither seemed like a good solution. So, we created this little appendix for you guys. Hope it helps out.

... WHAT'S THIS?
猪木
詩集
1
あのリング界の燃える闘魂
アントニオ猪木の初ポエム!!
2
オマリーの六甲おろし
PRISM 74
3
4
"I BET SHE LOVES POETRY BY RILKE."
5

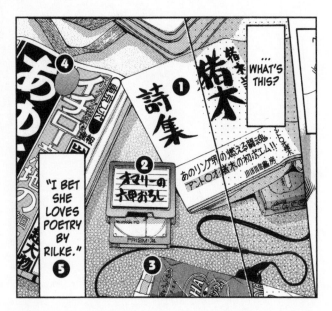

1) This is a book of poetry titled: *From the Demon of the Pro Wrestling Ring, Poetry by Antonio Inoki* (a variation on the translation is *From Pro Wrestling to Poetry, a Collection by Antonio Inoki*–if we had retouched out the Japanese, this is what I would have chosen.)

NOTE: Antonio Inoki is a famous pro wrestler in Japan, who already has at least one music CD on sale.

Gatcha Gacha Translation Notes

A bit of translation notes for page 18

2) The handwritten label on this MiniDisc reads: Omarii Rokkou Oroshi

NOTE: "Rokkou Oroshi" is a fight song for the wildly popular Hanshin Tigers baseball team, and it has been recorded by several dozen different musicians. The "Omarii" version is sung not only in Japanese, but also in English–and here are the English lyrics:

Dashing swiftly through the wind
blowin' from Mt. Rokkou
Like the big sun soaring
in the clear blue sky
Mighty spirit of the youth
shows the victor's grace
The name that shines in glory
"Hanshin Tigers"
Oh! Oh! Oh! Oh! Hanshin Tigers
Hooray, Hurray, Hurrah, Hurrah

3) A package of Fish Sausages.

4) This magazine is titled: *Tokyo Sports*

The caption reads:

Special Report
Mariners lose horribly but Ichiro smacks base hit in top of…

NOTE: Baseball right fielder Ichiro Suzuki played for seven years with the Orix Blue Wave in Japan's Pacific Leagues before signing with the Seattle Mariners. Ichiro is the first Japanese-born everyday position player in the U.S. Major Leagues.

5) "I bet she loves poetry by Rilke."

NOTE: Rainer Maria Rilke is considered one of the greatest lyric poets Germany has ever seen. He lived at the turn of the 20th century and is famous for his poems that go into extremely detailed description of physical objects.

TOKYOPOP SHOP

THIS FALL, TOKYOPOP CREATES A FRESH, NEW CHAPTER IN TEEN NOVELS...

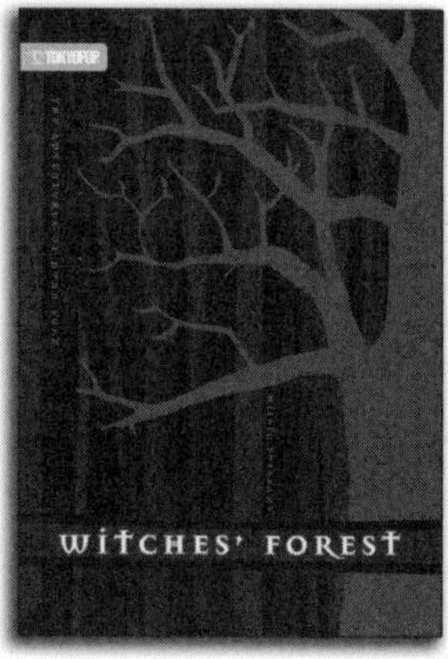
TOKYOPOP
witches' forest

For Adventurers...

Witches' Forest:

The Adventures of Duan Surk

By Mishio Fukazawa

Duan Surk is a 16-year-old Level 2 fighter who embarks on the quest of a lifetime—battling mythical creatures and outwitting evil sorceresses, all in an impossible rescue mission in the spooky Witches' Forest!

BASED ON THE FAMOUS *FORTUNE QUEST* WORLD

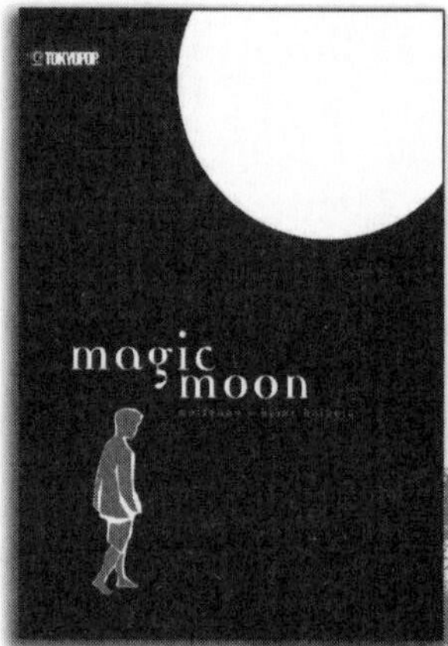
TOKYOPOP
magic moon

For Dreamers...

Magic Moon

By Wolfgang and Heike Hohlbein

Kim enters the engimatic realm of Magic Moon, where he battles unthinkable monsters and fantastical creatures—in order to unravel the secret that keeps his sister locked in a coma.

THE WORLDWIDE BESTSELLING FANTASY *THRILLOGY* ARRIVES IN THE U.S.!

TOKYOPOP PRESENTS

For Believers...

Scrapped Princess:
A Tale of Destiny

By Ichiro Sakaki
A dark prophecy reveals that the queen will give birth to a daughter who will usher in the Apocalypse. But despite all attempts to destroy the baby, the myth of the "Scrapped Princess" lingers on...

THE INSPIRATION FOR THE HIT ANIME AND MANGA SERIES!

For Thinkers...

Kino no Tabi:
Book One of The Beautiful World

By Keiichi Sigsawa
Kino roams the world on the back of Hermes, her unusual motorcycle, in a journey filled with happiness and pain, decadence and violence, and magic and loss.

THE SENSATIONAL BESTSELLER IN JAPAN HAS FINALLY ARRIVED!

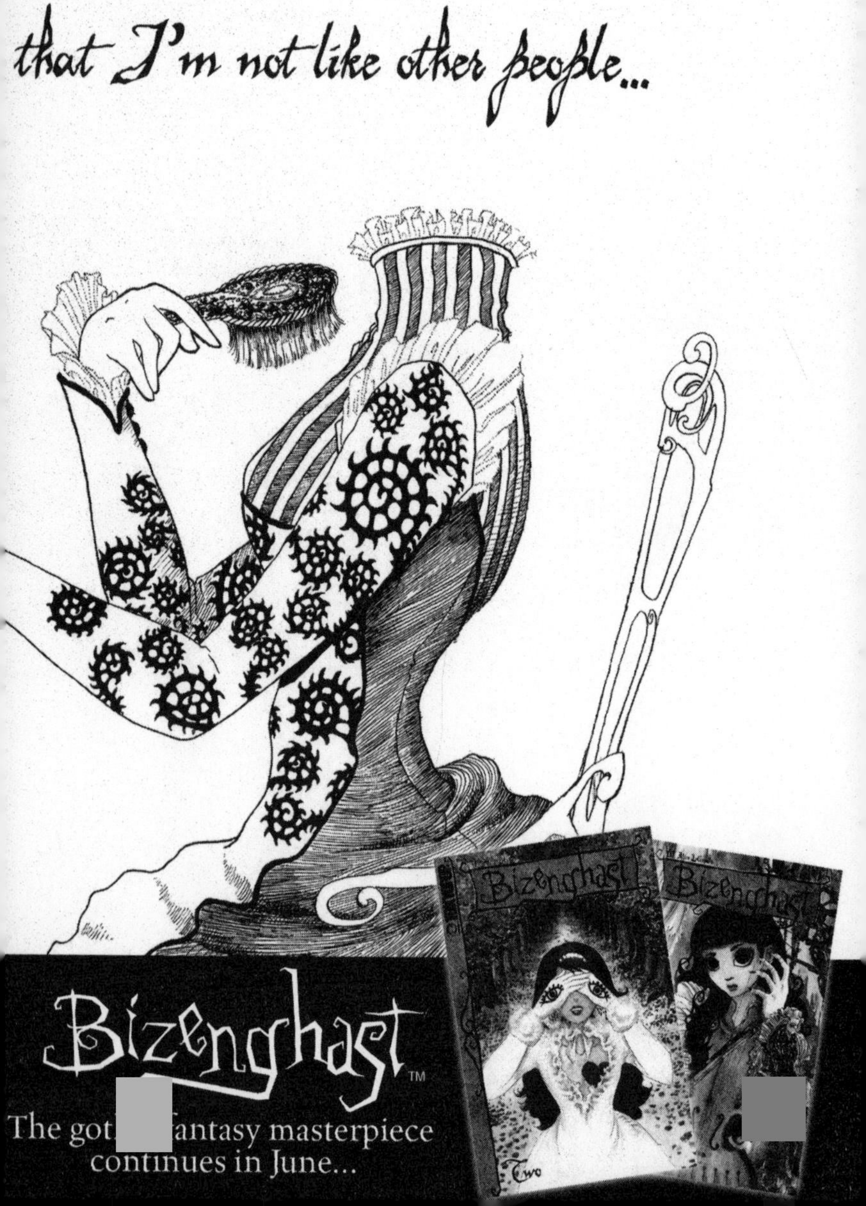
that I'm not like other people...
Bizenghast™
The got[redacted]fantasy masterpiece
continues in June...
Bizenghast
Bizenghast
Two

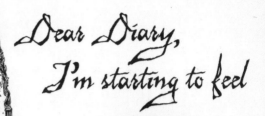

STOP!

This is the back of the book.
You wouldn't want to spoil a great ending!

This book is printed "manga-style," in the authentic Japanese right-to-left format. Since none of the artwork has been flipped or altered, readers get to experience the story just as the creator intended. You've been asking for it, so TOKYOPOP® delivered: authentic, hot-off-the-press, and far more fun!

DIRECTIONS

If this is your first time reading manga-style, here's a quick guide to help you understand how it works.

It's easy... just start in the top right panel and follow the numbers. Have fun, and look for more 100% authentic manga from TOKYOPOP®!